The Art of Digital Marketing for Fashion and Luxury Brands

"The digital revolution has forever changed the way people shop. The growing spread of smartphones, tablets and wearable technologies has generated new shopping habits. Consumers are increasingly experiencing a double life, analogue and digital, and are influenced not only by traditional media but also by social media. This has configured numerous challenges for fashion and luxury companies, which today are also grappling with the consequences of the Covid 19 pandemic, which have further modified models for evaluating, purchasing and receiving products. This book presents in an interesting and critical way all the crucial issues that companies in the sector must face in order to ensure an economically sustainable business."

—Elena Cedrola, *Professor of Marketing and Management, University of Macerata, Italy*

"The book introduces the theory and application of digital marketing and is a must-read for practitioners and researchers in the fashion and luxury industry. The book helps to understand the latest trends in the marketing of fashion and luxury brands. It will benefit most readers and students."

—Professor Xiaoting Zheng, *Dean of the School of Electronic Commerce at Jiujiang University*

"The difference between conventional and luxury brands is, that the latter master the art of building and maintaining deeply emotional relationships with their clients, based on unique, socially distinctive, holistic and memorable experiences. In times, when these experiences are happening in computer-mediated environments to an increasing extent and relationships are cultivated through multiple touchpoints, both online and offline, it is important to revisit the role, conceptualization and management of the fashion and luxury brand. By exploring the conceptual linkages between marketplace and marketspace, this book makes an important contribution to luxury and fashion management literature and provides relevant insight to academics and practitioners alike."

—Professor Fabio Duma, *Founder & President of Orbis Excellentiae; Principal at Luxury Observatory; Head Competence Team Luxury Management at Zurich University of Applied Sciences, School of Management and Law (ZHAW SML), Switzerland*

Wilson Ozuem · Silvia Ranfagni
Editors

The Art of Digital Marketing for Fashion and Luxury Brands

Marketspaces and Marketplaces

Editors
Wilson Ozuem
Institute of Business
Industry and Leadership
University of Cumbria
Lancaster, UK

Silvia Ranfagni
Department of Economics and
Business
University of Florence
Florence, Italy

ISBN 978-3-030-70323-3   ISBN 978-3-030-70324-0   (eBook)
https://doi.org/10.1007/978-3-030-70324-0

This Palgrave Macmillan imprint is published by the registered company Springer Nature
Switzerland AG
The registered company address is: Gewerbestrasse 11, 6330 Cham, Switzerland

*To Ann, Nathan, Jedd and Gabriella (With your love and patience,
nothing is impossible)*

—Wilson Ozuem

To Anna and Maurizio (Where life begins and love never ends)

—Silvia Ranfagni

FOREWORD BY TEODORA SEVASTAKIEVA

The market is transforming from market of masses to market of one, a concept well explained by Pine II and Gilmore in their book, *The Experience Economy*, published in 1999 by Harvard Business School Press. Although the theory is not totally accepted and its feasibility and applicability were criticized in some business segments, I consider the idea of market of one to be valid in today's environment. How can we interpret market of one? Market of one means that a company treats each customer as a unique consumer and the customer feels that they are receiving exclusive services, products, experiences and emotions. Brands offer customers personalization of their life: working day, shopping time, leisure time, family time and so on.

In 2020, due to COVID-19, there was a disruptive acceleration of the personalization of experience thanks to technologies already available and quickly developed for this purpose. Everyone can personalize their digital interaction with the world. All technological devices enable consumers to browse and navigate through any virtual experience, and personalization of this journey is work in progress; for example, Amazon and Google are highly focused on personalizing users' experiences, to enable ease of use and to give users the feeling that their journey is unique and they will find exactly what they are looking for.

Marketspace is the new dimension of marketplace. A marketplace is a physical place where consumers go to shop for products or services. However, in the era of e-commerce startups, the marketplace evolved into internet-based platforms, such as Tmall, Alibaba and Amazon, that offer products from multiple vendors. But, if a physical market and a digital market are called marketplaces, what is marketspace? The name is very evocative and is clearly differentiated from marketplace by the word "space". All people perceive space to be something that is not physically defined. It is something you cannot touch or embrace but you are conscious that you are part of it. When you add the word space to the word market, you automatically understand that it is a space where you can find something you are looking for. You can buy or sell. So, you imagine a space where your every need (material, emotional, etc.) can somehow be satisfied. Any kind of information can reach you and you can access anything you desire. In other words, you are an interactive part of the space. So, imagine the market as a space, you understand that it is global, multidimensional and extremely fluid. Now that you have a clear picture of my understanding of harmonious marketspace, you should be clear that if you want your brand to be successful you should connect all the dots that enable you to call, welcome, embrace and take care of the consumer forever. You need a direct relationship with the consumer. You need to know them.

It will be like creating music around the consumer, letting them think they created the music. A perfect orchestra delivered by your brand, conducted by your consumer.

I have identified 10 steps which brands need to follow in rethinking their strategy for marketspace:

1) Clarify if their **purpose** today is still relevant and in line with consumer needs. Identify, finetune or CHANGE the purpose (in these disruptive times, brands should probably rethink their purpose; to dress a woman from head to toe might have been relevant for luxury brands or department stores in the 1960s, but, today, brands need to reconsider and define a new purpose).
2) Clearly identify the **consumer target**.
3) Study the **consumer journey**; understand the space consumers move into and create a frictionless trajectory for them to attract them to your brand.
4) Implement relevant **territories of conversation** (values) for different touchpoints which fit the consumer journey of step 4.
5) **Create content** for the different touchpoints and territories of conversation of the consumer journey. You do not have to be pushy

but just helpful and supportive. Consumers will value this approach and it will create trust in the relationship they have with you in the space.

6) Implement **consistent and multiple communication strategies** that target the consumer and call attention to themes that are relevant to them at all touchpoints of their journey.

7) Welcome the consumer in the **brand's store or product presentation area** with attention, upscale the quality and the depth of the chosen "territory of conversation" when the consumer finally demonstrates interest in your brand, which means the consumer has started to connect the dots of the marketspace and is ready to convert their experience into a purchase.

8) **The purchase step** should occur naturally without any push; support and help should be offered to the consumer to complete their needs or experience. The environment of the brand's store should be cosy, intimate, made for feeling and faithful to the brand's purpose. The purchase step should be pleasant and easy, clear and **frictionless, as all the journey should be.**

9) **During purchase or after purchase** implement personalized immediate gratification and appreciation (use data to know more about your customer and engage with them with gratification and empathy after purchase).

10) **To retain the consumer, continue to engage** them with content that offers new opportunities for experiences.

These 10 steps also clearly show that it is irrelevant where the brand or product is purchased. What is important is the consistency of the message.

The "intermediation" of third party retail or e-tail is becoming either an opportunity or an obstacle for brands. The key differentiation between the old system of marketplace and the new system of marketspace is that it is the brand that reaches out to the consumer, not the consumer going to the brand in any retail or e-tail environment.

This is another reason to create an even stronger direct relation between brands and consumers where the network of distribution should just be able to complete the consumer journey. The marketspace could lead to a loss of identity of the new retail, which instead of leveraging on high-end luxury brands to drive consumers in store should start leveraging on key services to engage those new consumers who, for one reason or another, visit the physical space with services and experiences.

During this process of transition between retail and e-tail, third parties should be able to reinforce the brand message to the consumer coherently and consistently with what the brand is doing in the rest of the marketspace. Partners that are unable to complete the customer journey with the same tone of voice and "frictionless" experience can become an obstacle to the future development of the brand. This could seem annoying, because you wish for "amalgamation" of the market and no differentiation for consumers, but brands should find their way to deliver a "personalized" experience. How can personalization be created in order to be always relevant?

There are different ways but, from my point of view, brands mainly need the following tools to implement this strategy:

1) **Product for every life moment** of the identified customer target (offer to your target a "purpose of use" for each product or service you sell).
2) Content of communication that is a **real lifestyle broadcast**.
3) **Artificial intelligence for constantly recognizing the new needs** of the consumer.
4) **Agile organization** that is able to adapt quickly to the space.

The key message and the only important fact for brands and companies is that they have to be able to deliver a personalized journey to their consumers, transforming an anonymous experience standardized for a large consumer base, even in the luxury industry, to an individual experience in the "space". An experience which will emotionally transform and inspire your consumer, not only to buy your product, but also to feel they are contributing to or are part of something bigger and more important than just a purchase. If a brand is able to connect the dots of the consumer journey, then the brand's attractiveness will grow exponentially and consumers will be engaged forever. This engagement should be maintained and curated even if the consumer is not active.

Teodora Sevastakieva
General Manager Business Unit Parfums Salvatore Ferragamo
Florence, Italy

Foreword by Nicola Antonelli

This book deals with a very interesting theme: the integration of the management of an online market with an offline market. This is the challenge that Luisaviaroma has faced in the last 20 years, moving from a physical retail model to an omnichannel model where online and offline coexist and contribute to the success of the company. The concept of luxury and the behaviour of customers who buy luxury have changed profoundly over the years. Luisa Via Roma was one of the first international players in the marketing of luxury goods and it can be said that she has experienced practically all the phases that have characterized the fashion field. Luisaviaroma was an active player and protagonist of the creation and development of the "brand" concept, a real tsunami in the world of fashion: the product became the "background actor" on the scene, the brand became the real protagonist and the customers became followers of the brand itself. This has been a historical trend that we have always encountered in Luisa, especially since we started LUISAVIAR OMA.com, an e-commerce project in the early 2000s, which allowed the company to expand its reference market internationally. For many years, the behaviour of consumers of luxury products has been constant and extremely characterized by:

- Poor price sensitivity—up to 4 to 5 years ago, customers were clearly divided into two main clusters. The price sensitivity of the first cluster was very low, and indeed, they were almost bothered by the logic of the balance, which they experienced as a sort of class identification. The second cluster was composed of less affluent customers who were much more sensitive to the price of the product; they frequented the store (online and physical) only on the occasion of promotional sales or during the sales period, perhaps to buy a brand garment, a sort of "icon", to be placed in a wardrobe consisting mainly of non-brand products or fast fashion brands. These two clusters divided the season: the first months of distribution of the new collections were characterized by customers of the high-spending cluster, a cluster that practically disappeared when the sale period was coming.

- Ambition to be "first mover"—that is, having the iconic garment of a very famous brand or a much discussed new talent was a key element of the luxury customer of the 2000s. This was an important competitive advantage for Luisaviaroma: we have always been able to distribute our new collections well in advance of our main competitors due to our relationships of more than ten years with the main brands. Evidently, we could respond to the "first mover" syndrome by giving our customers the opportunity to be the first to receive the "must haves" of the season.

- Only luxury—this high-spending cluster was very "purist" about luxury brands and it was difficult to mix this type of product with other non-luxury brands or, even worse, fast fashion brands.

These three elements characterized the luxury consumer for many years but, starting from 2013/14 onwards, a radical change in the behaviour of this type of consumer began.

This change originated from and was driven by several factors: on the one hand, the slow but constant transfer of purchases from offline to online (accelerated considerably following the current pandemic) led to a significant increase in companies that started selling online and they started to work on the leverage of price and promos to acquire market share. Then, on the other hand, the customer worked out the equation online = savings and this generated the phenomenon known as the "good deal", a transversal phenomenon that affected all targets in terms of age, social background and spending capabilities.

The "thrill" of being able to make a deal, sometimes saving even a few euros, has become a determining element of the shopping experience; studies have found that a "good deal" can stimulate the production of serotonin in the consumer. This phenomenon gradually got the better of the trends that have guided luxury for many years: the "purity" of full-price purchase and at the same time the ambition to be among the first to own a certain object. Today, the consumer wants to feel "smart" and be able to "use the network" to make smart purchases. This phenomenon also had a great impact on physical stores because they are less flexible (for various reasons) regarding price changes than online stores, which generated another phenomenon, namely "showrooming": the customer begins the discovery phase in physical stores, trying and selecting the garment, and then finalizes the purchase in the online store that offers more advantageous commercial conditions.

The other big change concerned the consumer's ability to mix and match luxury brands with brands from other segments, typically street style. This new trend, mainly driven by the phenomenon of influencers, born and developed since 2010, has made luxury much more democratic and led the consumer to experiment much more than before, pushing towards different market segments, such as fast fashion and, in particular, as already mentioned, street style. What have been the effects of these changes on the sector? One of the main effects was a reduction in margins, driven on the one hand by the use of increasingly aggressive promotion policies and on the other by the introduction of brands and product categories with an average price much lower than those of luxury. Another effect is that brands have become more and more contaminated with realities extraneous to their world. Considering what Luisaviaroma is facing in terms of distribution strategies, it becomes interesting to view/read this book which, in the various chapters, highlights the challenges that luxury companies have to face in terms of omnichannel and new distribution models.

Nicola Antonelli
Project Manager in Luisaviaroma
Florence, Italy

PREFACE

Omnichannel fashion retailing has attracted considerable research attention in recent years. This is not surprising, since consumers' modes of fashion consumption are shifting towards a blend of computer-mediated marketing environments (CMMEs) and physical marketplaces. A book on the role and importance of CMMEs to fashion and luxury brands in determining a consumer's purchase and post-purchase trajectories has been conspicuous by its absence, particularly on the effects of emerging technologies. This is particularly surprising given the prominent roles played by the characteristics of emerging technologies in the fashion industry. Additionally, existing books on fashion and luxury brands offer limited or no conceptual linkages between marketplace and marketspace in these emerging dynamic phenomena. The current book was motivated by our desire to fill these important gaps in the academic and practitioner literature.

The organization of this book moves from the general to the specific. The book is divided into three main parts. Chapters in Part I, titled "The Question of Marketspace and Marketplace", discuss the foundational concepts for developing an effective omnichannel marketing strategy. Chapter 1, "The Key Drivers of Perceived Omnichannel Service Quality in Fashion" by Elena Patten, describes the tremendous increase in the complexity of the customer journey in the context of e-commerce because customers use various touchpoints at different channels when interacting with a retailer. In omnichannel retailing, a combination of different retail channels along the various customer touchpoints has become the predominant purchasing pattern of customers. The "research shopper phenomenon" describes a common tendency among customers to use one channel to search and another to purchase. This chapter aims to investigate the concept of integration in omnichannel retailing by considering the different elements of the retail mix. Furthermore, it elaborates the key drivers of perceived omnichannel service quality. This chapter presents an omnichannel customer typology of four different types of fashion customers.

Chapter 2, "Omnichannel Retailing and Brand Equity: A New Balance to Achieve" Claudio Becagli and Matilde Milanesi, examines how the premise of omnichannel retailing enhances brand equity. Over the last decades, consumers have started to use different channels and touchpoints at any stage of their shopping journey, and the internet and technologies have become relevant tools to ease their shopping experience. Many devices, such as smartphones and tablets, are increasingly used to search for product information, reviews and prices, to provide feedback and advocacy, to interact with a brand and, finally, to buy online. Consequently, traditional retailing had to gradually adapt itself to a new buying reality, first through the building of a multichannel environment and then through the adoption of an omnichannel approach aimed at providing a seamless shopping experience with the integration of channels and customer touchpoints. Starting from this background, this chapter delves into the shift from a multichannel to an omnichannel approach by retailing companies, and the implications for customer-based brand equity (CBBE). In particular, the chapter presents the main differences between multichannel and omnichannel retailing; then, the main features of the omnichannel approach are shown. The chapter discusses how to build and manage CBBE in omnichannel retailing, especially for luxury fashion companies, and proposes avenues for future research.

Chapter 3, "Opinion Leaders, Short Videos and Virtual Communities in the Fashion Industry" Peng Chen, offers some insights into the significance of opinion leaders in the development of an effective marketing strategy. Research on opinion leaders can be traced back to Lazarsfeld and colleagues' work in 1944. Research in the 1970s and 1980s focused on the characteristics, identity and influence of opinion leaders. In the past 20 years, with the development of internet technology, the role of opinion leaders in marketing, public affairs, medical treatment, management, tourism, fashion and other fields has attracted the interest of a large number of scholars. Short videos, as a form of social media, have become a new growth point of network marketing in recent years. Internet celebrities, as modern internet opinion leaders, are active in various virtual communities and attract the attention of internet users. They have a significant influence on the marketing campaigns of the fashion industry. Drawing on social influence theory, this chapter provides some insights into the relationship between internet celebrities and virtual communities in the fashion industry, and asks: How can fashion brands connect with consumers through a virtual community built by internet celebrities?

Chapter 4, "Fashion Bloggers: Temperament and Characteristics" Gordon Bowen and Deidre Bowen, provocatively discusses the persona and characteristics of fashion bloggers. The aim of the chapter is to build a consolidated view of fashion bloggers and understand how they differentiate themselves from other bloggers. Promoting fashion products differs from promoting other products that are functional and tangible. Fashion bloggers require abstract and innovative ideas to catch their audiences' attention to build a fruitful relationship. The success of fashion bloggers depends on whether they can become influential bloggers in the fashion blogosphere. Influential bloggers must deploy social and individual capital to build networks that enable them to change and evolve the content on their fashion blog. Building cross-social media networks in collaboration with other fashion bloggers is an important mechanism for them to become influential fashion bloggers. Failure to maintain and build their network will cause them to decouple from their followers and become lower in the social media rankings (e.g., Instagram). Influential fashion bloggers must continue to differentiate themselves in the online environment and this is achieved by creating personal and original content that draws on their social capital, which energizes their audience to engage.

Part II (Chapters 5–12) considers online brand communities (OBCs) and customer relationships. Chapter 5, "Online Brand Communities, Customer Participation and Loyalty in the Luxury Fashion Industry: Strategic Insights" Wilson Ozuem and Michelle Willis, presents a framework linking OBCs and customer satisfaction. Despite the proliferation of studies on the emerging CMMEs, particularly on the burgeoning role of OBCs in the luxury fashion industry, there is a paucity of knowledge on the ways in which the level of customer participation in OBCs affects customer loyalty. While previous research on OBCs mainly examined customer satisfaction and retention, it neglected the role and level of customer participation in complex OBCs, particularly in the luxury fashion industry. By drawing on existing studies, this chapter presents a customer participation filter model of participation in OBCs. The proposed model opens up interesting avenues for future research on the level of customer participation in OBCs and suggests practical lessons for the development of marketing strategies.

In Chapter 6, "Maintaining a Creative Brand Image in an Omnichannel World", Annette Kallevig focuses on the recent dynamics of maintaining a creative image in an omnichannel environment. The chapter discusses the need to optimize and coordinate digital marketing communications across multiple channels; digital marketing communications have received much attention in recent decades, but its integration with creativity has not. For trendsetting fashion and luxury brands, radical creativity is frequently at the core of their brand as well as their marketing communications. Marketing messages have always tended to be highly visual, building surreal dream environments for target groups to aspire to, visionary worlds unlikely to derive from user data. In today's complex omnichannel environments, where many dominant channels are user-driven, it is no longer sufficient to maintain a consistent brand image. A more agile approach is needed to harness the possibilities within dynamic marketing channels while maintaining the creative brand image. This chapter explores multichannel and creative marketing communication, and how they can be effectively integrated to strengthen fashion and luxury branding.

In Chapter 7, "Online Brand Communities and Brand Loyalty: Toward a Social Influence Theory", Michelle Willis affirms that OBCs are gaining traction in the development of marketing strategy within the fashion industry, but it is unclear how the dominant group of users, the millennials, is responding to the prevailing and varying customer loyalty programmes. Traditionally, customers' loyalty is measured by the volume of purchases. However, loyalty is not just based on the perceived materialistic and monetary gains a customer obtains. Loyalty also involves a strong feeling of support or allegiance that moves a customer to remain faithful to a brand despite the occurrence of a negative backlash on social media. However, not all customers have the same level of loyalty to a brand; some are even more loyal to the OBC than to the brand itself. Based on the understanding that loyalty differs among groups of people within the same OBC, this chapter contributes to existing literature and provides a conceptual insight into how OBCs activate customers' multidimensional loyalty intentions towards fashion brands. Based on customers' experience within OBCs from the fashion industry, this chapter identifies different levels of loyalty to fashion brands that can indicate millennial customers' loyalty intentions. From this, we can identify the diverse attitudes and actions that separate millennial customers into sub-groups based on their loyalty intentions.

In Chapter 8, "Exploring the Emergence of Luxury Smartphones and Switching Behaviour", Dominic Appiah and Alison Watson consider the emergence of luxury smartphones and switching behaviour. The chapter discusses how the evolution of the smartphone has influenced consumer behaviour and choice significantly in recent times. Mobile phone technology was initially used only for communication purposes, but has recently advanced to include additional features that have created a larger market which has altered the purchase behaviour of consumers. In this modern era of technological advancement, users of mobile phones expect other features such as media support, internet connectivity and special applications. Smartphones to a large extent have redefined our identities and remodelled our perspectives on our daily activities, including the delivery of education, how we communicate and our shopping experiences. A recent shift towards luxury smartphones means that luxury smartphone manufacturers are, ultimately, expected to consolidate customer loyalty through improved user experiences. Luxury is regarded by consumers as a value-added experience, which is an intangible benefit beyond functional utility that consolidates consumer–brand relationships. The management of luxury smartphones is a key marketing function. Hence, a strong and healthy brand is instrumental in creating sustainable competitive advantage and the transition to a relationship marketing paradigm that places brand loyalty at the heart of customer relational strength. It is widely accepted that brand loyalty has traditionally been perceived as a behavioural construct relating to intentions towards repeat purchases. This chapter aims to provide some insights into brand switching in the luxury smartphone industry and it offers insights for marketers and scholars interested in the development of related marketing plans.

In Chapter 9, "Digital Marketing in Luxury Fashion—From Crisis to Strength", Aster Mekonnen and Liz Larner offer a deep understanding of digital marketing in luxury fashion, particularly in a crisis situation. Digital technology has a key role to play in elevating luxury fashion, more so now than in the past. Historically, luxury fashion brands had been slow to embrace and capitalize on the opportunities of the digital era, but that has not been the case for their customers. Digital and online platforms are becoming more and more integrated into our daily lives and we spend a lot of time using the internet and digital devices. Internet technology and social media are known to have substantial impacts on the operations and success of businesses. We are witnessing unprecedented technological transformations in the way in which organizations and society communicate. The COVID-19 pandemic has made for a challenging 2020; this chapter aims to provide a general understanding of the way luxury fashion brands are transforming their strategies to adapt to digitalization in the industry to manage the crisis.

In Chapter 10, "The Effect of Social eWOM on Consumers' Behaviour Patterns in the Fashion Sector", Donata Tania Vergura, Beatrice Luceri and Cristina Zerbini consider how electronic word of mouth (eWOM) influences consumers' decision-making. This chapter aims to enhance knowledge on the influence of eWOM on consumers' decision-making processes. eWOM emerged as a key driver in consumers' decision-making processes given its greater impact on purchasing decisions than other communication channels. Specifically, the chapter focuses on the reviews of fashion products on social networks (SNs) and builds on the stimulus-organism-response (S-O-R) model in order to identify the determinants of social eWOM adoption and intention to buy the reviewed product. The chapter contributes both theoretically and empirically to the understanding of the role of social eWOM in influencing consumer behaviour. At the theoretical level, it supports the adequacy of the S-O-R model to explain the consumer decision-making process in the context of social eWOM. From a managerial perspective, the findings highlight the importance of taking into consideration both structural (accessibility) and social relationship variables while developing social media marketing strategies.

In Chapter 11, "Online Service Failure and Recovery Strategies: Examining the Influences of User-Generated Content", Samuel Ayertey, Silvia Ranfagni and Sebastian Okafor address the link between service failure recovery and user-generated content (UGC). The chapter discusses how the growth of UGC within fashion brands' online platforms has increased consumers' awareness of service failure and impacted their level of involvement and attitude towards recovery strategies. However, a limited number of studies have explored the value and antecedents of UGC on service failure and recovery strategies in the fashion industry. The aim of the chapter is to explore the online behaviour of fashion customers in relation to UGC and their attitudes towards a firm's response after a negative service experience, considering a range of recovery strategies that can be adopted. The chapter concludes with a discussion on the resulting managerial implications and solutions, and draws some conclusions for both marketing professionals and academics.

Part II concludes with Chapter 12, "Building a Sustainable Brand Image in Luxury Fashion Companies". Monica Faraoni discusses how building a sustainable brand image for a luxury fashion company is a very complex and tangled marketing process. Brand image is a set of perceptions and beliefs surrounding a particular brand fixed in the mind of the consumer. It represents the result of the associations that the consumer recognizes in a brand and summarizes the positioning, personality and reputation of the brand itself. The chapter seeks correspondences or discrepancies between consumer brand perceptions and the identity conveyed by the Ferragamo brand in terms of sustainability. By using a netnographic and text mining methodology, they found that the consumer associates the brand with a company committed to the environment and involved in social issues; a company that traditionally shows creative and experimental skills, using unusual materials, artisanry, innovative techniques and unique designs. The image that the company wants to convey, however, also includes other characterizations.

Part III focuses on complexities and possibilities: tactics and strategies. It discusses complementary perspectives that can be used to build a strong omnichannel competitive landscape. In Chapter 13, "Becoming Digital: The Need to Redesign Competences and Skills in the Fashion Industry", Lucia Varra focuses on how the digitalization of fashion companies has a significant impact on required staff skills and competences. This chapter aims to investigate, through the analysis of literature and business practices, how the development of Industry 4.0 affects organizational processes and staff competences, redefining the content of traditional jobs and creating new key roles in the fashion industry. The chapter identifies the set of skills and competences that the research has revealed to be necessary, distinguishing between technical competences and behavioural competences. Finally, this chapter reflects on the challenges that technological changes pose to companies in terms of organizational culture and the education and training system that must exist to support this new world of work.

In Chapter 14, "Luxury fashion in the Chinese marketplace and the new online channels: an emerging perspective" Serena Rovai and Jin Li explore how global luxury fashion brands have increasingly focused on social media marketing (SMM) to effectively compete in the Chinese luxury consumer market. Consequently, SMM in the Chinese market is attracting increasing interest from scholars in luxury fashion marketing. The highly diversified Chinese luxury customers have shown different shopping attitudes as well as mode of experiencing luxury shopping, mainly in the online marketplace; this implies that a new way of conceiving business operations for luxury fashion brands and a central role for the Chinese consumer is needed. The Chinese online marketplace seems to be a key phenomenon for luxury and fashion; academia has not sufficiently analysed the different components specific to the Chinese geographical context. The chapter examines conceptual studies in the field of online marketing in the Chinese luxury and fashion context and tries to provide an emerging research agenda related to the specificities of online Chinese luxury fashion channels for future empirical studies in the field.

In Chapter 15, "Managing Online Touchpoints for a Consistent Customer Experience; Cases From Fashion Retailing", Giada Salvietti, Marco Ieva and Cristina Ziliani address the role of online customer experience and online touchpoints in the customer journey. The chapter initially presents the online and in-store customer experience and discusses them comparatively in order to highlight similarities and differences. Second, the chapter focuses on the role of online and offline touchpoints and their relationships with consumer attitudes and behaviours. Third, best practices and successful cases in fashion and luxury retailing are discussed to analyse how best-in-class companies are managing online touchpoints. This analysis offers insights to guide practitioners in developing a compelling customer experience, both online and in store, with the goal of achieving long-term customer loyalty.

In Chapter 16, "Leveraging eWOM on Service Failure Recovery Strategy: An Insight into the Brand Perspective", Silvia Ranfagni and Wilson Ozuem offer a strategic approach on how leveraging eWOM on service failure recovery leads to competitive advantage. They begin by identifying consumers' power in the evolving CMMEs. Consumers are a source of eWOM that can influence other consumers and have an impact on their brand choices. eWOM is often produced when consumers experience an online service failure. Providers have to manage this with adequate recovery strategies. The value that fashion providers are able to create for consumers depends more and more on how they handle service failure situations. This chapter explores the relationship between UGC, as a basis of eWOM, and service failure and recovery strategies filtered through the brand. The analysis is carried out from a theoretical point of view and offers insights into the fashion industry.

The final chapter focuses on the evolving nature of the omnichannel landscape. Chapter 17, "Opera as Luxury in Culture: The Marketing Impact of Digitalization" Nicola Bellini, focuses on and extends the discussions of the omnichannel landscape to opera experience. The author provides a preliminary framework to analyse the process of digitalization in opera consumption, by exploring analogies with digitalization in luxury markets. Two main issues are discussed. First, we consider digitalization as a tool for market expansion and possibly "democratization" through increased accessibility. Evidence suggests that, rather than generating new opera audiences, digitalization provides an extension of the opera experience for the existing customer base, which is especially relevant for second and third "tier" customers. Second, we look at the early stages of the adoption of digital marketing approaches and especially the creation of online communities based on SNs.

Lancaster, UK   Wilson Ozuem
Florence, Italy   Silvia Ranfagni

Acknowledgements

This book would not have been possible without the support of its authors who generously gave their time and shared their wisdom, often at very short notice. We acknowledge the immensely valuable contributions and advice of the authors, especially their energy in moving things forward.

Several individuals deserve special acknowledgements for their sustained commitment to this book. We also appreciate their thoughtful reviews and comments. We could not have completed this book without the unstinting support of Palgrave Macmillan staff, especially Liz Barlow, who helped us to polish this book. We are also grateful for the support of the editorial team, especially Abarnay Antonyraj, who managed the production process. Finally, we thank, and appreciate, our families for their continued support and patience.

CONTENTS

Part I   The Question of Marketspace and Marketplace

1   The Key Drivers of Perceived Omnichannel Service
     Quality in Fashion   3
     Elena Patten

2   Omnichannel Retailing and Brand Equity: A New
     Balance to Achieve   31
     Claudio Becagli and Matilde Milanesi

3   Opinion Leaders, Short Videos and Virtual
     Communities in the Fashion Industry   51
     Peng Chen

4   Fashion Bloggers: Temperament and Characteristics   81
     Gordon Bowen and Deidre Bowen

**Part II   Online Brand Communities and Customer
          Relationships**

5   Online Brand Communities, Customer Participation
     and Loyalty in the Luxury Fashion Industry: Strategic
     Insights   107
     Wilson Ozuem and Michelle Willis

6   Maintaining a Creative Brand Image
in an Omnichannel World   131
Annette Kallevig

7   Online Brand Communities and Brand Loyalty:
Toward a Social Influence Theory   153
Michelle Willis

8   Exploring the Emergence of Luxury Smartphones
and Switching Behaviour   179
Dominic Appiah and Alison Watson

9   Digital Marketing in Luxury Fashion: From Crisis
to Strength   199
Aster Mekonnen and Liz Larner

10 The Effect of Social EWOM on Consumers'
Behaviour Patterns in the Fashion Sector   221
Donata Tania Vergura, Beatrice Luceri,
and Cristina Zerbini

11 Online Service Failure and Recovery Strategies:
Examining the Influences of User-Generated Content   243
Samuel Ayertey, Silvia Ranfagni, and Sebastian Okafor

12 Building a Sustainable Brand Image in Luxury
Fashion Companies   273
Monica Faraoni

Part III   Complexities and Possibilities: Tactics and
           Strategies

13 Becoming Digital: The Need to Redesign Competences
and Skills in the Fashion Industry   299
Lucia Varra

14 Luxury Fashion in the Chinese Marketplace
and the New Online Channels: An Emerging
Perspective   345
Serena Rovai and Li Jing

15 Managing Online Touchpoints for a Consistent
    Customer Experience: Cases from Fashion Retailing   365
    Giada Salvietti, Marco Ieva, and Cristina Ziliani

16 Leveraging EWOM on Service Failure Recovery
    Strategy: An Insight into the Brand Perspective   397
    Silvia Ranfagni and Wilson Ozuem

17 Opera as Luxury in Culture: The Marketing Impact
    of Digitalization   423
    Nicola Bellini

Index   441

Notes on Contributors

Dominic Appiah is currently a Business Lecturer at Arden University, where he leads various modules. Before joining Arden University, he was the global network learning coordinator at Pittsburgh University, London Campus. He holds a Ph.D. from Plymouth University, an M.B.A. from the University of Wales and a Bachelor of Arts degree from the University of Ghana.

Dominic is actively engaged in academic research. The plethora of his research investigates the dynamics of consumer purchase intentions in digitally disrupted markets and building resistance to brand switching in these competitive markets.

He has published extensively in academic books and journals, including *International Journal of Consumer Behaviour*, *International Journal of Retailing & Consumer Services*, *Journal of Sustainability* and *Interdisciplinary Journal of Economics & Business Law*. He also collaborates with leading researchers and has presented papers at reputable international conferences, notably the UK Academy of Information Services and Global Business and Technology Association. Dominic is an Associate Fellow of the Higher Education Academy (HEA), a member of the Chartered Institute of Marketing (CIM), Chartered Institute of Insurance (CII) and the British Academy of Management (BAM).

Samuel Ayertey is currently a Lecturer at Organisational Learning Centre (OLC) Europe. Samuel has a Ph.D. in Marketing from the University of Plymouth (UK) and an M.B.A. from the University of Wales (UK).

Samuel has worked in a number of companies across UK and Africa. His research interests include fashion industry and service recovery and the results of his research have been published in book chapters and International conference papers. He has also presented several conference papers in the field of digital marketing, particularly on the impact of emerging technologies on service failure and recovery strategies. Samuel is also a Fellow of the Higher Education Academy (HEA) and member of the Chartered Institute of Marketing (CIM).

Claudio Becagli is an Assistant Professor of Management in the Department of Economics and Management at the University of Florence (Italy). He is Lecturer of Fundamental of Management and Management of Cultural Businesses at the University of Florence, and has teaching experiences in other public and private institutions. Over the years, he has gained experience as a management consultant for companies operating in various sectors. His research interests include business strategy, corporate governance and brand management, with special reference to the utilities, fashion and cultural industries. He has participated in national and international management and marketing conferences and has published in national and international journals such as *Micro & Micro Marketing*, *Sinergie*, *Journal of Global Fashion Marketing*, *Journal of Cleaner Production* and *Business Strategy and the Environment*. He is a member of the Editorial Board of *Chinese Business Review* and of *China-USA Business Review*.

Nicola Bellini is Professor of Management at the Scuola Superiore Sant'Anna in Pisa (Italy) and Fellow of the Academy of Social Sciences (UK). He has been Visiting or Affiliate Professor at the Stanford University Center in Florence, the University of Sassari, the University of Pisa, the Gran Sasso Science Institute in L'Aquila, the Grenoble Ecole de Management and IULM University in Milan. He was Co-Director of the Confucius Institute in Pisa (2010–2014), Director of the Galileo Galilei Italian Institute at Chongqing University, China (2007–2014), Professor of Tourism and Director of the Tourism Management Institute at the La Rochelle Business School, France (2014–2018), and Director of the Regional Institute for Economic Planning of Tuscany—IRPET, Florence (2009–2011). He is author and editor of books and articles on regional innovation, place marketing and cultural tourism. Recent publications include: *Tourism in the City. Towards an Integrative Agenda on Urban Tourism* (editor with C. Pasquinelli), Berlin: Springer, 2017;

"Chinese Creative Entrepreneurs in Fashion and Luxury: An Exploratory Case Study of a Concept Store In Beijing" (co-author with S. Rovai), in Lazzeretti, L., Vecco, M. (ed.s) *Creative Industries, Entrepreneurship and Local Development: Paradigms in Transition in a Global Perspective*, Cheltenham: Edward Elgar, 2018, 221–238; *Gastronomy and Local Development. Quality of Products, Quality of Places, Quality of Experiences* (editor with C. Clergeau and O. Etcheverria), London: Routledge, 2019. He is currently developing a research project on the management and marketing of opera houses, with a focus on the impacts of digitalization.

Deidre Bowen holds a Masters in Applied Management (Henley Business School) with distinction, is a qualified solicitor and completed her degree at Oxford University. She is currently a Regional Manager for a charity, specializing in safeguarding and business development. Her research interests are strategy, social media, SMEs sustainability and leadership. More recently, Deidre has explored how business effectiveness is impacted in recessionary conditions, with particular focus on the role of employee engagement.

Gordon Bowen has a Doctorate in Business (University of Hull) and is a Chartered Marketer from the Chartered Institute of Marketing (UK). He is an Associate Lecturer at various universities and higher education institutions, including University of Gloucestershire, Regent's University London, Ulster University, Northumbria University, University of Hertfordshire, Warwick University and Grenoble Graduate Business School. His research interests are strategy, marketing, digital marketing, CSR and SMEs, and he supervises Ph.D. and DBA students in these areas. Gordon has held senior positions in the telecommunications industry, including strategy development, business development and training. He has also advised SMEs on business matters and co-edited a best seller with the publisher IGI-Global.

Peng Chen is a Lecturer in International Business at the School of Economics and Management of Jiujiang University (China). He is also a DBA candidate of the University of Wales Trinity Saint David (UK). Before this, he worked as the practical teaching administrator and member of International Trade Teaching and Research Team at the Business School of Jiujiang University (China). His main research interests include the development of social networks and social media marketing, social media influencer and consumer's purchase intention. He taught under-graduate courses and supervised students' dissertations. He has articles and conference papers in his specialist area of research in national journals and international conferences.

Monica Faraoni is an Associate Professor of Management at the University of Florence. She received a Ph.D. in Management from the University of Bologna and was Visiting Professor at the Wharton Business School of the University of Pennsylvania, Philadelphia. Her research interests centre around how new technologies and associated digitalization of information impact consumer and firm behaviour with particular attention to big data, online consumer purchasing process and brand management in fashion industry. She is the author of numerous publications in international journals such as *Journal of Business Research, Journal of Interactive Marketing* and *Journal of Knowledge Management.*

Marco Ieva, Ph.D. is Assistant Professor in Marketing at the University of Parma where he lectures in customer relationship management and customer analytics. He has been a Visiting Scholar at the University of Ghent, where he worked on analytical customer relationship management. His research spans retailing, loyalty marketing, customer experience and marketing innovation. He has published papers in Journal of Advertising Research, Industrial Marketing Management, Journal of Retailing and Consumer Services and International Journal of Retail and Distribution Management.

Li Jing is Associate Professor at Chongqing University and Executive Dean at the School of International Education. She has 25-year experience in International Relations at global level. She has contributed to the development of the international agreements and the international strategy at Chongqing University. Prof. Li spent several years in Italy as Co-Director of the Confucius Institute in Pisa—in partnership with Scuola Superiore Sant'Anna—reinforcing bilateral relations and research as well as pedagogical activities between the two institutions. She has an in-depth knowledge of internationalization policies and higher education in the Millennials context. She has been invited speaker and Visiting Professor at different Universities in Europe and in Asia.

Annette Kallevig is a Lecturer in Digital Marketing at the Institute of Marketing, Kristiania University College, Oslo (Norway). She holds a Masters in Strategic Marketing with Merit from Arden University (UK).

Her research interests are within digital marketing communication and especially issues associated with managing and inspiring creativity in the age of data-driven marketing communications, and how agile methodologies may be applied to the process. She draws upon her long, practical experience as advertising art director and digital consultant, and experience with clients from various sectors including fashion and beauty. Whether teaching or researching, her approach is practical and business oriented, always exploring areas of practical applicability for the business world of today.

Liz Larner was a marketing professional for more than 15 years, working in media and advertising for companies such as Leo Burnett and Bauer Media with clients across a range of sectors including luxury and fashion brands. Now working in academia Liz is Associate Dean Academic at Salford Business School work strategically to deliver ambitious academic and business targets and still teaches on marketing modules.

Beatrice Luceri is Full Professor of Marketing at the University of Parma, Italy. She teaches International Agribusiness Management and Consumer Behaviour Analysis. Her main research areas are consumer behaviour, retail marketing and product packaging. She is coordinator of the "Retailing & Service management" thematic group of the Italian Society of Management (SIMA). She is author of several papers published in scientific journals such as *International Journal of Retail & Distribution Management, British Food Journal, International Journal of Business and Management* and *Journal of Marketing Trends.*

Aster Mekonnen is a Senior Lecturer in Marketing, Research and Management areas, committed to ongoing education and curriculum development. Currently working at London College of Fashion (UAL) and the University of West Scotland (UWS). Her research interests include fashion marketing, digital marketing, consumer behaviour and affinity marketing. Aster is Fellow of the Higher Education Association, Fellow of the Academy of Marketing Science as well as other academic professional bodies. She was a Researcher at the Open University Business School (OUBS) Marketing and Strategy Unit where she gained her Ph.D. in Marketing Strategy. Prior to her research degree, she has acquired extensive experience in the service industry—particularly in the fashion sector and in charity organizations.

Matilde Milanesi is Postdoctoral Research Fellow at the University of Florence. She graduated in Economics and Management at the University of Florence, where she also received her Ph.D. in Economics in 2015, with a dissertation entitled "Liabilities and Business Relationships in Internationalization. Evidences From the Opening of Retail Stores in the Fashion Industry". She is also Lecturer of Marketing and Management at the University of Florence and has teaching experiences with many other public and private institutions. Over the years, she has gained experience as a marketing consultant for companies in various sectors, in particular fashion, luxury and pharmaceutical companies. She has been Visiting Researcher at the Centre for Science and Technology Studies, Department of Economic History, Uppsala University. Her research interests lie in the area of international business and international marketing, industrial marketing, buyer-supplier relationships, with a focus on the luxury and fashion industry. Her works are published in academic refereed journals such as *Journal of Business Research, Industrial Marketing Management, International Marketing Review, Journal of Business & Industrial Marketing, Journal of Cleaner Production* and *Journal of International Management*. She is reviewer for many international academic journals such as *Industrial Marketing Management, Journal of Business Research, Management Decision, Journal of Global Fashion Marketing* and *Journal of Business & Industrial Marketing*. She is also the author of chapters in edited books and has recently published a book entitled *Liabilities and Networks in the Internationalization of Fashion Retailing*.

Dr. Sebastian Okafor is a Lecturer at the University of Cumbria. Sebastian runs dissertation tutorials and supervises dissertations in several UK universities, including the University of Warwick, University of West London and Northampton University. Dr. Okafor's research interests are service failure recovery strategies and social media marketing. Dr. Okafor has several years of professional experience in business management, and education practice and policy. He is a specialist in interim management solutions for schools and colleges and has many years of experience in the UK public and private education sector. He has provided interim and project-based senior management support to international colleges and handles a wide range of client portfolios. Sebastian is a Fellow of the Higher Education Academy and Chartered Institute of Educational Assessors.

Prof Wilson Ozuem, Ph.D. is acknowledged as one of the international leaders in the study of digital marketing and multichannel retailing. His general area of expertise lies in digital marketing and fashion marketing. His specific research interest is: understanding the impacts of emerging computer-mediated marketing environments (CMMEs) on the fashion industry. His research has been published in key journals, including the *European Journal of Marketing*, *Journal of Business Research*, *Information Technology & People*, *Psychology & Marketing*, *International Journal of Market Research* and many others.

Elena Patten currently works as a Professor of Fashion Management at Macromedia University of Applied Sciences. Before that, Elena Patten worked in the German fashion retail industry for 17 years. Most recently, she was retail director for a major German fashion department store chain. Her research interests are omnichannel retailing and service quality especially in the fashion and luxury field. She has published several papers in these research areas.

Silvia Ranfagni, Ph.D. is Associate Professor of Marketing in the Department of Economics and Management at the University of Florence (Italy). Her research interests include innovation, internationalization and brand management with special reference to the fashion and cultural industry. She has participated in international marketing conferences and has published in national and international journals such as *Journal of Fashion Marketing and Management*, *Management Decision*, *European Journal of Marketing*, *Journal of Consumer Behaviour*, *Journal of Business Research* and *Journal of Interactive Marketing*.

Serena Rovai is currently Director of the BRaND LuxuryLab and the M.B.A. in Global Luxury Management and Innovation as well as Associate Professor in Luxury Brand Management at EXCELIA business School—FT ranked. Previously, Director of the International Affairs Division. Prof. Rovai is teaching and researching on Luxury Brand Management and she is Consultant for Luxury Brands—Cartier, Starwood Group, etc.—for China Markets Strategy. She has 20 years International Experience in Globalisation in Higher Education and Luxury Brand Management. She has founded the Europe-Asia Centre for Management and Innovation at Grenoble Ecole de Management—top 20 Business School in Europe and the Fashion and Luxury Management School special-izations. She is Visiting Professor in UK, US, China, Italian Higher Education Institutions for Luxury and Fashion Brand Management.

Giada Salvietti is PhD Candidate in Economics and Management of Innovation and Sustainability at the University of Parma. Her main research interest is Omnichannel and its influence on consumer behavior and management strategies, with a specific focus on the luxury sector. She has been Lecturer of Consumer Behavior and Retail Strategies at the FUA—Florence University of the Arts, and of Marketing Research within the Master in Digital Marketing at the University of Florence.

Lucia Varra is Associate Professor of Organization and Human Resource Management in the Department of Economics and Management of the University of Florence. She has a Ph.D. in "Economic and Business Doctrines, and Management". Her main research interests include organizational models and processes, innovation, decision-making and knowledge processes, organizational roles and competences. She has a consolidated experience in business consulting and training for private and public companies, on the issues of process redesign, organizational change, quality, communication processes and knowledge development. She has participated in important national and international conferences. Her scientific production includes books and articles in national and international journals.

Donata Tania Vergura is Researcher in Marketing. She teaches Communication and Digital Marketing and E-business and E-commerce at the University of Parma, Italy. Her main research fields are e-commerce, electronic word of mouth and sustainability, with a focus on consumer behaviour. She is author of a book on *E-commerce and Digital Trans-formation* and has published scientific articles in international journals such as *British Food Journal*, *Journal of Consumer Marketing*, *International Journal of Retail & Distribution Management*, *Food Research International* and *Health Policy*.

Dr. Alison Watson is the Head of School for Leadership and Management. She has been a Lecturer with Arden (RDI) for 15 years and has supported students on various management courses at all levels. Alison has also taught in a number of other higher and further education institutions. Prior to this, she was an operations and project manager for a number of large retailers and therefore has much experience in the field of business and management. She is a Chartered Marketer with the Chartered Institute of Marketing, a Senior Fellow of the Higher Education Academy and a member of the Chartered Management Institute. She gained her M.B.A. from the University of Leicester and her Ph.D. from Teesside University. Her research interests include: marketization of higher education, market segmentation, student recruitment and e-learning.

Michelle Willis is a Lecturer in International Business at the University of Cumbria (UK) where she is also undertaking a doctoral programme focusing on social media and customer loyalty in the luxury fashion sector. Her research interest focuses on emerging technologies, particularly on the interface between social networking sites (SNS) and the development of marketing programme, and online service failure and recovery strategies, in association with consumers of the millennial generation. She has co-authored chapters in textbooks, articles and conference papers in her specialist area of research that have been presented at the American Marketing Association and the European Marketing Academy conferences. Before this, she worked as a Student Information Officer at the Business School Undergraduate Administration Department at the University of Hertfordshire (UK) and managed student experience events and social media channels. At the same university, she received her M.Sc. in International Business with distinction and her B.A. in Business Studies with First-Class honours. In addition, she completed a one year study abroad programme at UH's partner university INTI International University in Malaysia where the consumer markets high usage of social media sparked her interest in consumer behaviour through social media marketing.

Cristina Zerbini is Research Fellow in Marketing at the University of Parma, Italy. She is Professor of Neuroshopping and International Marketing. Her main research fields are consumer behaviour, sustainability and neuromarketing. She is a member of the Editorial Board of the *International Journal of Nutrition and Food Sciences*. She has contributed to the marketing literature with publications appearing in *Food Research International, International Journal of Business & Management, British Food Journal, Food Quality and Preference* and *Health Policy*.

Cristina Ziliani, Ph.D. is Full Professor of Marketing at the University of Parma. She lectures on loyalty management at leading universities and business events around the world, including Japan, US, UK, France, Spain and Thailand. Her research focuses on loyalty marketing, customer relationship management, promotions and customer experience. She is the author of several books and numerous publications and is the scientific director of the Osservatorio Fedeltà UniPR (Loyalty Observatory) since 1999.

LIST OF FIGURES

Fig. 1.1   Terminology (*Source* Patten [2017])   5
Fig. 1.2   Sub-dimensions of integration quality (*Source* Patten
           [2017])   14
Fig. 1.3   Conceptual framework of omnichannel service quality
           (*Source* Patten [2017])   18
Fig. 1.4   Integration quality as a catalyst of omnichannel service
           quality (*Source* Patten [2017])   21
Fig. 1.5   Customer typology matrix (*Source* Patten [2017])   22
Fig. 5.1   *Customer participation filter model*   118
Fig. 6.1   Creativity motivation matrix   143
Fig. 7.1   Categorisation of millennial loyalists within online brand
           communities   161
Fig. 9.1   The web of expansion—From Web of things to the Web
           of Thought (*Source* www.Trendone.com)   205
Fig. 10.1 Conceptual model (*eWOM* Electronic word of mouth)   226
Fig. 10.2 Structural model with standardized coefficients (*eWOM*
           Electronic word of mouth, *ns* not significant, $*p <0.05$,
           $**p <0.01$)   233
Fig. 12.1 Common "luxury" and "sustainability" meanings   277
Fig. 13.1 A proposed model of skills and roles in the Industry 4.0
           fashion industry   315
Fig. 13.2 Summary of changes in jobs according to the level
           of specialisation   330
Fig. 14.1 The three D Chinese online luxury marketplace   353

LIST OF TABLES

Table 10.1	Measurement scales and reliability indices	228
Table 12.1	Company brand identity	285
Table 12.2	Consumer brand image	286
Table 12.3	Corporate brand identity related to the "sustainable" lemma	287
Table 12.4	Consumer brand identity related to the "sustainable" lemma	288
Table 13.1	Transversal competences common to all roles in the digital fashion industry	317
Table 13.2	Roles and competences that support the development of digital technology	318
Table 13.3	An emerging role and related skills in the material source development process	320
Table 13.4	Several traditional roles and related skills and competences in the digital manufacturing process	321
Table 13.5	Several emerging and new roles and related skills and competences in the digital manufacturing process	323
Table 13.6	A traditional role and related skills and competences in the retail and multichannel marketing process	325
Table 13.7	Several emerging and new roles and related skills and competences in the retail and digital marketing process	326
Table 13.8	Set of skills and competences for specialist roles in the retail and digital marketing process	327

Table 15.1   Fashion and luxury companies delivering
            an omnichannel customer experience   366
Table 17.1   Social networks' communities of selected opera houses
            (official accounts, thousands of followers, August 2020)   433
Table 17.2   Facebook followers of the official accounts of selected
            opera singers (August 2020)   435

PART I

The Question of Marketspace and Marketplace

The Key Drivers of Perceived Omnichannel Service Quality in Fashion

Elena Patten

INTRODUCTION

The increasing possibilities opened up by digitalization led to a fundamental change in consumer behaviour (Alexander & Cano, 2020; Huan,
Lobschat, & Verhoef, 2019). The combination of different retail channels
has influenced the predominant purchasing pattern of customers (Heinemann, 2019). Therefore, retailers nowadays need to find answers to this
changing behaviour (Verhoef, Kannan, & Inman, 2015). With respect
to service quality as an antecedent to customer satisfaction and loyalty,
there is a gap in the literature when it comes to understanding service
quality in omnichannel settings (Huan et al., 2019; Hult, Tomas, &
Zhang, 2019; Ozuem, Howell & Lancaster, 2008). This is surprising
since omnichannel service systems have become increasingly important
with the rise of e-commerce. Rezaei and Valaei (2017) empirically found
that retailers influenced by convergence of technology, customer expectations, and competition, now consider that their ability to offer their

E. Patten (✉)
Macromedia University of Applied Sciences, Munich, Germany

products through multiple channels is becoming indispensable (Rezaei & Valaei, 2017, p. 854).

This chapter will focus on omnichannel retailing and the service quality perception of omnichannel customers. It will, therefore, aim to investigate the concept of integration in omnichannel retailing by considering the different elements along the different customer touchpoints. Furthermore, it will elaborate the key drivers of perceived omnichannel service quality. This chapter will elaborate that omnichannel customers' service perception consists of six major themes: (1) physical stimulation, (2) affiliation, (3) value for physical service quality, (4) electronic stimulation, (5) utility for electronic service quality, and (6) choice optimization for the integration service quality. Finally, this chapter will present a customer typology of omnichannel fashion customers.

THEORETICAL CONTEXT

In recent years, companies' have developed their omnichannel retailing strategy (Lee, Chan, Chong, & Thadani, 2019; Lorenzo-Romero, Andrés-Martinez, & Mondéjar-Jiménez, 2020; Ozuem, Patel, Howell, & Lancaster, 2017). Retailers aim to offer their customers a seamless shopping experience and try to integrate their different retail channels; a switch between channels during one purchase at one retailer has got easier. Customers use different options, such as stores, computers, mobile devices, tablets, and social media, during the purchase process of transactions and these options can be a source of inspiration and communication (Verhoef et al., 2015). Borders between the different channels blur (Brynjolfsson, Hu, & Rahman, 2013).

The complexity of retail channel strategies has led to confusion regarding a coherent terminology for both academics and practitioners. Different concepts are used to describe retailing activities that operate across more than one retail channel, namely "multichannel", "cross-channel" , and "omnichannel" retailing. To date, the meanings of these concepts are blurred (Beck & Rygl, 2015).

The initial perception of multichannel retailing was of a system that administrated two or more parallel channels (Berman, 1996; Pelton, Strutton, & Lumpkin, 2002). During the next phase, the concept of integration became a topic of major interest both for practitioners and academia (Neslin et al., 2006). In this context, the terms "cross-channel" and "omnichannel" augmented the terminology of "multichannel" retailing. Yet, there has not been a focus on a conceptualization of these new terms (Verhoef et al., 2015). However, Beck and Rygl (2015) have published some initial research (see Fig. 1.1).

Beck and Rygl (2015) categorized the three different terms according to the degree of customer interaction options and degree of integration of a company's different retailing channels. They defined multichannel retailing as "the set of activities involved in selling merchandise or services through more than one channel or all widespread channels, whereby the customer cannot trigger channel interaction and/or the retailer does not control channel interaction" (Beck & Rygl, 2015, p. 175). Cross-channel retailing is a later stage of development of multichannel retailing in which the multiple channels of a retailer are integrated to a higher degree. In cross-channel retailing "the customer can trigger partial channel interaction and/or the retailer controls partial channel integration" (Beck & Rygl, 2015, p. 176). Omnichannel retailing refers to the most advanced stage of a multichannel retailing system; hence, there is full customer interaction and/or integration of a company's different retailing channels in omnichannel retailing (Beck & Rygl, 2015). Furthermore, Beck and Rygl (2015) elaborated a further form, which they called a hybrid

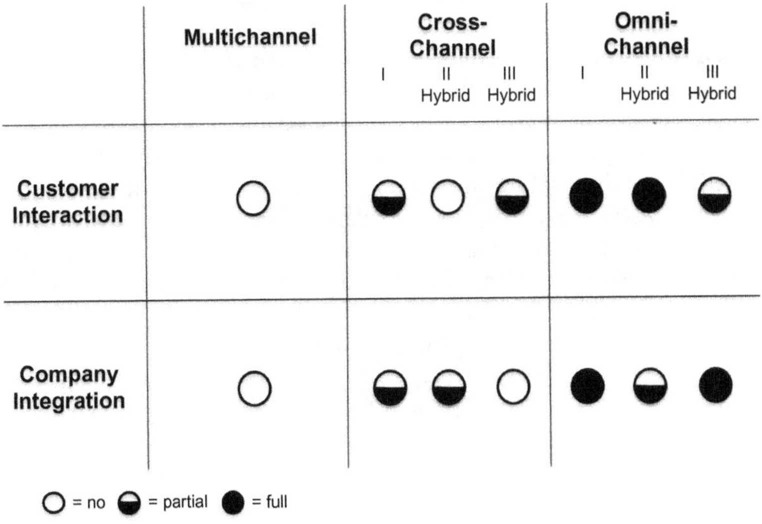

Fig. 1.1 Terminology (*Source* Patten [2017])

form, in which just one party (customer or retailer) fulfils the criterion of interaction/integration (Beck & Rygl, 2015, p. 174). For several reasons, this framework is a valuable contribution to retailing research in contexts in which retailers operate more than one channel. It helps to set clear boundaries for the classification of each of the three connected, but different, concepts. This conceptualization considers both perspectives: the customer's interaction with the different channels and the retailer's level of integration. Furthermore it gives a guideline for both researchers and practitioners to use the different terms more distinctively.

THE CONCEPT OF INTEGRATION

Research about omnichannel retailing embraces the concept of integration of the different operated channels within an organization (Huan et al., 2019). Channel integration initially meant that a retailer should provide a seamless customer experience between stores and online shops; customers should be able to easily switch channels during their interaction with the retailer (Goersch, 2002; Seck, 2013). However, important questions remain unanswered: Does a seamless customer experience automatically mean a full integration? In other words, does it mean the more integrated the better? For retailers, the level of integration is a difficult managerial decision. They face various challenges because different channels might have different purposes, features, cost structure, and competitors (Berry et al., 2010). Studies have investigated the optimal level of integration in certain areas. Related literature has focused on several aspects of the retail mix: integration of assortment (Emrich, Paul, & Rudolph, 2015; Mantrala et al., 2009), pricing and promotions (Bertrandie & Zielke, 2019; Vogel & Paul, 2015; Wolk & Ebling, 2010), fulfilment (Agatz, Fleischmann, & Van Nunen, 2008; Lang & Bressolles, 2013; Wolk & Ebling, 2010; Xing, Grant, McKinnon, & Fernie, 2010), and web design and store design integration (Emrich & Verhoef, 2015). However, none of the aforementioned areas have been completely resolved yet. Quite the contrary, there are still several areas requiring further investigation (Huan et al., 2019). The next three subsections discuss integration of assortment, pricing and promotions, and fulfilment.

Integration of Assortment

With regard to the assortment strategy of a retailer, it is deemed necessary to offer an attractive assortment on the one hand but avoid choice difficulty on the other hand (Mantrala et al., 2009). The reviewed literature revealed a lack of consensus on the degree of assortment integration across channels in omnichannel retailing. Some researchers argued that the assortment does not necessarily need to be fully integrated when the target customer of the two channels is different (Li et al., 2018). This is not the case for omnichannel customers, who switch retail channels during their purchases. However, other researchers argued that product consistency is crucial to provide a seamless shopping experience for the customer (Berman & Thelen, 2004). In practice, most of today's omnichannel retailers apply an asymmetrical assortment strategy, which means that they offer a larger assortment online than offline (Emrich et al., 2015).

Emrich et al. (2015) investigated the impact of multichannel assortment integration on underlying assortment relations. They classified three different assortment relations: assortments are substitutive (for instance, a retailer sells two different kinds of similar shoes), or complementary (shoes and shoe polish), or independent (shoes and sun lotion). Emrich et al. (2015) found that a lack of integration of assortment was detrimental to all three assortment structures. However, they argued that for a omnichannel retailer with a substitutive assortment, the perceived variety is lower when the assortment strategy is asymmetrical, and customers tend to have a low opinion of the decreased channel choice and autonomy.

Pricing and Promotions

In general, customers expect products online to be the same price or cheaper than products in-store (Zhang et al., 2010); however, at the same time, customers expect a consistent pricing strategy across channels (Seck, 2013). How can omnichannel retailers balance and meet these expectations without losing market share? In practice, retailers mostly tend towards a partial integration of their pricing (Wolk & Ebling, 2010). Retailers post the same prices across their different channels, because they fear that different prices might lead to customers' confusion and resentment. However, many retailers apply channel-specific price promotions or charge handling and shipping costs (Neslin et al., 2006). In the reviewed literature, most researchers argued in favour of a consistent pricing strategy across all channels of a retailer (Berman & Thelen, 2004; Vogel & Paul, 2015; Wolk & Ebling, 2010).

Vogel and Paul (2015) argued that channel-based price differentiation has certain positive and negative impacts on customer satisfaction; it positively affects their perceptions of value, increases relationship quality, and enhances repurchase intentions, but it also leads to perceptions of price unfairness and limits customer self-determination, which negatively affect retention outcomes (Vogel & Paul, 2015). It remains questionable, which of the mentioned criteria has more effect on the final choice of shopping location and, furthermore, on the long-term relationship with the retailer.

A possible pricing strategy for omnichannel retailers, which embraces both a high perception of value and price fairness, is "self-matching pricing" (Kireyev, Kumar, & Ofek, 2015). Here, the omnichannel retailer can set different prices across channels, but will offer the lower price to the customer if the customer can supply evidence of the lower price. Thus, "self-matching policies, by design, offer retailers the flexibility of setting different prices across channels, while affording consumers the possibility of a consistent experience, presumably in line with the omni-channel philosophy" (Kireyev et al., 2015, p. 29).

Price promotions at omnichannel retailers have several within and across channel implications: offline price promotions can reduce category sales online during the promotion period; furthermore, online promotions can reduce category sales offline during the promotion period; negative cross-channel effects are higher for loyal customers than for opportunists; and, the impact of online promotions on offline sales within the promoted category is higher than vice versa (Breugelmans & Campo, 2016).

One can conclude that successful management of pricing and promotions is a complex field in omnichannel retailing; effects within and across channels have to be considered, and pricing and promotion strategies must be coherent.

Fulfilment

A coherent omnichannel strategy should incorporate both the marketing mix and operations management (Agatz et al., 2008). In this respect, fulfilment is an important component of an omnichannel retailer's operations strategy. According to the reviewed fulfilment literature, omnichannel e-fulfilment is: fulfilling online or in-store orders, including warehousing, picking and order preparation, distribution, purchasing, delivery, and returns (Agatz et al., 2008; Lang & Bressolles, 2013). For omnichannel customers, the four most important dimensions of fulfilment are timeliness, availability, condition, and return (Xing & Grant, 2006; Xing et al., 2010). Timeliness refers to several aspects, such as speed of delivery, choice of delivery date, or delivery within a certain time slot. Availability refers to the confirmation of availability, order tracking, or waiting time. Condition refers to order accuracy, order completeness, or order damage. Return refers to return policies, such as ease of return and return channel options, and the promptness of collection and of replacement (Lang & Bressolles, 2013). For omnichannel retailers this means that their supply chain management needs to be adapted to these specific customer needs. This has several impacts: (1) an online channel not only provides a physical product but also several related services, most notably delivery. The delivery service may range from making the product available for pickup to time-specific home delivery. The management of this service component of e-fulfilment gives rise to novel planning issues. (2) The flexibility of an omnichannel retailer with respect to order promising and pricing requires an appropriate strategy. (3) The integration of different channels raises issues in inventory deployment, since different channels may require different service levels (Agatz et al., 2008). (4) E-fulfilment requirements differ across different product categories (Hu, Kumar, & Sumit, 2014).

The Omnichannel Customer Journey

In omnichannel retailing, the combination of different retail channels during the customer journey has become the predominant purchasing pattern for customers (Lee et al., 2019; Verhoef et al., 2015). Customers constantly switch channels; borders between channels are blurred (Lorenzo-Romero et al., 2020).

In the literature, the switch between different channels is called "ropo"; there are two types of ropo (Heinemann, 2019): (i) research online and purchase offline, and (ii) research offline and purchase online.

1. "Research online and purchase offline" means that internet users research online before making any purchase decision. They compare prices online, obtain information from the producer's webpage, or

read comments of other users of the same product. This trend is called "webrooming", a wordplay of "showrooming", where customers search for retail information online, then purchase offline (Verhoef et al., 2015). This purchase pattern has an important impact on the overall purchase process. In the past, customers first decided what retailer they would approach; then they decided what product they wanted to buy from this retailer. Customers would then visit the store to get information about the different products in the assortment of this retailer. Most customers would also visit other retailers in order to compare offers; then they would make their purchase decision. Nowadays, customers primarily decide what product they want and then choose an adequate retailer. Thus, when customers – after the initial phase of product decision – visit a retail store, they have already collected several pieces of information, such as product features, prices, online availability, and opinions from other users (Verhoef, Neslin, & Vroomen, 2007). The "point of decision" is nowadays often located on the internet, while the store is perceived as the "point of sale" (Heinemann, 2013; Shankar, 2011). Customers increasingly trust the opinions of other product users more than the recommendations made by in-store sales-people or advertisements. When customers enter a retail store, they already know a lot about products and their features. Hence, today's customers have high expectations regarding product availability, immediate accessibility to information, and service delivery.

2. Customers can also "research offline and purchase online". In this context, the store can be seen as a showroom, where customers can physically touch products, interact with salespeople, gather information, and enjoy a shopping experience (Verhoef et al., 2015). Customers are likely to try a product in-store if there are high mis-buy risks associated with buying the product (Heinemann, 2013).

Verhoef et al. (2007) proposed three reasons for ropo. First, customers prefer the channel that offers them the most advantages in each part of the purchase process; they switch among channels during the purchase process if another channel offers more advantages (attribute-based decision making). Second, it is seen as unlikely that customers will purchase via the channel with the most research advantages (lack of channel lock-in). Third, customers carry out research shopping when a channel switch increases their overall shopping experience (cross-channel synergy).

Other studies focussed on retention and free-riding behaviour: customers search for products on one channel of a retailer and buy the products from a different channel of the same retailer (cross-channel retention) or they search a channel of one retailer, but then purchase from a different channel of another retailer (cross-channel free-riding) (Heitz-Spahn, 2013). Chiu, Hsieh, Roan, Tseng, and Hsieh (2011) identified two major reasons for cross-channel free-riding: customers who have a high level of self-efficacy tend to switch channels and retailers during their purchasing process. Second, customers will buy at the retailer who offers good quality and a low risk (Chiu et al., 2011). Furthermore, Chiu et al. (2011) found that within-firm lock-in decreases cross-channel free-riding. This means that retailers can install switching barriers, which reduce customers' intention to switch channels. Heitz-Spahn (2013), however, stated that shopping convenience, flexibility, and price comparisons are the three major cross-channel free-riding motives. It is arguable whether these motives are similar across all industries or whether there are major differences regarding purchasing patterns. Heitz-Spahn (2013) argued that cross-channel free-riding behaviour is more likely for products with a high financial value that customers buy at a low frequency than for other product categories.

Kushwaha and Shankar (2013) investigated whether customers' purchasing behaviour differs for different product categories. They clustered product categories into hedonic and utilitarian categories. Kushwaha and Shankar (2013) found that customers of hedonic products, such as apparel, tended more towards impulse purchases and variety-seeking behaviour, and switched channel more often than customers of utilitarian products.

In addition to differing purchasing behaviour across product categories, the degree of maturity of online purchasing history plays an important role in omnichannel purchasing behaviour. Melis, Campo, and Breugelmans (2015) conducted research in the UK grocery omnichannel market. They found that when customers begin to purchase online, they tend to shop online with the retailer they prefer when purchasing offline, then, as they gain more experience, they start switching channels and retailers (Melis et al., 2015; Ozuem, Thomas & Lancaster, 2016).

Perceived Service Quality
in Omnichannel Retailing

In the context of omnichannel retailing, the evaluation and understanding of service quality has become a topic of major interest both for academics and practitioners (Badrinarayanan, Becerra, & Madhavaram, 2014; Banerjee, 2014; Seck & Philippe, 2013; Swaid & Wigand, 2012; Van Birgelen, De Jong, & Ruyter, 2006). "Owing to the intangible, heterogeneous and inseparable nature of services" (Martinez & Martinez, 2010, p. 30), several definitions of service quality have been built over the years. Zeithaml (1988, p. 3), for instance, saw service quality as "the consumer's judgment about a product's overall excellence or superiority"; Bitner and Hubbert (1994, p. 77) viewed service quality as "the consumer's overall impression of the relative inferiority/superiority of the organization and its services". The academic debate about how to evaluate service quality has developed extensively since the 1980s. In essence, the service quality literature can be divided into two streams: some researchers use a performance-only approach to evaluate service quality (Boulding, Kalra, Staelin, & Zeithaml, 1993; Cronin & Taylor, 1992; Teas, 1993), whereas the majority of researchers evaluate service quality based on the disconfirmation paradigm, that is, the gap between expected service and perceived service (Carr, 2007; Dabholkar, Thorpe, & Rentz, 1996; Grönroos, 1984; Parasuraman, Zeithaml, & Berry, 1988). These studies draw extensively on the work of Oliver (1980). Oliver saw himself in the tradition of Sherif and Hovland's assimilation theory (Sherif & Hovland, 1961) and Festinger's dissonance theory (Festinger, 1957), whereby "customers are posited to perceptually distort expectation-discrepant performance so as to coincide with their prior expectation level" and "post exposure ratings are primarily a function of the expectation level because the task of recognizing disconfirmation is believed to be psychologically uncomfortable" (Oliver, 1980, p. 460).

Several different service quality gap models, such as the Service Quality Model (Grönroos, 1984), SERVQUAL (Parasuraman et al., 1988), E-SQUAL (Parasuraman, Zeithaml, & Malhorta, 2005), and WebQual (Loiacono, Watson, & Goodhue, 2002) have been developed to conceptualize service quality and consumers' perception of it. Most approaches tend to take a single-channel perspective and do not consider multi-channel settings (Seck & Philippe, 2013; Sousa & Voss, 2012); however, omnichannel service quality should be viewed from multiple perspectives, including traditional (for instance retail stores) and electronic (for instance the internet) service settings, because perceived service quality results from all moments of contact between a retailer and its customers (i.e., across all channels) (Sousa & Voss, 2006).

In examining omnichannel service quality conceptualizations, the current chapter identifies five main elements of service quality, namely conceptual framework, dimension, method, perspective, and industry.

Regarding a **conceptual framework** for omnichannel service quality, Sousa and Voss (2006) were the first researchers to develop a framework that did not take a single-channel approach. In their Service Delivery System (SDS) framework they aimed to consider all moments of contact between a firm and its customers. Sousa and Voss distinguished between a physical and a virtual component of service delivery. In the physical component, non-automated operations take place and humans are directly involved. In the virtual component, operations are automated and humans do not play an active role. Sousa and Voss also distinguished between back office and front office operations. Back office operations are not directly visible to the customer whereas front office operations are visible. Sousa and Voss (2006) argued that existing service quality research has a single channel, which is a front office process. In their framework, the physical and the virtual service components (front office and back office) are linked to each other by integration mechanisms. These mechanisms function to integrate "the several service components and associated parts of the SDS" (Sousa & Voss, 2006, p. 359). According to Sousa and Voss, all front and back office physical and virtual operations enriched with integration mechanisms lead to overall perceived service quality. Sousa and Voss argued for a separate examination of physical, virtual, and integration quality: they emphasized the different nature of the three quality dimensions; they forecast a rapid technological development for the virtual dimension; and they saw advantages to examining the virtual dimension separately from the other two, more constant, dimensions of physical and integration quality.

Service quality attributes (**dimensions**) play a predominant role in service quality research, as perceived service quality is a function of different dimensions (Zeithaml & Berry, 1990). In the reviewed literature there is agreement that the key distinction between multichannel and single-channel service quality conceptualizations is the "integration quality" dimension. The contribution of the reviewed studies to the concept of integration quality is illustrated in Fig. 1.2.

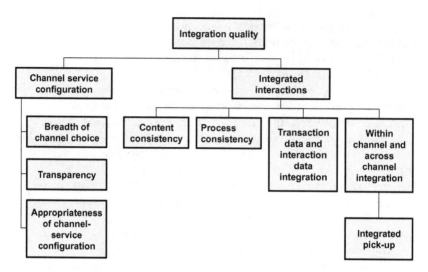

Fig. 1.2 Sub-dimensions of integration quality (*Source* Patten [2017])

In their multichannel SDS framework, Sousa and Voss established the integration quality dimension. They defined integration quality as providing a "seamless service experience across channels" (Sousa & Voss, 2006, p. 359). Sousa and Voss surmised that in a multichannel service system, even when the service quality of each channel is very high, the overall perception of service could be very low when the integration quality is perceived as low. Sousa and Voss proposed two sub-dimensions for integration quality: channel-service configuration and integrated interactions: (1) channel-service configuration is the degree of choice a customer has regarding a service offer in each of the channels (service breadth); (2) integrated interactions lead to a "consistency of interactions across channels" (Sousa & Voss, 2006, p. 366). The researchers emphasized two aspects of integrated interactions: content and process consistency. Content consistency means that customers receive the same information from the company across all channels. Process consistency means that customers expect the same handling of comparable processes.

Banerjee (2014) built up Sousa and Voss's framework and extended their findings on integration quality dimensions by adding three sub-dimensions. First, "the appropriateness of channel service configuration" refers to the degree to which a channel is suitable for different functions as a sub-dimension of channel-service configuration. Second, "transaction data and interaction data integration" refers to the degree to which customer transaction information and inbound and outbound interaction information are synthesized within and across channels. Third, "within channel and across channel integration" refers to the degree to which content and process information is integrated within parts of a channel and across channels (Banerjee, 2014, p. 461).

Swaid and Wigand (2012, p. 306) added "integrated pickup" as another omnichannel service quality sub-dimension: "the extent of smooth and easy pickup of products purchased online using a physical outlet/touchpoint". Swaid and Wigand concluded that integrated pickup is one of the key dimensions of omnichannel service quality.

In addition to integration quality, Sousa and Voss (2006) investigated virtual and physical quality as two other primary dimensions of omnichannel service quality. The definition of virtual quality can be considered equivalent to the definition of electronic service quality based on single-channel conceptualizations (for a review, see Ladhari, 2010). In an electronic setting, service quality means general perceived service in the virtual marketplace, with human intervention and without (Santos, 2003). Physical service quality can be considered equivalent to the definition of traditional service quality based on single-channel conceptualizations (for a review, see Martinez & Martinez, 2010).

Thus, from the reviewed literature, the extant knowledge about service quality dimensions can be synthesized as follows:

- Omnichannel service quality is a multidimensional construct, which consists of primary dimensions and corresponding sub-dimensions.
- There is evidence in the reviewed literature that the existing dimensions have not fully grasped the customer's perception of omnichannel service quality; however, new studies consistently investigate new dimensions.
- Omnichannel service quality consists of the quality that each channel can provide for the customer. However, omnichannel service quality is not a simple summation of service quality perceptions in each channel. Even when physical and electronic service quality are very high, a customer's perception of the overall service quality can be very low when the integration of each service channel is missing. Thus, the service quality dimensions that are experienced in any channel during the purchase process should be congruent online

and offline and should provide a seamless shopping experience for the customer.

- The key distinction between omnichannel and single-channel service systems is the integration quality dimension. The integration quality dimension has the ability to provide a "seamless service experience across channels" (Sousa & Voss, 2006, p. 359).

Regarding different **methods**, research into service quality in multi-channel settings is still in its early stages and few studies have examined service quality in an omnichannel context. The reviewed studies on the service quality of omnichannel settings applied different methods including a literature review (Sousa & Voss, 2006), qualitative methods (Banerjee, 2014), and mixed methods (Seck & Philippe, 2013; Swaid & Wigand, 2012). There are several implications of method choices. For example, Sousa and Voss (2006) conducted a literature review that set the foundation for their development of a framework of service quality in omnichannel services. At the time of their research, there was an absence of a sound conceptual foundation for omnichannel service quality. Sousa and Voss's study aimed to develop theory (Sousa & Voss, 2006). Banerjee (2014) selected qualitative methods and conducted in-depth interviews in order to develop a service quality conceptualization and to gain an in-depth understanding of the omnichannel service quality phenomenon. Generally, a qualitative research method has a non-numeric approach and helps to observe a phenomenon in depth (Saunders, Lewis, & Thornhill, 2009). It provides answers to "how" and "why" questions. In contrast, the quantitative method embraces a positivistic research paradigm and is applied either to analyse covariance or to test whether hypotheses are wrong or right (Guba & Lincoln, 1994). In the field of omnichannel service quality research, some researchers have applied mixed methods. They developed their theories applying a qualitative approach first before testing them in a quantitative manner.

Basically, there are two different **perspectives** regarding omnichannel service quality, namely organizational and customer. The perspective in the reviewed service quality literature is the customer's perspective. Grönroos (1984, p. 36) argued that it is particularly important to understand how the customer evaluates service, because "if we know this and the components of service quality, we will be able to develop service-oriented concepts and models more successfully". Factors that affect service quality are: customer satisfaction (Bitner & Hubbert, 1994), customer loyalty (Grönroos, 1984, p. 37), purchase intention (Bolton & Drew, 1991; Bressolles, Durrieu, & Senecal, 2014; Cronin, Brady, & Hult, 2000; Cronin & Taylor, 1992; Spreng & Mackoy, 1996), profitability (Cox & Dale, 2001; Cristobal, Flavian, & Guinaliu, 2007; Gummerus, Liljander, Pura, & Van Riel, 2004), and purchase retention (Cai & Jun, 2003; Parasuraman et al., 1988; Zeithaml, 2000). One can conclude from this that studies of customers' perspectives help retailers improve their service strategy and the performance of the service they offer (Cristobal et al., 2007; Fassnacht & Köse, 2007; Zeithaml, 2000).

In the reviewed literature, three different **industry** contexts of service quality can be identified: "pure" service industries (such as banking), the retail industry (such as clothing stores), and a mix of pure service and retail industries. The distinction between pure service and retail industries is that in pure service industries the service is the actual "product", whereas stores in the retail industry offer a mix of merchandise and service (Dabholkar et al., 1996; Kaynama, Black, & Keesling, 2000). The early service quality models were researched in the pure service industry (Kaynama et al., 2000). Later, researchers argued for a distinction to be made between different industries because, for instance, retail shopping has unique aspects of service, such as store image (Thang & Tan, 2003), store environment (Baker, Grewal, & Parasuraman, 1994; Dabholkar et al., 1996), in-store experiences (Dabholkar et al., 1996), and experiences related to the merchandise (Bishop Gagliano & Hathcote, 1994; Dabholkar et al., 1996). Mostly, these criteria can be translated to the online world (Kim & Stoel, 2004). However, online and offline shopping provide different shopping experiences. Online customers pay more attention to privacy/security; they appreciate some distinctive online capabilities such as interactivity, community, content, personalized experiences, increased product selection, and information (Wolfinbarger & Gilly, 2003). Offline customers, however, value the personal contact with salespeople in-store and the physical interaction with merchandise (Dabholkar et al., 1996).

An Omnichannel Retailing
Service Quality Conceptualization

This chapter builds on extant literature regarding omnichannel retailing and perceived service quality. Based on the current literature, this chapter proposes the following conceptualization as an approach towards omnichannel service quality, as presented in Fig. 1.3.

Omnichannel service quality conceptualization represents an interplay between omnichannel customers' interaction with the retailer and the omnichannel retailer's integration of assortment, pricing and promotions, fulfilment, and web and store design. Ultimately, omnichannel service quality involves three dimensions, namely physical, electronic, and integration quality. Or, as an equation, omnichannel service quality = integration quality − (physical channels' quality + electronic channels' service quality).

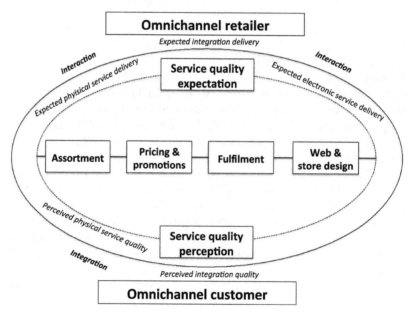

Fig. 1.3 Conceptual framework of omnichannel service quality (*Source* Patten [2017])

Omnichannel Customer Service Perception

In 2017, Patten (2017) conducted an empirical study of omnichannel customers' perception of service quality when purchasing a fashion product. According to Patten (2017), omnichannel customers' service perception consisted of six major themes: (1) physical stimulation, (2) affiliation, (3) value for physical service quality, (4) electronic stimulation, (5) utility for electronic service quality, and (6) choice optimization for the integration service quality.

The major themes that relate to the physical channel imply some emotional involvement on the part of omnichannel customers. Therefore, omnichannel customers seek physical stimulation from offline-mediated environments and, in particular, from store design, visual merchandising, and haptics.

Moreover, omnichannel customers tend to use offline-mediated environments to affiliate with others. This includes human relations, status, and advice. The first term expresses that omnichannel customers value meeting like-minded people in pleasant shopping environments. Such people can be familiar (e.g., friends, family, or familiar salespeople) or unfamiliar (other customers or unknown salespeople).

Westbrook and Black (1985, p. 90) defined affiliation (the second theme) as a dimension of shopping motivation that includes: (1) shopping alongside other customers who have similar tastes, (2) talking with salespeople and other shoppers who share interests, and (3) shopping with friends as a social occasion.

The third sub-dimension of physical service quality in an omnichannel retailing context is value. Omnichannel customers tend to be value-oriented when purchasing in offline-mediated environments.

Value orientation includes appreciation, honesty, trust, friendliness, and empathy. Salespeople have the most significant impact on these customers' value perceptions. In this context, three characteristics of omnichannel customers can be identified: (1) those who seek an individualistic and situation-related approach, (2) those who are enlightened by prior knowledge about a product before entering the retail store, and (3) those who retain a level of scepticism regarding advice received from sales employees (Patten, 2017).

The major themes that relate to the electronic channel context imply a mix of rational and emotional involvement on the part of omnichannel customers. Electronic stimulation refers to web design, content, and haptics. In terms of web design, omnichannel customers seek practicability, a clear structure, and filter options. These findings resonate with the "ease of use" service quality dimension that represents "the degree to which the functionality of the user interface facilitates the customer's retrieval of the electronic service" (Zeithaml, Parasuraman, & Malhotra, 2002, p. 363). However, the findings of this chapter go beyond this definition. Omnichannel customers also value the emotional aspects of web design. Accordingly, they cite attractive web design and video footage as strong product features.

In the context of online content, a retailer's assortment strategy can be seen as a controversial issue, both in the literature and in this chapter (Mantrala et al., 2009). It is a strategic managerial decision to offer an attractive assortment on the one hand but avoid choice difficulty on the other.

The concept of integration is the main difference between a single-channel and a multichannel service quality system. According to the literature, all physical and electronic elements enriched with integration mechanisms lead to overall perceptions of omnichannel service quality (Sousa & Voss, 2006). "Connection" and "linkage" are the terms that explain how customers express what is known in the literature as "integration quality". The emergent theme for integration quality is choice optimization.

Before the emergence of e-commerce and omnichannel retailing, Westbrook and Black (1985, p. 87) defined choice optimization as the "motivation to search for and secure precisely the right product to fit one's demands". In the context of service quality in omnichannel retailing, customers search for the "right" type of service and select the most suitable channel. Omnichannel customers tend to optimize their choices during the purchasing process. Integration quality is the essence of competitive advantage for omnichannel retailers compared to single-channel retailers. At omnichannel retailers, customers are able to switch channels without switching retailer. As the chapter suggests, they exploit this opportunity when the omnichannel retailer ensures optimized efforts, availability of items, price, and support (Patten, 2017).

As Fig. 1.4 illustrates, each retail channel provides different characteristics. In a well-integrated omnichannel system, customers are able to optimize their choice options. Hence, integration quality reinforces the characteristics of physical and electronic service quality in order to provide an optimized service quality experience. Therefore, integration can be

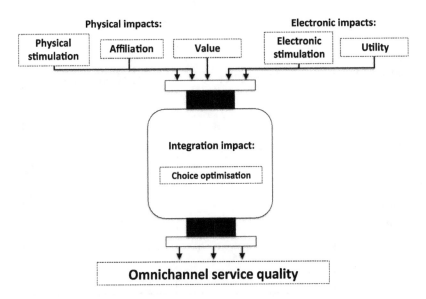

Fig. 1.4 Integration quality as a catalyst of omnichannel service quality (*Source* Patten [2017])

considered to be the competitive advantage enjoyed by an omnichannel retailer. Customers can exploit the full advantages of each channel, which has a positive impact on their overall service quality perception.

OMNICHANNEL CUSTOMER TYPOLOGY

Based on the findings on the service quality perception of omnichannel customers, Patten (2017) developed an omnichannel customer typology (see Fig. 1.5). "Each type of customer is distinguished by a specific pattern of social characteristics reflecting his position in the social structure" (Stone, 1954, p. 36). The generators of heterogeneity among omnichannel customers can be considered to be available income level and involvement with fashion products (Patten, 2017).

Hedonists were the largest customer segment. They had low or medium available incomes and they showed high emotional involvement. Their principal drivers were shopping experiences and amusement. For these customers, it is important to remain well informed about the latest fashion trends. They are price-sensitive due to their low available income,

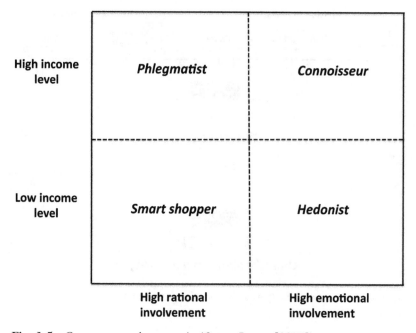

Fig. 1.5 Customer typology matrix (*Source* Patten [2017])

which is why they prefer to purchase from fast fashion discounters. A strong reference to affiliation and emotive stimulation are both indicators of high emotional involvement among this customer segment. Hedonists value omnichannel retailing for efficiency reasons. Since fashion trends are very short lived nowadays, they mainly use channel integration for availability checks across channels and they value fast delivery and an effortless purchasing process (Patten, 2019).

The connoisseur customer segment also demonstrates high emotional involvement in fashion purchases, but has a medium-high or high income. The connoisseur looks for indulgence when purchasing a fashion product. Connoisseurs can be considered the most demanding customer segment. They tend to have a clear idea of what they want. They are not dependent on the lower-priced retailing segment and they have high expectations concerning service quality. Generally, connoisseurs can be considered loyal customers, but if they migrate due to unsatisfying experiences it is hard for retailers to win them back. This customer segment seeks inspiration online and offline. They are receptive to aesthetic store design and visual merchandising. Furthermore, they follow lifestyle bloggers. However, in contrast to hedonists, who are influenced by bloggers and their fashion styles, connoisseurs look for bloggers who share a similar attitude and lifestyle. This segment appreciates competent personal advice and they avoid visiting stores that offer poor personal advice. When purchasing online, they value visual stories and editorials as well as aesthetic web design and sophisticated packaging. Connoisseurs have limited time and so they carry out omnichannel shopping to be efficient. They seek availability checks across channels and prefer the option to reserve items online and try them on in-store.

In contrast, smart shoppers have a low or medium available income and demonstrate higher rational involvement. They are principally driven by savings. Smart shoppers can be considered the least loyal segment because they show opportunistic buying behaviour at the retailer that offers them the cheapest price. Smart shoppers show a preference towards online shopping, since price comparisons are easier to complete online than offline. Furthermore, smart shoppers generally perceive prices to be lower online. They value integration quality for a more efficient comparison of prices across channels (Patten, 2019).

Phlegmatic shoppers are the second segment of higher rationally involved omnichannel customers. These shoppers have a medium to high income level. They are mainly driven by convenience. They can be considered loyal customers, except when they experience service failure at a retailer. Once they migrate, recovery is challenging for the retailer. Phlegmatic shoppers tend to have high expectations regarding the services they are offered. They value efficiency, convenience, practicability, and competence above all. These shoppers have a clear channel preference when it comes to purchasing fashion products. Switching barriers can be a helpful tool for omnichannel retailers to dissuade phlegmatic shoppers from cross-channel free-riding (Patten, 2019). Phlegmatic shoppers have a positive perception of channel integration because they value choice optimization for effort, availability, price, and support.

Managerial Implications and Recommendations

This chapter sets out a number of managerial implications. First, since omnichannel customers tend to constantly adjust their choices regarding retailer and retail channel during purchase, it is important for omnichannel retailers to set up coherent and integrated sales and communication strategies across channels. Retailers should cease working in silo organizations where one stream is in charge of online activities and another is in charge of offline activities. The different departments need to work in a cross-disciplinary manner, since omnichannel customers expect a seamless shopping experience.

Second, omnichannel retailers should employ managers who are in charge of the "integration" of the different channels, since it is a strategic managerial decision for omnichannel retailers to find the "right" level of integration, especially regarding assortment, pricing and promotions, fulfilment, and web and store design. In so doing, they will be able to fully leverage the competitive advantage of both channels.

Third, as this chapter suggests, salespeople still play an important role in the offline channel as a source of affiliation and furthermore to provide value. The more accessible a product is online and in-store, the more likely customers are to migrate to other retailers and/or retail channels when dissatisfied with the sales experience. Retailers need to train their sales teams to address the aforementioned attributes. Salespeople need to be better adjusted to the needs of "enlightened" omnichannel customers who already possess knowledge when entering a store. Furthermore, salespeople should address the various requests arising from the individualistic buying habits of omnichannel customers.

Fourth, the changed behaviour of omnichannel customers makes it necessary to identify a new approach towards service quality. At present, omnichannel retailers still tend to take a single-channel approach, and do not consider the distinctive requirements of multiple channel systems. So, managers of omnichannel retailers should not only place emphasis on enhancing and improving physical and/or electronic service quality, but also shift towards the integration of the service offers of both channels. The overall purchasing experience needs to be consistent for the customer at all moments of contact between the retailer and the customer in order for the customer to perceive a seamless service quality.

Fifth, this chapter suggests that omnichannel retailers should analyse their customer base by means of the four customer types proposed in this chapter, namely: (1) phlegmatic, (2) smart, (3) hedonist, and (4) connoisseur shoppers. There is no "one-size-fits-all" solution, since each customer group has distinctive drivers, behavioural characteristics, and perceptions regarding physical, electronic, and integration quality. Thus, to be able to set up an effective and successful strategy the fundamental question omnichannel retailers should be able to answer is, Which specific customer type do we want to target?

References

Agatz, N., Fleischmann, M., & Van Nunen, J. (2008). E-fulfilment and multi-channel distribution—A review. *European Journal of Operational Research, 187*(2), 339–356.

Alexander, B., & Cano, M. (2020). Store of the future: Towards a (re)invention and (re)imagination of physical store space in an omnichannel context. *Journal of Retailing and Consumer Services, 55,* 1–12.

Badrinarayanan, V., Becerra, E., & Madhavaram, S. (2014). Influence of congruity in store-attribute dimensions and self-image on purchase intentions in online stores of multichannel retailers. *Journal of Retailing and Consumer Services, 21,* 1013–1020.

Baker, J., Grewal, D., & Parasuraman, A. (1994). The influence of store environment on quality inferences and store image. *Journal of the Academy of Marketing Science, 22*(4), 328–339.

Banerjee, M. (2014). Misalignment and its influence on integration quality in multichannel services. *Journal of Service Research, 17*(4), 460–474.

Beck, N., & Rygl, D. (2015). Categorization of multiple channel retailing in multi-, cross-, and omni-channel for retailers and retailing. *Journal of Retailing and Consumer Services, 27,* 170–178.

Berman, B. (1996). *Marketing channels.* New York: John Wiley & Sons.

Berman, B., & Thelen, S. (2004). A guide to developing and managing a well-integrated multi-channel retail strategy. *International Journal of Retail & Distribution Management, 32*(3), 147–156.

Berry, L., Bolton, R., Bridges, C., Meyer, J., Parasuraman, A., & Seiders, K. (2010). Opportunities for innovation in the delivery of interactive retail services. *Journal of Interactive Marketing, 24*(2), 155–167.

Bertrandie, L., & Zielke, S. (2019). The influence of multichannel pricing strategy on price fairness and customer confusion. *The International Review of Retail, Distribution and Consumer Research, 29*(5), 504–517.

Bishop Gagliano, K., & Hathcote, J. (1994). Customer expectations and perceptions of service quality in retail apparel specialty stores. *Journal of Services Marketing, 8*(1), 60–69.

Bitner, M. J., & Hubbert, A. R. (1994). Encounter satisfaction versus overall satisfaction versus quality. In R. T. Rust & R. L. Oliver (Eds.), *Service quality: New directions in theory and practice* (pp. 72–94). London: Sage.

Bolton, R., & Drew, J. (1991). A multistage model of customers' assessments of service quality and value. *Journal of Consumer Research, 17,* 375–384.

Boulding, W., Kalra, A., Staelin, R., & Zeithaml, V. (1993). A dynamic process model of service quality: From expectations to behavioral intentions. *Journal of Marketing Research, 30,* 7–27.

Bressolles, G., Durrieu, F., & Senecal, S. (2014). A consumer typology based on e-service quality and e-satisfaction. *Journal of Retailing and Consumer Services, 21,* 889–896.

Breugelmans, E., & Campo, K. (2016). Cross-channel effects of price promotions: An empirical analysis of the multi-channel grocery retail sector. *Journal of Retailing, 92*(3), 333–351.

Brynjolfsson, E., Hu, Y. J., & Rahman, M. S. (2013). Competing in the age of omnichannel retailing. *MIT Sloan Management Review, 54*(4), 23–29.

Cai, S., & Jun, M. (2003). Internet users' perceptions of online service quality: a comparison of online buyers and information searchers. *Managing Service Quality, 13*(6), 504–519.

Carr, C. (2007). The FAIRSERV model: Consumer reactions to services based on a multidimensional evaluation of service fairness. *Decision Science, 38*(1), 107–130.

Chiu, H.-C., Hsieh, Y. C., Roan, J., Tseng, K.-J., & Hsieh, J.-K. (2011). The challenge for multichannel services: cross-channel free-riding behavior. *Electronic Commerce Research and Applications, 10,* 268–277.

Cox, J., & Dale, B. G. (2001). Service quality and e-commerce: an explanatory analysis. *Managing Service Quality, 11*(2), 121–131.

Cristobal, E., Flavian, C., & Guinaliu, M. (2007). Perceived e-service quality: measurement validity and effects on consumer satisfaction and web site loyalty. *Managing Service Quality, 17*(3), 317–340.

Cronin, J., Brady, M., & Hult, G. (2000). Assessing the effects of quality, value, and customer satisfaction on consumer behavioral intentions in service environments. *Journal of Retailing, 76*(2), 193–218.

Cronin, J., & Taylor, S. (1992). Measuring service quality: A reexamination and extension. *Journal of Marketing, 56*(3), 55–68.

Dabholkar, P., Thorpe, D., & Rentz, J. (1996). A measure of service quality for retail stores: Scale development and validation. *Journal of the Academy of Marketing Science, 24*(1), 3–16.

Emrich, O., Paul, M., & Rudolph, T. (2015). Shopping benefits of multichannel assortment integration and the moderating role of retailer type. *Journal of Retailing, 91*(2), 326–342.

Emrich, O., & Verhoef, C. P. (2015). The impact of a homogenous versus a prototypical web design on online retail patronage for multichannel providers. *International Journal of Research in Marketing, 32,* 363–374.

Fassnacht, M., & Köse, I. (2007). Consequences of web-based service quality: Uncovering a multi-faceted chain of effects. *Journal of Interactive Marketing, 21*(3), 35–54.

Festinger, L. (1957). *A theory of cognitive dissonance*. New York: Harper & Row.

Goersch, D. (2002). *Multi-Channel integration and its implications for retail web sites*. Paper presented at the The 10th European Conference on Information Systems, Gdansk.

Grönroos, C. (1984). A service quality model and its marketing implications. *European Journal of Marketing, 18*(4), 36–44.

Guba, E. G., & Lincoln, Y. (Eds.). (1994). *Paradigmatic controversies, contradictions, and emerging confluences*. Thousand Oaks: Sage.

Gummerus, J., Liljander, V., Pura, M., & Van Riel, A. (2004). Customer loyalty to content-based web sites: The case of an online health-care service. *Journal of Services Marketing, 18*(3), 175–186.

Heinemann, G. (2013). *No-Line-Handel*. Wiesbaden: Gabler Verlag.

Heinemann, G. (2019). *Handel mit Mehrwert*. Wiesbaden: Springer Gabler.

Heitz-Spahn, S. (2013). Cross-channel free-riding consumer behavior in a multichannel environment: an investigation of shopping motives, sociodemographics and product categories. *Journal of Retailing and Consumer Services, 20*(6), 570–578.

Hu, M., Kumar, R., & Sumit, C. (2014). Best pratices in strategic multichannel fulfillment. *Ivey Business Journal, Mar/Apr, 2014*, 1–6.

Huan, L., Lobschat, L., & Verhoef, P. (2019). Multichannel retailing: A review and research agenda. *Foundations and Trends in Marketing, 12*(1), 1–79.

Hult, G., Tomas, M., & Zhang, Y. (2019). Antecedents and consequences of customer satisfaction: do they differ across online and offline purchases? *Journal of Retailing, 95*(1), 10–23.

Kaynama, S., Black, C., & Keesling, G. (2000). Impact of the internet on internal service quality factors: the travel industry case. *The Journal of Applied Business Research, 19*(135–146).

Kim, S., & Stoel, L. (2004). Apparel retailers: Website quality dimensions and satisfaction. *Journal of Retailing and Consumer Services, 11*(2), 109–117.

Kireyev, P., Kumar, V., & Ofek, E. (2015). *Match your own price? Self-matching as a multichannel retailer's pricing strategy*. Watertown: Harvard Business Review.

Kushwaha, T., & Shankar, V. (2013). Are multichannel customers really more valuable? The moderating role of product category characteristics. *Journal of Marketing, 77*(3), 67–85.

Ladhari, R. (2010). Developing e-service quality scales: A literature review. *Journal of Retailing and Consumer Services, 17*, 464–477.

Lang, G., & Bressolles, G. (2013). Economic performance and customer expectation in e-fulfillment systems: A multichannel retailer perspective. *Supply Chain Forum, 14*(1), 16–27.

Lee, Z., Chan, T., Chong, A., & Thadani, D. (2019). Customer engagement through omnichannel retailing: The effects of channel integration quality. *Industrial Marketing Management, 77,* 90–101.

Li, Y., Liu, H., Lim, E., Goh, J., Yang, F., & Lee, M. (2018). Customer's reaction to cross-channel integration in omnichannel retailing: The mediating roles of retailer uncertainty, identity attractiveness, and switching costs. *Decision Support Systems, 109,* 50–60.

Loiacono, E., Watson, R., & Goodhue, D. (2002). WEBQUAL: A measure of website quality. *Journal of Marketing, 60*(2), 432–438.

Lorenzo-Romero, C., Andrés-Martinez, M., & Mondéjar-Jiménez, J. (2020). Omnichannel in the fashion industry: A qualitative analysis from a supply-side perspective. *Heliyon, 6,* 1–10.

Mantrala, M., Levy, M., Kahn, B., Fox, E., Gaidarev, P., Dankworth, B., et al. (2009). Why is assortment planning so difficult for retailers? A framework and research agenda. *Journal of Retailing, 85*(1), 71–83.

Martinez, J., & Martinez, L. (2010). Some insights on conceptualizing and measuring service quality. *Journal of Retailing and Consumer Services, 17*(1), 29–42.

Melis, K., Campo, K., & Breugelmans, L. (2015). The impact of the multichannel retail mix on online store choice: Does online experience matter? *Journal of Retailing, 91*(272–288).

Neslin, S., Grewal, D., Leghorn, R., Shankar, V., Teerlin, M., Thomas, J., et al. (2006). Challenges and opportunities in multichannel customer management. *Journal of Service Research, 9*(2), 95–112.

Oliver, R. L. (1980). A cognitive model of the antecedents and consequences of satisfaction decisions. *Journal of Marketing Research, 17*(4), 460–469.

Ozuem, W., Howell, K. E., & Lancaster, G. (2008). Communicating in the new interactive marketspace. *European Journal of Marketing, 42*(9/10), 1059–1083.

Ozuem, W., Patel, A., Howell, K. E., & Lancaster, G. (2017). An exploration of customers' response to online service recovery initiatives. *International Journal of Market Research, 59*(1), 97–116.

Ozuem, W., Thomas, T., & Lancaster, G. (2016). The influence of customer loyalty on small island economies: an empirical and exploratory study. *Journal of Strategic Marketing, 24*(6), 447–469.

Parasuraman, A., Zeithaml, V., & Berry, L. (1988). SERVQUAL: A multiple-item scale for measuring consumer perceptions of service quality. *Journal of Retailing, 64*(1), 12–40.

Parasuraman, A., Zeithaml, V., & Malhorta, A. (2005). E-S-QUAL: A multiple-item scale for assessing electronic service quality. *Journal of Service Research, 7*(3), 213–233.

Patten, E. (2017). *Conceptualizing service quality in multichannel fashion retailing* (PhD), University of Gloucestershire, Cheltenham.

Patten, E. (2019). Customer typology in German omni-channel fashion retailing. In W. Ozuem, E. Patten, & Y. Azemi (Eds.), *Harnessing Omni-channel marketing strategies for fashion and luxury brands*. Boca Raton, FL, USA: Brown Walker Press.

Pelton, L., Strutton, D., & Lumpkin, J. (2002). *Marketing channels—A relationship management approach* (2nd ed.). Chicago: Irwin/McGraw-Hill.

Rezaei, S., & Valaei, N. (2017). Branding in a multichannel retail environment: Online stores vs app stores and the effect of product type. *Information Technology & People, 30*(4), 853–886.

Santos, J. (2003). E-service quality: A model of virtual service quality dimensions. *Managing Service Quality, 13*(3), 233–246.

Saunders, M., Lewis, P., & Thornhill, A. (2009). *Research methods for business students* (5th ed., vol. 5). Harlow: Pearson.

Seck, A. (2013). The issue of multichannel integration, a key challenge for service firms in a context of multichannel services distribution. *International Business Research, 6*(2), 160–169.

Seck, A., & Philippe, J. (2013). Service encounter in multi-channel distribution context: Virtual and face-to-face interactions and consumer satisfaction. *The Service Industries Journal, 33*(6), 565–579.

Shankar, V. (2011). Innovations in shopper marketing: Current insights and future research issues. *Journal of Retailing, 87*(1), 29–43.

Sherif, M., & Hovland, C. I. (1961). *Social judgment: Assimilation and contrast effects in communication and attitude change*. New Haven: Yale University Press.

Sousa, R., & Voss, C. (2006). Service quality in multichannel services employing virtual channels. *Journal of Service Research, 8*(4), 356–371.

Sousa, R., & Voss, C. (2012). The impacts of e-service quality on customer behavior in multi-channel services. *Total Quality Management & Business Excellence, 23*(7), 769–787.

Spreng, R., & Mackoy, R. (1996). An empirical examination of a model of perceived service quality and satisfaction. *Journal of Retailing, 72*(2), 201–214.

Stone, G. (1954). City shoppers and urban identifications. Observation on the psychology of city life. *American Journal of Sociology, 60*(1), 36–45.

Swaid, S., & Wigand, R. (2012). The effective of perceived site-to-store service quality on perceived value and loyalty intentions in multichannel retailing. *International Journal of Management, 29*(3), 301–313.

Teas, K. (1993). Expectations, performance evaluation, and consumers' perceptions of quality. *Journal of Marketing, 57*, 18–34.

Thang, D., & Tan, B. (2003). Linking consumer perception to preference of retail stores: An empirical assessment of the multi-attributes of store image. *Journal of Retailing and Consumer Services, 10,* 193–200.

Van Birgelen, M., De Jong, A., & Ruyter, K. (2006). Multi-channel service retailing: The effects of channel performance satisfaction on behavioral intentions. *Journal of Retailing, 82*(4), 367–377.

Verhoef, P., Kannan, P. K., & Inman, J. J. (2015). From multi-channel retailing to omni-channel retailing: Introduction to the special issue on multi-channel retailing. *Journal of Retailing, 91*(2), 174–181.

Verhoef, P., Neslin, S., & Vroomen, B. (2007). Multichannel customer management: Understanding the research shopper phenomenon. *International Journal of Research in Marketing, 24*(2), 129–148.

Vogel, J., & Paul, M. (2015). One firm, one product, two prices: Channel-based price differentiation and customer retention. *Journal of Retailing and Consumer Services, 27,* 126–139.

Westbrook, R. A., & Black, W. C. (1985). A motivation-based shopper typology. *Journal of Retailing, 61*(1), 78–103.

Wolfinbarger, M., & Gilly, M. (2003). eTailQ: dimensionalizing, measuring and predicting etail quality. *Journal of Retailing, 79*(3), 183–198.

Wolk, A., & Ebling, C. (2010). Multichannel price differentiation: an empirical investigation of existence and causes. *International Journal of Research in Marketing, 27*(2), 142–150.

Xing, Y., & Grant, D. (2006). Developing a framework for measuring physical distribution service quality of multichannel and 'pure player' Internet retailers. *International Journal of Retail & Distribution Management, 34*(4), 278–289.

Xing, Y., Grant, D., McKinnon, A., & Fernie, J. (2010). Physical distribution service quality in online retailing. *International Journal of Physical Distribution and Logistics Management, 40*(5), 415–432.

Zeithaml, V. (1988). Consumer perceptions of price, quality, and value: A means-end model and synthesis of evidence. *Journal of Marketing, 52*(3), 2–22.

Zeithaml, V. (2000). Service quality, profitability, and the economic worth of customers: What we know and what we need to learn. *Journal of the Academy of Marketing Science, 28*(1), 67–85.

Zeithaml, V., & Berry, L. (1990). *Delivering quality service.* New York: Free Press.

Zeithaml, V., Parasuraman, A., & Malhotra, A. (2002). Service quality delivery through web sites: a critical review of extant knowledge. *Journal of the Academic Marketing Science, 30*(4), 362–375.

Zhang, J., Farris, P., Irvin, J., Kushwaha, T., Steenburgh, T., & Weitz, B. (2010). Crafting integrated multichannel retailing strategies. *Journal of Interactive Marketing, 24*(2), 168–180.

CHAPTER 2

Omnichannel Retailing and Brand Equity: A New Balance to Achieve

Claudio Becagli and Matilde Milanesi

INTRODUCTION

During the last twenty years, the retail world has experienced important changes. In particular, technological, telecommunication, and digital developments had a transformative and transversal role. These changes pushed companies to modify their organization and business models (Sorescu, Frambach, Singh, Rangaswamy, & Bridges, 2011) but, at the same time, they induced a transformation in the way customers raise information, take decisions, and buy products or services. To cope with these challenges, in addition to the traditional retail and communication channels, retailers are experimenting with new online and digital channels like mobile devices and social media (Verhoef, Kannan, & Inman, 2015). As defined by Neslin et al. (2006), a channel is a customer contact point or a medium through which a company and a customer interact. Keller (2010) distinguished between channels of distribution and marketing communications, where the first can be classified into direct and interactive channels

C. Becagli (✉) · M. Milanesi
University of Florence, Florence, Italy

© The Author(s), under exclusive license to Springer Nature
Switzerland AG 2021
W. Ozuem and S. Ranfagni (eds.), *The Art of Digital Marketing for Fashion and Luxury Brands*,
https://doi.org/10.1007/978-3-030-70324-0_2

(i.e., selling through personal contacts of the company to prospective customers by mail, phone, internet, mobile, etc.) and indirect channels (selling through third-party intermediaries), and the second can be classified into personal communications (i.e., personal selling, direct marketing, word of mouth, etc.) and mass communications (i.e., advertising, sales promotions, events, etc.). In certain retail markets, like music or movie distribution, online and other digital channels overtook traditional channels, almost entirely changing how products are distributed (Christensen & Raynor, 2003; Ozuem, Howell, & Lancaster, 2008). In other markets, the new distribution and communication channels represented new areas of intervention for companies.

In the first phase, traditional retail companies (the so-called bricks-and-mortar retailers) had to face the competition represented by the diffusion of new online distribution channels. This forced them to add new channels to their offline ones. At a later stage, the problem of channel diversification also became a priority for online operators who had to respond to the need to be also present offline (Avery, Steenburgh, Deighton, & Caravella, 2012). Nowadays, thanks also to the spread of mobile devices, the clear distinction among different channels has almost disappeared for consumers. Indeed, quite frequently, consumers simultaneously recourse to different channels during their research and purchase activity. In this regard, some authors have referred to two opposite phenomena: showrooming and webrooming. In the first case, consumers look for information in the physical store and buy online, where they can find more advantageous offers (Rapp, Baker, Bachrach, Ogilvie, & Beitelspacher, 2015), as frequently happens in luxury fashion retailers (Jebarajakirthy, Yadav, & Shankar, 2020), while in the second case, consumers collect information online and then buy offline (Verhoef, Neslin, & Vroomen, 2007). As Brynjolfsson, Hu, and Rahman (2013) observed, the retailing industry is evolving "toward a seamless 'omni-channel retailing' experience, in which the distinctions between physical and online will vanish, turning the world into a showroom without walls" (p. 2).

The possibility for the customer to use the various touchpoints in an integrated way represents for retailers both a threat and a great opportunity. It could, on the one hand, require companies to make important changes to their distinctive competencies, organization, culture, management, and marketing (Picot-Coupey, Huré, Piveteau, Towers, & Kotzab,

2016), on the other hand, it allows companies to propose innovative shopping journeys aimed at improving the value perceived by the customers, the consumer-based brand equity and, consequently, the overall value (Keller, 2010, 2016; Keller and Lehmann, 2003). The number and heterogeneity of the factors that can affect the interaction contexts between retailers and customers make it clear that there cannot be a one-fit-all solution, and companies will have to manage touchpoints by enhancing their resources and distinctive competencies. As observed by Keller (2010), companies tend to use multiple channels and communications because they are necessary to create an adequate reach and coverage of the target customers, and because different communications and channels play different roles and create different effects for each consumer. Furthermore, they also allow for differing levels of consumer engagement and involvement.

In this new omnichannel retail context, customer satisfaction is influenced by the customer experience not only with respect to a specific channel but with respect to the variety of channels used (Shen, Li, Sun, & Wang, 2018; Lee, Chan, Chong, & Thadani, 2019). Marketers must therefore define the best set of channel and communication options to maximize short-term sales and long-term brand equity, dedicating particular attention to managing retailing and communicating mix, trying to align every touchpoint with the brand fundamentals (Picot-Coupey et al., 2016; Verhoef, Kannan, & Inman, 2015; Ozuem, Patel, Howell, & Lancaster, 2017).

The difficulty of managing the interaction with consumers is particularly relevant since not all touchpoints are managed and controlled by the company. Lemon and Verhoef (2016) distinguished between touchpoints managed by the company, its partners, consumers, or external actors. Among those that are not under the control of the company, user-generated content can play a vital role in supporting or undermining the alignment between how the brand is perceived by consumers and how the brand is defined by the company (Becagli, Ranfagni, & Faraoni, 2020. The efficacy and the efficiency of the delivered shopping experience can be assessed referring to Keller's customer-based brand equity (CBBE) model (Keller and Lehmann, 2003; Keller, 2008, 2010, 2016) and brand resonance model (Keller, 2001, 2010). These models consider the brand equity from a consumer perspective and take into account many factors that may be influenced by any channel or communication marketing activity.

Starting from this background, this chapter delves into the shift from a multichannel to an omnichannel approach by retailing companies, and its implications for CBBE. In particular, the next section briefly shows the main differences between multichannel and omnichannel retailing, then, the main features of the omnichannel approach are analysed. The fourth section discusses how to build and manage CBBE in omnichannel retailing. The chapter ends with a discussion focused on luxury fashion companies and avenues for future research.

FROM MULTICHANNEL TO OMNICHANNEL RETAILING

Interest in digital consumers rose in the last two decades; data on digital retail support such interest. According to eMarketer, which provides statistics on digital retail, over 2.14 billion people worldwide are expected to buy goods and services online in 2021, compared to the 1.66 billion global digital buyers in 2016. In 2019, 63% of global internet users purchased products online. These figures clearly show that retailers must pay attention to consumers who use smartphones, tablets, and even social media for their buying process. Thus, the academic debate around this topic has stressed the need for retailers to move from a multichannel to an omnichannel approach.

Verhoef et al. (2015) showed that digital consumer behaviour has led retailers to move from multichannel to omnichannel retailing. Multichannel retailing means offering products in many different online and/or offline channels, while omnichannel retailing means offering seamless customer experiences across different channels and touchpoints. Verhoef et al. (2015, p. 175) stated that, on the one hand, multichannel retail management concerns "the design, deployment, coordination, and evaluation of channels to enhance customer value through effective customer acquisition, retention, and development", and, on the other hand, omnichannel retail management should focus on "the synergetic management of the numerous available channels and customer touchpoints, in such a way that the customer experience across channels and the performance over channels are optimized". The multichannel approach is characterized by a separation between online and physical channels, with a scarce degree of integration (Melero, Sese, & Verhoef, 2016). Conversely, the omnichannel approach focuses on customer touchpoints and channel integration aimed at providing a seamless holistic shopping experience to improve customer engagement (Beck and Rygl, 2015).

Thus, there are some relevant differences in the two approaches: coordination versus synergies, conversion (lead acquisition, retention, and development) versus holistic customer experience, and combination of channels versus focus on brand and touchpoints (Rosengren, Lange, Hernant, & Blom, 2018).

In the past, retailers started to use a multichannel approach to gain consumers' attention and respond to their demands (Rangaswamy and Van Bruggen, 2005), by managing a set of activities aimed at selling products or services across various channels without any interaction/integration among them. In other words, the multichannel approach draws on customers' willingness to explore more convenient ways to improve their shopping experience (Beck and Rygl, 2015; Ozuem, Thomas, & Lancaster, 2016). However, the growing use of the internet and new technologies has made the transition to an omnichannel approach almost inevitable. Even if, in the beginning, researchers discussed channel migration, namely the switch from offline to online stores, there is now a general understanding that most consumers use channels interchangeably and move back and forth between them, making an omnichannel approach indispensable. But why "omnichannel"? The word originates from the Latin word "omni" which means "all", "universal". The term was first used by business practitioners, but soon gained the attention of scholars, especially in the marketing domain. Parker and Hand (2009) and Ortis and Casoli (2009) used the term in the IDC's "Global Retail Insights" report and suggested an evolution from the multichannel consumer, who uses channels in parallel, to the omnichannel consumer, who uses channels simultaneously. The term then found its space in the academic debate when Rigby (2011) defined omnichannel retailing as "an integrated sales experience that melds the advantages of physical stores with the information-rich experience of online shopping" (Rigby, 2011, p. 4). It appears clear from the definition that it is not only a matter of simultaneity in the use of channels, but there is also a focus on the experience that derives from the integrated combination of several channels. Similarly, in 2013, Levy and colleagues (2013, p. 67) defined "omni-retailing" as "a coordinated multichannel offering that provides a seamless experience when using all of the retailer's shopping channels". The two definitions agreed around the idea of an integrated/seamless experience using all channels.

In the meantime, academic interest in the topic increased. Since then, an intense academic debate has begun aimed at outlining the contents and characteristics of omnichannel retailing, as well as the main strategies and implications in terms of brand management (Galipoglu, Kotzab, Teller, Hüseyinoglu, & Pöppelbuß, 2018).

Omnichannel Retailing: An Overview

Retail practices and consumers' shopping journeys have been deeply transformed in recent years by the diffusion of innovative retail settings besides the traditional ones, and the growing adoption of alternative business-to-consumer retail channels, resulting in a fast-evolving multichannel retail environment, which represents a challenge for retail managers, as well as a fertile ground for interesting research issues (Lazaris and Vrechopoulos, 2014).

The omnichannel retailing phenomenon originates from the multichannel retail infrastructure and is mainly based on the simultaneous use of many consumer–store interaction channels (e.g., the use of smartphones in the physical retail store to search for product information and/or compare prices) (Silva, Duarte, & Sundetova, 2020). The omnichannel approach (Carroll & Guzmán, 2013) refers to a seamless shopping experience delivered through the integration of customer touchpoints (Beck & Rygl, 2015). Consumers have the chance to choose the most suitable retail channel for themselves at any step of their shopping journey, without interrupting their shopping experience (Melero et al., 2016). The omnishopper (Yurova, Rippé, Weisfeld-Spolter, Sussan, & Arndt, 2017) can check the product characteristics using a mobile application, can compare prices on different websites using a tablet, a smartphone, or a computer, and complete the purchase at a physical store. From the retailer's point of view, the omnichannel approach calls for a redefinition of existing strategies to integrate the information provided from distinct channels and trace the consumer journey (Brynjolfsson et al., 2013).

It is interesting to trace the origins of the concept. Lazaris and Vrechopoulos (2014) proposed a review of the relevant literature, which revealed that omnichannel originated from the notion of "click and mortar". It all started in 2000 when Otto and Chung (2000) discussed a way to combine e-commerce techniques with traditional physical retailing, intending to enhance the value of the shopping experience. They defined "cyber-enhanced retailing" and proposed e-commerce practices to link with conventional retailing. Two years later, Burke (2002) focused on the

customer experience and conducted an empirical quantitative investigation on how consumers want to shop online and offline, considering 128
different aspects of the shopping experience. The results of his investigation showed that consumers were very much into multichannel shopping
(e.g., they searched online and purchased in-store, or they bought online
and collected in-store). Burke (2002) suggested that retailers should
integrate channels so that consumers could move transparently between
them.

Goersch (2002, p. 757) provided similar conclusions: "the goal
of multi-channel integration must be to provide a superior customer
experience that is consistent and seamless across channels". Again, a
similar suggestion is that of Bendoly, Blocher, Bretthauer, Krishnan,
and Venkataramanan (2005), who showed that companies that manage
both online and in-store channels should adopt seamless channel integration, which seemed to be associated with increased loyalty. Regarding
channel integration, synergies, and coordination, Steinfield (2002), when
discussing click and mortar e-commerce approaches, stressed the importance of seamless integration across channels, even if this appears like a
difficult task for retailers. Schoenbachler and Gordon (2002) investigated
the drivers of channel choice and focused attention on the consistency
of brand image. They suggested that advertising should keep the image
consistent, integrated across channels, with a focus on customers, not
channels. Kwon and Lennon (2009) conducted quantitative research and
reached similar results concerning seamless integration and the relevance
of consistent image management in multichannel environments. In the
same year, Cassab (2009) was one of the first to predict the disruptive impact of the mobile channel on channel integration, marketing,
and the customization of the retail offer. The role of new technologies
is undoubtedly relevant for omnichannel retailing, as shown by Nash,
Armstrong, and Robertson (2013), who underlined the importance of
enabling technologies to provide data-enabled customer interactions and
advanced analytics, useful to create enhanced customer experience that
leads to increased customer satisfaction, loyalty, and greater customer
lifetime value.

As already mentioned in the chapter, the integration of channels is the
main feature of omnichannel retailing (Bendoly et al., 2005). Retailing
companies should try to provide a more satisfactory shopping journey
through the understanding of the type of channels customers prefer at
each stage of their decision-making process. Even if the focus is more

and more on new digital technologies and digital consumers, in an omnichannel strategy, physical stores still play a crucial role in creating successful customer–brand relationships (Bell, Gallino, Moreno, Yoder, & Ueda, 2018). As shown by Larke, Kilgour, and O'Connor (2018), for some categories, like fashion and apparel, many consumers still require physical interaction with products and an offline sales experience. Offline shopping, especially in the fashion industry, allows consumers to touch, try, and feel the product, and the return policy is easier and more convenient in the physical store (Rigby, 2011). This is confirmed by data from Statista (2019) about the cross-channel purchases by omnishoppers in the USA in 2017: 66% of respondents searched for products online but purchased in physical stores, 61% ordered online and picked up in physical stores, and 74% purchased online after a search in physical stores. It appears clear that consumers prefer cross-channel purchasing. However, online channels have many advantages, such as price comparison, 24/7 access, reviews, and unlimited products (Agatz, Fleischmann, & Van Nunen, 2008; Rigby, 2011). Therefore, online and offline channels should complement each other, so that consumers and retailers can benefit from the advantages of both.

Concerning fashion and luxury, a recent contribution by Silva et al. (2020) underlines how fashion and apparel brands are adopting an omnichannel approach. There are some differences among low cost, mid-price, and luxury brands, even if, despite the different positioning of the brands, the strategies adopted have many points in common. Low-cost brands, such as Mango and H&M, use seven online and offline channels: store, catalogue, website, blog, newsletter, mobile app, and social networks. Much attention is given to the website, with: easy site navigation and accessibility from many countries; updated product and price information; several options of product delivery, return, and payments; in-store availability option; live chat; and links to social networks. Integration of online and offline channels is represented by the option "click and collect" to deliver products to the customer's home or the nearest store. As for the social networks (Instagram, Facebook, YouTube, Twitter, and Pinterest), they provide detailed product descriptions and prices (especially on Instagram), a link to the website, videos with campaigns, vlogs, interviews, and fashion shows. A high degree of channel integration is also testified by the features of the mobile application that, as in the case of H&M, includes in-store mode assistance to find the right colour or size of an item when the customer goes to the physical store and a "Scan and Find" function that allows finding a product online using a barcode from the price tag. Mid-priced brands, such as Guess and Massimo Dutti, use the same seven channels and have "click and reserve" services that allow consumers to reserve the product online, and pay and collect in the physical store. Even the use of social media and mobile applications is quite similar to low-cost brands (Silva et al., 2020). Luxury brands, such as Gucci and Burberry, show similar characteristics and a high degree of integration especially between the mobile application and their website.

Building and Managing CBBE in Omnichannel Retailing

Brand equity was defined, in general terms, as the marketing effects uniquely attributable to the brand. Many authors have tried their hand at this topic. Brand equity studies followed two main lines. On the one hand, the financial line, aimed at measuring the value of the brand for economic and financial purposes to provide useful support for business investment, acquisition, or merger decisions. On the other hand, the strategic line, aimed at identifying guidelines to pursue the improvement of the results of strategic and operational marketing choices thanks to the analysis and understanding of consumer behaviour.

As part of this second line, Keller (1993) proposed a conceptual model that served as a stimulus for marketing scholars and practitioners to reflect on how to build, measure, and manage brand equity. In this consumer-focused model, Keller (2016, p. 3) defined CBBE as "the differential effect that brand knowledge has on customer response to brand marketing activity". In other words, CBBE should explain a consumer's different reactions to one or more elements of the marketing mix of a given branded product and an unbranded product.

The central element of the CBBE model is the concept of brand knowledge. According to Keller, the value of a brand mainly depends on the knowledge that a company has been able to create in the customer's mind through previous marketing actions. According to this approach, brand knowledge consists of a brand node in memory to which a variety of associations are linked, and can be broken down into two components: *brand awareness* and *brand image*. The first one refers to brand recall and brand recognition and measures the consumer's familiarity with the brand. The second one refers to the strength, positivity, and uniqueness of the attributes and benefits that the consumer associates with the brand, and represents the meaning of the brand for consumers.

To broaden the analysis of brand knowledge, in a subsequent study Keller (2003) proposed a more detailed breakdown of its dimensions in terms of awareness, attributes, benefits, images, thoughts, feelings, attitudes, and experiences. The extension of the analysis was necessary considering that the variety of marketing activities available to companies affect different dimensions of brand knowledge and that, in turn, different dimensions of brand knowledge affect consumer reactions to different marketing actions.

In light of the importance of brand equity to businesses, marketers must therefore pay particular attention to building and managing client-based brand equity. For the construction of the CBBE, Keller (1993) indicated three actions to be implemented: choosing brand identities such as the name, logo, symbol, and so on; designing and implementing marketing programmes to strengthen brand awareness and develop positive, strong, and unique brand associations; and leveraging secondary associations that may arise from primary associations of attributes relating to the business, the country of origin, the distribution channels, a celebrity, or an event.

At the same time, Keller also proposed some guidelines for managing CBBE which can be summarized as follows: adopt a broad and long-term view of marketing decisions to develop over time consumers' ability to recall and recognize the brand; clearly define the knowledge structure and the specific benefits to be developed in the minds of consumers considering their expectations; take advantage of the different and new alternatives in terms of marketing communications ensuring careful coordination; conduct experiments to control changes in the knowledge structure over time; and evaluate potential extension candidates.

To support the difficult phase of brand creation, Keller (2001) proposed the brand resonance model which, focusing on the key aspects of brand knowledge, tries to explain how consumers develop their relationships with brands and how to generate a sort of synchronization between consumer feelings and the brand itself. This model describes how marketers can get an active engagement from customers that is more than simple repetition of purchases (behavioural loyalty), which consists in building a close relationship between consumers and the brand (attitudinal attachment) and in developing a sense of community with the company and other consumers (sense of community).

Different marketing decisions affect different dimensions of brand knowledge, which can generate direct or indirect effects on the brand. The direct effects are those that directly affect brand knowledge through customer interactions and experiences, while the indirect ones derive from the association of the brand with a certain distribution channel or with a particular communication media. To build the desired brand knowledge, marketers must therefore carefully design these experiences through the right combination and coordination of commercial channels, touchpoints, programmes, and marketing actions.

Distribution channels and marketing communication, while participating in the overall customer experience, have distinct characteristics and functions. Companies use several of them at the same time to obtain adequate coverage of their target audience. In fact, as noted by Keller (2010), different customers tend to shop in different channels and tend to use different media.

The adoption of an omnichannel distribution approach, characterized by the simultaneous use of multiple distribution channels and marketing communication and an increase in touchpoints between brands and consumers, offers marketers the opportunity to create original shopping experiences and to develop an active customer involvement through intervention on the various components of brand knowledge.

However, the definition and management of an effective and efficient mix, capable of making the most of the potential of omnichannel retailing, is not easy at all. If efficiency essentially depends on the marketer's ability to ensure the widest possible coverage of target consumers at the lowest possible cost, effectiveness can be assessed through the contribution that a channel can make independently from other channels in obtaining the desired consumer response, through: (1) the degree of commonality between the meanings attributed to the brand and those attributable to the channels used; (2) the complementarity between brand associations and channels which, however, make the brand knowledge more consistent with that expected by the customer; and, finally, (3) the versatility of the channel understood in terms of the ability to obtain the desired effects regardless of the specific characteristics of the customer (Keller, 2010).

The adoption of an omnichannel retailing approach should not be considered mandatory or preferable in absolute terms. It can result in conflict, control problems, and coordination problems.

For example, in terms of efficiency, marketers should integrate a new channel only if customers expect to be able to use it or that they still consider it useful for the satisfaction of their shopping experience. On the other hand, in terms of effectiveness, the addition of new channels involves increasing complexity in management and coordination and, if not managed properly, it could prove inconsistent with the brand knowledge that the company intends to promote. Furthermore, as the company may not be able to directly control all the channels used, as the breadth of the channel portfolio increases, the risk that some retailers pursue their objectives (turnover, margins, etc.) will increase, with negative consequences for the desired coherence and synergy between the channels. Likewise, by failing to impose the in-store atmosphere and desired commercial policies on the retailer, the omnichannel company risks undergoing brand associations that are not entirely consistent with those desired and making the customer's shopping experience more complex, less fluid, and, overall, less satisfying.

The risks associated with this retailing strategy depend on the business sector in which the company operates, the characteristics of the product offered on the market, and the segment of customers to which it is addressed. In the luxury sector, characterized by the marketing of specialty products or services, the use of an excessive number and an excessive variety of distribution channels could lead to overexposure of the brand and an excess of market coverage. The consequent deterioration of the brand's image of exclusivity, the possible cannibalization of sales among channels, and the consequent reduction in sales margins due to possible price wars among the various channels could lead to a worsening of both brand equity in the short term, and the economic-financial results in the medium/long term. Hence, luxury companies, especially those operating in the fashion sector, need to keep the flow of products to the end customer under strict control. The opportunistic behaviour that could push even a single independent retailer to offer the company's products at lower prices than those imposed, thanks to favourable exchange rates or tax savings obtained through commercial triangulations with countries with subsidized taxation, could negatively affect its brand image.

In light of the above, therefore, the omnichannel strategy can be pursued almost exclusively by vertically integrated companies, those operating both in the production of the good/service and in the distribution phase to the final customer, or by those operating in retailing, and this regardless of the sector of activity. It is clear that a company engaged in the sale of mass consumer products cannot by definition control and manage all the touching points with the customer.

LUXURY FASHION AND OMNICHANNEL RETAILING: EMERGING ISSUES AND FINAL REMARKS

This chapter has shown the rise of omnichannel retailing and its implications for CBBE. The luxury fashion sector certainly regards the features of the shopping experience as important, especially the emotional and experiential dimensions (Aiolfi & Sabbadin, 2019).

Luxury fashion companies have focused on the opening of physical stores for years (Milanesi, 2020), but in more recent years they have begun to invest in e-commerce and virtual spaces (Guercini & Runfola, 2015). Thus, the challenge now, under an omnichannel perspective, is to manage all the touchpoints to convey a unique brand image and a valuable brand experience, consistent with the company's identity and values. On the one hand, luxury fashion companies must develop a digital transformation that includes their website, dynamic and user-friendly e-commerce, a strategic presence in social networks, and the development of an overall digital marketing strategy (Guercini, Milanesi, Mir-Bernal, & Runfola, 2020). On the other hand, a priority of luxury fashion retailers is the integration of digital technologies in their stores, as the physical store still plays an important role for customers who want to live an exciting shopping experience (Alexander & Cano, 2020). Such a challenge appears even more urgent for luxury fashion retailers, given the intrinsic characteristics of luxury goods, such as exclusivity, top quality, prestige, symbolic and emotional meaning, and high prices, which seem to conflict with the accessibility and democracy of the internet (Kapferer, 2017). Additionally, despite the prevailing omnichannel approach, luxury fashion stores are still the key touchpoint for consumers (Aiolfi and Sabbadin, 2019; Arrigo, 2018; Guercini & Milanesi, 2017).

This scenario was strongly shaken by the arrival of the COVID-19 pandemic between the end of 2019 in China and the beginning of 2020 in the rest of the world. Luxury fashion companies have been strongly hit by the pandemic from many points of view, for example, the closure of retail stores during the lockdown, the shift from global travellers to local shoppers, and the cancelation—or in some cases digitalization—of fashion shows (Achille and Zipser, 2020).

So let us try to put forward some reflections. The contingent aspects of the pandemic require a rethinking regarding the management of the mix of retail channels. Social distancing, limits to the fitting of products, especially fashion goods in physical stores, reduction of the capacity of stores linked to social distancing rules, psychological aspects related to the fear of contagion, feelings of insecurity, and so on, seem to undermine the traditional preference for the physical store. These changes are not to be considered only temporary, limited to the duration of the pandemic. On the contrary, they will probably produce a deep change in consumer purchasing habits, which will not necessarily see the total abandonment of the physical store, but will probably promote a rethinking of its function within the omnichannel approach. No doubt this will lead to an increase in the weight of online channels at the expense of physical ones (as already demonstrated by the announcement of the closure of hundreds of physical stores by both fast fashion and luxury companies). This could pose new challenges to companies in managing CBBE (and the brand knowledge that underlies it) due to the greater difficulty of creating engaging experiences without the important support of the physical store, especially of flagship stores, in an online context in which luxury multibrand retailers (such as Luisaviaroma, Farfetch, Mytheresa, etc.) have greater experience and the ability to manage the customer journey. In this context, the ability to redefine the role of the physical store as a space more oriented towards showrooming where companies can recover part of their capacity to support their brand equity could play a fundamental role.

In light of the current pandemic situation that could lead to disruptive changes in the world of retailing and in the managing of an omnichannel approach, new avenues for academic research are opening up. These may concern: the study of technologies for retailers that can maximize the integration between channels, starting from the new role of the physical store as a showroom; the identification of the capabilities and skills necessary to support the transformation of physical stores and the enhancement of their role in the context of omnichannel; and the investigation of the changes to activities aimed at building CBBE in the omnichannel approach both for the industrial brand and the retailer brand.

References

Achille, A., & Zipser, D. (2020). *A perspective for the luxury-goods industry during—and after—coronavirus.* McKinsey & Company. https://www.mck

insey.com/industries/retail/our-insights/a-perspective-for-the-luxury-goods-industry-during-and-after-coronavirus.

Agatz, N. A., Fleischmann, M., & Van Nunen, J. A. (2008). E-fulfillment and multi-channel distribution–A review. *European Journal of Operational Research, 187*(2), 339–356.

Aiolfi, S., & Sabbadin, E. (2019). Fashion and new luxury digital disruption: The new challenges of fashion between omnichannel and traditional retailing. *International Journal of Business and Management, 14*(8).

Alexander, B., & Cano, M. B. (2020). Store of the future: towards a (re) invention and (re) imagination of physical store space in an omnichannel context. *Journal of Retailing and Consumer Services, 55,*.

Arrigo, E. (2018). The flagship stores as sustainability communication channels for luxury fashion retailers. *Journal of Retailing and Consumer Services, 44,* 170–177.

Avery, J., Steenburgh, T. J., Deighton, J., & Caravella, M. (2012). Adding bricks to clicks: Predicting the patterns of cross-channel elasticities over time. *Journal of Marketing, 76*(3), 96–111.

Becagli, C., Ranfagni S., & Faraoni, M. (2020). A research approach to combine brand alignment with social engagement: an insight into online fashion communities. *Interdisciplinary Journal of Economics and Business Law, 9,* 131–157, ISSN: 2047–8747.

Beck, N., & Rygl, D. (2015). Categorization of multiple channel retailing in Multi-, Cross-, and Omni-Channel Retailing for retailers and retailing. *Journal of Retailing and Consumer Services, 27,* 170–178.

Bell, D., Gallino, S., Moreno, A., Yoder, J., & Ueda, D. (2018). The store is dead—Long live the store. *MIT Sloan Management Review, Spring,* 59–66.

Bendoly, E., Blocher, J. D., Bretthauer, K. M., Krishnan, S., & Venkataramanan, M. A. (2005). Online/in-store integration and customer retention. *Journal of Service Research, 7*(4), 313–327.

Brynjolfsson, E., Hu, Y. J., & Rahman, M. S. (2013). *Competing in the age of omnichannel retailing* (pp. 1–7). Cambridge: MIT Press.

Burke, R. R. (2002). Technology and the customer interface: What consumers want in the physical and virtual store. *Journal of the Academy of Marketing Science, 30*(4), 411–432.

Carroll, D., & Guzmán, I. (2013). The new omni-channel approach to serving customers. *Accenture Consulting.* https://www.accenture.com/be-en/~/media/Accenture/Conversion-Assets/DotCom/Documents/Global/PDF/Industries_2/accenture-new-omni-channel-approach-serving-customers.pdf.

Cassab, H. (2009). Investigating the dynamics of service attributes in multi-channel environments. *Journal of Retailing and Consumer Services, 16*(1), 25–30.

Christensen, C. M., & Raynor, M. E. (2003). *The innovator's solution: Using good theory to solve the dilemmas of growth*. Boston: Harvard Business School Press.

Galipoglu, E., Kotzab, H., Teller, C., Hüseyinoglu, I. Ö. Y., & Pöppelbuß, J. (2018). Omni-channel retailing research—State of the art and intellectual foundation. *International Journal of Physical Distribution & Logistics Management, 48*(4), 365–390.

Goersch, D. (2002). *Multi-channel integration and its implications for retail web sites*. ECIS 2002 Proceedings, 11.

Guercini, S., & Milanesi, M. (2017). Extreme luxury fashion: Business model and internationalization process. *International Marketing Review, 34*(3), 403–424.

Guercini, S., Milanesi, M., Mir-Bernal, P., & Runfola, A. (2020). Surfing the waves of new marketing in luxury fashion: The case of online multi-brand retailers. In Martínez-López, F. J., & D'Alessandro, S. (Eds.), *Advances in digital marketing and ecommerce*. Springer Proceedings in Business and Economics.

Guercini, S., & Runfola, A. (2015). Internationalization through e-commerce. The case of multibrand luxury retailers in the fashion industry. *Advances in International Marketing, 26*, 15–31.

Jebarajakirthy, C., Yadav, R., & Shankar, A. (2020). Insights for luxury retailers to reach customers globally. *Marketing Intelligence & Planning, 38*(7), 797–811.

Kapferer, J. N. (2017). *Lusso: Nuove sfide, nuovi sfidanti*. Milano: FrancoAngeli.

Keller, K. L. (1993). Conceptualizing, measuring, and managing customer-based brand equity. *Journal of Marketing, 57*(1), 1–22.

Keller, K. L. (2001). *Building customer-based brand equity: A blueprint for creating strong brands* (pp. 3–27). Cambridge, MA: Marketing Science Institute.

Keller, K. L. (2003). Brand synthesis: The multi-dimensionality of brand knowledge. *Journal of Consumer Research, 29*(4), 595–600.

Keller, K. L. (2008). *Strategic brand management: Building, measuring and managing brand equity* (3rd ed.). Upper Saddle River, NJ: Pearson Prentice Hall.

Keller, K. L. (2010). Brand equity management in a multichannel, multimedia retail environment. *Journal of Interactive Marketing, 24*(2), 58–70.

Keller, K. L. (2016). Reflections on customer-based brand equity: Perspectives, progress, and priorities. *AMS Review, 6*(1–2), 1–16.

Keller, K. L., & Lehmann, D. R. (2003). How do brands create value?. *Marketing Management, 12*(3), 26.

Kwon, W. S., & Lennon, S. J. (2009). Reciprocal effects between multichannel retailers' offline and online brand images. *Journal of Retailing, 85*(3), 376–390.

Larke, R., Kilgour, M., & O'Connor, H. (2018). Build touchpoints and they will come: Transitioning to omnichannel retailing. *International Journal of Physical Distribution & Logistics Management, 48*(4), 465–483.

Lazaris, C., & Vrechopoulos, A. (2014, June). From multi-channel to "omnichannel" retailing: Review of the literature and calls for research. In 2nd International Conference on Contemporary Marketing Issues (ICCMI), Vol. 6.

Lee, Z. W., Chan, T. K., Chong, A. Y. L., & Thadani, D. R. (2019). Customer engagement through omnichannel retailing: The effects of channel integration quality. *Industrial Marketing Management, 77,* 90–101.

Lemon, K. N., & Verhoef, P. C. (2016). Understanding customer experience throughout the customer journey. *Journal of Marketing, 80*(6), 69–96.

Levy, M., Weitz, B., & Grewal, D. (2013). *Retailing management* (9th ed.). New York, NY, USA: McGraw-Hill Education.

Melero, I., Sese, F. J., & Verhoef, P. C. (2016). Recasting the customer experience in today's omni-channel environment. *Universia Business Review, 2016*(50), 18–37.

Milanesi, M. (2020). *Liabilities and networks in the internationalization of fashion retailing.* Milano: FrancoAngeli.

Nash, D., Armstrong, D., & Robertson, M. (2013). Customer experience 2.0: How data, technology, and advanced analytics are taking an integrated, seamless customer experience to the next frontier. *Journal of Integrated Marketing Communications, 1*(1), 32–39.

Neslin, S. A., Grewal, D., Leghorn, R., Shankar, V., Teerling, M. L., Thomas, J. S., et al. (2006). Challenges and opportunities in multichannel customer management. *Journal of Service Research, 9*(2), 95–112.

Ortis, I., & Casoli, A. (2009). *Technology selection: IDC retail insights guide to enabling immersive shopping experiences.* IDC Retail Insights. https://www.idg.co.uk/news/idc-retail-insights-publishes-a-guide-to-enabling-immersive-shopping-experiences-the-rise-of-omnichannel-shopping-requires-providing-an-immersive-and-superior-customer-experience-regardless-of-channe/.

Otto, J. R., & Chung, Q. B. (2000). A framework for cyber-enhanced retailing: Integrating e-commerce retailing with brick-and-mortar retailing. *Electronic Markets, 10*(3), 185–191.

Ozuem, W., Howell, K. E., & Lancaster, G. (2008). Communicating in the new interactive marketspace. *European Journal of Marketing, 42*(9/10), 1059–1083.

Ozuem, W., Patel, A., Howell, K. E., & Lancaster, G. (2017). An exploration of customers' response to online service recovery initiatives. *International Journal of Market Research, 59*(1), 97–116.

Ozuem, W., Thomas, T., & Lancaster, G. (2016). The influence of customer loyalty on small island economies: an empirical and exploratory study. *Journal of Strategic Marketing, 24*(6), 447–469.

Parker, R., & Hand, L. (2009). *Satisfying the omnichannel consumers whenever and wherever they shop.* IDC Retail Insights.

Picot-Coupey, K., Huré, E., Piveteau, L., Towers, N., & Kotzab, H. (2016). Channel design to enrich customers' shopping experiences: synchronizing clicks with bricks in an omni-channel perspective-the Direct Optic case. *International Journal of Retail & Distribution Management, 44*(3), 284–300.

Rangaswamy, A., & Van Bruggen, G. H. (2005). Opportunities and challenges in multichannel marketing: An introduction to the special issue. *Journal of Interactive Marketing, 19*(2), 5–11.

Rapp, A., Baker, T. L., Bachrach, D. G., Ogilvie, J., & Beitelspacher, L. S. (2015). Perceived customer showrooming behavior and the effect on retail salesperson self-efficacy and performance. *Journal of Retailing, 91*(2), 358–369.

Rigby, D. (2011). The future of shopping. *Harvard Business Review, 89*(12), 65–76.

Rosengren, S., Lange, F., Hernant, M., & Blom, A. (2018). Catering to the digital consumer: From multichannel to omnichannel retailing. In P. Andersson, S. Movin, M. Mähring, R. Teigland, & K. Wennberg (Eds.), *Managing digital transformation.* Stockholm School of Economics Institute for Research: Stockholm, Sweden.

Schoenbachler, D. D., & Gordon, G. L. (2002). Multi-channel shopping: Understanding what drives channel choice. *Journal of Consumer Marketing, 19*(1), 42–53.

Shen, X. L., Li, Y. J., Sun, Y., & Wang, N. (2018). Channel integration quality, perceived fluency and omnichannel service usage: The moderating roles of internal and external usage experience. *Decision Support Systems, 109,* 61–73.

Silva, S. C., Duarte, P., & Sundetova, A. (2020). Multichannel versus omnichannel: a price-segmented comparison from the fashion industry. *International Journal of Retail & Distribution Management, 48*(4), 417–4130.

Sorescu, A., Frambach, R. T., Singh, J., Rangaswamy, A., & Bridges, C. (2011). Innovations in retail business models. *Journal of Retailing, 87,* S3–S16.

Statista. (2019). *E-commerce share of omnichannel sales and growth in the United States as of December 2019.* https://www.statista.com/statistics/1110319/us-share-omnichannel-sales-growth-ecommerce/.

Steinfield, C. (2002). Understanding click and mortar e-commerce approaches: A conceptual framework and research agenda. *Journal of Interactive Advertising, 2*(2), 1–10.

Verhoef, P. C., Kannan, P. K., & Inman, J. J. (2015). From multi-channel retailing to omni-channel retailing: introduction to the special issue on multi-channel retailing. *Journal of Retailing, 91*(2), 174–181.

Verhoef, P. C., Neslin, S. A., & Vroomen, B. (2007). Multichannel customer management: Understanding the research-shopper phenomenon. *International Journal of Research in Marketing, 24*(2), 129–148.

Yurova, Y., Rippé, C. B., Weisfeld-Spolter, S., Sussan, F., & Arndt, A. (2017). Not all adaptive selling to omni-consumers is influential: The moderating effect of product type. *Journal of Retailing and Consumer Services, 34*, 271–277.

CHAPTER 3

Opinion Leaders, Short Videos and Virtual Communities in the Fashion Industry

Peng Chen

Introduction and Overview

With the arrival of the mobile internet era and the development of information technology, methods of communication, information acquisition and information transactions between people have changed significantly. According to Clement (2020a), the average daily social media usage of internet users worldwide amounted to 144 minutes per day in 2019. In 2020, the global penetration rate of social media reached 49%, with East Asia and North America having the highest penetration rates at 71 and 69%, respectively (Clement, 2020a). While social media connects consumers, it also provides an opportunity for marketers to interact and communicate with current and potential buyers (Clement, 2019), which has promoted the rapid development of social commerce. Social media platforms like YouTube, Facebook, Instagram, WeChat and TikTok have become the most popular and convenient sources for people to get access to information and share ideas (Turcotte, York, Irving, Scholl,

P. Chen (✉)
Jiujiang University, Jiujiang, China

© The Author(s), under exclusive license to Springer Nature Switzerland AG 2021
W. Ozuem and S. Ranfagni (eds.), *The Art of Digital Marketing for Fashion and Luxury Brands*,
https://doi.org/10.1007/978-3-030-70324-0_3

51

& Pingree, 2015). The huge change in consumers' information environment has had a big impact on consumers' behaviour (Lu & Zhou, 2005). Consumers acquisition of information has changed from passively accepting product information released by firms to actively seeking useful information (Deng, Wang, & Zhou, 2015). In addition, consumers' purchasing decisions are influenced by other people on social media platforms (Deng et al., 2015).

Among social media users, there is a small group of people who can have a big impact on other users. They have specialized knowledge or skills and are willing to share their reviews, with high-quality content, about products or brands in virtual communities. These people are called social media influencers or opinion leaders; they are active on social media platforms and are the main source of word-of-mouth messages (Haron, Johar, & Ramli, 2016). Marketers and brands should pay attention to the strategy of influencer marketing because opinion leaders play an important role in conveying information to consumers (Kotler & Armstrong, 2015).

Over the past few years, the rise of the short-video industry due to the development of the mobile internet and the updating of smartphones is another noteworthy phenomenon (Thomala, 2020a). Videos can tell stories in emotional or humorous ways, which most other forms of marketing cannot (Scott, 2015). The video format is also more effective than text and pictures at enhancing the engagement and interest of participants (Koehler, Yadav, Phillips, & Cavazos-Kottke, 2005). Short-video platforms are very popular; opinion leaders and multichannel network (MCN) organizations create high-quality content and attract millions of followers, which indicates an effective way for firms and brands to get access to consumers.

The fashion industry accounts for the largest proportion of the social commerce market in China and it attracts the most attention (Bu, Wang, Wei Wang, & Zipser, 2019). Fashion bloggers account for the second largest proportion of influencers on Sina Weibo (funny bloggers make up the largest proportion) (IResearch, 2018). These fashion bloggers share their videos and photos on social media, as well as their experiences with the products, which attract a large number of fans to like, favourite and repost.

The next section presents definitions and characteristics of opinion leaders, virtual communities and short videos; this is followed by a description of the development of virtual communities, including changes in consumers' information environment and a description of members of a virtual community. The next sections describe: the effect of opinion leaders on social commerce, virtual brand communities, and the characteristics and development of the short-video industry. The penultimate section offers suggestions for brand marketing in virtual communities, which is followed by a Conclusion section.

WHAT ARE OPINION LEADERS, VIRTUAL COMMUNITIES AND SHORT VIDEOS?

Opinion Leaders

Research on opinion leaders can be traced back to the work of Lazarsfeld, Berelson, and Gaudet (1944), who stated that the influence of mass communications on people's behaviours may not be as direct as had been previously thought. They suggested a two-step communication process in which opinion leaders first get news about a product from the mass media or business sources, and then pass on their opinions to others. Lazarsfeld et al. (1944) argued that opinion leaders are more involved in a certain field of consumption than others, so they are more willing to express their opinions to others.

Research in the 1970s and 1980s on opinion leaders focused on their characteristics, identity and influence (Childers, 1986; Darden & Reynolds, 1972; King & Summers, 1970; Myers & Robertson, 1972; Summers, 1970). In the past two decades, with the development of internet technology, the role of opinion leaders in marketing, management, tourism, fashion and other fields has aroused the interest of many scholars (Casaló, Flavián, & Ibáñez-Sánchez, 2018; Coulter, Feick, & Price, 2002; Thakur, Angriawan, & Summey, 2016; Van den Bulte & Joshi, 2007; Vernette, 2004; Zhao, Kou, Peng, & Chen, 2018).

According to Rogers and Cartano (1962), consumers consider the views of opinion leaders more credible than advertising because people think opinion leaders do not represent commercial sources; however, it can be argued that nowadays many opinion leaders who share their experiences about products on social media get commission from manufacturers.

Explaining and influencing consumer decisions is a never-ending pursuit for marketing researchers. As traditional advertising seems to become less effective (Trusov, Bucklin, & Pauwels, 2009; Van den Bulte & Wuyts, 2007) in the era of social media, marketers and firms continually seek new ways to promote products and influence consumers' adoption decisions.

In the digital era, opinion leaders have more platforms to disseminate information. At the same time, internet users can gather information through these platforms. Extant research indicates that social media opinion leaders have more influence over purchase decisions than other social media users (Godes & Mayzlin, 2009; Goldenberg, Han, Lehmann, & Hong, 2009; Iyengar, Van den Bulte, & Valente, 2011), and new customers influenced by consumer-to-consumer communication are more valuable to firms than customers acquired by other means (Schmitt, Skiera, & Van den Bulte, 2011; Trusov et al., 2009; Villanueva, Yoo, & Hanssens, 2008).

The continuous development of information technology has enabled people to post their own experiences and feelings about products and services and share them on various social media platforms. Social media has become an important channel for the dissemination of consumer information (Ansarin & Ozuem, 2015). In this context, face-to-face information exchange has been gradually transformed into online communication. Opinion leaders, who maintain an active presence on different kinds of social media platforms, are considered to be important links between manufacturers and ordinary consumers.

Virtual Communities

Definition
With the birth and development of the internet, people aggregated on the internet in chat rooms, online forums and bulletin boards, where individuals express and exchange opinions, experience or anything else for a period of time and with a certain degree of involvement (Baker, 2002; Blanchard, 2007; Dong, Huang, Hou, & Liu, 2020; Hsu, Wang, & Chih, 2018). These forms of social aggregation are called virtual communities, which were first defined by Rheingold (1993, p. xx) as "social aggregations that emerge from the net when enough people carry on those public discussions long enough, with sufficient human feeling, to form webs of personal relationships in cyberspace". Virtual communities enable users to communicate with each other and to establish a personal network with common interests, which allows them to interact regularly in a coordinated way over the internet. People can also keep a distance between

themselves and others in virtual communities, which can often overcome social and organizational barriers (Kiesler, 1986; Zhang, 2019).

Characteristics
Based on previous research (Fernback & Thompson, 1995; Hagel & Armstrong, 1997; Madupu & Cooley, 2010; Williams & Cothrel, 2000), several common characteristics of virtual communities can be summarized as follows:

- Virtual communities exist in cyberspace and are supported by information technology, which is the main difference between virtual communities and traditional communities.
- Virtual communities are used by members for communication and interaction around common interests.
- Virtual communities are made up of community members who generate most of the content.
- Communication and interaction among members leads to the formation of social relationships.

Categories
According to Armstrong and Hagel (2000), virtual communities can be categorized into four different types: interest communities, relationship communities, fantasy communities and transaction communities. These categories are not completely independent but overlap. Many virtual communities can be classified into more than one category.

Members
A virtual community is made up of its members, who can be classified into various types. Active user, passive user and lurker are the terms most commonly used by scholars to classify virtual community members according to their behaviours (Carlson, Suter, & Brown; 2008; Hartmann, Wiertz, & Arnould, 2015; Lai & Chen, 2014). Lurkers are those members who browse and read the messages posted by others within the virtual community but do not engage or respond (Ridings, Gefen, & Arinze, 2002; Madupu & Cooley, 2010). Active users and passive users are those who engage with the community by posting original content, sharing others' content, commenting, liking, replying and other interactive behaviours (Madupu & Cooley, 2010).

Although lurkers usually browse and read the content on websites or apps provided by others and do not actively participate in the community, they make up the majority of members in many communities (Nonnecke, Preece, & Andrews, 2004). According to Madupu and Cooley (2010), there are approximately 100 lurkers to one active member. It is important to note that although lurkers do not participate in interactive behaviour within the virtual community, they may spread the information outside the community through word of mouth and in other ways (Erkan & Evans, 2018).

Other terminology that is used to describe members and their level of engagement within the community includes the categorization of Felix (2012), which is based on members' level of identification: insiders, minglers, devotees and tourists. Moreover, the labels of lead users or influencers are assigned to those who actively access specialized new products and brand knowledge ahead of the general members (Kratzer, Lettl, Franke, & Gloor, 2016; Felix, Rauschnabel, & Hinsch, 2017; Marchi, Giachetti, & de Gennaro, 2011).

Short Videos

Sharing videos on the internet is nothing new. YouTube is one of the most successful video sharing platforms. YouTube was launched in February 2005 and made up approximately 10% of all internet traffic two years after its debut (Cheng, Dale, & Liu, 2007). YouTube now has two billion logged-in monthly users, who upload 500 hours of video every minute and spend 11 minutes 24 seconds per day on YouTube on average (Clement, 2020b).

With the decrease in barriers to internet video publishing, blogs consisting of short videos with a length of no longer than five or ten minutes became popular; these are called vlogs (Luers, 2007). According to Luers (2007), vlogs can fulfil some of the social needs of vloggers, and interactions between vloggers and followers are fundamental to vloggers' communities.

As an alternative to YouTube, on which videos range in length from a few minutes to several hours, some newly launched or newly designed social media platforms focus on the sharing of short videos lasting for seconds or minutes and have achieved great success in the market.

In the past decade, especially the last five years, there has been an explosion of growth in video on social media, and you may have noticed that the videos you would like to watch and share with friends have got shorter and shorter. These short videos often show moments of importance, fun, rarity or amazing performance. Sources for short videos include news reports, movies or television episodes, music videos and amateur-shot video.

According to iiMedia Report (2019), the number of short videos in China has expanded rapidly, with a growth rate of 107% in 2018, and the number of short-video users in China will reach 722 million by 2020. In the field of marketing, the size of the short-video market is expected to exceed 2.86 billion US dollars (iiMedia Report, 2019).

TikTok, an iOS and Android media app that can be used for creating and sharing 15-second short videos, has attracted 800 million active users worldwide since it was launched in September 2016 (Kemp, 2020). TikTok has attracted a large number of users not only in China, but also in other markets including the UK, USA and India, which indicates the popularity of short videos. Besides YouTube and TikTok, there are many apps such as Instagram, Twitter, Reddit and Snapchat which also integrate the function of sharing short videos.

As audiovisual narration helps to set up a profound connection with audiences, the development of video platforms has significantly improved the way fashion brands communicate with their customers (Diaz Soloaga & Garcia Guerrero, 2016). The fashion industry accounts for the largest proportion and attracts the most attention in China's social e-commerce market (Bu et al., 2019). Fashion bloggers share their videos and photos on social media, as well as their experiences with the products, which attract a large number of fans to like, favourite and repost.

As the popularity of short videos on social media platforms is only a few years old, there is no clear definition of a short video in academia. Some scholars argued that videos less than five minutes can be regarded as short videos, while others thought the criterion should be 20 minutes (iiMedia Report, 2017; Xu, Yan, & Zhang, 2019). In this chapter, short videos, including vlogs and video clips, are online videos lasting from several seconds to 20 minutes which can be played, shot and edited on mobile intelligent terminals and can be shared and interacted with in real time on social media platforms.

THE DEVELOPMENT OF VIRTUAL COMMUNITIES

Changes in Consumers' Information Environment

Consumers' behaviour is closely related to their information environment. Information environment refers to a collection of various elements related to information acquisition, communication, information sharing and information utilization, which constitute a consumer's information ecosystem (Lu & Zhou, 2005). With the development of mobile internet and social media technology, the information environment of consumers has undergone significant changes. Digital media enable an information-sharing environment (Lu & Zhou, 2005). Various social media platforms have become the most popular way for people to access information.

The development of social media also changed the structure of the information environment (Lu & Zhou, 2005). According to Christakis and Fowler (2009), everyone is an independent person as well as a node in their networks. People shape their social networks all the time and their networks affect other people in turn. Social networks and virtual communities have fundamentally changed consumers' information environment and transformed consumers' behaviours. In the era of the mobile internet, the virtual community has become a more important factor that influences consumers' behaviours (Lu & Zhou, 2005).

A virtual community is a concept that is widely used to describe a group of people who get together on internet platforms on the basis of a common interest (Madupu & Cooley, 2010). Social media platforms make it extremely easy to create or join virtual communities. Every social media user is a member of one or several virtual communities. Social media not only serves as a way to communicate online, but also has become the most convenient, the most efficient and the cheapest source of information.

Drawing on social influence theory, individuals are influenced by others and reference groups (Kelman, 1974). According to Kelman (1974, 2006), the attitudes, beliefs and behaviours of individuals can be changed. He also distinguished the different processes of social influence (Kelman, 2006). Social influence theory has been used to explain online anonymous user reviews (Zhao, Stylianou, & Zheng, 2018), social networks (Cheung, Chiu, & Lee, 2010), knowledge management (Wang, Meister, & Gray, 2013) and consumer purchase behaviour (Xu et al., 2017). In a virtual community, members, especially opinion leaders, post and share their experiences of products and services, which has a significant influence on others. As consumers constitute the vast majority of virtual community members, understanding why people are attracted to virtual communities will be beneficial to brands' marketing. Opinion leaders play an important role in spreading information and leading trends in virtual communities; investigating how opinion leaders influence consumers would help enterprises to promote brands in virtual communities.

Consumers in a Virtual Community

Based on common interests or aims, individuals aggregate on social media to communicate and interact with each other, and form virtual communities (Tamí-Maury, Brown, Lapham, & Chang, 2017). Virtual communities can form a huge social network and be an efficient word-of-mouth recommendation mechanism to provide individual users with high-quality product and service information, which, in a sense, surpasses the accuracy and credibility of search engines (Qualman, 2012).

People join a virtual community for different reasons. To get access to information is the most frequently cited reason to join a virtual community (Wellman et al., 1996), where social support, friendship and recreation are also provided to members depending on the type of the virtual community (Ridings & Gefen, 2004).

According to their level of engagement, members of a virtual community are most commonly classified into active users, passive users and lurkers (Hartmann et al., 2015), in which lurkers account for the majority of the total number of virtual community members (Madupu & Cooley, 2010). As lurkers are identified as silent members who read but seldom or never post messages, in some studies they are considered to be free-riders and of low value or even harmful to the virtual community (Nielsen, 2011; Rheingold, 2000; van Mierlo, 2014). In contrast, other studies argue that lurking is an important way to participate and is valuable (Edelmann, 2013; Nonnecke, Andrews, & Preece, 2006). From a marketing point of view, lurkers are also important potential customers, because they also join a virtual community to obtain the information they need, just the same as posters (Nonnecke et al., 2004; Tagarelli & Interdonato, 2018).

The connection or interaction between members is the most critical part of virtual communities. This connection can be an extension of real communities, a mix of virtual and real communities, or a purely online community without connections between members in the real world (Xu, 2011).

As members of virtual communities can move from one community to another at any time according to their needs, the connections within virtual communities are not static but dynamic. Members might leave the community when their interests or emotional communication changes or because they are dissatisfied with their community's service or other members. Moreover, as the openness of the internet gives the members of a virtual community much more autonomy than that of a real-world community, the cost of community migration in a virtual environment is very low.

OPINION LEADERS IN SOCIAL COMMERCE

Opinion leaders are those individuals who have a great influence on the decision making, attitudes and behaviours of others (Godey et al., 2016; Rogers & Cartano, 1962). In the two-step flow model of Lazarsfeld et al. (1944), opinion leaders get information from the mass media or business sources and then disseminate it to other members of their community via word of mouth, which constitutes an important part of consumers' information environment. Today, with the rapid development of information technology and social media, people communicate online and offline more frequently, which further magnifies the influence of opinion leaders (Turcotte et al., 2015).

Nowadays, the types of opinion leaders have become more diverse. Opinion leaders can be either people who have extensive knowledge of a particular field or people who have a lot of connections with others (Goldenberg, Lehmann, Shidlovski, & Barak, 2006). In addition to the traditional celebrities and industry elite, internet celebrities such as bloggers and network anchors also have a great influence on consumers' choices. On social media platforms, some content-oriented social media accounts focus on sharing interests rather than social relationships; these accounts attract a large number of followers due to their highly professional content and they are also opinion leaders or social media influencers (Yoo, Paek, & Hove, 2018).

Due to the influence of opinion leaders on consumers in virtual communities, brands and marketers see great marketing potential in the influence of opinion leaders on consumers in virtual communities and they try to convert the awareness opinion leaders generate on social media into purchases by using opinion leaders to drive a brand's message to a larger market (Tapinfluence, 2015). Social media influencers are not only able to attract large audiences, but also act as efficient marketers (Ge & Gretzel, 2018), as shown by the rapid development of social commerce in recent years (IResearch, 2019). Influencer marketing has become one of the most cost-effective approaches for brands to have more direct and organic contacts with potential consumers (Talavera, 2015), especially in the fashion industry.

As fashion clothing is a kind of good that is open for all to see and may indicate a person's personality and status to others (Kim, Lloyd, & Cervellon, 2016), leading figures are crucial in transmitting new fashion styles and clothing habits. Fashion opinion leaders are thought to have a powerful influence on consumers' buying behaviour (Goldsmith & Clark, 2008). In order to reduce the purchasing risk, fashion consumers seek information from opinion leaders, who are regarded as having more experience of the topic (Flynn, Goldsmith, & Eastman, 1996); fashion consumers also spread this information to other customers (Goldsmith & Clark, 2008). Therefore, opinion leaders in the fashion industry are considered the key to spreading new fashion trends because of their great influence on their followers. Their knowledge and expertise are regarded as reliable sources of information (Casaló et al., 2018).

Virtual Brand Communities

A brand community is an aggregation of admirers of a brand, which is based on a structured set of social relations and not restricted by geographical location (Muniz & O'Guinn, 2001). It can be created either by the consumers or the organization (Jang, Olfman, Ko, Koh, & Kim, 2008; Homburg, Ehm, & Artz, 2015). Products, brands and organizations are the objects of interest of these communities (Lima, Irigaray, & Lourenco, 2019).

With the development of information technology, organizations made use of social media to strengthen their relationship and interaction with consumers and built their brands using virtual brand communities (Hakala, Nummelin, & Kohtamäki, 2017; Islam, Rahman, & Hollebeek, 2017; Perren & Kozinets, 2018). Scholars have investigated the relationships in a virtual brand community; according to McAlexander, Schouten, and Koenig (2002), these relationships include those between the customer and the firm, brand, product and fellow customers. As these relationships indicate consumers' needs and brand loyalty, virtual brand communities are regarded as powerful instruments of marketing communication (Casaló, Flavián, & Guinaliu 2008; Xu & Ozuem, 2019).

A virtual brand community can benefit consumers in several ways. Like other virtual communities, a virtual brand community can provide members with the information they need and wide social benefits through communal interaction. Members can easily seek information about the brand from other members in an established virtual brand community (Muniz & O'Guinn, 2001). A brand community also represents a type of consumer agency, which can have a greater voice than individual consumers when needed (France & Muller, 1999).

From the perspective of the firms, a virtual brand community may affect brand equity, including perceived quality, brand loyalty, brand awareness and brand associations (Muniz & O'Guinn, 2001). A brand community differs from advertising in the mass media or new media because it enables two-way communications among users (Chi & Lieberman, 2011).

Users are more willing to trust, like and participate in a virtual brand community because of the interactivity and convenience of brand communities (Chi & Lieberman, 2011). Therefore, building a strong brand community could be an important part of brand marketing (Ozuem & Azemi, 2017).

CHARACTERISTICS AND DEVELOPMENT OF THE SHORT-VIDEO INDUSTRY

The popularity of short video has much to do with its characteristics and the technical support from social media platforms. Compared with words or pictures, video allows a person to tell a much richer story. Video enables bloggers to engage the viewer emotionally and to connect with people on a more personal level (Garfield, 2010). The following is an analysis of the characteristics of short videos on social media platforms.

First, short videos are easy to create and share online with smartphones.

In the past, when we talked about video shooting and video editing, we had images of a professional photographer working in a studio with a big camera and film editors editing videos on their computers with sophisticated software. Nowadays, more and more powerful smartphones and various intelligent apps provide great convenience to users who wish to make and share short videos. Compared to a long video, a short video is much more easily accepted by ordinary audiences, and the creation threshold is low.

According to Statista (2020), the number of global smartphone users will reach 3.5 billion by 2020, and this number will continue to grow in the next few years. In the last five years, the world's annual turnover of smartphones has been around 1.4 billion; China, India and the USA have been the countries with the largest number of smartphone users (Statista, 2020). The rapid development of 4G and 5G telecommunication technology provided people with faster mobile internet access speeds, which created the conditions for us to watch and share short videos on social media anytime and anywhere.

Moreover, many social media apps and video making apps on iOS and Android platforms have the functions of one-click photographing, portrait beautification, and text and music composition. For example, Instagram users can use an app's built-in filters and trimming functions when they post videos. If they wish to share videos in their stories, then there are more effects to help make their videos interesting. Therefore, short-video production and sharing have low requirements for technology and equipment. As long as a person has a smartphone, they can easily get started and become a content producer anytime and anywhere.

Second, short videos have the feature of fragmented content, which is in line with users' habits in the internet era.

Traditional long video requires users to have more leisure time to watch and it is also limited by network traffic and the appeal of the video itself to the audience. Short videos abandon the unique forms and logic of the traditional video and present the audience with simple and interesting features. People can watch short videos in their spare time, when they are waiting for a bus or need a break during work and study. In an era of information explosion, the internet has brought us masses of information, which has also gradually fragmented our way of life. A short video which lasts a few seconds to several minutes can give users much more information than simple text and pictures. This kind of fragmented content fills our trivial spare time and allows us to obtain a moment of pleasure. It has become the best choice for people with a fast-paced lifestyle.

Third, short videos are suitable for instant propagation and instant communication, which meets the real-time requirements of modern people.

Compared with traditional internet video, a short video has the characteristics of instant messaging and is more convenient for users to share.

Take TikTok for example, 95% of the TikTok videos uploaded by regular users are 15-seconds long or less, and 90% of TikTok videos are less than 1.5 MB (Chen, He, Mao, Chung, & Maharjan, 2019); the length and size are two of the most significant differences compared to traditional videos. Users of TikTok can combine voice, text, video and images and create unique content, which can spread on the internet very quickly. At the same time, the platform can also push content according to users' preferences and needs in real time, which creates an environment similar to face-to-face communication for users. In this way, the social media platform not only facilitates communication between users, but also saves a lot of cost and time, and the convenience captures the psychology of consumers.

Using these social media platforms, users can shoot, edit and upload short videos in a very short time. There can be two-way or multidirectional communication with others as they wish. Simple operations on a smartphone can abolish the time and space limitations of regular chat, narrow the communication distance between users and highlight the communication value of interpersonal relationships.

Fourth, short videos have a strong social interaction attribute.

With the rapid development of information technology, the apps market is constantly updating and launching new short-video social applications, which will bring better and better experiences to users. Compared with text and pictures, the visual nature of short videos enables universal understanding of the expression of the content and attracts more audiences to participate and interact with others. Videos generally lead to higher levels of emotional engagement and sympathy, and they elicit more affective responses (Koehler et al., 2005; Ozuem et al. 2017; Paivio & Clark, 1991). Moreover, as the majority of short-video creators are ordinary grassroots individuals, who also play the role of content recipients, they can shoot short videos that are popular from the perspective of the audience (Yang, Zhao, & Ma, 2019). Such videos can achieve good communication effects.

Although the length and content of a short video are limited, a good short video will strike a strong chord with countless netizens, and many of them will repost or comment. In this way, the huge social information generated from short videos will increase users' dependence on the short-video platform.

From the perspective of short-video apps, in order to capture the market and stimulate users' enthusiasm for participation, social media platforms position themselves as places not only for recording and sharing videos, but also a virtual community for communication and interaction, which benefits the users and platforms.

The Development of Short Videos

With the global spread of internet access, short videos have become very popular online. Since its launch in 2005 and acquisition by Google a year later, YouTube has grown from a repository of amateur videos into the biggest online video platform worldwide. After years of global orientation and constant growth, YouTube recorded an estimated 1.68 billion users in 2019 (Clement, 2020b).

Not all video platforms were as successful as YouTube. Viddy, once regarded as "the Instagram for video", launched on iOS app store in 2011 and shut down in 2014. After Viddy pioneered a social platform focus on short videos, many social media platforms, such as Twitter, Facebook and Instagram, added the function of shooting and sharing videos to compete for internet traffic. These social media platforms made the short-video format very popular.

In the era of the mobile internet, due to the technology upgrade of smartphones and the widespread popularization of 4G networks, mobile phones are becoming the main source of information for the public.

As the speed of the mobile internet increases and the price decreases, people are more willing to post and watch videos on social media platforms. In China, the short-video industry has achieved explosive growth since 2016. According to a survey conducted by McKinsey Digital (2019), Chinese consumers spend as much as 44% of their time on social media apps, a quarter of which is spent watching, sharing and creating short videos on apps such as the immensely popular Douyin (Chinese version of TikTok) and over-the-top video streaming services like Tencent Video and iQIYI. In 2019, the revenue of the online short-video market in China amounted to 18.6 billion US dollars, which indicates an increase of 179% from 2018 (Thomala, 2020b).

With the rapid development of the short-video industry, the video production mode has also changed greatly. In the past decade, the rapid development of digital technology and the increase of various short-video applications provided an opportunity for the development of user-generated content (UGC) videos. UGC refers to media content created or produced by the general public rather than by professionals and it is primarily distributed on the internet (Daugherty, Eastin, & Bright, 2008; Ozuem, Pinho, & Azemi, 2016). People are no longer merely receivers of video content, they can produce and disseminate videos, which breaks the previous one-way information transmission mode. With a smartphone, anyone can participate in the process of short-video production and dissemination. UGC has become the main production mode of short videos on social media platforms.

The development of UGC has led to the emergence of a large number of internet celebrities, who are also called social media influencers. "Regular people" can create and post videos on social media to show their expertise in specific areas, such as healthy living, travel, food, lifestyle, beauty or fashion (Lou & Yuan, 2019). Social media gives them an opportunity to be known and liked by others. Anyone can become an internet celebrity who attracts the public or a social media influencer who people trust. Traditional opinion leaders and celebrities also joined short-video platforms to increase their influence and attain fame. As they have a huge fan base, their videos are liked, commented on and reposted by numerous followers in a very short time (Abidin, 2018).

Because of the fierce market competition in the social media industry, high-quality videos are continuously needed to improve the appeal of short-video platforms and increase user stickiness. Therefore, to produce more professional-generated content (PGC) has become an important aim of social media platforms.

PGC refers to professional production content and expert production content that are produced by professional teams who produce videos of a high quality, which are similar to traditional TV programmes (Cai, 2019). PGC is usually produced by professional teams with high-end equipment and sophisticated design, which can attract a large audience and fans. The disadvantage is that PGC requires high-content production costs, complicated design and long production cycle (Cai, 2019).

In order to motivate users to produce high-quality videos, social media platforms have introduced a series of training and incentive programmes. For example, YouTube has set up a creator level and creator award system according to subscriber numbers to help and encourage creators to produce better content (YouTube, 2020). Sina Weibo, one of the most popular social media platforms in China, introduced a video creator plan in July 2020, which benefits 10,000 video creators and 130 MCNs (Weibo Video, 2020).

MCNs originated from YouTube. MCNs are intermediaries which sell advertising, manage internet celebrities and develop video brands (Cunningham, Craig, & Silver, 2016). Compared with UGC and PGC, MCNs enhance cooperation with social media platforms and the career development of internet celebrities, and provide better services to both the internet celebrities and social media platforms.

Short Videos and Virtual Communities

The increasing consumption of video content creates a variety of opportunities for content producers and marketers. Online video platforms allow brand marketers to reach their main audience through video consumption habits. The popularity of social media and the rapid development of the short-video industry have become the new battlefields of brand marketing, especially in the fashion industry. The opinions of social media influencers have a great impact on followers, and fashion celebrities' clothing provides a reference point for fans. The development of short videos on social media has gradually shifted from the perspective of entertainment to the perspective of commercial application.

The advantages of short-video marketing are largely attributed to the development of social media platforms and mobile internet (Peng, 2019). In this era of mobile social networking, the short video provides a marketing approach for the development of enterprises. Fashion enterprises can utilize this opportunity to promote their brands through short videos, so as to make the brands better penetrate consumers' lives while entertaining the public and achieving commercial goals. The following are some suggestions for brands to use short videos and influencers to construct a virtual community on social media platforms to increase market share and customer retention.

Customization of Video Content

Compared with UGC and PGC, MCNs have the advantage of abundant resources and comprehensive technology. In recent years, the rapid development of MCNs has had a strong influence on the short-video industry. According to the statistics of Topklout (2020), in 2019 there were more than 5000 MCN organizations in China, which is a tenfold increase from 2017. MCN organizations are familiar with the rules of short-video platforms and have experience of cooperating with many internet celebrities on various platforms. MCN organizations also have the resources of world-class tools and technology, which ensures the production of high-quality video content. These content providers have a much stronger ability to produce and promote than ordinary UGC and PGC teams. In terms of content, MCN organizations can strictly control the quality, and realize the standardization and scale of content. In operation, their professional promotion and their whole network marketing ability will achieve rapid traffic realization for brands.

From the perspective of brand enterprises, due to their lack of familiarity with short-video platforms and internet celebrities, it could be difficult to work with internet celebrities to generate direct benefits. Working with MCN organizations could greatly improve efficiency and effectiveness for brands.

Selection of Brand Influencers

Influencers have a large number of fans on social media platforms. Fans that follow the same influencers will have some similar characteristics, such as age, occupation, hobbies and so on. It is these common characteristics that make fans pay attention to the same influencers. Fans' fashion consumption is significantly influenced by fashion influencers' recommendations, short videos or vlogs (Zou & Peng, 2019).

As grassroots internet celebrities are much closer to the lives of ordinary people, the influence and communication ability of these short-video bloggers may exceed that of some stars.

There are thousands of different influencers offering different topical interests, numbers of followers and other characteristics (Swant, 2016). Similar to selecting celebrity endorsement, an enterprise's selection of an internet celebrity to promote its brand needs to consider the matching of an internet celebrity's characteristics to the brand. How to choose the best-suited and most effective influencer is a challenge for brand managers (Chahal, 2016), which may vary depending on the specific goals of the brand.

As a medium between brands and fans, social media influencers can subtly promote products to consumers and improve the conversion rate of brand products. When the fans of an internet celebrity and the consumers of a brand have a high degree of compatibility, both the brand and the internet celebrity will benefit from cooperation.

Social Platform and Multidimensional Communications

The development of information technology has also promoted the diversification and rapid development of social networking platforms all over the world. In January 2020, there were 3.80 billion social media users, an increase of more than 321 million new users in one year (Kemp, 2020). These users are distributed across different social media platforms.

It has been proved that effective application of social media in the fashion industry could lead to a wider market share and customer retention (Stokinger & Ozuem, 2018). In the new media era, multiplatform and multidimensional content distribution is a typical content distribution model of brands to maximize dissemination. Multiplatform distribution means videos of the same or similar content can be uploaded to various social media platforms to obtain more network traffic. Although users on these platforms may overlap to some degree, every social media platform has a different algorithm for pushing content, and the way followers and bloggers interact also differs. In this way, brands can save their costs and expand their influence. Multidimensional distribution means a combination of different levels of internet celebrities as well as the official community of the brand.

The brand community is an important place to display brand culture and products; it also has the functions of product forecasts, official promotion activity releases and after-sales service. The virtual communities of internet celebrities focus on the internet celebrities' experiences with products and their interactions with followers. Therefore, brands and internet celebrities can construct different virtual communities on different platforms, as well as different ways for brands to communicate with users.

CONCLUSION

Due to the combination and development of social media and e-commerce, social commerce has become the new trend of e-commerce (Jascanu, Jascanu, & Nicolau, 2007). Consumers can easily obtain product information and share experiences of products in various virtual communities, which also play an important role in communication and interaction between consumers and brands. Opinion leaders are active on social media platforms and they have a huge impact on followers. The short video has become the most popular form of content on social media platforms.

As traditional advertising seems to become less effective (Trusov et al., 2009; Van den Bulte & Wuyts, 2007) in the era of social media, enterprises and brands should follow the trend and take measures to attract customers and increase customer engagement in a virtual brand community. This chapter suggests that firms build virtual communities and influence consumers through opinion leaders. It is suggested that firms cooperate with MCNs to customize video content, select influencers who match their brand and utilize social platforms to realize multidimensional communication.

As the popularity of short videos on social media platforms is still a new phenomenon, literature on marketing practice that combines short video with a virtual community is scarce. This topic involves knowledge of many disciplines, including communication science, sociology, psychology and marketing; so, quantitative and qualitative studies are needed to provide more theoretical and practical support for brands.

FURTHER READINGS

Felix, R., Rauschnabel, P. A., & Hinsch, C. (2017). Elements of strategic social media marketing: A holistic framework. *Journal of Business Research, 70*, 118–126.

Hakala, H., Nummelin, L., & Kohtamäki, M. (2017). Online brand community practices and the construction of brand legitimacy. *Marketing Theory, 17*(4), 537–558.

Kratzer, J., Lettl, C., Franke, N., & Gloor, P. A. (2016). The social network position of lead users. *Journal of Product Innovation Management, 33*(2), 201–216.

Lima, V. M., Irigaray, H. A. R., & Lourenco, C. (2019). Consumer engagement on social media: Insights from a virtual brand community. *Qualitative Market Research, 22*(1), 14–32.

Ozuem, W., & Azemi, Y. (Eds.). (2017). *Digital marketing strategies for fashion and luxury brands*. IGI Global.

Perren, R., & Kozinets, R. V. (2018). Lateral exchange markets: How social platforms operate in a networked economy. *Journal of Marketing, 82*(1), 20–36.

References

Abidin, C. (2018). *Internet celebrity: Understanding fame online.* Emerald Publishing Limited.

Ansarin, M., & Ozuem, W. (2015). Social media and online brand communities. In G. Bowen & W. Ozuem (Eds.), *Computer—Mediated marketing strategies: Social media and online brand communities* (pp. 1–27). IGI Global.

Armstrong, A., & Hagel, J. (2000). The real value of online communities. *Knowledge and Communities, 74*(3), 85–95.

Baker, G. (2002). The effects of synchronous collaborative technologies on decision making: A study of virtual teams. *Information Resources Management Journal (IRMJ), 15*(4), 79–93.

Blanchard, A. L. (2007). Developing a sense of virtual community measure. *CyberPsychology & Behavior, 10*(6), 827–830.

Bu, L., Wang, J., Wei Wang, K., & Zipser D. (2019). *China digital consumer trends in 2019.* Retrieved from https://www.mckinsey.com/featured-insights/china/china-digital-consumer-trends-in-2019.

Cai, Z. (2019). A comparative study of Pgc and Ugc modes in video websites based on mirror theory—Taking "Iqiyi" and "Tencent Video" as an example. *Frontiers in Art Research, 1*(6).

Carlson, B. D., Suter, T. A., & Brown, T. J. (2008). Social versus psychological brand community: The role of psychological sense of brand community. *Journal of Business Research, 61*(4), 284–291.

Casaló, L. V., Flavián, C., & Guinalíu, M. (2008). Promoting consumer's participation in virtual brand communities: A new paradigm in branding strategy. *Journal of Marketing Communications, 14*(1), 19–36.

Casaló, L. V., Flavián, C., & Ibáñez-Sánchez, S. (2018). Influencers on Instagram: Antecedents and consequences of opinion leadership. *Journal of Business Research, 117*, 510–519.

Chahal, M. (2016). Four trends that will shape media in 2016. *Marketing Week.* Retrieved from http://www.marketingweek.com/2016/01/08/four-trendsthat-will-shape-media-in-2016/. Accessed 21 August 2020.

Chen, Z., He, Q., Mao, Z., Chung, H. M., & Maharjan, S. (2019). *A study on the characteristics of douyin short videos and implications for edge caching.* In Proceedings of the ACM Turing Celebration Conference-China (pp. 1–6).

Cheng, X., Dale, C., & Liu, J. (2007). Understanding the characteristics of internet short video sharing: YouTube as a case study. *arXiv preprint* arXiv: 0707.3670.

Cheung, C. M. K., Chiu, P., & Lee, M. K. O. (2010). Online social networks: Why do students use Facebook? *Computers in Human Behaviour, 27*, 1337–1343.

Chi, P. Y., & Lieberman, H. (2011). *Raconteur: Integrating authored and real-time social media*. In Proceedings of the SIGCHI Conference on Human Factors in Computing Systems (pp. 3165–3168).

Childers, T. L. (1986). Assessment of the psychometric properties of an opinion leadership scale. *Journal of Marketing Research, 23*(2), 184–188.

Christakis, N. A., & Fowler, J. H. (2009). *Connected: The surprising power of our social networks and how they shape our lives*. Little, Brown Spark.

Clement, J. (2019). *Global social media usage reasons 2018 | Statista*. Retrieved from https://www.statista.com/statistics/715449/social-media-usage-reasons-worldwide/. Accessed 5 August 2020.

Clement, J. (2020a). *Daily social media usage worldwide | Statista*. Retrieved from https://www.statista.com/statistics/433871/daily-social-media-usage-worldwide/. Accessed 8 August 2020.

Clement, J. (2020b). *YouTube - Statistics & Facts | Statista*. Retrieved from https://www.statista.com/topics/2019/youtube/. Accessed 30 July 2020.

Coulter, R. A., Feick, L. F., & Price, L. L. (2002). Changing faces: Cosmetics opinion leadership among women in the new Hungary. *European Journal of Marketing, 36*(11/12), 1287–1308.

Cunningham, S., Craig, D., & Silver, J. (2016). YouTube, multichannel networks and the accelerated evolution of the new screen ecology. *Convergence, 22*(4), 376–391.

Darden, W. R., & Reynolds, F. D. (1972). Predicting opinion leadership for men's apparel fashions. *Journal of Marketing Research, 9*(3), 324–328.

Daugherty, T., Eastin, M. S., & Bright, L. (2008). Exploring consumer motivations for creating user-generated content. *Journal of Interactive Advertising, 8*(2), 16–25.

Deng, Q., Wang, C., & Zhou, Z. (2015). Research review of social media marketing. *Foreign Economics and Management, 37*(1), 32–42.

Diaz Soloaga, P., & Garcia Guerrero, L. (2016). Fashion films as a new communication format to build fashion brands. *Communication & Society, 29*(2), 45–61.

Dong, L., Huang, L., Hou, J., & Liu, Y. (2020). Continuous content contribution in virtual community: The role of status-standing on motivational mechanisms. *Decision Support Systems*, 113283.

Edelmann, N. (2013). Reviewing the definitions of "lurkers" and some implications for online research. *Cyberpsychology, Behavior, and Social Networking, 16*(9), 645–649.

Erkan, I., & Evans, C. (2018). Social media or shopping websites? The influence of eWOM on consumers' online purchase intentions. *Journal of Marketing Communications, 24*(6), 617–632.

Felix, R. (2012). Brand communities for mainstream brands: the example of the Yamaha R1 brand community. *Journal of Consumer Marketing, 29*(3), 225–232.

Fernback, J., & Thompson, B. (1995). *Virtual communities: Abort, retry, failure?* Originally presented as "Computer mediated communication and the American Collectivity: The dimensions of community within Cyberspace" at the annual meeting of the International Communication Association, Albuquerque, New Mexico. Retrieved March 24, 1997, from http://www.well.com/user/hlr/texts/VCcivil.html.

Flynn, L. R., Goldsmith, R. E., & Eastman, J. K. (1996). Opinion leaders and opinion seekers: Two new measurement scales. *Journal of the Academy of Marketing Science, 24*(2), 137.

France, M., & Muller, J. (1999). A site for soreheads. *Business Week,* 69–70.

Garfield, S. (2010). *Get seen: Online video secrets to building your business.* John Wiley & Sons.

Ge, J., & Gretzel, U. (2018). Emoji rhetoric: A social media influencer perspective. *Journal of Marketing Management, 34*(15–16), 1272–1295.

Godes, D., & Mayzlin, D. (2009). Firm-created word-of-mouth communication: Evidence from a field test. *Marketing Science, 28*(4), 721–739.

Godey, B., Manthiou, A., Pederzoli, D., Rokka, J., Aiello, G., Donvito, R., et al. (2016). Social media marketing efforts of luxury brands: Influence on brand equity and consumer behavior. *Journal of Business Research, 69*(12), 5833–5841.

Goldenberg, J., Han, S., Lehmann, D. R., & Hong, J. W. (2009). The role of hubs in the adoption process. *Journal of Marketing, 73*(2), 1–13.

Goldenberg, J., Lehmann, D. R., Shidlovski, D., & Barak, M. M. (2006). The role of expert versus social opinion leaders in new product adoption. *Marketing Science Institute Report, 6*(4), 67–84.

Goldsmith, R. E., & Clark, R. A. (2008). An analysis of factors affecting fashion opinion leadership and fashion opinion seeking. *Journal of Fashion Marketing and Management, 12*(3), 308–322.

Hagel, J., & Armstrong, A. (1997). *Net gain: Expanding markets through virtual communities.* Harvard Business School.

Haron, H., Johar, E. H., & Ramli, Z. F. (2016). *Online opinion leaders and their influence on purchase intentions.* In 2016 IEEE Conference on e-Learning, e-Management and e-Services (IC3e) (pp. 162–165). IEEE.

Hartmann, B. J., Wiertz, C., & Arnould, E. J. (2015). Exploring consumptive moments of value-creating practice in online community. *Psychology & Marketing, 32*(3), 319–340.

Homburg, C., Ehm, L., & Artz, M. (2015). Measuring and managing consumer sentiment in an online community environment. *Journal of Marketing Research, 52*(5), 629–641.

Hsu, L. C., Wang, K. Y., & Chih, W. H. (2018). Investigating virtual community participation and promotion from a social influence perspective. *Industrial Management & Data Systems, 118*(6), 1229–1250.

iiMedia Report. (2017). *China micro-video market trend research report*. Retrieved from https://www.iimedia.cn/c400/56105.html. Accessed 21 August 2020.

iiMedia Report. (2019). *China micro-video innovation trend research report*. Retrieved from https://www.iimedia.cn/c400/66047.html. Accessed 21 August 2020.

IResearch. (2018). *2018 China's internet celebrity economy development report*.

IResearch. (2019). *2019 China's social e-commerce sector report*. iResearch Consulting Group.

Islam, J. U., Rahman, Z., & Hollebeek, L. D. (2017). Consumer engagement in online brand communities: A solicitation of congruity theory. *Internet Research, 28*(1), 23–45.

Iyengar, R., Van den Bulte, C., & Valente, T. W. (2011). Opinion leadership and social contagion in new product diffusion. *Marketing Science, 30*(2), 195–212.

Jang, H., Olfman, L., Ko, I., Koh, J., & Kim, K. (2008). The influence of online brand community characteristics on community commitment and brand loyalty. *International Journal of Electronic Commerce, 12*(3), 57–80.

Jascanu, N., Jascanu, V., & Nicolau, F. (2007). A new approach to e-commerce multi-agent systems. *The annals of "Dunarea de Jos" University of Galati. Fascicle III, electrotechnics, electronics, automatic control, informatics*, 8–11.

Kelman, H. C. (1974). Social influence and linkages between the individual and the social system: Further thoughts on the processes of compliance, identification, and internalization. In J. Tedeschi (Ed.), *Perspectives on social power* (pp. 125–171). Chicago: Aldine.

Kelman, H. C. (2006). Interests, relationships, identities: Three central issues for individuals and groups in negotiating their social environment. *Annual Review Psychology, 57*, 1–26.

Kemp, S. (2020). *More than half of the people on Earth now use social media: DataReportal*. Global Digital Insights. Retrieved from https://datareportal.com/reports/more-than-half-the-world-now-uses-social-media. Accessed 21 August 2020.

Kiesler, S. (1986). *The hidden messages in computer networks* (pp. 46–47). Harvard Business Review Case Services.

Kim, J. E., Lloyd, S., & Cervellon, M. C. (2016). Narrative-transportation storylines in luxury brand advertising: Motivating consumer engagement. *Journal of Business Research, 69*(1), 304–313.

King, C. W., & Summers, J. O. (1970). Overlap of opinion leadership across consumer product categories. *Journal of Marketing Research, 7*(1), 43–50.

Koehler, M. J., Yadav, A., Phillips, M., & Cavazos-Kottke, S. (2005). What is video good for? Examining how media and story genre interact. *Journal of Educational Multimedia and Hypermedia, 14*(3), 249–272.

Kotler, P., & Armstrong, G. (2015). *Principles of marketing* (16th ed.). Toronto: Pearson Prentice Hall.

Lai, H. M., & Chen, T. T. (2014). Knowledge sharing in interest online communities: A comparison of posters and lurkers. *Computers in Human Behavior, 35*, 295–306.

Lazarsfeld, P. F., Berelson, B., & Gaudet, H. (1944). *The people's choice: How the voter makes up his mind in a presidential campaign.* New York, NY: Duell, Sloan and Pierce.

Lou, C., & Yuan, S. (2019). Influencer marketing: How message value and credibility affect consumer trust of branded content on social media. *Journal of Interactive Advertising, 19*(1), 58–73.

Lu H., & Zhou Y. (2005). *Consumer insight in China consumer behaviour.* Renmin University of China Press.

Luers, W. (2007). *Cinema without show business: a poetics of vlogging* (Vol. 5, No. 1). Ann Arbor, MI: MPublishing, University of Michigan Library.

Madupu, V., & Cooley, D. O. (2010). Antecedents and consequences of online brand community participation: A conceptual framework. *Journal of Internet Commerce, 9*(2), 127–147.

Marchi, G., Giachetti, C., & De Gennaro, P. (2011). Extending lead-user theory to online brand communities: The case of the community Ducati. *Technovation, 31*(8), 350–361.

McAlexander, J. H., Schouten, J. W., & Koenig, H. F. (2002). Building brand community. *Journal of Marketing, 66*(1), 38–54.

McKinsey Digital. (2019, September) (pp. 1–24). Retrieved from https://www.mckinsey.com/~/media/McKinsey/FeaturedInsights/China/Chinadigital consumertrendsin2019/China-digital-consumer-trends-in-2019.ashx.

Muniz, A. M., Jr., & O'Guinn, T. C. (2001). Brand community. *Journal of Consumer Research, 27*(4), 412–432.

Myers, J. H., & Robertson, T. S. (1972). Dimensions of opinion leadership. *Journal of Marketing Research, 9*(1), 41–46.

Nielsen, J. (2011). Participation inequality: Encouraging more users to contribute, 2006. Online: http://www.useit.com/alertbox/participation_i nequality.html. 1 March 2012.

Nonnecke, B., Andrews, D., & Preece, J. (2006). Non-public and public online community participation: Needs, attitudes and behavior. *Electronic Commerce Research, 6*(1), 7–20.

Nonnecke, B., Preece, J., & Andrews, D. (2004). *What lurkers and posters think of each other.* In Proceedings of the 37th Annual Hawaii International Conference on System Sciences (HICSS'04), Track 7.

Ozuem, W., Pinho, C. A., & Azemi, Y. (2016). User-generated content and perceived customer value. In W. Ozuem (Ed.), *Competitive social media marketing strategies* (pp. 50–63). IGI Global.

Ozuem, W., Patel, A., Howell, K. E., & Lancaster, G. (2017). An exploration of customers' response to online service recovery initiatives. *International Journal of Market Research, 59*(1), 97–116.

Paivio, A., & Clark, J. M. (1991). Static versus dynamic imagery. In C. Cornoldi, et al. (Eds.), *Imagery and cognition* (pp. 221–245). New York, NY: Springer.

Peng, A. (2019). Development process, characteristic and trend of short video industry. *Media Observer, 9,* 3.

Qualman, E. (2012). *Socialnomics: How social media transforms the way we live and do business.* John Wiley & Sons.

Rheingold, H. (1993). *The virtual community: Homesteading on the electronic frontier.* Reading, MA: Addison-Wesley.

Rheingold, H. (2000). *The virtual community: Homesteading on the electronic frontier.* MIT press.

Ridings, C. M., & Gefen, D. (2004). Virtual community attraction: Why people hang out online. *Journal of Computer-mediated communication, 10*(1), JCMC10110.

Ridings, C. M., Gefen, D., & Arinze, B. (2002). Some antecedents and effects of trust in virtual communities. *The Journal of Strategic Information Systems, 11*(3–4), 271–295.

Rogers, E. M., & Cartano, D. G. (1962). Methods of measuring opinion leadership. *Public Opinion Quarterly, 26,* 435–441.

Schmitt, P., Skiera, B., & Van den Bulte, C. (2011). Referral programs and customer value. *Journal of Marketing, 75*(1), 46–59.

Scott, D. M. (2015). *The new rules of marketing and PR: How to use social media, online video, mobile applications, blogs, news releases, and viral marketing to reach buyers directly.* John Wiley & Sons.

Statista (2020). *Smartphone users worldwide 2020 | Statista.* Retrieved from https://www.statista.com/statistics/330695/number-of-smartphone-users-worldwide/. Accessed: 1 August 2020.

Stokinger, E., & Ozuem, W. (2018). Social media and customer retention: implications for the luxury beauty industry. In M. Khosrow-Pour (Ed.), *Social media marketing: Breakthroughs in research and practice* (pp. 733–755). IGI Global.

Summers, J. O. (1970). The identity of women's clothing fashion opinion leaders. *Journal of Marketing Research, 7*(2), 178–185.

Swant, M. (2016). *Twitter says users now trust influencers nearly as much as their friends.* Retrieved from https://www.adweek.com/digital/twitter-says-users-now-trust-influencers-nearly-much-their-friends-171367/. Accessed 5 August 2020.

Tagarelli, A., & Interdonato, R. (2018). *Mining lurkers in online social networks: Principles, models, and computational methods.* Springer.

Talavera, M. (2015). 10 Reasons why influencer marketing is the next big thing. Retrieved June 3, 2019, from https://www.adweek.com/digital/10-reasons-why-influencer-marketing-is-the-next-big-thing/.

Tamí-Maury, I., Brown, L., Lapham, H., & Chang, S. (2017). Community-based participatory research through virtual communities. *Journal of Communication in Healthcare, 10*(3), 188–194.

Tapinfluence. (2015). *What is influencer marketing? | Read the ultimate guide.* Retrieved from https://www.tapinfluence.com/blog-what-is-influencer-marketing/. Accessed 21 August 2020.

Thakur, R., Angriawan, A., & Summey, J. H. (2016). Technological opinion leadership: The role of personal innovativeness, gadget love, and technological innovativeness. *Journal of Business Research, 69*(8), 2764–2773. https://doi.org/10.1016/j.jbusres.2015.11.012.

Thomala, L. L. (2020a). *China: Number of social media users 2017–2025 | Statista.* Retrieved from https://www.statista.com/statistics/277586/number-of-social-network-users-in-china/. Accessed 8 August 2020.

Thomala, L. L. (2020b). *China: short video market revenue 2016–2022 | Statista.* Retrieved from https://www.statista.com/statistics/874562/china-short-video-market-size/#statisticContainer. Accessed: 3 August 2020.

Topklout. (2020). *White paper on MCN industry development in China.* Retrieved from https://img.topklout.com/website/report/5eb9043a258d5.pdf. Accessed 13 August 2020.

Trusov, M., Bucklin, R. E., & Pauwels, K. (2009). Effects of word-of-mouth versus traditional marketing: Findings from an Internet social networking site. *Journal of Marketing, 73*(5), 90–102.

Turcotte, J., York, C., Irving, J., Scholl, R. M., & Pingree, R. J. (2015). News re- commendations from social media opinion leaders: Effects on media trust and in- formation seeking. *Journal of Computer-Mediated Communication, 20*(5), 520–535.

Van den Bulte, C., & Joshi, Y. V. (2007). New product diffusion with influentials and imitators. *Marketing Science, 26*(3), 400–421.

Van den Bulte, C., & Wuyts, S. (2007). *Social networks and marketing.* Cambridge, MA: Marketing Science Institute.

Van Mierlo, T. (2014). The 1% rule in four digital health social networks: an observational study. *Journal of Medical Internet Research, 16*(2),

Vernette, E. (2004). Targeting women's clothing fashion opinion leaders in media planning: an application for magazines. *Journal of Advertising Research, 44*(1), 90–107.

Villanueva, J., Yoo, S., & Hanssens, D. M. (2008). The impact of marketing-induced versus word-of-mouth customer acquisition on customer equity growth. *Journal of Marketing Research, 45*(1), 48–59.

Wang, Y., Meister, D. B., & Gray, P. H. (2013). Social influence and knowledge management systems use: Evidence from panel data. *MIS Quarterly, 37*, 299–313.

Weibo Video. (2020). *Weibo Video_Weibo.* Retrieved from https://weibo.com/u/5186027114?refer_flag=1005055013&is_all=1. Accessed 4 August 2020.

Wellman, B., Salaff, J., Dimitrova, D., Garton, L., Gulia, M., & Haythornthwaite, C. (1996). Computer networks as social networks: Collaborative work, telework, and virtual community. *Annual Review of Sociology, 22*(1), 213–238.

Williams, R. L., & Cothrel, J. (2000). Four smart ways to run online communities. *MIT Sloan Management Review, 41*(4), 81.

Xu, C. (2011). Characteristics of network communities as social organizations. *Journal of Huaihai Institute of Technology (Social Science Edition), 9*(05), 122–126.

Xu, J., & Ozuem, W. (2019). Building brands together: Online brand community and commitment in the luxury fashion industry. In W. Ozuem, E. Patten, & Y. Azemi (Eds.), *Harnessing Omnichannel retailing strategies for fashion and luxury brands.* Boca Raton, FL: Brown Walker Press.

Xu, L., Yan, X., & Zhang, Z. (2019). Research on the causes of the "Tik Tok" app becoming popular and the existing problems. *Journal of Advanced Management Science, 7*(2), 59–63.

Xu, X., Li, Q., Peng, L., Hsia, T. L., Huang, C. J., & Wu, J. H. (2017). The impact of informational incentives and social influence on consumer behavior during Alibaba's online shopping carnival. *Computers in Human Behavior, 76*, 245–254.

Yang, S., Zhao, Y., & Ma, Y. (2019). Analysis of the reasons and development of short video application—Taking Tik Tok as an example. In Proceedings of the 2019 9th International Conference on Information and Social Science (ICISS 2019), Manila, Philippines (pp. 12–14).

Yoo, W., Paek, H. J., & Hove, T. (2018). Differential effects of content-oriented versus user-oriented social media on risk perceptions and behavioral intentions. *Health Communication, 35*(1), 99–109.

YouTube. (2020). *Creators | YouTube.* Retrieved from https://www.youtube.com/intl/en-GB/creators/benefits-and-awards/. Accessed 4 August 2020.

Zhang, Z. (2019). Sustained participation in virtual communities from a self-determination perspective. *Sustainability, 11*(23), 6547.

Zhao, K., Stylianou, A. C., & Zheng, Y. (2018a). Sources and impacts of social influence from online anonymous user reviews. *Information & Management, 55*(1), 16–30.

Zhao, Y., Kou, G., Peng, Y., & Chen, Y. (2018b). Understanding influence power of opinion leaders in e-commerce networks: An opinion dynamics theory perspective. *Information Sciences, 426,* 131–147.

Zou, Y., & Peng, F. (2019). 'Key opinion leaders' influences in the Chinese fashion market. In N. Kalbaska, et al. (Eds.), *Fashion communication in the digital age* (pp. 118–132). Cham: Springer.

CHAPTER 4

Fashion Bloggers: Temperament and Characteristics

Gordon Bowen and Deidre Bowen

INTRODUCTION

Bloggers are rudimentary diarists on one level, but more sophisticated bloggers are individuals who maintain regular commentary on diverse phenomena, products, services and special interest groups. Bloggers allow blog visitors to leave comments in an interactive format. Some bloggers use blogs in preference to traditional media, whereas others are like mainstream journalists and view blogs as an additional communication medium (Steyn, van Heerden, Pitt, & Boshoff, 2008).

The public relations community has not been slow to realise the importance of blogging and the impact the new media could have on the practice of the public relations discipline (Croft, 2007). Lifestyle products, such as fashion, could benefit enormously from blogging, because

G. Bowen (✉)
Northumbria University, Northumbria, UK

D. Bowen
POW, Oxford, UK

© The Author(s), under exclusive license to Springer Nature Switzerland AG 2021
W. Ozuem and S. Ranfagni (eds.), *The Art of Digital Marketing for Fashion and Luxury Brands*,
https://doi.org/10.1007/978-3-030-70324-0_4

81

commentary and ideas are central to promoting fashion brands and blog visits are interactively engaging. If the values of lifestyle products and services are based on intangible benefits, then commentaries and fashion blogs are more likely to successfully promote products and persuade blog visitors than a journalistic blog. This suggests that fashion bloggers require a certain temperament to write engaging commentary using abstract ideas and opinions. The need for innovation is an important driver of a blog's success.

The market for bloggers is huge with the number in the USA set to reach 31.7 million, which is up from 28.3 million in 2015 (Statista, 2020). Bloggers who have strong content are the most successful at engagement. The types of content that are the best for engagement based on a 30% benchmark are (blogtyrant, 2020):

how to articles (34%)
guides and e-books (40%)
gated content (36%)
infographics (37%)
original research (33%)
roundups (32%)
interviews (33%).

Opinion (29%) and news and trends (28%) are laggards when it comes to audience engagement online. Certainly, there are content lessons for fashion bloggers but, due to the nature of the product, other qualities are required to engage visitors and potential visitors. This chapter suggests that fashion brands drive content to a lesser degree than other products; thus, bloggers' characteristics as influencers, the politics of blogging, and an understanding of the psychology of blogging and language are the more important drivers of fashion bloggers' success.

THEORETICAL FRAMEWORK

Fashion Blogging

Fashion bloggers are individuals with a fashion blog; they write and share information about fashion to their community (SanMiguel & Sádaba, 2017). Fashion bloggers form the largest segment of the blogosphere to date and communicate about fashion brands, fashion products, street style and personal style (Halvorsen, Hoffmann, Coste-Manière, & Stankeviciute, 2013). Akritidis, Katsaros and Bozanis (2009) stated that fashion blogs can be authored by individuals or be multi-authored (community blogs). Categorisation of fashion blogs includes ordinary people interested in fashion, celebrities, media blogs and corporate blogs (Sádaba & SanMiguel, 2015). Fashion influence has changed and evolved because of the individual fashion blogger (Pedroni, Sádaba, & SanMiguel, 2017). Fashion bloggers are influential because of their ability to create trust and credibility (Hsu, Chuan-Chuan Lin, & Chiang, 2013). It is likely that fashion bloggers influence purchase decisions because they are viewed as a credible source by their readers and followers (Haugtvedt, Machleit, & Yalch, 2005). Blogs are more effective at changing attitudes to accept or reject a new product, because blogs are interpersonal channels and are viewed as credible sources (Rogers, 2010).

Fashion bloggers' influence on readers is due to their unique position. They are regarded as fashion gods and at the same time readers are fascinated with the bloggers and involve them in their everyday personal lives, which indicates they are also considered friends (Belch & Belch, 2011). Engagement could be a key method that enables fashion bloggers to establish a close and qualified relationship with their readers. Engagement is an important tool for the fashion blogger (Sádaba & SanMiguel, 2016). In fact, a study of luxury products concluded that 75% of consumers consult a blog before purchasing a luxury item, while 87% ask for other readers' comments about a given brand (Okonkwo, 2010). Recent studies have highlighted the importance of electronic word of mouth in the online environment at the time of purchase (Han, Song, & Han, 2013).

Characteristics of Fashion Bloggers on Social Media (Instagram)

According to Statista (2017), out of the 15 most popular Instagram accounts, 7 are fashion-related brands (Nike, Victoria's Secret, Nike Football, H&M, ZARA, Adidas, Louis Vuitton), engaging millions of fans in the online environment. According to the Pew Research Center, Instagram users are mainly women ranging from 18- to 29-years old (Greenwood, Perrin, & Duggan, 2016). Becker (2016) coined the term "Instagrammer"; Instagrammers check Instagram for content at least twice a day, which creates a demand for content (Greenwood et al., 2016). What is considered entertaining or useful content is subjective, but globally significant trends will attract many users. In the fashion world, the most noticeable trends are makeup tips, outfit of the day posts and funny narrative, surprisingly (Lungeanu & Parisi, 2018).

Successful fashion bloggers must prove they have both individual and social capital (Bourdieu, 1980). Fashion bloggers have more chance of success if they are female, young adults or teenagers and have regular posts that confirm their interest in fashion. Social capital is generated in three ways (Nahapiet & Ghoshal, 1998): structural (e.g., network links), relational (e.g., trust) and cognitive (e.g., shared goals and shared paradigms). This supports the idea of being "authentic" and trustworthy as put forward by Marwick (2013, p. 4). Therefore, successful fashion bloggers are individuals who have relationships with others in the community, disclose personal information about themselves, and share their personal opinions on trends and products online (Lungeanu & Parisi, 2018). Another social capital trait is empathy (Wiedmann, Henning, & Langner, 2010). Instagram fashion bloggers' main traits are: act as opinion leaders and trendsetters, establish interactive and collaborative relationships with users and other fashion bloggers, and produce authentic content to foster closeness with users (Lungeanu & Parisi, 2018).

According to Ramos-Serrano and Martínez-García (2016, p. 90), fashion bloggers are opinion leaders who "exercise greater influence on people's opinions than mass media or those media which are controlled by the fashion industry". Fashion bloggers consider themselves to be experts, which is a mechanism to legitimise their position and standing in a field in which not all have the requisite knowledge (Lungeanu & Parisi, 2018), which blurs the boundary between journalism and non-journalism (Carlson, 2007). Fashion bloggers become opinion leaders and trendsetters by self-analysis and promotion (Tomiuc & Stan, 2015). Fashion bloggers who use the internet for storytelling that combines interpersonal communication with brand communication, leading to content creation in which personal life connections are used to connect with others, will potentially become a success (Ramos-Serrano & Martínez-García, 2016).

Social media and blogs are termed as interconnected platforms that enable users to modify content in a collaborative manner (Laurell, 2014). Linking information on social media and blogs is considered a first step, providing the right environment and getting users to use it is when interaction occurs. Fashion bloggers take up the invitation to be very interactive (Lungeanu & Parisi, 2018). On Instagram "mentions" (also known as tagging) is a mechanism to link profiles or keywords (hashtags). The acquisition of mentions boosts a blogger's profile, thus gaining more attention, which leads to more followers. Fashion bloggers use the mentions to attract brand attention, in order to promote their products to customers (Tomiuc & Stan, 2015). Tagging is also a way to drive fashion bloggers' followers to subscribe to their friends' accounts (Koughan & Rushkoff, 2014).

Digital technologies have led to increasingly higher rates at which "fashion information is spread from various sources through multiple media outlets" (Laurell, 2014, p. 523). Keeping up with fashion movements is becoming increasingly more difficult, resulting in fashion bloggers becoming intermediaries between customers and companies, directing their followers to websites of the brand they are using and talking about (Lungeanu & Parisi, 2018). Fashion bloggers also require a certain status and visibility on the social media platform, which is mediated by the number of followers and by the quality of the interactions (Lungeanu & Parisi, 2018; Wiedmann et al., 2010; Ozuem, Howell, & Lancaster, 2008). Being unsociable or unknown in the fashion world sends a negative signal to the audience: that they do not care enough or are not considered worthy by the rest of the community (Lungeanu & Parisi, 2018; Marwick, 2013).

How can fashion bloggers differentiate themselves? They achieve this by producing and sharing original and personal content with their audiences (Bruns, 2005). Fashion bloggers create a false reality based on mass media images, to create "pseudo-needs", which are continuously made and hoisted onto customers (Lungeanu & Parisi, 2018). A current problem is that fashion blogs reinforce hierarchies of aesthetics, taste and knowledge (Pham, 2011). Adopting a fashion persona online takes place within a commercial context of branding and advertising practices (Lungeanu & Parisi, 2018). Marwick (2013) suggested that fashion bloggers can differentiate themselves from one another by being authentic not only in their blogs, but also on other fashion platforms, such as magazines or corporate pages. Fashion bloggers can play a vital role in shaping the influencing process; they can interpret corporate messages and add their personal touch (Lungeanu & Parisi, 2018). Jenkins, Ford and Green (2013) suggested that fashion bloggers act as cultural intermediaries between brands and consumers' needs. Through social media, fashion bloggers contribute to the establishment of the cultural meaning of fashion products by taking over and modifying the symbolic meanings they carry. Audiences can get suspicious if a blog is too perfect, because of its high similarity to corporate pages (Marwick, 2013; Ozuem,

Patel, Howell, & Lancaster, 2017). An insincere Instagram profile can cost a fashion blogger their audiences' trust and the same is true if the fashion blogger is engaging with brands just for money, without genuinely endorsing the brand (Lungeanu & Parisi, 2018; Marwick, 2013).

Digital technologies have enabled a new kind of value co-creation through co-creation and co-creation of brand, involving fashion bloggers and customers. In this new environment, fashion bloggers can call upon the type of power and influence associated with firms; points of interaction offer opportunities for both value creation and value extraction for their customers (Laurell, 2014). Interactions taking place on fashion bloggers' sites produce a common social world that shapes the meaning of fashion trends and habits (Arvidsson, 2006).

An authentic fashion blogger must be willing to discuss intimate details about theirself to create a sense of a personal relationship with their audience while using self-branding techniques to get attention and visibility (Marwick, 2013). By publicising their lives, fashion bloggers offer immediate gratification to their followers (Rocamora, 2012). Importantly, the ability of followers to interact with fashion bloggers is the main facet of their differentiation, which companies cannot offer; fashion blogs offer connectiveness and show that the fashion blogger is a "real" person who cares about others (Marwick, 2013). The nature of content on fashion blogs "favors informality, direct conversational modes of address, and a certain assumption of intimacy (sometimes even of ironic complicity) with the audience" (Tomlinson, 2007, p. 100). According to Marwick (2013), audiences' value honest and personal thoughts that provide useful information to "real" people, answering their questions and meeting their needs.

Research by Lungeanu and Parisi (2018) found that in the fast moving and changing fashion environment, fashion bloggers maintain a constant and regular engagement (with an average of 4.37 feed posts/day) through social media. Drawing on the research of Koughan and Rushkoff (2014), the most famous Romanian fashion bloggers on Instagram make constant use of tags to aid interaction and collaborations. There are regular interactions and postings with other fashion bloggers, which increase the influence of audiences and the fashion bloggers. Those fashion bloggers who did not engage got fewer followers, which affected their ranking positions.

Another interesting finding from Lungeanu and Parisi (2018) is the importance of transmedia storytelling (i.e., multiplatform storytelling) among various social media platforms (Jenkins, 2006; Lungeanu & Parisi, 2018). Fashion bloggers who work across social media networks, such as Facebook, Instagram and YouTube, earned more followers on Instagram than those who did not. Vlogging is a lucrative communication tool that attracts attention; it pushes engagement and generates advertising revenues for the bloggers themselves. Too much professionalism tends to scare followers away, as it brings the fashion blogger closer to a fashion professional and further away from being an individual. Although fashion bloggers engage in collaborations, they need to ensure authenticity and that the opinions are genuine with the use of hyper-mediated authenticity based on sophisticated marketing techniques and informal posts that reinforce the consumerist society in which we live.

Opinion Leaders and Influencers

People tend to confer and consult when making decisions in the real world. Making purchases, event attendance, selecting travel destinations and even political voting involve a decision-making process. The blogosphere is a virtual environment that enables visitors to ask questions or to listen to opinions and perspectives to aid them in their decision making (Akritidis, Katsaros, & Bozanis, 2011). Consequently, visitors are influenced by others in their decision making and actors that assist in the decision process are influencers (Gruhl Guha, Kumar, Novak, & Tomkins, 2005).

Influencers are likely to have the interest of commercial organisations, because of the political capital and respect they hold. Influencers could become "unofficial spokespersons", saving an organisation from making investments in advertising, which is expensive (Akritidis et al., 2011), and requiring less coordination and time than an advertising campaign would entail. The popularity of blogs has attracted users because of their high functionality, and publication is straightforward (Akritidis et al., 2011). Blogs have become popular because of the psychology of blogging, that is, blogs are a communication tool to inform others about their activities or work and to provide commentary and opinion, to explain their whereabouts and to express deeply held emotions (Nardi, Schiano, Gumbrecht, & Swartz, 2004).

Identifying influential bloggers has given rise to a specific model, which is the influence flow method, which explicitly identifies the influential from the active bloggers. The model considers the features relevant to the blogsphere, such as size of the blog post, the number of comments, and the incoming and outgoing links (Agarwal, Liu, Tang, & Yu, 2008). The blogosphere is a changing environment and the model fails to recognise time-related factors, which are crucial in understanding the influence of bloggers. Furthermore, the model does not consider the productivity factor (active bloggers), which impacts influence (Akritidis et al., 2011).

Factors that measure the influence of bloggers include the incoming links. The number and length of comments are strong indicators of the importance of the blog to a community. However, the outgoing links are more subtle, they are used to recognise or convey authority (Akritidis et al., 2011). It is generally accepted that longer documents have more informational value than short ones. This is assigned an intuition value on most successful web ranking functions (Ozuem, Thomas, & Lancaster, 2016; Robertson, Walker, Jones, Hancock-Beaulieu, & Gatford, 1994).

The temporal factor is an important indicator of a blogger's influence in a rapidly changing blogsphere. Time is related to the age of the blog post and the age of the incoming link to the post. The age of the comment on the post is also significant. Influential bloggers are recognised if they made influential posts recently or if the posts had impact (Akritidis et al., 2011).

Temporal impact is defined by the following (Akritidis et al., 2011):

Proximal impact – identifies the impact that a blogger has on the regular members or readers of the community. It is measured by the comments made to the posts.

Wide impact – identifies the influence a blogger has on other bloggers outside the community. The incoming links that a post receives are a significant indicator of this type of impact. Other indicators of this impact are the quantity of posts on social media, such as Twitter and Facebook.

Blogger productivity and influence have unique characteristics in the blogosphere. The definition of productivity for bloggers is the number of long posts that were posted recently. Productivity needs to be viewed in the context of rapid changes in the blogosphere, where posts will only be productive for a certain period. New bloggers enter the blogosphere and others leave. The date a blog post was submitted is crucial to determining whether it becomes old, after two months it could be considered totally outdated.

Improvement in the temporal impact and productivity calculations altered the original influence flow method and identified bloggers with potential commercial and advertising significance. Thus, the modified influence flow method accounts for the rapidness and dynamism of the blogosphere (Akritidis et al., 2011).

Other models that take account of the characteristics of bloggers are classified as feature-based models and are non-temporal models. Feature-based models take into account blog posts to gauge the influence of bloggers. For example, the number of in-links and comments received by a blogger's blog are considered direct influence on the blogger's post. The H index is used to measure the quality of the blog posts and is used to measure the influence of the blog post based on citations of the blogger's research output (Hirsch, 2010).

How can the different models be used in the blogging community? The models help to identify influential bloggers who can be used to find identify applications in different fields, such as finding trendsetters, viral marketing, product promotion, revealing effectors in political domains and changing others' lives on social issues. The above applications are discussed below.

Finding Trendsetters

Firms are attracted to the social web. Some multinational corporations need to find celebrities who have large followings; these particular celebrities are known as trendsetters. Influential bloggers are market movers and trendsetters, who can help in the analysis of trends in technology, online marketing and fashion (Goyal, Bonchi, & Lakshmanan, 2010). Trend analysis helps firms to predict sales of their products in a sophisticated way. It also enables personalisation research and it can be used to improve blogs. This is achieved by asking users to share their wish list, which could include their interests, which can be modelled to make book recommendations to users based on their personalised interests (Lu, Hao, & Jing, 2016). The latest application is the use of influential bloggers in the identification of radical, extremist elements, which pose a threat of harm (Anwar & Abulaish, 2015).

Viral Marketing

Viral marketing is a modern technique that uses social media channels to promote marketing for various products. Viral marketing is known by many names, such as viral advertising or buzz marketing. The use of blogs presents unique and innovative opportunities. Companies target influential bloggers to gain their trust and turn them into reliable campaigners for their products and services. Blogs are free to the users, which is a big advantage and traditional media (television) and new media are synergistic (Chewning & Montemurro, 2016). Blogs are a major source of advertisement and viral marketing, and they are supportive of brand awareness and the role of the product. Pre-launch advertising on products and services stimulates blogging activities and thus makes the advertising and marketing more effective (Wu, Wu, & Chang, 2016). Viral marketing is one of the major areas of influence for bloggers. Bloggers' views and opinions are considered trustworthy. Influential bloggers can also help a company's customer support service by sharing reviews about products to increase interest in them. Users of social media with extensive social connections are likely to spread reviews to social networks (Kaur, Dhir, & Rajala, 2016). Influential bloggers exhibit predictive abilities that can assist in understanding future popularity levels (Zhang, Tomonaga, Nakajima, Inagaki, & Nakamoto, 2015). Analysis of the blogosphere can provide valuable insight into understanding user engagement and its relationship to blog post content. This, in turn, can help in advertising and viral marketing (Khan & Sapra, 2014).

Political Domain

The social web is an important component of political campaigns. Political leaders and activists use social networks, such as Twitter, for spreading information quickly to their followers. There is also a spillover effect to the population at large. Identification of influential bloggers has an impact on other users' opinions on things such as government policies and political campaigns (Farrell & Drezner, 2008). A contemporary example is the use of Twitter by President Trump, the president of the USA, to wage political campaigns against his political opponents and firms that have disappointed him. Keller and Berry (2003) suggested that influential bloggers can change voters' behaviour. Political blogs are creating a new political blog space, which is giving rise to a new form of political representation (Karlsson & Astrom, 2016).

Social Issues

The social web not only influences the participation of users, but it also has a direct influence on areas of their lives. People share their experiences and personal stories on social media, which is a useful starting point for sociologists and psychologists to gain insight into people's everyday life (Gordon & Swanson, 2009). The identification of influential bloggers can save valuable time for users, because they will not have to review too much content that may be irrelevant. Blogs present diverse views on news stories and readers can keep track of important stories (Lee, Jung, Song, & Lee, 2010). Influential bloggers can assist in health awareness campaigns such as anti-smoking movements (Gharlipour et al., 2015). Influential bloggers can facilitate businesses to address customers' complaints and improve customer service (Munger & Zhao, 2015).

Emotional and Sentiment Analysis
Emotions and sentiment analysis are part of social media, which has given rise to the emergence of opinion mining as an active research area. The influence of emotional arousal has been explored on the stock exchange using Chinese micro-blogs (Dong, Chen, Qian, & Zhou, 2015). Models that measure sentiment score (Alghobiri, Ishfaq, Khan, & Malik, 2015) for influential bloggers found a correlation between bloggers' activities and their influence (Ishfaq, Khan, & Iqbal, 2016). Machine learning techniques have been applied to separate the subjective as well objective content in social web forums (Gharlipour et al., 2015).

Research on influential bloggers who are also influential in other social web channels is an interesting area that needs to be explored (Khan et al., 2017).

Language and Politics of the Fashion Blogger

A growing area of interest in fashion blogging, which has not been researched in great depth, is how fashion bloggers create influence (SanMiguel & Sádaba, 2017). Fashion bloggers have found it difficult to gain full acceptance. This is captured by a quote from *Vogue*, "Note to bloggers who change head-to-toe, paid-to-wear outfits every hour: Please stop. Find another business. You are heralding the death of style" (*Vogue*, October 2016, as cited in SanMiguel & Sádaba, 2017). Fashion blogging is designated a sub-field in the fashion world, by which, "more research is needed to better understand how social media has altered the brand relationships, in particular how it influences consumers to make choices and recommend products to their social networks" (Kontu & Vecchi, 2014, p. 211).

Fashion bloggers are considered to have considerable influence, but this is a taken for granted approach. This still leaves marketing professionals and researchers wondering how fashion bloggers influence fashion brands. Understanding the characteristics of influential fashion bloggers from a personal perspective (i.e., on knowledge criteria) and from their social activities is challenging using a quantitative approach (SanMiguel & Sádaba, 2017).

Research concluded that opinion leaders can be found in small and informal groups and they exercise a face-to-face and personal leadership role. These informal groups constitute friends, family and neighbours. The influence of these informal groups moved beyond mere words by motivating their audience to act and behave in a certain way. The influencing of the informal group is done in a manner that is involuntary, invisible and unconscious. Leadership is not linked to position or status but is based on know-how and trust (SanMiguel & Sádaba, 2017). Personal factors are the key relationship driver over the Web, giving rise to e-influence (Sádaba & SanMiguel, 2015).

Fashion bloggers play a key role as opinion leaders by influencing the fashion process in the following ways, as: mediators of standards of cultural and social values (Simmel, 1923), sources of information (Katz & Lazarsfeld, 2006), sources of advice (Katz & Lazarsfeld, 2006), sources of reliability (Rogers, 1962), models of behavioural patterns (Katz & Lazarsfeld, 2006) and diffusers of innovation (Goldsmith, Freiden, & Kilsheimer, 1993).

The defining features of fashion bloggers consist of an interest in fashion information and a commitment to being "in fashion", such influencers are usually young women and they usually belong to a high social class (Katz & Lazarsfeld, 2006). Fashion opinion leaders tend to be more interested in clothes, have access to more sources of information and belong to a high socioeconomic class (MiKyeong, Seung, & Sun, 2003). Opinion leaders in fashion regard being fashionable important and they change their wardrobe to keep up with the fashion; thus, they follow fashion closely and influence others to do the same (SanMiguel & Sádaba, 2017). Fashion leadership plays a key role in the diffusion of new fashions (Goldsmith et al., 1993). Fashion leadership is linked to younger age groups; fashion leaders are younger than non-leaders (Bertrandias & Goldsmith, 2006; Goldsmith et al., 1993).

SanMiguel and Sádaba (2017) in their research found that 16% of bloggers could be classed as influential fashion bloggers. Only a small percentage of fashion bloggers exert influence. The most effective fashion blogger's profile is: female, between 24 and 39 years of age, single and university educated.

Fashion bloggers read more fashion blogs than fashion magazines. Fashion blogs feed off each other, using more blogs than conventional sources, such as fashion magazines or books. This implies that fashion bloggers influence each other (Agarwal et al., 2008). Influential fashion bloggers read more fashion magazines; fashion magazines are still an important source of information for them because they provide them with the information they need to influence others (SanMiguel & Sádaba, 2017).

Influential fashion bloggers not only influence online, but also go on to become opinion leaders in the offline environment. This could be because of their professionalism and their position as key players in the fashion industry. Influential fashion bloggers are active in closed social circles and are not just active in the online environment (SanMiguel & Sádaba, 2017).

Influential fashion bloggers update their looks fortnightly, which could be in sympathy with the latest trends they have read about. The fashion industry is event-oriented: presentations, catwalks, product presentations, magazine parties and awards. Influential fashion bloggers attend these events to gather new content, expand their social network, and act as a model of behaviour and a source of security for others (SanMiguel & Sádaba, 2017).

Fashion and fashion blogging have been condemned by feminists in the past. However, fashion blogs play a key communication role for women to express feminist messages. The feminist woman uses fashion to express an identity. The feminist woman acts and performs her gender, and this can lead to a stronger empowered version of one's self. The feminist self is infused in the blog post and shared with her readers. Feminist fashion bloggers create a niche audience that is created around feminist ideals (Sofra, n.d.).

Psychology of the Blogger

The internet is a rich environment to study the psychology of blogging in computer-mediated situations. Hiltz and Turoff's (1978) book, *The Network Nation*, which was reprinted in 1993, noted several observations about the online environment. Their observations included how users interact, and the impersonal nature and the freedom to "to be one's self" (Hiltz & Turoff, 1978, p. 27) in the digital environment. They also noted the social and psychological difference between online and offline (face-to-face) communications. These differences included the use of pen names and anonymity online, and the insertion of gestures and other forms of conversational discourse, which they referred to as "written vocalization" (Hiltz & Turoff, 1978, p. 90). Licklider and Taylor (1968, p. 28) referred to online communications as "distributed intellectual resources". The features these authors referred to, although about distributed computer access and shared programmes, are true for bloggers today, who share personal stories, opinions, recipes and technical information (Gurak & Antonijevic, 2008). There is a lack of social cues in the digital world, but this is not a barrier to people expressing a range of opinion and emotion (Rice & Love, 1987).

Research by Pew Internet and American Life Project (2006) concluded that the most popular topic among bloggers is "me". Speed, reach, anonymity and interactivity provide the foundation for blogging (Gurak & Antonijevic, 2008). Bloggers invite the intersection of private and public life (Miller & Shepherd, 2004). The sharing of an unprecedented amount of information with strangers via blogs is noted by Miller and Shepherd (2004). The character of blogs is simultaneously private and public, enabling group and individual identities (Wei, 2004). The blog community develops a group identity that emerges (Blanchard, 2004). Blogs as a communicative event are generally identified as online diaries. Blogs, therefore, enable temporal structuring of a person's activities, experiences and/or thoughts, which is the function of traditional diaries (Gurak & Antonijevic, 2008; Harris, 1995). Blogging is the rewriting of oneself through interaction with the audience. Unlike writing traditional diaries, blogging is the linking of two or more individuals. This is why blogs are both private and public and cannot be either public or private (Gurak & Antonijevic, 2008). The introduction of new technology has extended the boundary of writing (Harris, 1995). It is easier to hold a type of blogger identity through text-based social interaction than through visual social interaction. It is easier to hold an invented identity using text-based communications than visual communication. In visual communications, you must look the part (Gurak & Antonijevic, 2008).

Blogging gives back some control to the users, they can make the decision to share information that is of a personal nature or not. Consequently, they can decide if personal information should remain private or public. Blogging allows a fusing of sharing information and creating an identity, which is shared with the community (Gurak & Antonijevic, 2008).

IMPLICATIONS

Fashion bloggers are not like "ordinary" bloggers, they need to deploy relationship-building skills, empathy, grow a social network, evolve and refresh the content of their blog frequently. Ideas and innovation are necessary characteristics of fashion bloggers, but they must be of interest to their followers, which necessitates them to be extrovert in nature and be central to social crowds so as to gain the insight required to refresh and engage their online audience. Bloggers on products or services also need to be opinionated, but this is based on expertise on equipment or services, which legitimises their presence online. Fashion bloggers need to create legitimacy to gain acceptance in the fashion blogosphere, which is built on trust, collaborative partnership and authentic content.

Empathy is a characteristic that fashion bloggers require to differentiate themselves from the crowd. One can argue that empathy is less important for other bloggers who promote non-fashion brands. Fashion is about intangible qualities (e.g., style) and fashion sends cues about the individual. Successful fashion bloggers have empathetic antennae to judge and understand what fashion products will catch on and how to entice their audience to adopt different fashion trends. Earlier in the chapter, the social capital that fashion bloggers need to acquire in order to develop authentic blogs was discussed. The social capital environment is enriched by fashion bloggers attending events, parties and corporate entertainment. If fashion bloggers are to capitalise on the social capital environment and engage with the attendees, then an empathetic nature would help them to become an active member of the group, to solicit ideas and encourage the attendees to be open about their experiences. This would suggest that an outgoing nature and extrovert character would help fashion bloggers.

However, the fashion blogger must be able to distil the myriad of information they will gather and identify what is important to the fashion world and to their audience. Fashion bloggers must be able to read trends and nurture them, so they become mainstream. Moreover, fashion bloggers represent brands, which is a mechanism to gain advertising revenue, but they need to do their market research on how the adopted brands will play with their audience. Fashion bloggers must be able to read their audience and assess what will work and what will not, which means fashion bloggers must be flexible and open to learning from their audience. The trick for the fashion blogger is getting the balance right so that most of the audience is satisfied with the blog, because the last thing a fashion blogger wants is to lose members. Presentation of the ideas gathered from social capital meetings is important and may require "manipulation" of the audience to gain their compliance and trust. Fashion blogs portray a "different universe" to the everyday life of their audience. It is reasonable to suggest that most of the audience understand that fashion blogs are, in many respects, describing a parallel universe to their everyday life. Nevertheless, the audience needs to feel comfortable in the fashion blog environment and over-the-top or unbelievable experiences will sour the relationship between the fashion blogger and the audience. The fashion blogger creates a fantasy world that the audience can relate to and feel comfortable with. This fantasy world needs to evolve and refresh to hold and grow the audience.

Keeping an audience committed, engaged and loyal is more challenging for products that are based on intangible ideas. The authenticity of the fashion blogger must not just be based on new ideas; these ideas must energise the audience to stay and encourage them to engage with family and friends so they become members of the fashion blog. The audience for fashion bloggers matures and evolves; because fashion trends are connected to age groups, fashion bloggers must replenish their audience over time. Maintaining diverse fashion blogs would be challenging and, probably, satisfy few of the audience. This does beg the question will fashion bloggers be able to still have the same degree of influence as they grow older and will they maintain their ability to read the audience and exploit social capital meetings effectively to deliver the messages their audience want to read? Afterall, fashion bloggers tend to be young women who are fully engaged with the fashion scene. Will older fashion bloggers be accepted at social capital events? Gaining useable information in a social setting is a political process and requires fashion bloggers to be politically astute and consummate networkers.

Fashion bloggers can hide their persona from their audience, because they operate in a digital computer-mediated environment. Fashion bloggers cannot have an anonymous personality, because their messages are built on private experiences, which must become public. However, the persona they are presenting online might not be the "real" person, and this could be perceived as manipulation. Fashion bloggers develop an online personality that is attractive to the audience. The rewriting of oneself could appear dishonest and fashion bloggers might not give truthful opinions in what they are writing. Fashion bloggers are now entering the world of marketing and specifically marketing communication, namely, advertising. This could lead to a conflict of interest for fashion bloggers; successful fashion bloggers (influential fashion bloggers) will be able to use their skills to sell brands and products in which they may not necessarily believe. The fashion bloggers' audience needs to be able to read between the lines but, it will not be easy. However, if fashion bloggers were found to be misleading their audience, then their audience could dissipate; this risk will need weighing by the fashion bloggers. There is a tension between advertising by the fashion bloggers and legitimately sending verifiable messages to the audience. Breaking of the tension by fashion bloggers could damage their reputation as an influential fashion blogger. The tension between fashion bloggers and their audience could help to establish an equilibrium that ensures honesty, truthfulness and "authenticity with truth". Fashion bloggers need to understand the psychology of blogging to become influential fashion bloggers.

CONCLUSION

Fashion bloggers like (need) to share information like ordinary bloggers. However, fashion bloggers do not have a choice when it comes to the private and public intersection. It is necessary for fashion bloggers to put personal experiences (storytelling) into the public domain for their audiences, if the blog is to have any hope of success. This is not the case for ordinary blogs, such as writing about technical equipment. Furthermore, to be an influential fashion blogger requires shared personal experiences that are refreshed using the fashion blogger's social network and collaboration with other fashion bloggers. The need to refresh fashion blogs quickly puts more pressure on fashion bloggers to maintain their authenticity to differentiate themselves from other fashion bloggers. Replenishing of social capital is time consuming and intrudes on work–life balance, which suggests that fashion bloggers have a shelf life, which is determined by the commitments one accumulates as one gets older.

RESEARCH LIMITATIONS AND FUTURE RESEARCH

The chapter is a review of the literature on fashion bloggers from different perspectives (opinion leader, psychology of blogging, language and politics of blogging, and becoming a successful or influential fashion blogger) to build a consolidated view of fashion bloggers. However, further research is required to understand how the dimensions considered will vary in the offline environment of lockdown (an effect of the pandemic). The frequency of reading fashion blogs may change and the nature of the information that audiences may want could be different. How can fashion bloggers obtain the social capital for their blogs? Social meetings are interactive and the vibes inform the messages, but meeting online to gather social capital is much more challenging. What strategies did the fashion bloggers adopt to overcome the communication challenges?

REFERENCES

Agarwal, N., Liu, H., Tang, L., & Yu, P. S. (2008). *Identifying the influential bloggers in a community.* In Proceedings of the 2008 International Conference on Web Search and Data Mining (pp. 207–218).

Akritidis, L., Katsaros, D., & Bozanis, P. (2009). Identifying influential bloggers: Time does matter. *IEEE/WIC/ACM International Joint Conferences on Web Intelligence and Intelligent Agent Technology, 1,* 76–83. IET.

Akritidis, D., Katsaros, D., & Bozanis, P. (2011). Identifying the productive and influential bloggers in a community. *IEEE Transactions on Systems, Man, and Cybernetics—Part C Applications and Reviews, 41*(5), 759–764.

Alghobiri, M., Ishfaq, U., Khan, H. U., & Malik, T. A. (2015). *Exploring the role of sentiments in identification of active and influential bloggers.* In International Conference on Computer Science and Communication Engineering, Durres.

Anwar, T., & Abulaish, M. (2015). Ranking radically influential web forum users. *IEEE Transactions on Information Forensics and Security, 10*(6), 1289–1298.

Arvidsson, A. (2006). *Brands: Meaning and value in media culture.* New York: Routledge.

Belch, G. E., & Belch, M. (2011). *Advertising and promotion: An integrated marketing communications perspective* (9th ed.). New York, NY: McGraw-Hill, Irwin.

Bertrandias, L., & Goldsmith, R. E. (2006). Some psychological motivations for fashion opinion leadership and fashion opinion seeking. *Journal of Fashion Marketing and Management: an International Journal, 10*(1), 25–40.

Bourdieu, P. (1980). Le capital social: Notes provisoires. *Actes de La Recherche En Sciences Sociales, 3,* 2–3.

Bruns, A. (2005). *Gatewatching.* New York: Peter Lang.

Carlson, M. (2007). Blogs and journalistic authority. *Journalism Studies, 8*(2), 264–279.

Chewning, L. V., & Montemurro, B. (2016). The structure of support: Mapping network evolution in an online support group. *Computers in Human Behavior, 64,* 355–365.

Croft, A. C. (2007). Emergence of new media moves PR agencies in new directions. *Public Relations Quarterly, 52*(1), 16–20.

Dong, Y., Chen, H., Qian, W., & Zhou, A. (2015). Micro-blog social moods and Chinese stock market: The influence of emotional valence and arousal on Shanghai composite index volume. *International Journal of Embedded Systems, 7*(2), 148–155.

Farrell, H., & Drezner, D. W. (2008). The power and politics of blogs. *Public Choice, 134*(1–2), 15–30.

Gharlipour, Z., Hazavehei, S. M. M., Moeini, B., Nazari, M., Beigi, A. M., & Tavassoli, E. (2015). The effect of preventive educational program in cigarette smoking: Extended Parallel Process Model. *Journal of Education and Health Promotion, 4*(4). https://doi.org/10.4103/2277-9531.151875.

Goldsmith, R., Freiden, J., & Kilsheimer, J. (1993). Social values and female fashion leadership: A cross-cultural study. *Psychology & Marketing, 10*(5), 399–412.

Gordon, A. S., & Swanson, R. (2009). *Identifying personal stories in millions of weblog entries.* In Third International Conference on Weblogs and Social Media, San Jose, CA.

Goyal, A., Bonchi, F., & Lakshmanan, L. V. S. (2010). *Learning influence probabilities in social networks.* In Proceedings of the third ACM international conference on Web search and data mining (WSDM), New York.

Gruhl, D., Guha, R., Kumar, R., Novak, J., & Tomkins, A. (2005). *The predictive power of online chatter.* In Proceedings of the Eleventh ACM SIGKDD International Conference on Knowledge Discovery in Data Mining (pp. 78–87).

Gurak, L. J., & Antonijevic, S. (2008). The psychology of blogging you, me, and everyone in between. *American Behavioral Scientist, 52*(1), 60–68.

Halvorsen, K., Hoffmann, J., Coste-Manière, I., & Stankeviciute, R. (2013). Can fashion blogs function as a marketing tool to influence consumer behavior? Evidence from Norway. *Journal of Global Fashion Marketing*, 4(3), 211–224.

Han, S. L., Song, H., & Han, J. J. (2013). Effects of technology readiness on prosumer attitude and eWOM. *Journal of Global Scholars of Marketing Science*, 23(2), 159–174.

Harris, R. (1995). *Signs of writing*. New York: Routledge.

Haugtvedt, C. P., Machleit, K. A., & Yalch, R. F. (2005). *Online consumer psychology: Understanding and influencing consumer behaviour in the virtual world*. Mahwah, NJ: Lawrence Erlbaum Associates.

Hiltz, S. R., & Turoff, M. (1978). *The network nation: Human communication via computer*. Cambridge: MIT Press.

Hirsch, J. (2010). An index to quantify an individual's scientific research output that takes into account the effect of multiple coauthorship. *Scientometrics*, 85(3), 741–754.

Hsu, C. L., Chuan-Chuan Lin, J., & Chiang, H. S. (2013). The effects of blogger recommendations on customers' online shopping intentions. *Internet Research*, 23(1), 69–88.

Ishfaq, U., Khan, H. U., & Iqbal, K. (2016). *Modeling to find the top bloggers using sentiment features*. In IEEE ICE CUBE 2016 (pp. 227–233). Quetta, Pakistan.

Jenkins, H. (2006). *Convergence culture*. New York: New York University Press.

Jenkins, H., Ford, S., & Green, J. (2013). *Spreadable Media: Creating value and meaning in a networked culture*. New York: New York University Press.

Karlsson, M., & Astrom, J. (2016). The political blog space: A new arena for political arena. *New Media & Society*, 18(3), 465–483.

Katz, E., & Lazarsfeld, P. F. (2006). *Personal influence, the part played by people in the flow of mass communications*. Pistcataway, NJ: Transaction Publishers.

Kaur, P., Dhir, A., & Rajala, R. (2016). Assessing flow experience in social networking site based brand communities. *Computers in Human Behavior*, 64, 217–225.

Keller, E., & Berry, J. (2003). *The Influentials: One American in ten tells the other nine how to vote, where to eat, and what to buy*. New York: Free Press.

Khan, A., & Sapra, R. (2014). The systematic survey on influential users in a blog network. *International Journal of Emerging Trends & Technology in Computer Science* (IJETTCS), 3(1), 237–239.

Khan, H. U., Daud, A., Ishfaq, U., Amjad, T., Aljohani, N., Abbasi, R. A., et al. (2017). Modelling to identify influential bloggers in the blogosphere: A survey. *Computers in Human Behavior*, 68, 64–82.

Kontu, H., & Vecchi, A. (2014). The strategic use of social media in the fashion industry. In B. Christiansen, S. Yildiz, & E. Yildiz (Eds.), *Transcultural marketing for incremental and radical innovation* (pp. 209–233). IGI Global.

Laurell, C. (2014). *Commercializing social media: A study of fashion (Blogo)spheres* (Doctoral thesis). Stockholm University School of Business. Stockholm, Sweden.

Lee, Y., Jung, H.-Y., Song, W., & Lee, J.-H. (2010). *Mining the blogosphere for top news stories identification.* In Proceedings of the 33rd international SIGIR Conference on Research and Development in Information Retrieval, Geneva.

Licklider, J. C. R., & Taylor, R. W. (1968). The computer as a communications device. *Science and Technology, 76,* 21–31.

Lu, J., Hao, Q., & Jing, M. (2016). Consuming, sharing, and creating content: How young students use new social media in and outside school. *Computers in Human Behavior, 64,* 55–64.

Lungeanu, I., & Parisi, L. (2018). What makes a fashion blogger on Instagram? The Romanian Study. Observatorio (OBS*). 028-053 1646-5954/ERC123483/2018 028. Special issue on The co-option of audiences in the attention economy Guest Editors: Ana Jorg, Inês Amaral, & David Mathieu.

MiKyeong, B., Seung, S. L., & Sun, Y. P. (2003). The brand name effect of consumer's evaluation on intrinsic attributes: A case study of clothing market. *International Journal of Human Ecology, 4*(1), 45–54.

Miller, C. R., & Shepherd, D. (2004). *Blogging as social action: A genre analysis of the weblog.* University of Minnesota. Retrieved from the University of Minnesota Digital Conservancy. http://hdl.handle.net/11299/172818.

Munger, T., & Zhao, J. (2015). *Identifying influential users in on-line support forums using topical expertise and social network analysis.* In Proceedings of the 2015 IEEE/ACM International Conference on Advances in Social Networks Analysis and Mining, Paris.

Nahapiet, J., & Ghoshal, S. (1998). Social capital, intellectual capital and the organizational advantage. *Academy of Management Review, 23,* 242–266.

Nardi, B. A., Schiano, D., Gumbrecht, J. M., & Swartz, L. (2004). Why we blog. *Communications: ACM, 47*(12), 41–46.

Okonkwo, U. (2010). *Luxury online: Styles, systems, strategies.* New York, NY: Palgrave Macmillan.

Ozuem, W., Howell, K. E., & Lancaster, G. (2008). Communicating in the new interactive marketspace. *European Journal of Marketing, 42*(9/10), 1059–1083.

Ozuem, W., Patel, A., Howell, K. E., & Lancaster, G. (2017). An exploration of customers' response to online service recovery initiatives. *International Journal of Market Research, 59*(1), 97–116.

Ozuem, W., Thomas, T., & Lancaster, G. (2016). The influence of customer loyalty on small island economies: an empirical and exploratory study. *Journal of Strategic Marketing, 24*(6), 447–469.

Pedroni, M., Sádaba, T., & SanMiguel, P. (2017). Is the golden era of fashion blogs over? An analysis of the Italian and Spanish. In E. Mora & P. Pedroni (Eds.), *Fashion tales: Feeding the imaginary* (pp. 105–124). New York, NY: Peter Lang.

Pew Internet and American Life Project. (2006). *Bloggers: A portrait of the Internet's new storytellers*. Retrieved January 2, 2007, from http://www.pewint ernet.org/pdfs/PIP%20Bloggers%20Report%20July%2019%202006.pdf.

Pham, M.-H. T. (2011). Blog ambition: Fashion, feelings, and the political economy of the digital raced body. *Camera Obscura, 26*(1[76]), 1–37.

Ramos-Serrano, M., & Martínez-García, A. (2016). Personal style bloggers: The most popular visual composition principles and themes on Instagram. *Observatorio (OBS*) Journal, 10*(2), 89–109.

Rice, R. E., & Love, G. (1987). Electronic emotion: Socioemotional content in a computer-mediated communication network. *Communication Research, 14,* 85–108.

Robertson, S. E., Walker, S., Jones, S., Hancock-Beaulieu, M., & Gatford, M. (1994). Okapi at TREC-3. In Proceedings 3rd Text REtrieval Conference (pp. 109–126).

Rocamora, A. (2012). Hypertextuality and remediation in the fashion media. *Journalism Practice, 6*(1), 92–106. https://doi.org/10.1080/17512786. 2011.622914.

Rogers, E. M. (1962). *Diffusion of innovations*. New York, NY: Free Press a Division of Macmillan Publishing.

Rogers, E. M. (2010). *Diffusion of innovations* (5th ed.). New York, NY: Free Press.

Sádaba, T., & SanMiguel, P. (2015). Fashion Influentials: Prescripción y liderazgo en moda. In T. Sádaba (Ed.), *Moda en el entorno digital* (pp. 111–122). Eunsa.

Sádaba, T., & SanMiguel, P. (2016). Fashion blog's engagement in the customer decision making process. In A. Vecchi & C. Buckley (Eds.), *Handbook of research on global fashion management and merchandising* (pp. 211–230). London: IGI.

SanMiguel, P., & Sádaba, T. (2017). Nice to be a fashion blogger, hard to be influential: An analysis based on personal characteristics, knowledge criteria, and social factors. *Journal of Global Fashion Marketing*. https://doi.org/10. 1080/20932685.2017.1399082.

Simmel, G. (1923). Filosofía de la moda. *Revista de Occidente, 1,* 42–66.

Sofra, I. (n.d.). *Fashion and feminism: Materially relative designing of everyday life female behaviour the bloggers' contribution* (Dissertation). Guglielmo Marconi University, Rome.

Steyn, P., van Heerden, G., Pitt, L., & Boshoff, C. (2008). Meet the bloggers: some characteristics of serious bloggers in the Asia-Pacific region and why

PR professionals might care about them. *Public Relations Quarterly*, 52(3), 39–44.

Tomiuc, A., & Stan, O. (2015). The fashion blogosphere in Romania: Fashionscape and fashion bloggers. *Postmodern Openings*, 6(1), 161–174.

Tomlinson, J. (2007). *The culture of speed*. London: Sage.

Wiedmann, K.-P., Henning, N., & Langner, S. (2010). Spreading the word of fashion: Identifying social influencers in fashion marketing. *Journal of Global Fashion Marketing: Bridging Fashion and Marketing*, 1(3), 142–153.

Wu, L.-H., Wu, L.-C., & Chang, S.-C. (2016). Exploring consumers' intention to accept smartwatch. *Computers in Human Behavior*, 64, 383–392.

Zhang, J., Tomonaga, S., Nakajima, S., Inagaki, Y., & Nakamoto, R. (2015). *Finding prophets in the blogosphere: Bloggers who predicted buzzwords before they become popular*. In 17th International Conference on Information Integration and Web-Based Applications & Services, Brussels.

WEBSITES

Becker, T. (2016, January 26). How and why 13–24 year-olds use Instagram. Retrieved August 24, 2020, from https://socialmediaweek.org/blog/2016/01/how-why-13-24-year-olds-use-instagram/.

Blanchard, A. (2004). Blogs as virtual communities: Identifying a sense of community in the Julie/Julia Project. In L. J. Gurak, S. Antonijevic, L. Johnson, C. Ratliff, & J. Reyman (Eds.), *Into the blogosphere: Rhetoric, community, and culture of Weblogs*. Retrieved August 26, 2020, from http://blog.lib.umn.edu/blogosphere/women_and_children.html.

Blogtyrant. (2020). *The latest blogging trends and statistics for 2020 (and beyond)*. https://www.blogtyrant.com/new-blogging-statistics/. Accessed 28 June 2020.

Greenwood, S., Perrin, A., & Duggan, M. (2016, November 11). *Social media update 2016*. Retrieved August 24, 2020, from http://www.pewinternet.org/2016/11/11/social-media-update-2016/.

Koughan, F., & Rushkoff, D. (Writers). (2014, February 18). *Generation like [documentary]*. United States: Frontline. Retrieved August 15, 2020, from http://www.pbs.org/wgbh/frontline/film/generation-like/.

Marwick, A. (2013). *They're really profound women, 'they're entrepreneurs':* Conceptions of authenticity in fashion blogging. In International Conference on Weblogs and Social Media (ICWSM), 1–8. Retrieved August 19 2020, from http://www.tiara.org/wp-content/uploads/2018/05/amarwick_fashionblogs_ICWSM_2013.pdf.

Statista (2017, December). *Leading brands ranked by number of Instagram followers as of December 2017 [Statistics]*. Retrieved August 23, 2020, from https://www.statista.com/statistics/253710/leading-brands-ranked-by-number-of-instagram-followers/.

Statista. (2020). Number of bloggers in the US from 2014 to 2020. https://www.statista.com/statistics/187267/number-of-bloggers-in-usa/#:~:text=3%20million%20internet%20users%20updated%20a%20blog%20at,set%20to%20reach%2031.7%20million%20users%20in%202020. Accessed 28 June 2020

Wei, C. (2004). Formation of norms in a blog community. In L. J. Gurak, S. Antonijevic, L. Johnson, C. Ratliff, & J. Reyman (Eds.), *Into the blogosphere: Rhetoric, community, and culture of Weblogs.* Retrieved August 26, 2020, from http://blog.lib.umn.edu/blogosphere/women_and_children.html.

PART II

Online Brand Communities and Customer Relationships

Online Brand Communities, Customer Participation and Loyalty in the Luxury Fashion Industry: Strategic Insights

Wilson Ozuem and Michelle Willis

INTRODUCTION

Customers' participation within online brand communities (OBCs) is critical for the long-term success and continued existence of OBCs and luxury brands' social media presence (Kumar, 2019). Customer participation refers to the involvement of members of an OBC in activities that keeps them connected to the community (Malinen, 2015), including sending regular online posts and replies, searching for information and sharing information. Research has found that active participation in OBCs can lead to positive outcomes for brands, including members' commitment to the brand, brand loyalty and word-of-mouth communication (Relling, Schnittka, Sattler, & Johnen, 2016). However, not all forms of customers' online participation will directly benefit luxury

W. Ozuem · M. Willis (✉)
Institute of Business, Industry and Leadership, University of Cumbria, Lancaster, UK

© The Author(s), under exclusive license to Springer Nature Switzerland AG 2021
W. Ozuem and S. Ranfagni (eds.), *The Art of Digital Marketing for Fashion and Luxury Brands,*
https://doi.org/10.1007/978-3-030-70324-0_5

fashion brands or motivate loyalty towards the brand (Ozuem, Thomas, & Lancaster, 2016). Motivations for participating in OBCs vary from search for information related to the brand to seeking entertainment by socially interacting with others. However, the motivations that encourage customers to participate in OBCs do not necessarily oblige them to place the brand as the central factor influencing their participation.

The importance of the brand to a customer affects participation outcome. If a customer's loyalty is aligned with the brand, then it may positively influence other customers' loyalty. If online participation does not align favourably with the brand, the level of customer participation gradually becomes irrelevant. A large number of social media users may be participating within OBCs but not positively engaging or connecting with the brand, whereas others may be passively participating but engaging positively with the online content related to the brand. From this we can identify two groups of participants in OBCs: active and passive participants (this is discussed in more detail in the section "Dichotomies: passive and active participation". Passive participants generally observe content rather than create and publish content like active participants do. However, their passive participation can positively impact their engagement with the brand directly: they consume content that may impact their purchasing decisions and the appeal of the brand. The same can be said for active participants; they will consume the content they encounter but will actively respond to the content through replies, pictures and other visual content. However, active participants come with higher threats than passive members. They have the ability to share negative information related to the brand as well as positive information; therefore, brand managers need to critically examine whether active participants' loyalty aligns with the brand itself or with other non-loyalists.

Despite the positive outcomes of customer participation through OBCs, the success of customers' participation can backfire on a luxury fashion brand (Park, Im, & Kim, 2018). Content and information shared by some participating members, which may be prompted by posters who do not positively identify with the brand but are willing to share such information, can contradict the image of the luxury brand. It is important to examine not only the level of participation customers develop but the context and impact of their participation both on themselves and on other customers. Every motivation and experience of participation is subjective and leads to different outcomes. Regardless of the level of participation, customers' loyalty can be identified based on how they participate, what content they contribute and what messages they communicate regarding the brand. The examination of online participation within this chapter is influenced by the behaviour and attitudes of the millennial generation. Millennials are significantly involved in social media activity, including brand-related posts and social interactions, and they regularly purchase products online, which places them at the centre of social media activity (Azemi, Ozuem, & Howell, 2020; Bi, 2019; de Kerviler & Rodriguez, 2019; Liu, Wu, & Li, 2019). They are also critical about the brands they consume, justifying their choice based on whether the brand suits their image and is socially friendly, which makes them an important customer segment in understanding the effect and outcome of online participation on loyalty within OBCs. The next section discusses luxury fashion and OBCs, which leads to a discussion of customer participation in OBCs, including customers' online behaviours, attitudes and motivations for participating in OBCs. This is followed with a discussion of the customer participation filter model developed from the discussed literature.

Luxury Fashion and OBCs

A luxury brand is often defined as having a set of unique factors, such as exclusivity, high price, quality and symbolic attributes (Park et al., 2018), which causes customers to psychologically perceive them as different from mass-marketed brands (Wiedmann, Hennigs, & Siebels, 2009). Customers who purchase luxury fashion brands are driven by the need to enhance their social status and own a product that only a handful of people can actually possess (Wiedmann et al., 2009). Advertisements of luxury fashion brands have strongly emphasised the exclusivity and superiority of their products, evoking social segregation between customers (Park et al., 2018). Luxury fashion brands like Armani, Chanel, Louis Vuitton and Tiffany & Co. are, for a majority of customers, financially difficult to acquire; hence, their reputation as rare and exclusive and available only to the elite market in contrast to the mainstream market.

Whereas luxury fashion brands separate elite fashion taste from the mass market, social media emphasises the building of interpersonal relationships between members through interactions and exchanges (Willis, 2018), which has motivated luxury fashion brands to build interpersonal relationships with customers (Kim & Ko, 2012). Platforms like Instagram have dominated the communication channels of luxury fashion industries, and, as the showcasing of luxury brands on social media increases, the perceived psychological distance between the luxury brand's status and the consumer's status lessens. Engagement within social media leads to greater intimacy between brands and consumers (Hudson, Huang, Roth, & Madden, 2016), prompting a feeling of friendship. However, while social media has reduced the distance between customers and brands, the status of luxury fashion brands and the status of mainstream fashion products can still impact the level of interaction between low-income customers and brands and between customers with elite status and brands. Social distance represents a symbolic space between individuals with different lifestyles, connecting people who have similar lifestyles and dividing them from those who have different lifestyles. This leads to less interactions between customers and less psychological attachment to brands with luxury status (Park et al., 2018). This psychological distance between customers and luxury brands can be reduced by two important factors: (1) the brand's image aligns with the customer's personality and identity, and/or (2) the brand or other community members encourage customers or give customers reasons to participate within OBCs. The next section discusses customer participation in OBCs; in particular, customers' goals and trajectories in OBCs and the effect they have on an OBC's value.

CUSTOMER PARTICIPATION IN OBCS

Customer participation indicates the degree to which customers are willing to invest time and resources into services, which will consequently impact the production, delivery and outcomes of products and services, thus contributing to the overall value of the products and services firms offer (Nysveen & Pedersen, 2014). Customer participation has been examined based on the physical actions between the brand and the customer, emphasising the co-production of product designs, service delivery and knowledge sharing based on the collaborative actions of the firm and the customer. However, customer participation activities are not limited to activities between the firm and the customer, they also involve group level activity within OBCs. In OBCs, customer participation refers to the members' involvement and engagement in online activities that keep them connected in the long term (Malinen, 2015; Tsai, Huang, & Chiu, 2012). Participation in OBCs includes contributing content, such as online posts and replies, and investing time observing, searching and exchanging information within OBCs (Kumar, 2019; Sun, Rau, & Ma,

2014). Participation can also refer to community group activity, following the feelings of "we-intentions" among members (Dholakia, Bagozzi, & Pearo, 2004), which can lead to integration, a consistent unity within the community, enhanced brand knowledge and brand relationships.

Customer participation does not happen without a purpose. When a customer searches an online shopping website it is with the intention to purchase an item; when considering participation in OBCs, the customer needs a goal that motivates them to participate. Customers will participate within an online community if they think that their goals will be achieved following online participation (Relling et al., 2016). Research identifies two sets of goals that motivate customers to participate in communities: functional goals and social goals (Baldus, Voorhees, & Calantone, 2015; Nambisan & Baron, 2007). When customers pursue such goals, they are more likely to engage in community participation (de Almeida, Scaraboto, dos Santos Fleck, & Dalmoro, 2018; Mathwick & Mosteller, 2016); thus, encouraging the regular involvement of customers within OBCs.

Goals and Trajectories in OBCs

Participation within OBCs is arguably a result of customers' individual goals that indicate a need to engage with OBCs. As mentioned earlier, customers' goals can be divided into social goals or functional goals that could include gaining benefits from participating in OBCs. Customers may seek social benefits, such as social enhancement, support and approval from other members (Relling et al., 2016), which they obtain by establishing close ties with other community members (Dholakia et al., 2004). Customers with such social goals, benefit from participating in OBCs as they connect them to other customers who share a passion for a brand and they can obtain social support and approval from those members (Dholakia et al., 2004; Nambisan & Baron, 2007; Wang, Stoner, & John, 2019). In contrast, other customers may seek functional benefits, such as information obtained from observing information shared by other customers, to help accomplish specific tasks such as purchasing decisions. These customers are primarily interested in brand-related information, which may not be available on company websites, that OBC members can provide, such as other customers' overall perception of the brand's quality and their general purchasing experience. Customers with functional goals typically seek objective information about a brand (Relling et al., 2016);

so, they may have lower intentions to socialise with others on a personal level.

Effect of Customer Participation on the Value of OBCs

As the usage of OBCs increases, so do the perceived benefits customers obtain from participating in OBCs, thus, motivating them to continue using OBCs. This increases the perceived value of the OBC, including the functional, emotional, relational and entitativity values of the OBC. In using OBCs for functional benefits, customers' participation generates value, such as high quality experience, personalised services and increased control (Chan, Yim, & Lam, 2010). Customers' active involvement in OBC activity that revolves around problem solving, purchasing decisions and evaluations, and searching and sharing brand-related information (Davis, Piven, & Breazeale, 2014), promotes a positive interactive learning environment, which can have an impact on how customers perceive consumption experiences through OBCs in contrast to the traditional methods of online shopping. The completion of functional goals can lead to the development of emotional value that contributes to OBCs' success. Customers may experience enjoyment in participating in the services OBCs facilitate (Shukla & Drennan, 2018) and feel empowered in using an OBC due to the control it allows customers (Yim, Chan, & Lam, 2012). Members of OBCs are able to shape their own brand experiences by contributing their own resources, such as personal pictures and messages, making them more personalised, thus, enhancing enjoyment when browsing through OBCs. Furthermore, the interactive nature of OBCs and the closeness to the brand and other customers they enable make them a fun and entertaining environment for customers (Carlson, Rahman, Taylor, & Voola, 2019); thus, customers derive emotional value from participating in OBCs.

Social media enables customers to interact with brands regardless of geographical distances; thus, a purchase and delivery exchange develops into a close personal relationship with the brand. OBCs enable customers to engage in personalised communication with a brand's daily activities. This activity can be linked to relational consumption; the customer enjoys their interactions with the brand (Davis et al., 2014; Ramaswamy & Ozcan, 2016; Ozuem, Howell & Lancaster, 2008), particularly through OBCs, which enhances their consumption experiences with the brand (Merz, Zarantonello, & Grappi, 2018; Prahalad & Ramaswamy, 2004).

Relational brand connections promoted through OBCs can influence brand-related outcomes, such as brand attitudes, purchase intentions, brand affect and brand separation distress (Kara, Vredeveld, & Ross, 2018), which reveals that customers' active participation in an OBC increases their emotional attachment to the brand. This attachment can also be developed between the community's members. Entitativity values refers to situations where people act as a whole coherent unit (Lickel et al., 2000; Vock, Dolen, & Ruyter, 2013). Consumers may use OBCs to share personal experiences with others, not only for their own benefit but for the benefit of others, which, over time, helps members to build strong links with each other, thus encouraging them to continue participating in OBCs. In using OBCs, customers add value to an OBC by portraying it as an environment that enables members to develop interpersonal relationships with the brand and its members.

Social Identification and Commitment

OBC identification can be linked to group identification, which is a type of social identification in which people describe their character based on their membership of groups (Mael & Ashforth, 1992). Membership may include being a regular follower of Chanel or Louis Vuitton through Instagram, a subscriber to a fashion influencer through YouTube or a subscriber to a premium monthly membership that gives access to exclusive jewellery, bought online, but showcased through social media. What do these types of groups have in common? Shared value between a follower and a brand and between a subscriber and a fashion influencer, and shared experiences with the brand through social media platforms; shared value is considered a major source of brand community identification (Carlson, Suter, & Brown, 2008). Membership of communities can create a feeling of belongingness causing a commitment to the brand community (Zhou, Zhang, Su, & Zhou, 2012). From the previous discussion, we found that perceived social and functional values of OBCs can impact community participation, which can lead to members becoming committed to the OBC (Mathwick, Wiertz, & De Ruyter, 2008). Likewise, when members with shared brand experiences and useful knowledge are linked together, participation within the OBC is more likely to develop into a long-term commitment.

Similarly, customers' identification with the OBC can potentially lead them to commit to the brand itself (Willis, Ng, & Chitran, 2019).

Bhattacharya and Sen (2003) found that when customers identify with a company, loyalty outcomes are more likely to occur in contrast to individuals who do not identify with the company (Willis, Ozuem, & Ng, 2019). A long-term brand relationship is likely to develop when customers perceive a similarity between their individual personality and the brand. Fashion brands are described as having human personality traits (Thompson & Haytko, 1997) that reflect the characteristics of a person. In order for a customer to identify with a brand, they must first feel that it aligns with their self-image and personality (Aaker, 1997; Ranfagni, Crawford Camiciottoli, & Faraoni, 2016; Sirgy, 1982). For instance, Armani evokes feelings of sophistication, glossiness and exclusiveness, whereas Valentino promotes a modernised and contemporary young image. The source of influence for both brands is luxury but they promote different personalities and images. Customers' commitment to these brands depends on how they identify with them and whether they satisfy the intended status they want to deliver to their peers through social media (Helal, Ozuem, & Lancaster, 2018).

There exists contrasting arguments regarding the order of influence between OBC identification and brand identification (Zhou et al., 2012). One argument is that brand community identification influences brand identification (Bagozzi & Dholakia, 2006), the other is that brand identification leads to brand community identification (Algesheimer, Dholakia, & Herrmann, 2005). Arguably, a significant number of customers around the world were loyal customers to luxury fashion brands before the major movement of brands' social presence to social media. However, the efforts of luxury fashion brands to connect with young adults who have more luxury personality than luxury income, along with the use of social media, has redefined younger customers' attachment to brands that they may have only dreamed of being associated with. With more online communities connecting customers with shared brand experiences and values, it is arguably the brand community that continues to reinforce customers' positive brand attitudes, thus, enhancing identification with brands (Stokburger-Sauer, 2010). When consumers develop a commitment to a brand through OBCs, their purchasing intentions consistently tend to narrow to the same brand (Algesheimer et al., 2005; Zhou et al., 2012). Purchasing from a competing brand leads to disagreement among the members, thus lessening the connection between them (Scarpi, 2010). This issue highlights a concern for brands, as it indicates that though consumers may commit to an OBC, they may not neces-sarily commit to the brand. Customers without an emotional attachment to a brand will not automatically develop loyalty or brand commit-ment, causing them to be classified as OBC participants rather than loyal customers within OBCs.

Dichotomies: Passive and Active Participation

An important aspect of OBCs is the type of participation members prac-tice; members perceive OBCs differently and the type of member they choose to be acts as a mediator in the type of participation they prac-tice (Mathwick et al., 2008). In the literature, the types of participation membership in OBCs are divided into two groups: passive members and active members. Passive members are non-interactive members, often known as "lurkers" , who silently browse and read messages and posts (Kumar, 2019; Mousavi, Roper, & Keeling, 2017). Active members, also known as posters of content in OBCs, interact with other commu-nity members (Kumar, 2019; Mousavi et al., 2017). While both of these groups feel a sense of community towards a brand or other members, active members participate much more within OBCs than passive members. Passive members have a lower frequency rate in regards to content posting and prefer to observe the content than actively engage with it. OBCs embed collective activity and values; active members prefer the interactive and community goal orientation of OBCs, whereas passive members, who do not regularly participate in these community activities, are less affected by the collective environment the OBC promotes.

The issue associated with passive members of OBCs is the assumption that because they are less interactive with other community members, then they cannot be engaging with the brand. However, in reality, this is far from the case. Passive members can develop cognitive and emotional bonds with others, but their rare social interactions limit their motivation to participate in OBC activity (Kumar, 2019). Passive members prefer activities that involve less social contact, such as brand purchasing, but this does not make them less engaged than active members. It is impor-tant to note that OBCs are not just channels to network and socialise, they also consist of brand-related information, including product and promo-tion updates. Members of online social network sites aim to socialise, whereas members of OBCs can socialise, seek information or both. Passive members can thus be referred to as information seekers, who actively visit OBCs to find information related to the brand by examining the online comments published by active members. OBCs are an ideal platform to transform information seekers into socialisers, which is possible over time given the communities' shared language, vision and reciprocal exchanges that appeal to the information seeker (Meek, Ryan, Lambert, & Ogilvie, 2019). Not all members will evolve into active participants of OBCs, but their motivation to continue seeking information through OBCs maintains the behaviour that keeps them engaging with the brand's information, even if it is not noticeably obvious.

OBCs thrive on the relationships members develop with each other following social interactions. Thus, the continued success of OBCs depends on the ability of their members to interact with each other (Meek et al., 2019). This is important for brands that rely on existing customers to share brand knowledge and other information related to the brand to encourage social engagement between members (Aksoy et al., 2013; Chiu, Hsu, & Wang, 2006; Ozuem et al., 2017). To facilitate this within OBCs, the development of network ties is encouraged; network ties can be defined as people who send information to and receive information from each other. Network ties are essential for OBCs as they promote the creating and sharing of knowledge and have an impact on attracting new members to OBCs and retaining existing ones (Meek et al., 2019). Several researchers have investigated the importance of developing connections between community members, emphasising a "we" or "us" culture that encourages a shared feeling of belonging within the community (Bergami & Bagozzi, 2000; Fournier, 1998; He, Chen, Lee, & Pohlmann, 2017; van Meter, Syrdal, Powell-Mantel, Grisaffe, & Nesson, 2018). The ties individuals develop with other community members encourage a perceived sense of belonging, potentially leading to participative behaviour within OBCs (Muniz & O'Guinn, 2001).

Within OBCs, the impact of network ties can be measured by their strength, immediacy and number of people within the network. Luxury fashion brands and fashion influencers can be found on a variety of social media channels, like Instagram or Twitter, with a high volume of followers and subscribers. According to Statista, Chanel had 34.9 million Instagram followers, Louis Vuitton had 32.07 million and Dior had 25.55 million followers in 2019 (Clement, 2019). When considering brands, social influencers and customers, their level of status on social media, also referred to as online rank and popularity, is often determined by the number of social ties they have (Muller & Peres, 2019). Research encourages social media managers to attract individuals with a high status to encourage more potential members (Hanaki, Peterhansl, Dodds, & Watts, 2007; Hinz, Skiera, Barrot, & Becker, 2011; Kupfer, Pähler vor der Holte, Kübler, & Hennig-Thurau, 2018). A perceived critical mass of members has been proven to be effective in encouraging individuals to adopt technology channels and purchasing behaviour (van Slyke, Ilie, Lou, & Stafford, 2007). However, because luxury fashion brands have a unique personality, social network ties need to emphasise a unique personality and identification with members (Dholakia et al., 2004), which can be negatively impacted if there are too many social network ties. It is important to encourage personal interactions between network ties when discussing brand-related information through OBCs. It is important that customers feel genuinely connected to the discussion and are able to relate to the sender of the information, so that individuals' participation evolves from simple information exchange into the sharing of values and goals in regards to commitment to OBCs. This will ultimately create empathy between community members, which will motivate them to become attached to the community.

CUSTOMER PARTICIPATION FILTER MODEL

There are many important characteristics that are important to understanding the outcome and effect of customer participation, including the willingness to participate, vividness of the content and users' brand attitude. OBC members could be passive or active. While there are important features linked to passive participants, it is the active participants who illustrate the level of brand loyalty that emerges based on their participation, and it can impact the loyalty of others based on the messages they publish. From this we outline three key characteristics: participation effort, participants' intended audience and brand mentions. Using these, we can determine whether a participant is active or passive, whether they intend to communicate with the brand itself or other users, and if the content reflects positive, negative or neutral attitudes towards the brand. By considering these, we can filter out individuals who participate in brand-related or non-brand-related participation and whether the participation positively aligns with the brand as shown below in Fig. 5.1.

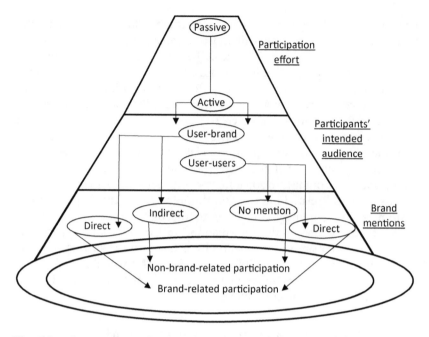

Fig. 5.1 *Customer participation filter model*

Participation Effort

Participation within social media is not a mandatory activity to remain connected with brands, unless a customer, psychologically attached to the brand and OBC, is convinced otherwise. Customers' willingness to participate can be linked to their motivations; they could have a single or several motivations for participating, such as curiosity, interest in creativity, to gain knowledge, enthusiasm to present their own ideas or to gain monetary rewards. Customers' specific motivations and their current mind-set of the brand, causes them to tailor their participation within OBCs. While there are several individual motivations for participating in OBCs, millennial customers generally seek information, entertainment or social benefit values or a combination of these within OBCs.

Information value within OBCs aligns with searches for content, information, experience, ideas and other resources related to the brand published either by the brand or other OBC members (Dessart, Veloutsou, & Morgan-Thomas, 2015). Specific brands are the central topic within OBCs, making them an attractive platform containing information majorly related to the brand. Customers follow social media brand pages to retrieve information related to a brand's products, pre-purchase information, sales and promotions, brand events and product reviews. Such information links to highly observant and passive behaviour in regards to online participation. Participants who seek information do not generally create and contribute; those who do, may comment with questions to fill in knowledge gaps related to products or brand services. Participants with information goals usually rely heavily on members who actively share knowledge and self-created content. While looking for information can be deemed an active act and part of an individual's motivation to participate in OBCs, information seekers develop more passive levels of participation as their informational needs can be satisfied without having to actively contribute or create content.

Therefore, it can be argued that customers motivated by information seeking, which requires less effort than active participation, are likely to contribute the bare minimum of content. However, it is important to note that though some millennials do not actively comment within OBCs, they can engage with the information they encounter when seeking information, by using the information they observe to influence their purchasing decisions as well as their knowledge of the brand. In contrast, they may simply avoid or scroll past the information they encounter, thus causing them to be classified as disengaged participants within OBCs. Of course, this also means that for customers to engage in information-related content, they must have a motivational goal to search for the information with the intention of using it for additional purposes.

The entertainment value of OBCs is embedded in their ability to provide pleasurable experiences and enjoyment to participants observing their visual content. Entertainment activities within OBCs can evoke emotions that can encourage observers to not only consume but also create and contribute content online. Customers who have entertainment goals provide more creative content, such as pictures and explicit comments, and they engage more in sharing. Unlike customers whose motive is information seeking, customers with entertainment seeking motives do not necessarily have a specific goal in mind in regards to the brand, which places their loyalty to the brand into question. The entertainment value of OBCs encourages OBC members to become involved in online activities, like social media campaigns, content or games, which can eventually lead to social interactions with other members. These social interactions can strengthen relationships between members, leading to a strong network of ties within OBCs. However, meeting entertainment value is more complex than meeting informational value. What is considered entertaining is subjective. Social media enables customers to engage in personalised interactions, which can become less about the brand and align more with the topic on which the discussion is based. The values that emerge from these interactions can often shape a brand through the OBC; however, this can threaten the image of exclusivity and uniqueness that a luxury fashion brand aims to retain online. Consequently, though high participation is strongly encouraged in luxury fashion brands' OBCs, brand managers have to take care to ensure the participation efforts of OBC members appropriately represent the image of the brand.

Participants' Intended Audience

The transformation of social media platforms has allowed millennials control regarding what they share and who they share it with. In the luxury market, social media content does not simply comprise interactions between the firm and the customer, it includes interactions with owners of luxury brand products, opinion leaders, the informed and bias-aligned OBC members, and the owners of the brand itself. When luxury brand consumers participate in OBCs, they may have different target audiences depending on the self-created content contributed. Luxury fashion brand consumers' online engagement with the brand may differ from their engagement with other brand consumers and social peers.

The term "user–brand interactions" describes the relationship between a brand and its customers or users of its social media channels. This relationship is built on interactions in which a customer/user directly posts a comment and the firm/brand responds with information beneficial to the customer, such as events, product promotions and collection updates. Customer-to-customer, or user–user interactions, allow more flexibility in the exchange of positive and negative information and responses shared between the members. The majority of exchanges between luxury customers and the brand involve liking, sharing and posting short comments, and the customers do not expect brands to directly respond to them. Customers' engagement that is directed towards social peers and other brand users presumes a response (i.e., positive responses to comments, answers to product and brand enquiries, and discussions of photos and videos). Content that is delivered to a broader audience is likely to develop a greater reaction than content directly aimed at the brand. When content is directed towards the brand, the interactions are usually brief. Arguably, there are two reasons for this: (1) the risks of over-exposing millennials' interactive comments and (2) the socioeconomic market the brand is aligned with.

Though luxury fashion brands are transforming their one-sided communication platforms, they deliver varying levels of online brand–consumer engagement. Some deliver a low level of brand–consumer engagement and selectively respond to customers' comments and focus on communicating brand image and messages. Whereas others deliver a high level of engagement, focusing on building intimate and close relationships with all consumers. High engagement between the brand and all customers may seem like a good thing. However, in the luxury sector, it can threaten to downgrade the perceived exclusivity of the brand, causing it to be perceived as a brand for just anyone. Louis Vuitton classifies its target market as "self-indulgers", "quality seekers" and "status seekers". Coach targets the "affordable luxuries" market, whereas Michael Kors aims to reach the "high earners, not rich yet" consumers. When communicating with brands, customers adjust their content according to the marketing messages and segment category the brand promotes. The 2013 #WhatsInYourKors campaign encouraged fans to upload photos of what they were carrying around in their handbag, promoting a fun and interactive way for Michael Kors customers to share pictures of their bags. Though the images were shared publicly, the content was arguably tailored to align with the Michael Kors personality. Chanel updated followers on a new line of pink shades of makeup, the responses: "The colour is very beautiful", "Love Chanel! Beautiful Fall" and "Once again they don't disappoint...a masterpiece" to name a few along with happy emojis. Once again, this content is arguably for Chanel and other brand users, and not for social peers, who would likely engage in counterarguments related to the brand or perhaps have low association with the brand.

Brand Mentions

Luxury fashion brands are very interested in engaging in social media activities to obtain benefits, such as positive brand reputation, brand image and brand awareness. Many customers of luxury fashion brands rely on the reputation and equity of a brand to express aspects of their self-identity, which social media has allowed to be made more visible to a larger audience (Bernritter, Verlegh, & Smit, 2016; Wilcox & Stephen, 2013). Brand mentions on social media have been a major method of communication to present information and identities that can be traced back to the brand itself (Hu, Chen, Chen, & He, 2020); they are often found in the form of a hashtag or through a comment. Brand mentions are very important in identifying the extent to which social media users are engaging in relation to the brand. It is common for millennials, the generation most active on social media, to come across brand mentions in other users' posts.

The mention of brands can differ depending on the nature of the post: the mention of the brand could be either direct or indirect. For instance, in blogs or review sites, a customer's review of a new makeup collection can draw direct attention to the brand itself, whereas a picture post through Instagram or Facebook of a recent dining and holiday event may feature a branded handbag, jewellery or clothing item that the poster does not directly mention because the holiday or dining event is the focus of the poster, so the observer may not see a hashtag or additional comment in reference to the brand. As the number of mentions of a brand grows, the level of interactions related to the brand becomes more visibly evident. For the active publisher, a brand mention can identify the perception they have of the brand. Often, posters who hashtag a brand add additional hashtags to briefly, yet powerfully, summarise their feelings about having a luxury fashion brand item (e.g., #louisvuitton #pureromance #business-woman #justneededit). This indulges their desire to socially stand out based on the luxury fashion product and identifies their positive perception of the brand, which companies often adopt as a useful and authentic social media marketing tool in relation to other potential customers.

Many luxury fashion brands have reached their goal in getting their brand name mentioned, but they are not free from negative publicity, which is easily generated through brand mentions. Although a luxury fashion brand can make use of positive brand messages that customers share through hashtags and comments, they also have to deal with the unexpected negative messages added to the mention of the brand. Social issues and events, which may not necessarily be connected to the brand, can draw the brand as the centre of focus of these issues, negatively impacting the image and following of the brand. This shows that high participation within OBCs is not always a good thing for luxury fashion brands if, for example, the intention of the conversations is to boycott the company. Brand managers must always check not only the level of participation, but what the sentiment is and whether it aligns positively or negatively with the brand. This is important because brand mentions do not only concern active posters, they also concern the passive observer. How the brand comes across through customers' mentions of the brand when participating in OBCs can impact the perceptions of other potential customers; the passive information seeking individual may be influenced to reconsider their purchasing decisions, and the active poster may be encouraged to contribute further negative information.

Conclusion and Future Outlook

From the discussion of the identified characteristics of customer participation within OBCs, and the different motivations for participation, considering the number of participants alone is not a feasible measurement to justify the success of online participation within the luxury fashion sector or for it to be classified as loyalty to the brand itself. The term quality over quantity may come to mind when considering the effect of customer participation on brand loyalty. Luxury fashion brands have no issue attracting high numbers of followers and commenters to their OBCs. However, this does not mean that all are loyal customers or followers of the brand itself. Luxury brand managers must examine the sentiment of the messages community members share regarding whether they align positively or negatively with the brand. Millennials are impacted by what their close peers and other social networks share through social media. So, it is important to examine what the active posters are sharing about the brand, as the perception of individuals who engage passively, who mostly observe content, will be impacted by what they read.

The chapter finds that though an individual may be highly active in contributing content within OBCs it may not be beneficial to the brand; for instance, they could post negative messages that are directly related to the brand, or engage in conversations that are not related to the brand but influential enough to motivate other active members to participate. The chapter also finds that passive participants, though they participate less actively in OBCs, engage with the published information by using it for other activities, like finalising purchasing decisions or enhancing brand knowledge. This can over time impact the long-term loyalty they may develop with the brand, and though passive participants encounter negative information delivered through other individuals' online participation, they are unlikely to actively share negative information themselves.

Although online participation is important to luxury fashion brands, satisfaction with the brand remains a key factor in loyalty in the short and long term. Customers may participate within OBCs, but they may not necessarily become more satisfied with the brand, and participating in many online activities may have only a short-term effect on loyalty. However, it is important to remember that all customers have different motivations for engaging in OBCs and have different past experiences with the brand. Future research should not only consider the motivations to participate within OBCs, but also consider the perceived attachment or relationship customers have with the brand and how it impacts their decision to participate within OBCs and the actions they perform. This will support further understanding of millennial customers' individual behaviours expressed through OBCs and how their loyalty is impacted by their participation within OBCs. This will also help to further conceptualise passive participants by explaining why they might not actively participate but continue to visit OBCs.

Recommended Further Reading

Fang, C., & Zhang, J. (2019). Users' continued participation behavior in social Q&A communities: A motivation perspective. *Computers in Human Behaviour, 92*, 87–109.

Kübler, R. V., Colicev, A., & Pauwels, K. H. (2019). Social media's impact on the consumer mindset: When to use which sentiment extraction tool? *Journal of Interactive Marketing, 50*, 136–155.

Meek, S., Ryan, M., Lambert, C., & Ogilvie, M. (2019). A multidimensional scale for measuring online brand community social capital (OBCSC). *Journal of Business Research, 100*, 234–244.

Muniz, A. M., & O'Guinn, T. C. (2001a). Brand community. *Journal of Consumer Research, 27*(4), 412–432.

Ozuem, W., Thomas, T., & Lancaster, G. (2016a). The influence of customer loyalty on small island economies: An empirical and exploratory study. *Journal of Strategic Marketing, 24*(6), 447–469.

Pansari, A., & Kumar, V. (2017). Customer engagement: The construct, antecedents, and consequences. *Journal of the Academy of Marketing Science, 45*(3), 294–311.

REFERENCES

Aaker, J. L. (1997). Dimensions of brand personality. *Journal of Marketing Research, 34*(3), 347–356.

Aksoy, L., van Riel, A., Kandampully, J., Wirtz, J., den Ambtman, A., Bloemer, J., et al. (2013). Managing brands and customer engagement in online brand communities. *Journal of Service Management, 24*(3), 223–244.

Algesheimer, R., Dholakia, U. M., & Herrmann, A. (2005). The social influence of brand community: Evidence from European car clubs. *Journal of Marketing, 69*(3), 19–34.

Azemi, Y., Ozuem, W., & Howell, K. E. (2020). The effects of online negative word-of-mouth on dissatisfied customers: A frustration—Aggression perspective. *Psychology & Marketing, 37*(4), 564–577.

Bagozzi, R. P., & Dholakia, U. M. (2006). Antecedents and purchase consequences of customer participation in small group brand communities. *International Journal of Research in Marketing, 23*(1), 45–61.

Baldus, B. J., Voorhees, C., & Calantone, R. (2015). Online brand community engagement: Scale development and validation. *Journal of Business Research, 68*(5), 978–985.

Bergami, M., & Bagozzi, R. P. (2000). Self-categorization, affective commitment and group self-esteem as distinct aspects of social identity in the organization. *British Journal of Social Psychology, 39*(4), 555–577.

Bernritter, S. F., Verlegh, P. W., & Smit, E. G. (2016). Why nonprofits are easier to endorse on social media: The roles of warmth and brand symbolism. *Journal of Interactive Marketing, 33,* 27–42.

Bhattacharya, C. B., & Sen, S. (2003). Consumer–company identification: A framework for understanding consumers' relationships with companies. *Journal of Marketing, 67*(2), 76–88.

Bi, Q. (2019). Cultivating loyal customers through online customer communities: A psychological contract perspective. *Journal of Business Research, 103,* 34–44.

Carlson, J., Rahman, M. M., Taylor, A., & Voola, R. (2019). Feel the VIBE: Examining value-in-the-brand-page-experience and its impact on satisfaction and customer engagement behaviours in mobile social media. *Journal of Retailing and Consumer Services, 46,* 149–162.

Carlson, B. D., Suter, T. A., & Brown, T. J. (2008). Social versus psychological brand community: The role of psychological sense of brand community. *Journal of Business Research, 61*(4), 284–291.

Chan, K. W., Yim, C. K., & Lam, S. S. (2010). Is customer participation in value creation a double-edged sword? Evidence from professional financial services across cultures. *Journal of Marketing, 74*(3), 48–64.

Chiu, C. M., Hsu, M. H., & Wang, E. T. (2006). Understanding knowledge sharing in virtual communities: An integration of social capital and social cognitive theories. *Decision Support Systems, 42*(3), 1872–1888.

Clement, J. (2019). Leading luxury brands with the most followers on Instagram as of May 2019 (in millions). *Statista* [Online] Available at: https://www.statista.com/statistics/483753/leading-luxury-brands-instag ram-followers/. Accessed 13 July 2020.

Davis, R., Piven, I., & Breazeale, M. (2014). Conceptualizing the brand in social media community: The five sources model. *Journal of Retailing and Consumer Services, 21*(4), 468–481.

de Almeida, S., Scaraboto, D., dos Santos Fleck, J., & Dalmoro, M. (2018). Seriously engaged consumers: Navigating between work and play in online brand communities. *Journal of Interactive Marketing, 44,* 29–42.

de Kerviler, G., & Rodriguez, C. M. (2019). Luxury brand experiences and relationship quality for Millennials: The role of self-expansion. *Journal of Business Research, 102,* 250–262.

Dessart, L., Veloutsou, C., & Morgan-Thomas, A. (2015). Consumer engagement in online brand communities: a social media perspective. *Journal of Product & Brand Management, 24*(1), 28–42.

Dholakia, U. M., Bagozzi, R. P., & Pearo, L. K. (2004). A social influence model of consumer participation in network-and small-group-based virtual communities. *International Journal of Research in Marketing, 21*(3), 241–263.

Fournier, S. (1998). Consumers and their brands: Developing relationship theory in consumer research. *Journal of Consumer Research, 24*(4), 343–373.

Hanaki, N., Peterhansl, A., Dodds, P. S., & Watts, D. J. (2007). Cooperation in evolving social networks. *Management Science, 53*(7), 1036–1050.

He, Y., Chen, Q., Lee, R., & Pohlmann, A. (2017). Consumers' role performance and brand identification: Evidence from a survey and a longitudinal field experiment. *Journal of Interactive Marketing, 38*(2), 1–11.

Helal, G., Ozuem, W., & Lancaster, G. (2018). Social media brand perceptions of millennials. *International Journal of Retail & Distribution Management, 46*(10), 977–998.

Hinz, O., Skiera, B., Barrot, C., & Becker, J. U. (2011). Seeding strategies for viral marketing: An empirical comparison. *Journal of Marketing, 75*(6), 55–71.

Hu, M., Chen, J., Chen, Q., & He, W. (2020). It pays off to be authentic: An examination of direct versus indirect brand mentions on social media. *Journal of Business Research, 117,* 19–28.

Hudson, S., Huang, L., Roth, M. S., & Madden, T. J. (2016). The influence of social media interactions on consumer–brand relationships: A three-country study of brand perceptions and marketing behaviors. *International Journal of Research in Marketing, 33*(1), 27–41.

Kara, S., Vredeveld, A. J., & Ross, W. T., Jr. (2018). We share; we connect: How shared brand consumption influences relational brand connections. *Psychology & Marketing, 35*(5), 325–340.

Kim, A. J., & Ko, E. (2012). Do social media marketing activities enhance customer equity? An empirical study of luxury fashion brand. *Journal of Business Research, 65*(10), 1480–1486.

Kumar, J. (2019). How psychological ownership stimulates participation in online brand communities? The moderating role of member type. *Journal of Business Research, 105*, 243–257.

Kupfer, A. K., Pähler vor der Holte, N., Kübler, R. V., & Hennig-Thurau, T. (2018). The role of the partner brand's social media power in brand alliances. *Journal of Marketing, 82*(3), 25–44.

Lickel, B., Hamilton, D. L., Wieczorkowska, G., Lewis, A., Sherman, S. J., & Uhles, A. N. (2000). Varieties of groups and the perception of group entitativity. *Journal of Personality and Social Psychology, 78*(2), 223.

Liu, H., Wu, L., & Li, X. (2019). Social media envy: How experience sharing on social networking sites drives millennials' aspirational tourism consumption. *Journal of Travel Research, 58*(3), 355–369.

Mael, F., & Ashforth, B. E. (1992). Alumni and their alma mater: A partial test of the reformulated model of organizational identification. *Journal of Organizational Behavior, 13*(2), 103–123.

Malinen, S. (2015). Understanding user participation in online communities: A systematic literature review of empirical studies. *Computers in Human Behavior, 46*, 228–238.

Mathwick, C., & Mosteller, J. (2016). Online reviewer engagement: A typology based on reviewer motivations. *Journal of Service Research, 20*(2), 204–218.

Mathwick, C., Wiertz, C., & De Ruyter, K. (2008). Social capital production in a virtual P3 community. *Journal of Consumer Research, 34*(6), 832–849.

Merz, M. A., Zarantonello, L., & Grappi, S. (2018). How valuable are your customers in the brand value co-creation process? The development of a Customer Co-Creation Value (CCCV) scale. *Journal of Business Research, 82*, 79–89.

Mousavi, S., Roper, S., & Keeling, K. A. (2017). Interpreting social identity in online brand communities: Considering posters and lurkers. *Psychology & Marketing, 34*(4), 376–393.

Muller, E., & Peres, R. (2019). The effect of social networks structure on innovation performance: A review and directions for research. *International Journal of Research in Marketing, 36*(1), 3–19.

Muniz, A. M., & O'Guinn, T. C. (2001b). Brand community. *Journal of Consumer Research, 27*(4), 412–432.

Nambisan, S., & Baron, R. A. (2007). Interactions in virtual customer environments: Implications for product support and customer relationship management. *Journal of Interactive Marketing, 21*(2), 42–62.

Nysveen, H., & Pedersen, P. E. (2014). Influences of cocreation on brand experience. *International Journal of Market Research, 56*(6), 807–832.

Ozuem, W., Howell, K. E., & Lancaster, G. (2008). Communicating in the new interactive marketspace. *European Journal of Marketing, 42*(9/10), 1059–1083.

Ozuem, W., Patel, A., Howell, K. E., & Lancaster, G. (2017). An exploration of customers' response to online service recovery initiatives. *International Journal of Market Research, 59*(1), 97–116.

Ozuem, W., Thomas, T., & Lancaster, G. (2016b). The influence of customer loyalty on small island economies: an empirical and exploratory study. *Journal of Strategic Marketing, 24*(6), 447–469.

Park, M., Im, H., & Kim, H. Y. (2018). "You are too friendly!" The negative effects of social media marketing on value perceptions of luxury fashion brands. *Journal of Business Research, 117*, 529–542.

Prahalad, C. K., & Ramaswamy, V. (2004). Co-creation experiences: The next practice in value creation. *Journal of Interactive Marketing, 18*(3), 5–14.

Ramaswamy, V., & Ozcan, K. (2016). Brand value co-creation in a digitalized world: An integrative framework and research implications. *International Journal of Research in Marketing, 33*(1), 93–106.

Ranfagni, S., Crawford Camiciottoli, B., & Faraoni, M. (2016). How to measure alignment in perceptions of brand personality within online communities: Interdisciplinary insights. *Journal of Interactive Marketing, 35*, 70–85.

Relling, M., Schnittka, O., Sattler, H., & Johnen, M. (2016). Each can help or hurt: Negative and positive word of mouth in social network brand communities. *International Journal of Research in Marketing, 33*(1), 42–58.

Scarpi, D. (2010). Does size matter? An examination of small and large web-based brand communities. *Journal of Interactive Marketing, 24*(1), 14–21.

Shukla, P., & Drennan, J. (2018). Interactive effects of individual-and group-level variables on virtual purchase behavior in online communities. *Information & Management, 55*(5), 598–607.

Sirgy, M. J. (1982). Self-concept in consumer behavior: A critical review. *Journal of Consumer Research, 9*(3), 287–300.

Stokburger-Sauer, N. (2010). Brand community: Drivers and outcomes. *Psychology & Marketing, 27*(4), 347–368.

Sun, N., Rau, P. P. L., & Ma, L. (2014). Understanding lurkers in online communities: A literature review. *Computers in Human Behavior, 38*, 110–117.

Thompson, C. J., & Haytko, D. L. (1997). Speaking of fashion: Consumers' uses of fashion discourses and the appropriation of countervailing cultural meanings. *Journal of Consumer Research, 24*(1), 15–42.

Tsai, H. T., Huang, H. C., & Chiu, Y. L. (2012). Brand community participation in Taiwan: Examining the roles of individual-, group-, and relationship-level antecedents. *Journal of Business Research, 65*(5), 676–684.

van Meter, R., Syrdal, H. A., Powell-Mantel, S., Grisaffe, D. B., & Nesson, E. T. (2018). Don't just "Like" me, promote me: How attachment and attitude influence brand related behaviors on social media. *Journal of Interactive Marketing, 43*, 83–97.

van Slyke, C., Ilie, V., Lou, H., & Stafford, T. (2007). Perceived critical mass and the adoption of a communication technology. *European Journal of Information Systems, 16*(3), 270–283.

Vock, M., Dolen, W. V., & Ruyter, K. D. (2013). Understanding willingness to pay for social network sites. *Journal of Service Research, 16*(3), 311–325.

Wang, Y., Stoner, J. L., & John, D. R. (2019). Counterfeit luxury consumption in a social context: The effects on females' moral disengagement and behavior. *Journal of Consumer Psychology, 29*(2), 207–225.

Wiedmann, K. P., Hennigs, N., & Siebels, A. (2009). Value-based segmentation of luxury consumption behavior. *Psychology & Marketing, 26*(7), 625–651.

Wilcox, K., & Stephen, A. T. (2013). Are close friends the enemy? Online social networks, self-esteem, and self-control. *Journal of Consumer Research, 40*(1), 90–103.

Willis, M. (2018). The dynamics of social media marketing content and customer retention. In G. Bowen & W. Ozuem (Eds.), *Leveraging computer-mediated marketing environments*. IGI Global: Hershey.

Willis, M., Ng, R., & Chitran, V. (2019). Exploring the relationship between customer participation and online brand community and consumer loyalty. *Interdisciplinary Journal of Economics and Business Law, 9*(special issue), 72–111.

Willis, M., Ozuem, W., & Ng, R. (2019b). Enhancing online brand relationship performance in the fashion industry. In W. Ozuem, E. Patten, & Y. Azemi (Eds.), *Harnessing Omnichannel retailing strategies for fashion and luxury brands*. Boca Raton, FL: Brown Walker Press.

Yim, C. K., Chan, K. W., & Lam, S. S. (2012). Do customers and employees enjoy service participation? Synergistic effects of self-and other-efficacy. *Journal of Marketing, 76*(6), 121–140.

Zhou, Z., Zhang, Q., Su, C., & Zhou, N. (2012). How do brand communities generate brand relationships? Intermediate mechanisms. *Journal of Business Research, 65*(7), 890–895.

CHAPTER 6

Maintaining a Creative Brand Image in an Omnichannel World

Annette Kallevig

INTRODUCTION

The age of digital marketing has presented several new opportunities for luxury fashion brands. Influencer marketing, search engine optimization and precise targeting are but a few, and represent an always-on approach to marketing. Previously, marketing communications were executed in campaign cycles, similar to the seasonal collections of the fashion houses. Mass marketing communication was primarily one way, with little direct interaction with the consumer, which left the brands with a high level of control over their brand message (Straker & Wrigley, 2016a). Today's consumers engage directly with the brands across several media and platforms simultaneously, both offline and online, making brand management complex, with considerably less control. At the same time, digital marketing collects data so that it can be continually optimized based on performance and measurable customer behaviour (Braun & Moe, 2013; Bruce et al., 2017; Kumar et al., 2013). This development has

A. Kallevig (✉)
Kristiania University College, Oslo, Norway

© The Author(s), under exclusive license to Springer Nature Switzerland AG 2021
W. Ozuem and S. Ranfagni (eds.), *The Art of Digital Marketing for Fashion and Luxury Brands*,
https://doi.org/10.1007/978-3-030-70324-0_6

brought on a need for more iterative, continuous work processes with an ever-increasing focus on integrated marketing communication (IMC) (Havlena et al., 2007; Tevi et al., 2019).

Over the past decades, much research has been conducted on the effects and effectiveness of using IMC processes (Batra & Keller, 2016; Calder & Malthouse, 2005; Ots & Nyilasy, 2015). The role of creativity and content within IMC has been largely overlooked in these studies, however, although one of the few early studies on the subject revealed a positive effect of creative content on IMC (Sasser et al., 2007). A need for updated constructs within creativity research as it relates to digital marketing communications has been identified (Bruce et al., 2017; West et al., 2019).

To build a resilient brand in this complex and highly competitive marketing climate, creative marketing communication is as important as ever to obtain attention, build loyalty and separate the brand from its competitors (Ozuem et al., 2008; Turnbull & Wheeler, 2017). The question then, is, how to integrate creativity coherently across the many and varied touchpoints in the various customer journeys.

With much of its value proposition tied to immaterial, emotional attributes, creativity has always played an important role in luxury marketing. Along with quality and exclusivity, social constructs such as psychological value, identity and customer awareness have been identified as key attributes of a luxury brand (Fionda & Moore, 2009). For such immaterial social constructs to contribute to a perceived consumer value that transcends the physical attributes of the product and its parts, creative and emotionally evocative marketing communication is necessary (Straker & Wrigley, 2016a) In fashion luxury brands, creativity is not only at the core of the external brand image, but of the product and the entire industry (Dion & Arnould, 2011).

Fashion, comprising couture, ready-to-wear and accessories, is the largest of the four dominant categories within the luxury sector, the other three being perfumes/cosmetics, wines/spirits and watches/jewellery (Fionda & Moore, 2009). According to a report "Luxury Fashion Worldwide 2020" (Statista, 2020), the luxury apparel segment held a market volume of €55,036 million in 2020 and annual revenue growth is expected to continue. While not all segments within the luxury category need to continually introduce novel products, the luxury fashion segment is required to present high frequency innovation across many products at a time (Fionda & Moore, 2009; Marcone, 2014; Miller & Mills, 2012).

Two seasonal collections per brand per year, each comprising several new products, is rather the norm than the exception (Alexander, 2016).

While both luxury fashion production and marketing communication are considered creative disciplines, the ways in which they use and manage creativity are not necessarily aligned. There has frequently been friction regarding their perception and management of creativity (Leclair, 2017). As many luxury fashion brands administer their marketing communications in-house (Fionda & Moore, 2009), friction is likely between departments in the same company. In maintaining the luxury fashion brand, a marketing communication department can experience dissonance within the department because different roles may have different tasks that require varying degrees of adoption of the overall brand, which requires adapting the core of the brand to the various marketing communication efforts. In addition, the department frequently needs to balance the creative brand interests with financial requirements. Over recent years, previously independent luxury brands have grouped under luxury group holding companies that now dominate the market, and these groups may impose financial and other business requirements affecting marketing communication. While imparting broad luxury marketing expertise across the individual brands in which the luxury group has an interest, it is not unlikely that the holding company also wishes to ensure that a strong brand positioning is executed without compromising other brands in their investment portfolios (Fionda & Moore, 2009; Miller & Mills, 2012).

Although not all brands in the luxury category have the same complexity and creativity requirements as luxury fashion, most have their value proposition in immaterial assets that are subject to some of the same dynamics (Miller & Mills, 2012). They will have the same need to convey these creatively through IMC. The trends and observations in this chapter are therefore likely to be applicable to the broader luxury and fashion brand categories, in varying degree.

Brand and Creative Brand Image

From the early stages of marketing, when brand and trademark were more or less synonymous, brand and brand value have been interpreted in many ways. The purpose, however, has always been recognition, and, ultimately, to encourage customer commitment. In recent times, the importance of brand values has integrated the brand more deeply within the organization, and the ideal is often to increase the value of the brand beyond its product or offer (De Chernatony, 2009).

A clear and well-developed brand concept is considered fundamental within the luxury category, with special emphasis on brand name and identity. A brand identity rooted in values may be the best way to differentiate and engage consumers on an emotional and functional level, especially long term (Fionda & Moore, 2009). While congruity between consumer self-perception and brand personality is a deciding factor in all brand identity perception (Klipfel et al., 2014), it is likely to be a requirement when the goal is to build long-term engagement that leads to customer loyalty and, ultimately, advocacy, which is the foundation on which most successful luxury fashion brands are built. Luxury brand performance is a balancing act, where brand management is concerned with creating growth while retaining the exclusivity that is key to the luxury brand (Dubois & Paternault, 1995; Kapferer & Valette-Florence, 2018).

Authenticity, high quality and exclusivity characteristics of iconic coveted products associated with the luxury category are aspects of the product itself. Of these three, the characteristics of exclusivity have the potential to differentiate products within the category; marketing communication is concerned with exclusivity. The exclusivity characteristics are often tied to the vision of the founders or creators, and often become core aspects of the brand signature, sometimes called the "brand DNA" (Fionda & Moore, 2009).

Iconic and coveted are social constructs related to a consumer's realization of their social self and personal self (Kapferer & Valette-Florence, 2018), and product attributes are not likely to evoke such a psychological effect alone. Creative marketing and marketing communication are called upon to build a desirable culture the consumer wants to be a part of, which aligns with and enhances the brand DNA to a coveted status. This coveted culture at the perilous intersection of brand awareness and brand penetration has been referred to as an aspirational dream environment, which signals the complex need to create and communicate experiential value beyond the product itself through marketing and marketing communication (Dubois & Paternault, 1995; Kapferer & Valette-Florence, 2018). With creativity from the fashion product embedded in the brand DNA, accentuated by marketing communication creativity to create and maintain immaterial psychosocial value beyond that of the product itself, the brand image becomes creative, in and of itself.

IMC and Creative Brand Image

The omnichannel marketing communication environment has become increasingly complex, and a growing need for IMC has inspired much academic research on the subject over the past two decades (Calder & Malthouse, 2005; Kerr & Patti, 2015; Kitchen et al., 2008; Ots & Nyilasy, 2015; Sasser et al., 2007; Tafesse & Kitchen, 2017). IMC can be defined as the optimal result of a company's efforts to inform, persuade purchase, and remind consumers about their brands and products, consistently (Batra & Keller, 2016). In a multichannel marketing environment, this means across media, channels, messages and the various disciplines of the people involved.

Although plentiful, IMC research can be difficult to apply in practice, since much of it takes an abstract, managerial standpoint, with practical suggestions only as it applies to overarching brand management. This can lead to top-down brand management (Keller, 2016; Ozuem et al., 2017). With more specialists in various disciplines working in increasingly complex processes, integration between them rather than in vertical silos is likely to be more efficient (Kitchen et al., 2008). To seamlessly deliver the customer experience level expected of a luxury brand across multiple channels in a complex, competitive digital environment requires, at the least, a multichannel strategy, but possibly also a digital-first approach (Straker & Wrigley, 2016b; Patten et al., 2020).

Even when most participants in a process work towards integration, IMC is not always successful in practice. It has been suggested that this may be due to varying interpretations of IMC by participants and consequent different mental models, but research has also suggested that this may be due to a lack of standards (Gronstedt & Thorson, 1996; Ots & Nyilasy, 2015). Ots and Nyilasy identified four main types of IMC dysfunction: compartmentalization, lack of trust, communication and context.

Creativity research yields few theories regarding the role of creativity in IMC. Focusing not only on initial creative development but also taking into account a system's resources and their interactions over time by adopting a systems approach to creativity (Csikszentmihalyi, 1996) is recommended (Lee & Östberg, 2013; Sasser et al., 2013). This approach is also likely to be relevant for creative IMC (CIMC). To fully understand how creativity can be integrated in IMC, however, comprehensive, holistic theories are needed (West et al., 2019).

The fashion industry as a whole represents an integration of many different specialties, several of which are creative within their fields. Marketing communication has always played an integral part. The first presentation of a new collection, frequently referred to as a runway show, is held fairly early in the production process; it is at the core of both product development and marketing communication. However, the centralized coordination of the various competences involved is top down and highly hierarchical. This may lead to dysfunctions in internal integration similar to those listed for IMC above, and might be less conducive to meeting the creative integrated marketing demands of today (Ots & Nyilasy, 2015).

With its immaterial and psychological value to the consumer, experience has always been a key attribute of the luxury proposition, and is at the core when building and maintaining a luxury fashion brand identity. For luxury fashion brands, the full brand experience was initially limited to small, privileged groups, receiving exceptional personal service at various points in the supply chain. This gave high levels of exclusivity and control over the brand image, but may have limited growth potential (Kapferer & Valette-Florence, 2018). Today, most luxury fashion brands share their brand experience with a broader public. Through flagship stores, for example, luxury environments deeply engrained in the brand image are available to consumers in major cities around the world (Fionda & Moore, 2009). As a broader consumer base has gained access to brands as well as to interactive technology, the demand for an integrated luxury experience available anywhere is expected, and transfer of the creative brand image to new and often digital platforms is needed to maintain interactive emotional engagement (Atwal & Williams, 2009; Straker & Wrigley, 2016b). This broad integration leaves the luxury brands with less control of their brand image, and since key characteristics of the category are rarity and perceived exclusivity, there is a risk that luxury brand desirability may diminish over time. A balance needs to be struck between brand awareness and brand penetration to avoid negative consequences (Kapferer & Valette-Florence, 2018).

CREATIVITY IN THE FASHION INDUSTRY

Researching creativity can be challenging, even when narrowing its scope to business applications (Sternberg & Lubart, 1991; Steiner & Prettenthaler, 2015; West et al., 2019). While creativity has been defined in many ways, most research agrees that originality and appropriateness for what it is intended to achieve are key components (Sasser et al., 2013; Sternberg & Lubart, 1996). Original and appropriate as social constructs are quite open to interpretation, and different interpretations can prevail even within the same marketing communication environment (Koslow et al., 2003). Different stakeholders and contributors to the creative production may have different interpretations as well. Indirect stakeholders with financial influence may have a propensity towards appropriateness over originality in response to financial and market conditions, for example (Kilgour et al., 2013). As luxury and fashion brands are frequently owned by large, category-specific holding companies that own competing brands, this may be especially applicable (Fionda & Moore, 2009).

Within marketing communication and research, advertising is frequently associated with creativity. Creativity, as it pertains to advertising, has been defined as using imagination and originality strategically in solving a marketing communication problem (El-Murad & West, 2004; Koslow et al., 2003). In suggesting this form of creativity to solve any marketing communication problem, it is implied that the definition can be extended beyond advertising to all forms of marketing communication. This may be a useful expansion, since a growing need for integration has led to advertising losing ground as a separate entity (Laurie & Mortimer, 2019). This definition of marketing communication creativity is used in this chapter.

Common to all luxury fashion brands is an engrained culture for luxury and innovation, embedded in a clear creative direction, throughout the company (Fionda & Moore, 2009). This serves as a creative platform to all competencies working within, from product developer to social media manager.

While fashion and marketing communications are both considered to be creative disciplines as well as industries (Wijngaarden et al., 2019), they are quite different, also with regard to creativity. Creativity as a social construct has many interpretations, even between industries utilizing it commercially, so how fashion and marketing communication professionals perceive, define and valuate creativity is likely to differ (Kirsch et al., 2016).

The haute couture tradition within luxury fashion is frequently associated with fine art, for example, implying a more exclusive form of creativity (Dion & Arnould, 2011). When comparing originality and appropriateness in terms of creativity, requirements for originality are paramount in haute couture, while ready-to-wear is likely to prioritize appropriateness because of its broader market orientation. While creative marketing communication tasks may require various degrees of originality and appropriateness, the inherent market orientation will always require higher levels of appropriateness compared to haute couture.

The creative director represents a key role found in many creative industries, including fashion and marketing communications. In most contexts, the title of creative director generally refers to a leadership role responsible for coordinating various creative competences in a creative production. In the luxury fashion industry, the creative director role has a special significance, however, frequently with direct implications for the brand. Sometimes called the artistic director, the role refers to the person responsible for the creative vision behind the fashion collection. While many luxury fashion brands bear the names of the initial fashion creative director, many of today's most powerful creative directors represent the next generation. While still highly visionary fashion experts, the creative directors of today are also expected to understand business and especially brand management (*What luxury fashion brands want in a creative director—Vogue Business Talent*, 2019). This means they are responsible for all aspects of creativity within the organization and the brand image specifically. With today's complex marketing communication requiring many specialists applying different kinds of creativity and brand communication, such a centralized, top-down creative marketing approach is likely to hinder efficient CIMC.

Where creativity used to be considered a scarce personal trait, there has been a democratization of the term "creative person" in recent years. Florida (2004) proposed that anyone who performs an economic function in creating new ideas is a creative. By this definition, data scientists handling data-driven marketing are as creative as a film director, or luxury brand creative director for that matter, but in a different area.

Although Florida's macro perspective has been challenged, it has also been elaborated upon. It has been proposed that creativity is not a company or industry classification, but rather a function of the people within. A creativity index for the characteristics of creative products and services has been proposed (Steiner & Prettenthaler, 2015). Using such an index, a fashion creative director and a data scientist can have different degrees or types of creativity, while the creative value of their work may be equal in relation to their role and environment. This perspective as it applies to creative leadership is supported by other studies (Shalley & Gilson, 2017; Sternberg et al., 2003, 2004).

Motivational Theories of Creativity

Creativity in people is generally considered an intrinsically motivated personal trait. There is little agreement regarding what motivates creativity in some people more than others, nor is there consensus on how best to encourage the desired type of creativity extrinsically in intense business environments. While creativity cannot be induced in individuals without intrinsic creative motivation, there is evidence that creative behaviour can be incentivized in creative individuals (Sasser & Koslow, 2012). Recent research by Malik et al. (2019) indicated that intrinsic motivation and extrinsic incentives can both contribute to enhanced creative output. They were found, however, to motivate different types of creativity.

Several creativity research studies have identified a willingness to take risks as a common attribute in creative people (El-Murad & West, 2003; Sasser et al., 2013; Sternberg et al., 2003). This is supported by the fact that proposing something new is a requirement of their creative contribution, which carries a risk of rejection.

In their investment theory of creativity, Sternberg et al. (1997) took it one step further and elevated risk to a motivational factor in and of itself. Their research indicated that highly creative people are often motivated by the risk associated with defending and developing seemingly inappropriate ideas with the chance to turn them into successful, creative executions. Once this aim is achieved, they move on to the next unrealized idea. This motivational relationship between creativity and risk may appear more relevant for a fashion creative director in luxury fashion rather than for creatives in marketing communications. Although risk has not been isolated as a motivational factor, other research has revealed that advertising creatives tend to assume a positive correlation between risk and creativity (El-Murad & West, 2003; Sasser et al., 2013).

With different types and levels of creativity, various risk profiles and diverse interpretations of risk within an organization, the investment theory of creativity seems applicable only to some individuals, not to creative leadership (Sternberg et al., 2004). Hence, the theory may apply to the fairly autonomous fashion creative director role of the luxury fashion house without providing a useful framework for managing creativity in the organization at large. While willingness to take risks is necessary in most creative leadership within luxury fashion branding, the type and level of risk may vary. Furthermore, financial stakeholders, marketing management teams as well as creative individuals may all hold different risk perspectives.

RADICAL VERSUS INCREMENTAL CREATIVITY

In data-driven marketing communication, risk is minimized by using data to inform fact-based decisions. Strategies and tactics can be continually optimized based on proven effects or results (Kumar et al., 2013). If we were to return to the investment perspective, the data-driven scientist can now be placed at opposite ends of the risk scale as compared to, for example, the fashion creative director.

To better adapt to the rapid changes in marketing communication, it may be useful to look to agile methodologies when integrating digital marketing. An agile approach is likely to provide the flexible framework needed to continually adapt the degree of radical and incremental creativity to the task being performed. While some roles and personality types predominantly perform incremental creativity, others may have roles that require more radical creativity (Lynch & West, 2017; Malik et al., 2019). For daily data-driven marketing communication and social media management, incremental creativity is likely to be the most relevant, while developing new brand concepts for content marketing and campaigns may require more radical creativity, for example. From an integrated and dynamic marketing perspective, radical and incremental creativity may also be useful at different stages of a problem-solving process, so the same roles and resources may draw on different types of creativity when needed.

The fashion creative director is likely to be the main representative for radical creativity. Although luxury fashion is one of the rare industries where the investment theory may be useful in understanding the dynamics surrounding this radically creative individual, it does not seem relevant to other forms or degrees of creativity within the organization (Florida,

2004). The theory may therefore need to be modified (Sternberg et al., 1997). Limiting valuable creative contribution to this type of creativity may describe the past of luxury fashion marketing more than the future, and hinder rather than further CIMC in the luxury fashion industry.

Managing the Creative Organization

Creativity in leadership may not be necessary to successfully lead creative individuals towards creative end products and solutions; however, certain leadership styles are more likely than others to inspire and cultivate different types of creativity. In modern leadership, qualities such as the ability to handle and nourish originality, openness to new ideas and experiences, and willingness to take risks to scaffold and protect creative solutions are among the qualities associated with creative leadership excellence (Sternberg et al., 2004). Fashion comes from a tradition of apprenticeship, which is still common within the industry. In this form of leadership, a master trains apprentices (Guile, 2006). This may partially explain the spearhead role the fashion creative director holds as creative leader, and why it is still fairly common for their successors to have started their careers as protégés of the creative director (*What luxury fashion brands want in a creative director—Vogue Business Talent*, 2019).

Team creativity is a dynamic and complex collaborative work form that requires careful management (Lynch & West, 2017). Whether homogenous or multidisciplinary, working on radical or incremental creative tasks, team creativity is influenced by the environment in which it is performed; so, creative team management frequently involves building and nurturing creativity-inducing environments. Elements to be considered in building and maintaining such environments are not only physical workspace characteristics, such as location and interior design, but also the psychological workspace, including team autonomy, support and recognition for creative ideas, and incentives to inspire creative performance (Dul & Ceylan, 2014). To inspire collaboration needed for CIMC, facilitating co-creation both physically and psychologically may positively affect the creative process. Since creativity is deeply engrained throughout the luxury fashion brand, from product development and production through to marketing and communication, an approach that draws on both supply chain management and marketing management may be called for (Marcone, 2014; Ozuem et al., 2016).

CREATIVITY AND LUXURY FASHION BRANDS

To avoid polarization, and ensure that incremental creative contributions are encouraged in an environment optimized for radical creativity, the different roles and/or tasks must first be identified and arranged. Since different roles are likely to hold various degrees of radical and incremental creativity, adopting a broad spectrum approach may be useful.

In the dynamic creative environment of a modern luxury fashion brand, a broad spectrum of creativity profiles are at play at any given time. Although the fashion creative director is the highly visible representative of the most radical creativity, there are several other types of creativity at play throughout the organization, both in realizing the product, as well as in other supporting functions, such as marketing communication. At the opposite end of the spectrum from the fashion creative director may be a marketing data scientist (Florida, 2004) performing incremental creativity. All other creative roles may be placed between the extremes. Since the various types of creativity are likely to be motivated intrinsically, extrinsically or both, it may be useful to add this dimension once roles have been placed, resulting in a matrix model (Fig. 6.1).

To identify the various creative resources in the organization in order to motivate them, they can be positioned in the matrix. Vertical placement signifies degree of creativity type, while horizontal placement signifies likely motivational structure.

The placement of the roles may vary from fashion house to fashion house, so the population shown in Fig. 6.1 represents an example. Since the current focus is on marketing communication in relation to the overall creative product, these roles are prioritized, but the creativity motivation matrix can be populated with all relevant creative roles within the brand community (in grey, exemplified by tailor in this model). Based on this, appropriate motivational resources may be applied. To motivate radical creativity in intrinsically motivated marketing creatives, award show entries may be appropriate. Extrinsically motivated incrementally creative data scientists may be more motivated by management acclaim and action based on the statistics regarding their latest accomplishments. Further research should be performed on procedures related to incentivizing the various combinations of intrinsic and extrinsic motivation and how they relate to the various degrees of radical and incremental creativity. Due to the number of possible combinations, determination of incentives is likely to be granular and highly individual. The various

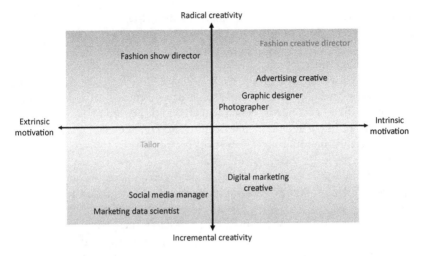

Fig. 6.1 Creativity motivation matrix

specialities within areas of professional expertise extend the number of combinations further.

ENCOURAGEMENT OF CREATIVE CONTRIBUTIONS

Creativity is a multifaceted social construct, and as such is subject to interpretation and defined by the environment in which it is performed. What the environment values and incentivizes may contribute to further variations (Sue-Chan & Hempel, 2016). The incentives within a discipline such as design, forecasting or marketing will vary in form, but the type of creativity they reward is likely to vary as well. If a fashion house, an advertising agency and an industrial design department enter different creative award competitions specific to their disciplines, they may all still incentivize a similar type of creativity (West et al., 2013). This is because annual creative award shows in most industries tend to prioritize originality and reward radical, attention-getting creativity within the field. Other awards may prioritize the two aspects of the creativity definition—original and appropriate (Sue-Chan & Hempel, 2016)—differently, and thereby incentivize other forms of creativity. Awards for effectiveness or structural design, as well as People's choice awards, for example, are likely to incentivize appropriateness over originality. Still, there are many other forms of creativity at play in companies within these creative industries, and not all creatives are motivated by winning awards. If a company only rewards creativity in the form of awards, types of creativity requiring other incentives may suffer.

Most creative industries are likely to have a strategic framework for encouraging the prevalent form of creativity, especially if it is a radical type of creativity that needs to be protected and nurtured throughout the organization. In particular, luxury fashion and creative marketing communication environments have a tradition for nurturing various degrees of radical creativity. As new, incremental forms of creativity are called for within digital marketing, such as social media management, new strategic frameworks and creativity measurement standards are called for (Lynch, 2019).

One managerial approach may be to address the goal orientation of the various creative roles and how they relate to radical and incremental creativity. Creative individuals primarily involved in radical creativity seem to have an intrinsic learning goal orientation (LGO); this means that discovering and exploring are goals in and of themselves (Malik et al., 2019). While creatives primarily involved in incremental creativity might also have this LGO, they are not necessarily dependent upon it and may also be motivated by performance goal orientation. Since performance goals are extrinsic and frequently measurable, they can be incentivized more directly by management. This is not to suggest an either/or orientation, but rather both. Since both types of creativities have some LGO, it may be beneficial to map similarities and differences between radical and incremental LGO. Creative performance goals can also be identified and incentivized accordingly.

CONCLUSION AND MANAGERIAL IMPLICATIONS

Luxury fashion is a highly creative industry. Companies competing in the luxury fashion industry need to produce highly original and appropriate items with high frequency on a regular basis. Creativity is at the core of their product offer, as well as engrained in the culture of the company. Exclusive characteristics contribute to a distinctive luxury brand signature, sometimes called the brand DNA. For the brand and products to reach the coveted, iconic status associated with luxury brands, creative marketing communication is necessary. Creativity is multifaceted and deeply engrained at all levels of the brand experience; hence, brand image becomes creative in and of itself.

Although luxury fashion brands are strongly associated with and defined by radical creativity that emanates from the product itself, other more incremental types of creativity are present and necessary throughout the company, not only to realize the product, but to market and communicate it. With the growing demand for integration, especially in multichannel marketing, a more holistic approach to creativity is needed if the brand is to retain a unified creative brand image across various platforms, devices and communications types, including interactive ones beyond the direct control of the marketing communications department. To secure integration not only of the overall creative brand image top down, but also of the distributed, specialized creative application across the organization, a more democratic distribution of creativity may need to be acknowledged.

Creating something original will always involve a level of risk, so it is not possible to deliver on the luxury fashion brand promise without risk. Willingness to take risks is an attribute of the entire creative industry company, not just its designated creative resources. There appears, however, to be an asymmetrical relationship between creativity and risk as it pertains to different roles within the luxury fashion environment that may be unique to the industry. While risk orientation is rarely evenly distributed throughout a company, nor even across the creative resources, few industries have so much of the risk associated with one individual in a way that directly influences brand perception as does the role of the fashion creative director.

Thus, luxury fashion houses may be among the few commercially oriented companies that employ creative individuals who seem to hold the personality traits described by the investment theory of creativity (Sternberg & Lubart, 1991) and, in fact, invest their brand in them. The fashion creative director, although not working alone, takes on high risk on a regular basis, an investment on behalf of the brand that frequently also holds strong personal ramifications. Whether risk itself, vanity or ambition is the intrinsic motivation in this case is not clear, and further research is needed to support the theory. It is, however, evident that the personal investment in terms of risk and creative responsibility the fashion creative director takes also gives the role extreme creative influence. While the many creative roles within the organization invest their creativity in the overall creative vision of the fashion creative director with varying degrees of risk, the risk seems disproportionately absorbed by the role of the fashion creative director. During the creative director's tenure, the personal brand of the creative director has a brand value of its own that frequently becomes deeply engrained in the brand, which, in turn, affects the collective luxury brand image. This strong personal investment in the brand may lead to a need for creative control beyond the individual's area of expertise, possibly at the cost of expertise-specific creativity throughout the organization.

To gain empirical insight into this unusual dynamic, further luxury fashion-specific research is recommended. Although iconic fashion creative directors are the subject of documentaries and movies (Leclair, 2017), there is at present little academic research on the creativity and role of the modern fashion creative director and their influence on the brand, so this may be a good place to start.

Suggestions for CIMC Management

Prioritizing the radical form of creativity emanating from the product and using marketing communication merely as a vehicle to disseminate this creativity to the audience may have sufficed in the age of mass media. Today, however, the marketing communication department is responsible for a wide and varied range of marketing communication services on a continuous basis, and not all creative contributions emanate directly from the current collection or product range to convey the underlying brand image. If creativity is to be applied to maintain a creative brand image in all marketing communication channels on a regular, continual basis, then incremental forms of creativity must be encouraged as well. The overall, creative brand position emanating from the radically creative products needs to be engrained in an omnichannel approach for a coherent brand, and it must also adopt a more flexible approach suitable for incremental, interactive marketing communication.

The fashion creative director role does not need to be diminished for management to encourage and acknowledge other types of creativity in the company overall and in marketing communication specifically. While luxury fashion brand managers need to protect the radical creativity emanating from the core of the brand, they also need to build systems that support and encourage more incremental creative contributions. Since extrinsic motivation can be affected directly, incentivizing the creativity associated with it can be managed, and may need to be so, to a greater degree. This may require a more active, distributed creative management than what has been the norm in an industry built on radical, centralized creative management. There seems to be untapped potential in encouraging many creative contributions within the various areas of expertise at play in the luxury fashion industry, beyond marketing communication.

Assessing the overall creative resources of the luxury fashion brand may provide a useful first step. Operationalizing a form of spectrum model may provide a tool to assess resources and likely incentives in the micro environment (see Fig. 6.1). The determination of incentives is likely to be granular and highly individual, most likely developed in collaboration with each individual. Further research towards a framework and operationalization is needed.

References

Alexander, B. (2016). Inter-industry creative collaborations incorporating luxury fashion brands. *Journal of Fashion Marketing and Management, 20*(3), 254–275.

Atwal, G., & Williams, A. (2009). Luxury brand marketing—The experience is everything! *Journal of Brand Management, 16*(5–6), 338–346.

Batra, R., & Keller, K. L. (2016). Integrating marketing communications: New findings, new lessons, and new ideas. *Journal of Marketing, 80*(6), 122–145.

Braun, M., & Moe, W. W. (2013). Online display advertising: Modeling the effects of multiple creatives and individual impression histories. *Marketing Science, 32*(5), 753–767.

Bruce, N. I., Murthi, B. P. S., & Rao, R. C. (2017). A dynamic model for digital advertising: The effects of creative format, message content, and targeting on engagement. *Journal of Marketing Research, 54*(2), 202–218.

Calder, B. J., & Malthouse, E. C. (2005). Managing media and advertising change with integrated marketing. *Journal of Advertising Research, 45*(4), 356–361.

Csikszentmihalyi, M. (1996). *Creativity: The psychology of discovery and invention* (1st ed.). HarperCollins.

De Chernatony, L. (2009). Towards the holy grail of defining "brand". *Marketing Theory, 9*(1), 101–105.

Dion, D., & Arnould, E. (2011). Retail luxury strategy: Assembling charisma through art and magic. *Journal of Retailing, 87*(4), 502–520.

Dubois, B., & Paternault, C. (1995). Understanding the world of international luxury brands: the "dream formula" (Special Issue: Research Input into the Creative Process). *Journal of Advertising Research, 35*(4), 69–77.

Dul, J., & Ceylan, C. (2014). The impact of a creativity-supporting work environment on a firm's product innovation performance. *Journal of Product Innovation Management, 31*(6), 1254–1267.

El-Murad, J., & West, D. C. (2003). Risk and creativity in advertising. *Journal of Marketing Management, 19*(5–6), 657–673.

El-Murad, J., & West, D. C. (2004). The definition and measurement of creativity: What do we know? *Journal of Advertising Research, 44*(2), 188–201.

Fionda, A. M., & Moore, C. M. (2009). The anatomy of the luxury fashion brand. *Journal of Brand Management, 16*(5–6), 347–363.

Florida, R. L. (2004). *The rise of the creative class: And how it's transforming work, leisure, community and everyday life.* 1st Paperb. Basic Books.

Gronstedt, A., & Thorson, E. (1996). Five approaches to organize an integrated marketing communication agency. *Journal of Advertising Research, 36*(2), 48–57.

Guile, D. (2006). Access, learning and development in the creative and cultural sectors: From "creative apprenticeship" to "being apprenticed". *Journal of Education and Work, 19*(5), 433–453.

Havlena, W., Cardarelli, R., & de Montigny, M. (2007). Quantifying the isolated and synergistic effects of exposure frequency for TV, print, and internet advertising. *Journal of Advertising Research, 47*(3), 215–221.

Kapferer, J. N., & Valette-Florence, P. (2018). The impact of brand penetration and awareness on luxury brand desirability: A cross country analysis of the relevance of the rarity principle. *Journal of Business Research, 83*, 38–50.

Keller, K. L. (2016). Unlocking the power of integrated marketing communications: How integrated is your IMC program? *Journal of Advertising, 45*(3), 286–301.

Kerr, G., & Patti, C. (2015). Strategic IMC: From abstract concept to marketing management tool. *Journal of Marketing Communications, 21*(5), 317–339.

Kilgour, M., Sasser, S., & Koslow, S. (2013). Creativity awards: Great expectations? *Creativity Research Journal, 25*(2), 163–171.

Kirsch, C., Lubart, T., & Houssemand, C. (2016). Comparing creative profiles: Architects, social scientists and the general population. *Personality and Individual Differences, 94*, 284–289.

Kitchen, P. J., Kim, I., & Schultz, D. E. (2008). Integrated marketing communications: Practice leads theory. *Journal of Advertising Research, 48*(4), 531–546.

Klipfel, J. A. L., Barclay, A. C., & Bockorny, K. M. (2014). Self-Congruity: A determinant of brand personality. *Journal of Marketing Development & Competitiveness, 8*(3), 130–143.

Koslow, S., Sasser, S. L., & Riordan, E. A. (2003). What is creative to whom and why? *Journal of Advertising Research, 43*(1), 96–110.

Kumar, V., Chattaraman, V., Neghina, C., Skiera, B., Aksoy, L., Buoye, A., & Henseler, J. (2013). Data-driven services marketing in a connected world. *Journal of Service Management, 24*(3), 330–352.

Laurie, S., & Mortimer, K. (2019). How to achieve true integration: The impact of integrated marketing communication on the client/agency relationship. *Journal of Marketing Management, 35*(3–4), 231–252.

Leclair, M. (2017). "Dior and I": Understanding the combination of creativity and economy in fashion industry. *Society and Business Review, 12*(3), 274–284.

Lee, Y. J., & Östberg, J. (2013). A case study of the Swedish fashion industry from the systems perspective of creativity. *Journal of Global Fashion Marketing, 4*(2), 128–143.

Lynch, J. (2019). Advertising industry evolution: Agency creativity, fluid teams and diversity. An exploratory investigation. *Journal of Marketing Management, 35*(9–10), 845–866.

Lynch, J., & West, D. C. (2017). Agency creativity: Teams and performance. *Journal of Advertising Research, 57*(1), 67–81.

Malik, M. A. R., Choi, J. N., & Butt, A. N. (2019). Distinct effects of intrinsic motivation and extrinsic rewards on radical and incremental creativity: The moderating role of goal orientations. *Journal of Organizational Behavior, 40*(9–10), 1013–1026.

Marcone, M. R. (2014). Creativity–decision processes: The case of Italian luxury fashion. *Journal of Global Fashion Marketing, 6*(1), 60–74.

Miller, K. W., & Mills, M. K. (2012). Contributing clarity by examining brand luxury in the fashion market. *Journal of Business Research, 65*(10), 1471–1479.

Mondalek, A. (2019). *What luxury fashion brands want in a creative director—Vogue Business Talent, Vogue Business*. Available at: https://www.vogueb usiness.com/talent/articles/luxury-fashion-brands-creative-director-balmain-louis-vuitton-virgil-abloh/. Accessed 27 September 2020.

Ots, M., & Nyilasy, G. (2015). Integrated Marketing Communications (IMC): Why does it fail? *Journal of Advertising Research, 55*(2), 132–145.

Ozuem, W., Howell, K. E., & Lancaster, G. (2008). Communicating in the new interactive marketspace. *European Journal of Marketing, 42*(9–10), 1059–1083.

Ozuem, W., Patel, A., Howell, K. E., & Lancaster, G. (2017). An exploration of customers' response to online service recovery initiatives. *International Journal of Market Research, 59*(1), 97–116.

Ozuem, W., Thomas, T., & Lancaster, G. (2016). The influence of customer loyalty on small island economies: An empirical and exploratory study. *Journal of Strategic Marketing, 24*(6), 447–469.

Patten, E., Ozuem, W., & Howell, K. (2020). Service quality in multichannel fashion retailing: An exploratory study. *Information Technology and People, 33*(4), 1327–1356.

Sasser, S. L., & Koslow, S. (2012). Passion, expertise, politics, and support: Creative dynamics in advertising agencies. *Journal of Advertising, 41*(3), 5–17.

Sasser, S. L., Koslow, S., & Kilgour, M. (2013). Matching creative agencies with results-driven marketers. *Journal of Advertising Research, 53*(3), 297–312.

Sasser, S. L., Koslow, S., & Riordan, E. A. (2007). Creative and interactive media use by agencies: Engaging an IMC media palette for implementing advertising campaigns. *Journal of Advertising Research, 47*(3), 237–256.

Shalley, C. E., & Gilson, L. L. (2017). Creativity and the management of technology: Balancing creativity and standardization. *Production and Operations Management, 26*(4), 605–616.

Statista. (2020). *Luxury fashion—Worldwide.* Available at: https://www.statista.com/outlook/21030000/100/luxury-fashion/worldwide?currency=eur. Accessed 21 September 2020.

Steiner, M., & Prettenthaler, F. (2015). Creativity reconsidered—so your firm is creative, but how much? A trans-sectoral and continuous approach to creative industries[†]. *Regional Studies, Regional Science, 2*(1), 275–289.

Sternberg, R. J., Kaufman, J. C., & Pretz, J. E. (2003). A propulsion model of creative leadership. *Leadership Quarterly, 14*(4–5), 455–473.

Sternberg, R. J., Kaufman, J. C., & Pretz, J. E. (2004). A propulsion model of creative leadership. *Creativity and Innovation Management, 13*(3), 145–153.

Sternberg, R. J., & Lubart, T. I. (1991). An investment theory of creativity and its development. *Human Development, 34*(1), 1–31.

Sternberg, R. J., & Lubart, T. I. (1996). Investing in creativity. *American Psychologist, 51*(7), 677–688.

Sternberg, R. J., O'Hara, L. A., & Lubart, T. I. (1997). Creativity as investment. *California Management Review, 40*(1), 8–21.

Straker, K., & Wrigley, C. (2016a). Designing an emotional strategy: Strengthening digital channel engagements. *Business Horizons, 59*(3), 339–346.

Straker, K., & Wrigley, C. (2016b). Emotionally engaging customers in the digital age: The case study of "Burberry love". *Journal of Fashion Marketing and Management, 20*(3), 276–299.

Sue-Chan, C., & Hempel, P. S. (2016). The creativity-performance relationship: How rewarding creativity moderates the expression of creativity. *Human Resource Management, 55*(4), 637–653.

Tafesse, W., & Kitchen, P. J. (2017). IMC—An integrative review. *International Journal of Advertising, 36*(2), 210–226.

Tevi, A., Koslow, S., & Parker, J. (2019). Can media neutrality limit creative potential? *Journal of Advertising Research, 59*(3), 312–328.

Turnbull, S., & Wheeler, C. (2017). The advertising creative process: A study of UK agencies. *Journal of Marketing Communications, 23*(2), 176–194.

West, D., Caruana, A., & Leelapanyalert, K. (2013). What makes win, place, or show? Judging creativity in advertising at award shows. *Journal of Advertising Research, 53*(3), 324–338.

West, D., Koslow, S., & Kilgour, M. (2019). Future directions for advertising creativity research. *Journal of Advertising, 48*(1), 102–114.

Wijngaarden, Y., Hitters, E., & Bhansing, P. V. (2019). "Innovation is a dirty word": Contesting innovation in the creative industries. *International Journal of Cultural Policy, 25*(3), 392–405.

CHAPTER 7

Online Brand Communities and Brand Loyalty: Toward a Social Influence Theory

Michelle Willis

INTRODUCTION

Customers' role in marketing messages is no longer restricted to being passive receivers of brand messages, their role has extended, allowing them to become creators of marketing information and awareness (Cheng et al., 2020; Meek et al., 2019). This development of customer behaviour is a result of the transformation of traditional media to new online social platforms (Trusov et al., 2009). Social media has provided users with the ability to freely share and distribute information across different communication channels, such as blogs and social networking sites. However, OBCs are not just simple social media tools used for communication purposes, they are important entities in building relationships between brands and customers (Meek et al., 2019). Customer engagement has been found to promote greater marketing efficiency, such as

M. Willis (✉)
Institute of Business, Industry and Leadership, University of Cumbria, Lancaster, UK

© The Author(s), under exclusive license to Springer Nature Switzerland AG 2021
W. Ozuem and S. Ranfagni (eds.), *The Art of Digital Marketing for Fashion and Luxury Brands*,
https://doi.org/10.1007/978-3-030-70324-0_7

building brand trust and evaluation (Hajli et al., 2017). Most importantly, customer engagement within OBCs has been found to be a positive predictor of customer loyalty (McAlexander et al., 2002; Pansari & Kumar, 2017).

Loyalty is a significant factor for OBCs; customers' intention to remain committed to a valuable relationship is essential to maintaining successful long-term relationships (Garbarino & Johnson, 1999). Customers can freely join and participate in online communities, but this does not necessarily make them loyal customers. The engagement within OBCs is aligned to a specific brand. Social media users may passively observe brand pages or actively engage within the pages without having an emotional attachment to the brand itself. Engagement within OBCs is affected by factors such as brand influence and community belonging (Yuan et al., 2020) that are motivated by customers' attachment to the brand through the community. Psychological attachment to an online community arguably influences the dependence individuals have on the relationships developed through OBCs (Cheng et al., 2020), which arguably creates a distinction between an active loyal customer and a passive observer. This highlights the major importance of using OBCs to encourage customers to develop online relationships that motivate them to remain attached to a specific brand, rather than simply using it as a communication tool to share basic marketing messages.

Previous studies have identified the significance of encouraging emotional relationship development within OBCs and influencing members' sense of belonging (Fournier, 1998; Bagozzi & Dholakia, 2006). However, relationships within OBCs are not limited to other customers, they can also involve the brand itself. Brand communities can facilitate the development of brand loyalty and the brand's long-term relationships with customers (Muniz & O'Guinn, 2001; Ozuem et al., 2017). Brands with the use of social media pages have attracted millions of followers; in 2019, Chanel had obtained 34.9 million Instagram followers, Louis Vuitton had 32.07 million and Dior had 25.55 million (Clement, 2019). Arguably, a key antecedent that has impacted the high volume of followers these brands have is the brand itself. This along with the "sense of belonging" to an OBC can be linked to individual customers' biased brand preferences (Coelho et al., 2019), as a specific brand preference can influence customers' alignment to a community that features the specific brand (Algesheimer et al., 2005). Fashion brands are symbols of unique identities; therefore, customers' alignment to an

OBC is likely to be directed by their favoured brands. This shows that while engagement is significantly important in maintaining loyalty within an active community, continuing usage of OBCs is strongly motivated by the specific brand the OBC revolves around. However, the question remains, If all OBC members favour the brand, why do they not demonstrate the same kind of loyalty? Despite the awareness of different loyalty categories and diverse customer behaviours, loyalty intentions are still universally generalised causing millennial customers to be regarded the same as other customer segments. For this reason, this chapter considers loyalty behaviours within OBCs that apply to the millennial generation.

The Millennial Generation

Millennials' early introduction to social media has greatly impacted their mass usage of online platforms causing social media to become part of their social lives and activities, including online shopping for fashion. In regards to online shopping, millennials are more likely to search for information through social media and participate in online interactions than any other previous generation (Ladhari et al., 2019). However, attempts to provide generic definitions of millennials' behaviour and attitudes have to led to a variety of definitions creating contradictions across research. For instance, one group of researchers defined them as highly consumption-oriented, materialistic and confident in spending (Butcher et al., 2017), whereas others found them to be very conscious of financial losses (Deloitte, 2020), which motivated them to limit unnecessary spending or select products more cautiously (Kemp et al., 2020). Others reported that millennials are conscious about the brands they purchase, placing status consumption at the centre of their purchasing decisions, and are eager to influence others (Butcher et al., 2017; Helal et al., 2018); however, in contrast, others claimed that millennials are less interested in impressing others and brands with heritage credentials than other generations are (Deloitte, 2017).

Millennials have been the subject of focus in studies linked to understanding social identity within social media and the impact of brands on millennials' social identity. Millennials' capability to socially influence behaviours directly and indirectly through social media is still in the process of being fully understood. Millennials' significant involvement in social media has encouraged investigation into how it impacts their brand loyalty (Bi, 2019). Studies have identified that millennials' involvement within OBCs and electronic word of mouth (WOM) can influence their purchasing decisions (Liu et al., 2019). Findings also support that millennials can be influencers of other millennials' purchasing decisions (Azemi et al., 2020; Butcher et al., 2017). Millennials are greatly influenced by the online information they encounter (Kim et al., 2012), but how they use it varies; some seek approval from their peers, thus relying on others' recommendations (Ladhari et al., 2019), whereas others seek to maintain their unique self-created identity in social media, believing their involvement and identity created within OBCs to be independent from the influence of other customers. It is clear that millennials are not the same; however, they are often grouped as one large homogenous segment. This chapter considers the various levels of social media engagement and loyalty towards brands, and the diverse effects of social influence on customers. These are the key to conceptualising millennial customers and their diverse habits within OBCs.

THEORETICAL FOUNDATION AND CONTEXT

OBCs

Brand community refers to a non-geographically bound community that is dedicated to a specific brand, which is formed by the collective creation of brand fans (Kozinets, 2001; Muniz & O'Guinn, 2001). Similar to other communities, which can be identified based on various characteristics such as age, culture or hobbies, brand communities concentrate on a specific brand. The membership of these brand communities consists of individuals who have a biased preference towards the brand and are willing to express their perceptions of the brand to others (Merz et al., 2009; Zaglia, 2013). The digital age transformed the ways in which people communicate, socialise and purchase products, which prompted the digitalisation of brand communities; this enabled firms to better understand their customers' behaviour (Adjei et al., 2010) and customers to develop closer relationships with the brands through interactive experiences. OBCs differ from the other digital platforms companies have adopted, including corporate websites and product channels. Brand websites and product channels are limited to providing information through a one-way communication channel; although customers are encouraged to post reviews on brand websites and product channels, they do not offer the interactive experiences that online communities accommodate.

OBCs allows customers to provide honest and open information regarding brand's products and services (Mathwick et al., 2008; Ozuem et al., 2008) and to partake in social exchanges. OBCs are no longer restricted to being simple text-sharing forums (Baldus et al., 2015) or sites on which members can search for products and services, they now provide an ideal environment for members to socialise within the community (Meek et al., 2019; Thompson & Sinha, 2008). This encourages brands to provide meaningful experiences through social media (Kim & Ko, 2012) to develop long-term relationships with customers. A brand's willingness to facilitate relationship development through OBCs can leave a positive impression on customers (Verhagen et al., 2015). Emotion as well as information quality are key attributes of OBCs that can impact customers' loyalty (Cheng et al., 2020; Pattern et al., 2020). This is important for a brand because gaining customers' attention through an OBC is only the first step, influencing them to stay with an OBC is challenging. In many cases, customers' membership of OBCs is temporary (Liao et al., 2017), which can be due to a lack of psychological attachment between the customer and the community.

Online Consumer Engagement

OBCs can be considered a network of formed relationships between customers and the brand and other customers (McAlexander et al., 2002; Yuan et al., 2020). In a simple definition, customer engagement can be referred to as a customer's participation with an organisation's marketing activities (Vivek et al., 2012). Yet, consumer engagement has been defined and interpreted from several perspectives. For example, some researchers refer to it as an individual's psychological state which will affect the degree to which that individual will interact with communities (Bowden, 2009), including their involvement with and interest in a brand community (Ibrahim et al., 2017). Others examined consumer engagement based on customers' behavioural outcomes, such as interactions and WOM between users and product review sharing (Wu et al., 2018). Baldus et al. (2015) conceptualised a way to measure consumer engagement by focusing on consumers' motivations for interacting in online communities.

Despite the difference in definitions, the underlining outcome of online consumer engagement is co-created values and interactive experiences through the users' learning, sharing, influencing and socialising (Yuan et al., 2016). The interaction it encourages between customers strengthens the OBC's perceived reliability for consumer-to-consumer and consumer-to-brand engagement ensuring the long-term existence of the brand within social media (Yuan et al., 2020). Pansari and Kumar (2017) even referred to customer engagement as a key determinant for generating firm's value, either directly through customer purchases or indirectly through positive WOM in social media. Researchers have explored a range of antecedents and consequences of online consumer engagement that are brand-related or beneficial to community members (Bazi et al., 2020; Willis, 2019). Brand-related factors may include brand identification and the symbolic significance the brand has to the customer (Giakoumaki & Krepapa, 2020). Other researchers explored the functional benefits of online engagement to customers; the mass volume of information generated by customers' interactions and the convenient access to it make social media an appropriate platform for customers to learn and process the information (Gruner et al., 2014). The perceived functional benefits of participating in OBCs can lead to engagement intentions, such as the need to be entertained or informed about the brand (Yuan et al., 2020).

Attitudinal and Behavioural Loyalty

Loyalty can generally be described as a customer's commitment to repurchase a product or service from the same brand as much as possible (Cossío-Silva et al., 2016). In early research, loyalty has been examined from either an attitudinal (Guest, 1944) or behavioural perspective (Cunningham, 1956) and these perspectives remain relevant to this day. The attitudinal perspective of loyalty emphasises the importance of customers' attitude towards an entity, such as a preference or liking towards it. This aligns with Oliver's (1999) description of loyalty as a deep commitment to patronise a preferred product or service in the future; it thereby establishes same-brand purchasing, despite situational influences and marketing efforts of competing brands. Loyalty from a behavioural perspective represents the customers' actual repeat purchasing of a brand over a period of time (Yi & Jeon, 2003).

Some researchers perceived behavioural loyalty to be more important than attitudinal loyalty due to its direct effect on brands' overall income (Bemmaor, 1995; Chandon et al., 2005; Liu, 2007). However, other researchers argued that a purely behavioural definition of loyalty fails to fully explain the reasons for loyalty and they suggested that attitudinal loyalty is the essence of true loyalty (Dick & Basu, 1994a). It can be argued that a lack of psychological elements, such as satisfaction and trust, can make motivating customers' purchase intentions more challenging (Kamran-Disfani et al., 2017). However, measuring loyalty from a purely attitudinal perspective can also cause issues for marketers (Sharp et al., 2002), especially when there is an absence of clear and obvious signs of emotions from customers within OBCs. Thus, neither behavioural nor attitudinal loyalty is more important than the other (Sharp et al., 2002), but one of the two categories may be more relevant to one group of millennials than it is for another group.

Social Influence Theory

OBCs are made up of a large network of individuals who have developed strong personal relationships with each other or with the brand (McAlexander et al., 2002; Yuan et al., 2020). Individuals in this online network can influence others to imitate community behaviours (Lucero-Romero & Arias-Bolzmann, 2019; Venkatesh & Davis, 2000) and make decisions that they may not have necessarily made independently. Social influence theory refers to an individual's change in behaviour and attitudes in response to others' influence. Social influence takes many forms and is familiar through socialisation, peer influence, leadership, persuasion, sales and marketing. In some cases, people alter their attitudes and behaviour to feel accepted and to meet others' expectations (Gass, 2015); for others, it is to obtain rewards, such as community acceptance (Kelman, 1958; Warshaw, 1980), and avoid negative outcomes, such as community disapproval (Bagozzi & Lee, 2002). However, behaviour and attitude alterations occur not just as a result of community pressure or the need to feel accepted; in many cases, individuals may conform to the influence of others because they agree with the communicated information (Kelman, 1958).

When considering customers of the millennials generation, there are several key issues that highlight the varying effect of social influence on their behaviour and attitudes. From one perspective, millennials are considered distinct from other generation cohorts based on their display of rejecting social norms (Lazarevic, 2012). They are also expected to be less inclined to accept the influence of company sources. In place of company-generated websites, social media has been the major influencer of millennials' behaviour and plays a significant role in keeping them connected with their peers (Bilgihan et al., 2013). The strong connection they have with their peers influences their motivation to seek their peers' approval of their fashion brand choices using social media (Ladhari et al., 2019). This means that they are likely to be aware of their product purchasing and will be particular in their brand choices to ensure they reflect status and personality (Helal et al., 2018). Another perspective is that they are less concerned about impressing others (Deloitte, 2017) and are confident in making their own purchase decisions (Butcher et al., 2017), making it hard to influence their behaviours. However, millennial customers could also be confident in their fashion brand choices and seek to socially influence others (Butcher et al., 2017). As well as being capable of having attitudinal loyalty towards their preferred brands, millennials are able to showcase their choices of brands through user-generated content which can impact community participation and loyalty (Kumar et al., 2016). Any content they share can influence the observing customers' sentiment towards the brand (Willis et al., 2019).

Discussion: Millennial Customer Loyalty Conceptualisation

A review of the extant literature resulted in the categorisation of four different categories of loyalty towards a fashion brand and fashion OBC: status loyalists, follower loyalists, brand loyalists and price loyalists. Each of these groups practice different behaviours and attitudes that reflect different levels of loyalty towards a brand within OBCs. The lower the loyalty for the brand itself, the higher the loyalty towards the online community itself, as presented in Fig. 7.1.

The level of loyalty millennial customers have towards a fashion brand can be measured by considering their actions and attitudes regarding loyalty towards a fashion brand, which can be linked back to the literature concerning the different types of loyalty and the level of online engagement within OBCs. Some millennial customers will communicate through the social media channels of fashion brands indicating favouritism towards that brand, but they might not necessarily actively purchase from

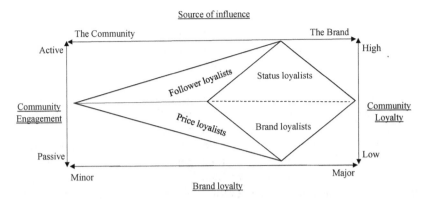

Fig. 7.1 Categorisation of millennial loyalists within online brand communities

the brand. In contrast, another group of millennial customers might not communicate through the brand's social media channels, but they may frequently purchase from the same brand. Although a customer following base in social media is important for any brand, it is important for companies to distinguish which millennial groups would generate sales before or after online engagement in OBCs and which will remain passive observers of fashion brands' social media content. Additionally, it is important to understand how millennials are affected by other millennials within OBCs. Millennials can be grouped as being either an influencer or a follower, and it is important to differentiate millennials based on the potential impact they may have on other millennials' decision making. In addition to understanding the different loyalty categories and varying levels of social influence, it is important to understand the groups of millennials and the level of loyalty they have for the fashion brand itself or the OBC.

Status Loyalists (High Loyalty–High Engagement)

Brand followers who seek to maintain status typically display the majority of positive support for a specific brand through OBCs. They aim to distinguish themselves from other customers based on their perceived association with the brand through social media. They do not necessarily have a high purchase frequency with the brand, as behavioural loyalty would indicate, but they are key influencers within OBCs. For this group of millennials, they are significantly influenced by the symbolic aspects of a brand, which makes it an essential element of their online social identity (Kara et al., 2018; Mousavi et al., 2017; Willis et al., 2019). Some millennials value being perceived as unique and different from others through their choice of fashion brands. Throughout history, people's wealth, or lack of wealth, would be displayed through the styles and brand of the fashion they wore, which identified their social rank. This occurs very much to this day and is becoming more visible through social media. Status consumption is no longer just for the wealthy, it is for anyone who aims to make a statement about their personality through the fashion items they wear. Millennials, with their high usage of social media, have made status consumption a relevant factor in their generation. Today, many millennials on social media have a large social network of "friends" viewing their lives through the messages and pictures they upload and share. How these "friends" perceive the individual is influenced by what that individual shares on their social media pages, including their fashion brand preferences.

Sometimes, individuals observing the content of millennials who are seeking to maintain status through social media messages linked to a fashion brand, do not respond positively. This may be because they perceive the individual as being vain and even quite amateur. Fashion brands consist of both professional and amateur influencers, and it is expected that all their followers are actual purchasers of the brand. That said, social media users who observe may be sceptical of constant status posts that indicate too much favouritism towards the brand without proof of actual usage. However, millennials whose loyalty is influenced by the need for status, are not necessarily affected by these critics. While status is important to them, so is their perceived independence from their peers' influence; the brand itself is the core influence. Customers who have a significant level of attitudinal loyalty to the brands they follow harbour favourable attitudes towards those specific brands (Böttger et al., 2017; Dick & Basu, 1994; Olsen, 2007; Siebert et al., 2020). When they have favourable emotional support for the brand, they are more likely to engage in positive WOM (Eelen et al., 2017) and refer the brand to other potential customers. They are less likely to engage in negative WOM about the brand and may even defend the brand if negative information emerges within OBCs (Wilson et al., 2017). This positive attitude they hold towards the brand reduces the effect of other millennials on their attitudes and their actions, making this group less compliant to social influence.

If they are affected by social influence, then identification is likely to have an effect on this group. Identification refers to the acceptance of influence from someone who is liked and respected (Kelman, 1958). Sources of influence that are likely to appeal to status loyalists would be representatives of the brand or other status loyalists, as well as the brand itself, compared to individuals who are not loyal to the brand. Information from other brands' marketing messages is also less likely to have an effect on millennials concerned about their social status through OBCs due to their psychological belief that the brand supports their status. Additionally, they are most likely to act as influencers themselves, both directly and indirectly. Social media is where users can express their identity, and the content related to the brand they share can potentially motivate others to consider how they might be seen if they follow specific brands others are following (Fuchs et al., 2013); customers aiming to uphold their social status play a role in influencing that perspective.

Follower Loyalists (Low Loyalty–High Engagement)

There are two ways to describe follower loyalists: they may seek to follow others to support purchase decisions or to simply feel part of a community. Novice customers are in a position where they have noticed a fashion brand but are indecisive regarding whether to actively purchase from that brand. This group of millennials seek support in their decision making from other millennials through the information they share through OBCs. When observing customers' suggestions, expressed through comments or through shared pictures, following loyalists typically follow suggestions that are supported by the majority of the members of an OBC. This group, in the early stages, does not have a strong emotional attachment towards the brand. A brand relationship may be compared to real-life relationships replicating human-like behaviours like trust and commitment (MacInnis & Folkes, 2017), which can impact the commitment customers are willing to deliver towards specific brands (Beatty & Kahle, 1988; Morgan & Hunt, 1994). Customers who are mostly followers do not have the past experience with the brand, both in purchasing and in online engagement, to have such a connection. Instead, they may develop connections with other members of the OBC who have actual experience and are active socialisers. Followers may then gradually build a sense of belonging that encourages them to seek support from the OBC members with whom they have connected.

Studies have supported the finding that customers with positive purchasing experience and a strong attachment to a brand are most likely to engage in positive WOM through social media, thus indirectly generating value for the firm (Kupfer et al., 2018). This means that experienced shoppers will be able to confirm the value and quality of a fashion brand to other potential customers. With customers' increased ability to share their experience openly with their peers in their social networking sites, in addition to the increased usage of social media, purchasing experience and other brand-related information are made easily available for online followers to access. Millennial customers, especially novice customers, are more sceptical of company websites or social media channels that mainly contain firm-generated content. Thus, they are more inclined towards other customers' comments, which are perceived to be more trustworthy as they are created in an online platform over which the firm has limited control, thus making the platform appear more genuine.

Customers who are follower loyalists cannot be categorised as having high loyalty for the brand itself. They have not yet developed an attachment to the brand, nor have they actively purchased from the brand to confirm the benefits associated with purchasing from the brand. Instead, this chapter defines them as having a relatively high loyalty towards the community of the fashion brand. When individuals find others who share values, personalities and are willing to exchange support, they are more likely to commit to remaining with that community because of the members. Eventually, it is possible that members who grow attached to the community itself, may, over time, develop an attachment to the fashion brand. This decision to align with the brand will be determined by the brand sentiment indicated by other customers within the OBC. One important factor related to consumers' behaviour in online buying is perceived critical mass (Cheng et al., 2020). This is a form of social influence that affects customers' adoption behaviour. If a large group of people are consuming a specific brand or share a certain perspective related to the brand, others will likely follow the mass/crowd. The higher the number of brand fans within an OBC, then the more likely that millennials who were originally followers become customers of that brand themselves. Eventually they will develop their own initiative to determine their future loyalty intentions following their experience, but they may continue to rely on information from other OBC members when the need arises.

Regardless of the equity of the brand, follower loyalists will prioritise their loyalty to the community rather than to the brand itself.

Brand Loyalists (High Loyalty–Low Engagement)

Millennials who do not comment or socially engage within an OBC may appear to have no preference towards a brand, but their actions and their attitude says otherwise. This group of millennials have a past purchasing history with a brand and intend to continue consuming the brand's products and services. Unlike millennials who follow and engage within fashion OBCs for status, customers who are loyal to the brand through purchasing behaviour, do not actively attempt to showcase their preference towards the brand through OBCs. This group's loyalty is therefore examined through behavioural loyalty measures, meaning their number of purchases and possible purchase behaviour is counted by marketers. Often, this causes them to be perceived as seeking monetary value from the brand's products rather than an emotional connection with the brand. Generally, millennials' decision making is often based on emotions, especially in the case of fashion consumption. However, they also seek the functional values gained from continuing their patronage of a specific brand (Luo et al., 2018; Ozuem et al 2016), but not necessarily just for financial reasons.

Monetary prices are not the only components of perceived brand value, they can include the perceived quality and performance of a brand (Broyles et al., 2009; Gallarza & Saura, 2006). Fashion is not just commodity items for consumption, fashion is a symbol of expression and promotes experience of emotions. A fashion brand's quality and performance are delivered when a customer feels a positive experience when wearing the brand. This builds their confidence in the branded products they purchase, which motivates them to remain with the brand. Consumption that involves experience thus means that brand value should be measured by both the functional benefits it provides and the enjoyment customers feel when using the brand's products or services. Some millennials value the experience brands provide and, compared to older generations, they are more willing to pay premium prices to maintain that experience (Deloitte, 2017). Millennials perceive this experience to come directly from the brand; therefore, they are selective of fashion brands that provide experience as well as a desirable clothing item.

Within OBCs, customers who are loyal to the brand may appear emotionless, which is due to their low level of online engagement with other customers. Nevertheless, they are determined to remain with a brand due to their past purchasing experience that has left a positive impression on them. Evidence supports the finding that emotions have a direct effect on consumers' behavioural responses, including their willingness to patronage a brand (Lee et al., 2008; Zeelenberg & Pieters, 2004). Although this group of millennial customers may not show obvious signs on OBCs of having a preference towards a brand, their attitude restrains them from choosing alternative brands. Arguably, they can be viewed as the group of millennials who do not seek to share their social life for the whole social network to see. Their positive preference for a fashion brand maintains their intention to remain with the same brand, even if they encounter negative brand sentiment within the OBC and even if they have a negative purchasing experience themselves. This means that as well as not actively publishing content in OBCs that reflects a positive attitude towards the brand, they will not publish negative messages either. Initially, this group of millennials could be referred to as "lurkers". Lurkers are social media users who observe online activity, including posts, comments and other visual content, but will not actively engage in the activity themselves (Fang & Zhang, 2019). This indicates that they will not be easily influenced by other customers' comments published through OBCs. They may enjoy viewing social media content, but their loyalty is not to the community itself; however, they do intend to maintain personal relations with the members of a fashion OBC. For millennials who are loyal to the brand, the key sources of influence that impact their level of brand loyalty are their own individual purchasing experiences and the functional and emotional benefits the brand delivers.

Price Loyalists (Low Loyalty–Low Engagement)

Compared to the other millennial customers' groups, this group of millennials, price loyalists, have little or zero direct intention of becoming emotionally attached to a specific fashion brand or the community dedicated to the brand, offline or online. Similar to the previously discussed millennials who are loyal to the brand, the behaviour of this group of millennials can be examined based on their purchasing behaviour. However, as the category indicates, they are not necessarily loyal to the brand but to the price that is offered. Literature on behavioural loyalty indicates that customers may divide their loyalty between various brands (DuWors & Haines, 1990) because customers may have a preference for different brands or shops based on the price setting of the products the different brands offer. This typically means that the customer is not searching for products based on the name of the brand but on the quality of the clothing product and its price. Therefore, their loyalty to a specific brand will be relatively weak compared to the other millennial customer groups.

In addition to having weak loyalty towards a specific brand, millennial customers may not necessarily feel the need to personally connect with members of an OBC other than for learning purposes. OBCs include individuals who share information online; other individuals who observe that content often attempt to learn and process the information related to products or services, especially when purchasing products online. Product reviews, consumers' messages, tweets and images related to products and services are among the many forms of information published by online consumers that online millennial shoppers search for (Klostermann et al., 2018; Moon & Kamakura, 2017; Netzer et al., 2012). Millennial customers who shop online search for these messages that identify the quality and price of fashion products.

Although this group of millennial customers may be satisfied when they see a desirable clothing item and be satisfied with its price, this will not automatically make them loyal long-term customers of the brand. As mentioned earlier, some millennials appear to be less interested in brands with high equity image (Deloitte, 2017) and are concerned about financial losses (Deloitte, 2020) if product quality expectations are not met. These characteristics identify a segment of shoppers who are economically orientated, where the purchase choice is solely based on price (Ladhari et al., 2019). Economic shoppers or shoppers who are less interested in the brand image the product represents, seek the maximum monetary value they can achieve from brands; therefore, they will highly favour promotion deals or product and service value that exceeds the expense. If the brand continues to meet their expectations, they will continue to purchase from that brand. However, their lack of mental attachment to that brand means they will easily switch to another brand if they perceive it has a better offer.

Due to their low level of loyalty and attachment to a brand, they are highly sceptical of firms' marketing messages that are not related to promotional or discount deals. As well as being economic shoppers they are also critical analysis shoppers. This means they are sceptical about brand-related messages published by the company that owns the brand. Trust in a brand's product is a significant factor for millennials, especially if they do not have high loyalty towards a brand. Although millennial customers are concerned about prices they may not actively engage within an OBC or seek to develop interpersonal relationships with other customers, rather they will observe the content that is provided by other customers related to purchasing experiences. However, rather than simply following what positive customers say, they will check for negative comments before making their decision. Rather than observing the community's positive sentiment towards the brand, they will examine customers' practical experience. Their decision will be determined based on whether other customers received high value from the spending investment; therefore, this group is expected to be socially compliant to other customers' influence, but only if accepting that influence leads to monetary value and reduces economic losses.

Conclusion and Future Outlook

In the context of loyalty within OBCs, millennial customers' behaviour has developed into a complex construct. Their diverse behaviours and attitudes in response to social media activity in the fashion industry indicate the complexity of grouping them purely based on either attitudinal or behavioural loyalty. By examining the literature on behavioural and attitudinal loyalty, and levels of engagement in OBCs, this chapter has identified different levels of loyalty towards a fashion brand that can be used to categorise the loyalty intentions of millennial customers towards fashion brands. By adding the level of online engagement alongside the level of loyalty, we can critically examine the reasons for customers' usage of OBCs and how it affects their loyalty. The discussion shows that millennial customers have different motivations for engaging within OBCs as well as varying levels of loyalty for a brand; thus, they can be separated into sub-groups based on their levels of loyalty and engagement: high loyalty with high engagement, high loyalty with low engagement, low loyalty with high engagement and low loyalty with low engagement. Individuals with high brand loyalty and high online engagement indicate not only favour towards the brand but the need to promote their brand preference to others. Whereas low loyalty and low engagement indicate an absence of loyalty for either the brand or community, suggesting that the individual's membership of OBCs will be temporary. When a millennial individual has low brand loyalty but strongly engages within OBCs, they probably intend to socialise with community members; this indicates their loyalty is aligned more with the community than with the brand itself. Likewise, a millennial with high brand loyalty but who does not significantly engage in OBCs is likely to be more loyal to the brand than to the community.

By examining millennial customers' unique characteristics and behaviour through social media we can predict the possible loyalty intentions millennial customers will have towards an OBC or towards a brand. Customers who are loyal because of the status the brand gives through OBCs typically have attitudinal loyalty. Although attitudinal loyalty indicates the positive emotions brands desire from customers, it does not guarantee intentions to purchase from the brand. Anyone can love Chanel, Valentino and Nike, but do they love them enough to pay for them? Customers may post constant status updates about the next product showcased by a brand they claim to love, but are they actually buying? This is the case for millennials with genuine loyalty for a brand. Although they may not quickly reveal their love for a brand on social media, they feel committed to maintaining a long-term purchasing commitment to a specific brand.

When customers have high loyalty to a brand but have little intention to engage online, companies miss out on customers who would be great sources of influence in their social media communication channels. However, customers who are loyal because of the status they can achieve, practice a high level of engagement in OBCs. They strongly emphasise the brand in their social media activity, which can influence brand image; this can directly impact other customers' perception of the brand. The other millennial group who show loyalty to social media channels by following their content have a lack of experience with the brand and are greatly affected by the social influence of other customers, including those who are concerned about their online status. Marketers can connect these two groups of customers together as customers with high loyalty and high engagement can socially influence followers through social engagement, which may eventually extend customers' loyalty beyond the simple following stage and encourage them to consider promoting and purchasing from the brand. Millennial customers who are loyal because of the price can also be socially influenced; however, because they are more concerned about the monetary value of purchasing, they will communicate with others to seek practical information rather than to socialise. Marketers should therefore consider connecting them with customers with actual experiences who can justify the brand as a good choice to purchase from as well as inform about promotion deals. Overall, fashion marketers should examine the actions and attitudes of millennials within OBCs to identify their loyalty intentions and to find whether their loyalty aligns with the brand or the community connected to it. This will help them adapt social media strategies to individuals who seek either community socialisation or specifically brand-related information and experiences.

REFERENCES

Adjei, M. T., Noble, S. M., & Noble, C. H. (2010). The influence of C2C communications in online brand communities on customer purchase behavior. *Journal of the Academy of Marketing Science, 38*(5), 634–653.

Algesheimer, R., Dholakia, U. M., & Herrmann, A. (2005). The social influence of brand community: Evidence from European car clubs. *Journal of Marketing, 69*(3), 19–34.

Azemi, Y., Ozuem, W., & Howell, K. E. (2020). The effects of online negative word-of-mouth on dissatisfied customers: A frustration–aggression perspective. *Psychology & Marketing, 37*(4), 564–577.

Bagozzi, R. P., & Dholakia, U. M. (2006). Antecedents and purchase consequences of customer participation in small group brand communities. *International Journal of Research in Marketing, 23*(1), 45–61.

Bagozzi, R. P., & Lee, K. H. (2002). Multiple routes for social influence: The role of compliance, internalization, and social identity. *Social Psychology Quarterly, 65*(3), 226–247.

Baldus, B., Voorhees, C., & Calantone, R. (2015). Online brand community engagement: Scale development and validation. *Journal of Business Research, 68*(5), 978–985.

Bazi, S., Filieri, R., & Gorton, M. (2020). Customers' motivation to engage with luxury brands on social media. *Journal of Business Research, 112*, 223–235.

Beatty, S. E., & Kahle, L. R. (1988). Alternative hierarchies of the attitude-behavior relationship: The impact of brand commitment and habit. *Journal of the Academy of Marketing Science, 16*(2), 1–10.

Bemmaor, A. C. (1995). Predicting behavior from intention-to-buy measures: The parametric case. *Journal of Marketing Research, 32*(2), 176–191.

Bi, Q. (2019). Cultivating loyal customers through online customer communities: A psychological contract perspective. *Journal of Business Research, 103*, 34–44.

Bilgihan, A., Okumus, F., & Cobanoglu, C. (2013). Generation Y travelers' commitment to online social network websites. *Tourism Management, 35*, 13–22.

Böttger, T., Rudolph, T., Evanschitzky, H., & Pfrang, T. (2017). Customer inspiration: Conceptualization, scale development, and validation. *Journal of Marketing, 81*(6), 116–131.

Bowden, J. L. H. (2009). The process of customer engagement: A conceptual framework. *Journal of Marketing Theory and Practice, 17*(1), 63–74.

Broyles, S. A., Schumann, D. W., & Leingpibul, T. (2009). Examining brand equity antecedent/consequence relationships. *Journal of Marketing Theory and Practice, 17*(2), 145–162.

Butcher, L., Phau, I., & Shimul, A. S. (2017). Uniqueness and status consumption in Generation Y consumers. *Marketing Intelligence & Planning, 35*(5), 673–687.

Chandon, P., Morwitz, V. G., & Reinartz, W. J. (2005). Do intentions really predict behavior? Self-generated validity effects in survey research. *Journal of Marketing, 69*(2), 1–14.

Cheng, F. F., Wu, C. S., & Chen, Y. C. (2020a). Creating customer loyalty in online brand communities. *Computers in Human Behavior, 107*,.

Clement, J. (2019). Leading luxury brands with the most followers on Instagram as of May 2019 (in millions). *Statista* [Online] Available at: https://www.statista.com/statistics/483753/leading-luxury-brands-instagram-followers/. Accessed 13 July 2020.

Coelho, A., Bairrada, C., & Peres, F. (2019). Brand communities' relational outcomes, through brand love. *Journal of Product and Brand Management, 28*(2), 154–165.

Cossío-Silva, F. J., Revilla-Camacho, M. A., Vega-Vázquez, M., & Palacios-Florencio, B. (2016). Value co-creation and customer loyalty. *Journal of Business Research, 69*, 1621–1625.

Cunningham, R. M. (1956). Brand loyalty—What where how much? *Harvard Business Review, 34*, 116–128.

Deloitte. (2017). *Bling it on. What makes a millennial spend more?* [Online]. Available at: https://www2.deloitte.com/ch/en/pages/consumer-industrial-products/articles/young-premium-consumer.html. Accessed 14 July 2020.

Deloitte. (2020). *The Deloitte Global Millennial Survey 2020 resilient generations hold the key to creating a "better normal"*. [Online] Available at: https://www2.deloitte.com/global/en/pages/about-deloitte/articles/millennialsurvey.html#insight. Accessed 14 July 2020.

Dick, A. S., & Basu, K. (1994a). Customer loyalty: Toward an integrated conceptual framework. *Journal of the Academy of Marketing Science, 22*(2), 99–113.

DuWors, R. E., Jr., & Haines, G. H., Jr. (1990). Event history analysis measures of brand loyalty. *Journal of Marketing Research, 27*(4), 485–493.

Eelen, J., Özturan, P., & Verlegh, P. W. (2017). The differential impact of brand loyalty on traditional and online word of mouth: The moderating roles of self-brand connection and the desire to help the brand. *International Journal of Research in Marketing, 34*(4), 872–891.

Fang, C., & Zhang, J. (2019). Users' continued participation behavior in social Q&A communities: A motivation perspective. *Computers in Human Behaviour, 92,* 87–109.

Fournier, S. (1998). Consumers and their brands: Developing relationship theory in consumer research. *Journal of Consumer Research, 24*(4), 343–373.

Fuchs, C., Prandelli, E., Schreier, M., & Dahl, D. W. (2013). All that is users might not be gold: How labeling products as user designed backfires in the context of luxury fashion brands. *Journal of Marketing, 77*(5), 75–91.

Gallarza, M. G., & Saura, I. G. (2006). Value dimensions, perceived value, satisfaction and loyalty: An investigation of university students' travel behaviour. *Tourism Management, 27*(3), 437–452.

Garbarino, E., & Johnson, M. S. (1999). The different roles of satisfaction, trust, and commitment in customer relationships. *Journal of Marketing, 63*(2), 70–87.

Gass, R. H. (2015). Social influence, sociology of. In J. Wright (Ed.), *International Encyclopedia Of The Social & Behavioral Sciences* (2nd ed.). Elsevier.

Giakoumaki, C., & Krepapa, A. (2020). Brand engagement in self-concept and consumer engagement in social media: The role of the source. *Psychology & Marketing, 37*(3), 457–465.

Guest, L. P. (1944). A study of brand loyalty. *Journal of Applied Psychology, 28,* 16–27.

Gruner, R., Homburg, C., & Lukas, B. (2014). Firm-hosted online brand communities and new product success. *Journal of the Academy of Marketing Science, 42*(1), 29–48.

Hajli, N., Shanmugam, M., Papagiannidis, S., Zahay, D., & Richard, M. O. (2017). Branding co-creation with members of online brand communities. *Journal of Business Research, 70,* 136–144.

Helal, G., Ozuem, W., & Lancaster, G. (2018a). Social media brand perceptions of millennials. *International Journal of Retail & Distribution Management, 46*(10), 977–998.

Ibrahim, N. F., Wang, X., & Bourne, H. (2017). Exploring the effect of user engagement in online brand communities: Evidence from Twitter. *Computers in Human Behavior, 72,* 321–338.

Kamran-Disfani, O., Mantrala, M. K., Izquierdo-Yusta, A., & Martínez-Ruiz, M. P. (2017). The impact of retail store format on the satisfaction-loyalty link: An empirical investigation. *Journal of Business Research, 77,* 14–22.

Kara, S., Vredeveld, A. J., & Ross, W. T., Jr. (2018). We share; we connect: How shared brand consumption influences relational brand connections. *Psychology & Marketing, 35*(5), 325–340.

Kelman, H. (1958a). Compliance, identification, and internalization three processes of attitude change. *Journal of Conflict Resolution, 2*(1), 51–60.

Kemp, E., Cowart, K., & Bui, M. M. (2020). Promoting consumer well-being: Examining emotion regulation strategies in social advertising messages. *Journal of Business Research, 112,* 200–209.

Kim, A. J., & Ko, E. (2012). Do social media marketing activities enhance customer equity? An empirical study of luxury fashion brand. *Journal of Business Research, 65*(10), 1480–1486.

Kim, K. H., Ko, E., Xu, B., & Han, Y. (2012). Increasing customer equity of luxury fashion brands through nurturing consumer attitude. *Journal of Business Research, 65*(10), 1495–1499.

Klostermann, J., Plumeyer, A., Böger, D., & Decker, R. (2018). Extracting brand information from social networks: Integrating image, text, and social tagging data. *International Journal of Research in Marketing, 35*(4), 538–556.

Kozinets, R. V. (2001). Utopian enterprise: Articulating the meanings of Star Trek's culture of consumption. *Journal of Consumer Research, 28*(1), 67–88.

Kumar, A., Bezawada, R., Rishika, R., Janakiraman, R., & Kannan, P. K. (2016). From social to sale: The effects of firm-generated content in social media on customer behavior. *Journal of Marketing, 80*(1), 7–25.

Kupfer, A. K., Pähler vor der Holte, N., Kübler, R. V., & Hennig-Thurau, T. (2018). The role of the partner brand's social media power in brand alliances. *Journal of Marketing, 82*(3), 25–44.

Ladhari, R., Gonthier, J., & Lajante, M. (2019). Generation Y and online fashion shopping: Orientations and profiles. *Journal of Retailing and Consumer Services, 48,* 113–121.

Lazarevic, V. (2012). Encouraging brand loyalty in fickle generation Y consumers. *Young Consumers, 13*(1), 45–61.

Lee, Y. K., Lee, C. K., Lee, S. K., & Babin, B. J. (2008). Festivalscapes and patrons' emotions, satisfaction, and loyalty. *Journal of Business Research, 61*(1), 56–64.

Liao, J., Huang, M., & Xiao, B. (2017). Promoting continual member participation in firm-hosted online brand communities: An organizational socialization approach. *Journal of Business Research, 71,* 92–101.

Liu, H., Wu, L., & Li, X. (2019). Social media envy: How experience sharing on social networking sites drives millennials' aspirational tourism consumption. *Journal of Travel Research, 58*(3), 355–369.

Liu, Y. (2007). The long-term impact of loyalty programs on consumer purchase behavior and loyalty. *Journal of Marketing, 71*(4), 19–35.

Lucero-Romero, G., & Arias-Bolzmann, L. G. (2019). Millennials' use of online social networks for job search: The Ecuadorian case. *Psychology & Marketing, 37*(3), 359–368.

Luo, J., Dey, B. L., Yalkin, C., Sivarajah, U., Punjaisri, K., Huang, Y. A., et al. (2018). Millennial Chinese consumers' perceived destination brand value. *Journal of Business Research, 116,* 655–665.

MacInnis, D. J., & Folkes, V. S. (2017). Humanizing brands: When brands seem to be like me, part of me, and in a relationship with me. *Journal of Consumer Psychology, 27*(3), 355–374.

Mathwick, C., Wiertz, C., & De Ruyter, K. (2008). Social capital production in a virtual P3 community. *Journal of Consumer Research, 34*(6), 832–849.

McAlexander, J. H., Schouten, J. W., & Koenig, H. F. (2002). Building brand community. *Journal of Marketing, 66*(1), 38–54.

Meek, S., Ryan, M., Lambert, C., & Ogilvie, M. (2019). A multidimensional scale for measuring online brand community social capital (OBCSC). *Journal of Business Research, 100,* 234–244.

Merz, M. A., He, Y., & Vargo, S. L. (2009). The evolving brand logic: A service dominant logic perspective. *Journal of the Academy of Marketing Science, 37,* 328–344.

Moon, S., & Kamakura, W. A. (2017). A picture is worth a thousand words: Translating product reviews into a product positioning map. *International Journal of Research in Marketing, 34*(1), 265–285.

Morgan, R. M., & Hunt, S. D. (1994). The commitment-trust theory of relationship marketing. *Journal of Marketing, 58*(3), 20–38.

Mousavi, S., Roper, S., & Keeling, K. A. (2017). Interpreting social identity in online brand communities: Considering posters and lurkers. *Psychology & Marketing, 34*(4), 376–393.

Muniz, A. M., & O'Guinn, T. C. (2001). Brand community. *Journal of Consumer Research, 27*(4), 412–432.

Netzer, O., Feldman, R., Goldenberg, J., & Fresko, M. (2012). Mine your own business: Market-structure surveillance through text mining. *Marketing Science, 31*(3), 521–543.

Oliver, R. L. (1999). Whence consumer loyalty? *Journal of Marketing, 63* (Special issue), 33–44.

Olsen, S. O. (2007). Repurchase loyalty: The role of involvement and satisfaction. *Psychology & Marketing, 24*(4), 315–341.

Ozuem, W., Howell, K. E., & Lancaster, G. (2008). Communicating in the new interactive marketspace. *European Journal of Marketing, 42*(9–10), 1059–1083.

Ozuem, W., Patel, A., Howell, K. E., & Lancaster, G. (2017). An exploration of customers' response to online service recovery initiatives. *International Journal of Market Research, 59*(1), 97–116.

Ozuem, W., Thomas, T., & Lancaster, G. (2016). The influence of customer loyalty on small island economies: An empirical and exploratory study. *Journal of Strategic Marketing, 24*(6), 447–469.

Pansari, A., & Kumar, V. (2017). Customer engagement: The construct, antecedents, and consequences. *Journal of the Academy of Marketing Science, 45*(3), 294–311.

Patten, E., Ozuem, W., & Howell, K. (2020). Service quality in multichannel fashion retailing: An exploratory study. *Information Technology & People, 33*(4), 1327–1356.

Sharp, A., Sharp, B., & Wright, M. (2002). Questioning the value of the "true" brand loyalty distinction. *International Journal of Research in Marketing, 19*(1), 81–90.

Siebert, A., Gopaldas, A., Lindridge, A., & Simões, C. (2020). Customer experience journeys: Loyalty loops versus involvement spirals. *Journal of Marketing,* p. 0022242920920262.

Thompson, S. A., & Sinha, R. K. (2008). Brand communities and new product adoption: The influence and limits of oppositional loyalty. *Journal of Marketing, 72*(6), 65–80.

Trusov, M., Bucklin, R. E., & Pauwels, K. (2009). Effects of word-of-mouth versus traditional marketing: Findings from an internet social networking site. *Journal of Marketing, 73*(5), 90–102.

Venkatesh, V., & Davis, F. (2000). A theoretical extension of the technology acceptance model: Four longitudinal field studies. *Management Science, 46*(2), 186–204.

Verhagen, T., Swen, E., Feldberg, F., & Merikivi, J. (2015). Benefitting from virtual customer environments: An empirical study of customer engagement. *Computers in Human Behavior, 48,* 340–357.

Vivek, S. D., Beatty, S. E., & Morgan, R. M. (2012). Customer engagement: Exploring customer relationships beyond purchase. *Journal of Marketing Theory and Practice, 20*(2), 122–146.

Warshaw, P. (1980). A new model for predicting behavioral intentions: An alternative to Fishbein. *Journal of Marketing Research, 17*(2), 153.

Wilson, A. E., Giebelhausen, M. D., & Brady, M. K. (2017). Negative word of mouth can be a positive for consumers connected to the brand. *Journal of the Academy of Marketing Science, 45*(4), 534–547.

Willis, M. (2019). The dynamics of social media marketing content and customer retention. In G. Bowen & W. Ozuem (Eds.) *Leveraging computer-mediated marketing environments.* IGI Global.

Willis, M., Ng, R., & Chitran, V. (2019). Exploring the relationship between customer participation and online brand community and consumer loyalty. *Interdisciplinary Journal of Economics and Business Law, 9*(special issue), 72–111.

Willis, M., Ozuem, W., & Ng, R (2019). Enhancing online brand relationship performance in the fashion industry. In W. Ozuem, E. Patten, & Y. Azemi (Eds.), *Harnessing Omnichannel retailing strategies for fashion and luxury brands*. Brown Walker Press.

Wu, J., Fan, S., & Zhao, J. L. (2018). Community engagement and online word of mouth: An empirical investigation. *Information & Management, 55*(2), 258–270.

Yi, Y., & Jeon, H. (2003). Effects of loyalty programs on value perception, program loyalty, and brand loyalty. *Journal of the Academy of Marketing Science, 31*(3), 229–240.

Yuan, D., Lin, Z., Filieri, R., Liu, R., & Zheng, M. (2020). Managing the product-harm crisis in the digital era: The role of consumer online brand community engagement. *Journal of Business Research, 115,* 38–47.

Yuan, D., Lin, Z., & Zhuo, R. (2016). What drives consumer knowledge sharing in online travel communities? Personal attributes or e-service factors? *Computers in Human Behavior, 63,* 68–74.

Zaglia, M. E. (2013). Brand communities embedded in social networks. *Journal of Business Research, 66*(2), 216–223.

Zeelenberg, M., & Pieters, R. (2004). Beyond valence in customer dissatisfaction: A review and new findings on behavioral responses to regret and disappointment in failed services. *Journal of Business Research, 57*(4), 445–455.

Recommended Further Reading

Cheng, F. F., Wu, C. S., & Chen, Y. C. (2020b). Creating customer loyalty in online brand communities. *Computers in Human Behavior, 107,.*

Dick, A. S., & Basu, K. (1994b). Customer loyalty: Toward an integrated conceptual framework. *Journal of the Academy of Marketing Science, 22*(2), 99–113.

Helal, G., Ozuem, W., & Lancaster, G. (2018b). Social media brand perceptions of millennials. *International Journal of Retail & Distribution Management, 46*(10), 977–998.

Kelman, H. (1958b). Compliance, identification, and internalization three processes of attitude change. *Journal of Conflict Resolution, 2*(1), 51–60.

Willis, M. (2019). The dynamics of social media marketing content and customer retention. In G. Bowen & W. Ozuem (Eds.) *Leveraging computer-mediated marketing environments*. IGI Global.

Willis, M., Ozuem, W., & Ng, R. (2019). Enhancing online brand relationship performance in the fashion industry. In W. Ozuem, E. Patten, & Y. Azemi (Eds.), *Harnessing Omni-channel marketing strategies for fashion and luxury brands*. Brown Walker Press.

CHAPTER 8

Exploring the Emergence of Luxury Smartphones and Switching Behaviour

Dominic Appiah and Alison Watson

INTRODUCTION AND CONTEXT

Luxury brands are not naturally luxurious in themselves; rather, they need to be perceived as luxurious by consumers (Hudders, 2012). This makes the management of consumers' perceptions of particular importance for luxury brands. Romanuik and Huang (2020) shared the view that luxury brand perceptions arise from three main sources namely, direct brand experience (buying the brand, experiencing its retail outlets), word-of-mouth communications from others, and advertising or other marketing communications exposure. Direct experience of a luxury brand is the most powerful source of brand perceptions; there is extensive evidence that consumers of a luxury brand are two to three times more likely to hold perceptions about a brand than non-consumers of that particular brand (Bird et al., 1970; Romaniuk et al., 2012) and that brand experiences are correlated with loyalty and satisfaction (Brakus et al., 2009).

D. Appiah (✉) · A. Watson
Arden University, Coventry, UK

W. Ozuem and S. Ranfagni (eds.), *The Art of Digital Marketing for Fashion and Luxury Brands*,
https://doi.org/10.1007/978-3-030-70324-0_8

179

Luxury brands rely on strong brand identities to establish loyalty among consumers. Loyalty and luxury consumption are built on the relationships that consumers establish with luxury brands. The power of strong brands is increasing and is absolutely critical in the high-tech luxury industry. Appiah and Ozuem (2019) stated that a brand is a name, design, symbol or major feature that helps to distinguish one or more products or services of a particular organization from others within the same product category. Hence, branding remains a powerful tool as consumers recognize that brands provide them with focused information, such as identity and value, as well as some unique features of branded products or services. Broadly, research on brand loyalty focuses on two main schools of thought: behavioural and attitudinal loyalty (e.g., Dick & Basu, 1994; Ringberg & Gupta, 2003). Nam et al. (2011) confirmed that brand loyalty has traditionally been perceived as a behavioural construct relating to intentions towards repeat purchases. Indeed, consumer behaviour tends to be based on repeat purchases of particular products or services (Hallowell, 1996; Homburg & Giering, 2001). However, this chapter considers attitudinal loyalty to be a form of long-term and emotional commitment to a brand (Bennett & Rundle-Thiele, 2002; Shankar et al., 2003). This is why attitudinal loyalty is referred to as "emotional loyalty", and is regarded as much stronger and longer lasting (Hofmeyr & Rice, 2000). This chapter reviews the literature on luxury brands, then presents a discussion of brand switching based on two contrasting perspectives, it then reviews the literature on luxury smartphones and brand loyalty. An evaluation of both behavioural and attitudinal loyalty is carried out to establish the latter as a more sustainable choice. Switching behaviour is then discussed in more detail. Finally, the chapter concludes with a discussion of managerial implications.

CONCEPTUAL CLARIFICATION OF LUXURY BRANDS

Branding is important in the hyper-competitive luxury industry because the brand is a significant influencer of product loyalty (Ahn et al., 2018; Appiah et al., 2019; Ozuem et al., 2016). Luxury brands are often associated with high-income consumers, and this category of consumers is typically willing to pay larger premiums compared to middle-income consumers. The emergence of new technologies has given luxury brands higher visibility, and such technologies continue to attract more attention from consumers all over the world (Appiah & Ozuem, 2018a). Luxury brands are characterized as one of the fastest-growing brand segments in the world, generating high profits in various markets. Luxury brands are defined and categorized based on different perspectives. Vickers and Renand (2003) defined luxury brands as symbols of personal identity, and emphasized that consumers' luxury consumption is dependent on personal, social and individual attachments. For the purposes of this chapter, and in line with the above clarification, luxury brands are defined as the outward expression of a consumer's own identity. However, the intentions of consumers to purchase luxury brands are complex and multifaceted (Giovannini et al., 2015). Luxury brands are considered to be conspicuous possessions categorized by exclusivity, prestige and premium pricing (Berthon et al., 2009; Miller & Mills, 2012). They possess distinct brand identities and meanings distinguished by specific associations (Tynan et al., 2010). Luxury brands benefit from associations utilized by firms in developing strong brand identities which typically include: (a) authenticity, (b) stylistic consistency, (c) quality commitment, (d) unique aesthetic symbolism, and (e) hedonic and emotional promotional appeals (Okonkwo, 2009).

Aaker (1996) insisted that luxury brands carry a deeper identity compared to ordinary brands. Luxury branding is a strategic marketing tool that provides competitive advantage for manufacturers (Keller, 2009). Conventionally, luxury denotes excellence, creativity and exclusivity (Okonkwo, 2009), based on these attributes, luxury brands build and harness consumer identity by connecting the consumer's inner self with the external world (Belk, 1988; Jenkins, 2004).

Innovation and Disruption

The ultimate causes of brand switching are market disruptions. Market disruptions are key occurrences in a market that, more often than not, impede customer–brand relationships (Christensen, 2013; Fournier, 1998; Jung et al., 2017). Disruption therefore occurs when markets cease to operate routinely. It is characterized by steep and prolonged market declines. This chapter focuses on disruptions that occur within product markets. As noted by McGrath and Cliffe (2011), the concept of market disruption that occurs in the market can be understood by drawing on research in two significant areas: technology and innovation. In recent times, these areas have attracted significant attention from firms in the smartphone industry. Disruptions displace and alter how we think, behave, transact business, learn and go about our daily business. This is echoed by Christensen (2013), who stated that disruptions displace existing markets, industries and technology; markets, industries and technology then develop into something unique, more efficient and more useful.

The theory of disruptive innovation introduced by Christensen (2013) provides an explanation of the displacement of industry giants by lesser competitors and the opening of channels to new entrants (Bower & Christensen, 1995; Christensen, 2013; Giovanisa & Athanasopouloub, 2018). Disruptive innovation creates a new market and disrupts existing markets. The term is used in the business and technology literature to describe innovations that improve products or services in ways that markets do not expect: first by generating a different set of consumers in the new market (Christensen, 2013; Giovanisa & Athanasopouloub, 2018; Ozuem et al., 2008), and later by lowering prices in the existing market.

Luxury Smartphones and Brand Loyalty

The personal lives of contemporary individuals have become largely reliant on advanced information communication technologies. In particular, smartphones have permeated every arena of today's society. Smartphones are supported by the development of communication infrastructures, especially that of high-speed communication networks. The ownership of smartphones as well as the use of smartphone apps has significantly increased (Smith, 2013). Furthermore, as the internet of things (IoT), a network of wireless connections across devices that enables information to be conveyed without the intentional involvement of humans, continues to be applied to an increasing number of devices, the domains converging with smartphone apps have also broadened and diversified. According to a Cisco report conducted by Bradley et al. (2016), the number of devices based on IoT will reach 50 billion by the end of 2020. This implies that the function of smartphone apps as technological hubs for IoT devices will also intensify.

The emergence of a networked world, in which the smartphone plays a significant part, has led to smartphones becoming a basic necessity and a shift in attention towards high-end luxury smartphones. The Solarin smartphone is a luxury smartphone. The Solarin smartphone stands out because of its sleek surface, and leather and titanium exterior. Luxury devices often boast technology that provides protection to thwart cyber-attacks and military grade chip-to-chip 256-bit encryption. By flicking a unique security switch on the back of the device, the smartphone enters a special shielded mode which allows end-to-end encrypted calls and messages. These unique features make Solarin smartphones physically different from other phones (http://www.solarin.com).

Another luxury smartphone is the Fantôme Arcane. According to a PR Newswire (2015) report, the Fantôme Arcane is a high-performance luxury smartphone built to satisfy the increasing demands of consumers seeking security and privacy features. It has very unique features and functions, including a secure space to enrich the mobile user experience that allows multiple virtual phones to co-exist on the device. Each virtual phone created on the device can be paired to one of the two SIMs available on the Arcane. Each virtual phone isolates the accounts and data from other virtual phones on the device. This allows device owners to use the same app with different accounts in each virtual phone making it easy to maintain personal, public and work accounts and identities all on a single premium device (http://www.fantom3.com/arcane).

In line with the above developments, and the shift towards luxury smartphones, the expectation of these luxury smartphone firms is to ultimately consolidate customer loyalty through improved user experience. Loyalty to a brand is expressed based on a positive attitude, which drives consumers to repeatedly demand goods or services of a particular brand or a limited number of brands within a suitably defined period of time. Consistent with this view, Appiah (2014) suggested that positive attitudes may have a strong effect on consumers' behaviour towards a particular brand. Brand loyalty is a "deeply held commitment to rebuy or repatronize a preferred product or service consistently in the future, causing repetitive same-brand or same-brand-set purchasing, despite situational influence and marketing efforts having the potential to cause switching behaviour" (Oliver, 1999, p. 34). Dimitriades (2006) shared a similar view in noting that it is widely accepted that satisfied consumers are less sensitive to price changes, less influenced by competitor attacks and increasingly more loyal to firms than dissatisfied customers.

Arguably, no recent technological innovation has had a more transformative effect on consumers' lives than the virtually indispensable smartphone, with one-third of all consumer purchases, over US$1 trillion, now occurring on mobile platforms (Melumad & Pham, 2020).

Behavioural and Attitudinal Loyalty

While functionalities undoubtedly play an important role in explaining why consumers form attachments to their smartphones, there is a deeper psychological explanation for this special relationship (Melumad & Pham, 2020). Luxury smartphone consumers are drawn to their devices because they offer a unique combination of functional, haptic and personal ownership benefits that allow these devices to serve as a source of psychological comfort. Thus, although the very notion of "smartphone addiction" frames the relationship that people have with their smartphone in an exclusively negative light, consumers also derive emotional and psychological benefits from use of their luxury smartphone devices (Ball & Tasaki, 1992).

Despite the large number of studies on brand loyalty, much of the research over the past three decades investigates consumer loyalty from two perspectives; so, broadly, there are two schools of thought underlining the definition of brand loyalty: behavioural loyalty and attitudinal loyalty (Dick & Basu, 1994).

The early marketing studies perceived customer loyalty in a behavioural way, measuring the concept as a behaviour involving repeat purchases of a particular product or service. This behaviour was evaluated in several ways: by the sequence in which goods and services were purchased, as a proportion of purchases, as an act of recommendation or as a measure of several of these criteria combined (Hallowell, 1996; Homburg & Giering, 2001). Nam et al. (2011) confirmed the above-mentioned perception by stating that loyalty has traditionally been conceived of as a behavioural construct relating to intentions towards repeat purchase. Put simply, Nam et al. (2011) referred to behavioural loyalty as the frequency of repeat purchases, and, repeat purchases may, to a certain degree, capture consumers' loyalty towards their brand of interest. Kuusik and Varblane (2009) identified three sub-segmented reasons for customers' loyalty: (i) those who are forced to be loyal (e.g., by monopoly or high exit costs), (ii) those who are loyal due to inertia, and (iii) those demonstrating functional loyalty. Oliver (1999) attached the concept of inert loyalty to routine purchases in which a sense of satisfaction is not experienced and purchasing becomes a task. From a marketing perspective, this would suggest that as long as there are no specific "triggers" to compel behaviourally loyal customers to change providers, they will remain passively loyal (Roos, 1999). According to Liu et al. (2007), even when presented with more attractive alternatives, consumers who have high inertia will be reluctant to change, and this behaviour can be linked to a consumer's familiarity and a perception that frequenting a familiar service vendor requires less effort. They stated that consumer inertia has greater influence on repeat purchase intentions, and they recommended that managers make efforts to develop consumer consumption inertia.

Day (1969) criticized this one-dimensional view as behaviourally centred, and therefore not particularly useful to distinguish true loyalty from "spurious loyalty". Since then, many researchers have recognized the need to add an attitudinal component to the behavioural one (Berné et al., 2001; Dick & Basu, 1994; Oliver, 1997). Day's criticism was embraced by Uncles and Laurent (1997) who argued that by classifying these behavioural observations as a form of loyalty, there is a tendency to overlook customers who are emotionally attached to products and services. This can lead to overestimations of loyal customer bases and the stability of portfolios (Crouch et al., 2004). Significantly, Dick and Basu (1994) contended that a favourable attitude and repeat purchase is ideal to define loyalty. They viewed loyalty as an attitude–behaviour relationship in their framework.

Attitudinal loyalty, on the other hand, can be defined as capturing the emotional and cognitive components of brand loyalty (Kumar & Shah, 2004; Ozuem et al., 2016). Brand commitment is the pledging or binding of a person to his or her brand choice within a product class (Appiah et al., 2019). Brand commitment is synonymous with attitudinal loyalty.

Attitudinal loyalty represents a long-term and emotional commitment to an organization or brand (Bennett & Rundle-Thiele, 2002; Ozuem et al., 2016; Shankar et al., 2003). Sadeghi et al. (2014) supported this view and argued that loyalty is gained from affective commitment and emotional attachments. The idea of attitudinal loyalty has been compared with marriage (Albert & Merunka, 2013).

Consistent with the above, attitudinal loyalty refers to the psychological commitment that a consumer makes in the purchase act, such as intentions to purchase and recommend without necessarily taking repeat purchase behaviour into account (Jacoby, 1971). Jacoby and Kyner (1973) defended Jacoby's (1971) definition of brand loyalty. Their definition offers a set of six necessary and collectively sufficient conditions. According to Jacoby and Kyner (1973) brand loyalty is: (1) biased (i.e., non-random), (2) a behavioural response (i.e., purchase), (3) expressed over time, (4) undertaken by some decision-making unit, (5) fulfilled with respect to one or more alternative brands out of a set of such brands, and (6) a function of psychological (decision-making, evaluative) processes. They stated that it is the evaluation process (the sixth condition) that makes an individual develop a commitment towards a brand. It is this notion of commitment, they argued, that provides an essential basis for differentiating brand loyalty from other forms of repeat purchasing behaviour.

Attitudinal loyalty is preferred by marketers to behavioural loyalty (Appiah & Ozuem, 2018a; Day, 1969; Dick & Basu, 1994) for the following reasons. Customers who are behaviourally loyal customers are considered spuriously loyal; hence, they remain loyal until they find an alternative in the same product or service category (Dick & Basu, 1994). An attitudinally loyal customer, on the other hand, is strongly committed to a brand or service, and does not switch to an alternative easily. Customers are influenced through trust and affective commitment, leading to a positive relationship with the brand (Aurier & Lanauze, 2010). Attitudinal loyalty not only indicates higher repurchase intent, but also resistance to counter-persuasion and adverse expert opinion. It is an indicator of a willingness to pay a price premium and to recommend the service provider or brand to others.

Based on the reasons established above, this chapter adopts the idea of attitudinal loyalty towards a brand or service provider and defines brand loyalty as the consumer's intention to repurchase or their willingness to recommend a particular brand regardless of price change. Shankar et al. (2003) viewed attitudinal loyalty as similar to the type of affective or cognitive loyalty proposed by Oliver (1999). This represents a higher order or a long-term commitment of a customer to an organization or brand, which cannot be inferred by merely observing customer repeat purchase behaviour (Appiah & Ozuem, 2018b).

BRAND SWITCHING FROM SOCIAL INFLUENCE THEORY PERSPECTIVE

Brand switching occurs when a customer is motivated to review available alternatives in the marketplace due to a change in competitive activities (Matzler et al., 2015; Seiders & Tigert, 1997). Socially, switching occurs when a customer's belief in a brand is externally influenced within the social setting. The customer's belief then impacts his or her attitude towards using a specific brand, which leads to changes in purchase intentions.

For the purposes of this chapter, social influence refers to the extent to which customers are influenced by the actions of others within the same social environment (Karikari et al., 2017; Osei-Frimpong & McLean, 2018; Risselada et al., 2014). Similarly, Deutsch and Gerard (1955) offered further insight into informational and normative social influence as two major types of social influence. They shared the view that informational social influence is about accepting information that is acquired within a social setting based on another customer's experience. On the other hand, normative social influence denotes the adaptation of other customers' preferences and expectations in a similar social environment. In the smartphone industry, normative social influence occurs within groups due to the desire of users of specific brands to identify with, or maintain, self-congruency with positive positions considered favourable by group members (Kaplan & Miller, 1987). The symbolic values of brands extend deeper than their role as a signalling device, in that they help consumers to retain a sense of the past, to categorize themselves in society, and to communicate cultural meanings such as social status and group identity (Belk, 1988). Switching occurs when customers are exposed to normative influence; that is, social pressure causes them to accept certain purchase behaviour irrespective of their beliefs and attitudes towards the behaviour. This compares with informational influence in which some customers in a particular group re-evaluate their decisions to switch when other forms of information relevant to the decision are discussed in the same group (Lee, 2009).

Functional Utility and Consumer Switching Behaviour

Switching happens at the point where customers are driven to consider available alternatives (Appiah et al., 2017; Seiders & Tigert, 1997). Therefore, brand switching may be defined as an act of showing loyalty to a product or service, but opting for an alternative as a result of dissatisfaction. This is further supported by Biedenbach et al. (2015) who found that satisfaction is crucial in order to retain customers. Therefore, management needs to constantly evaluate and redirect its resources and capabilities in order to maintain a strong position relative to competitors (Itami & Roehl, 1987).

Consumer loyalty is defined as the degree to which a consumer exhibits repeat purchasing behaviour from a service provider, possesses a positive attitudinal disposition toward the provider, and considers using only this provider when a need for the service arises (Gremler & Brown, 1996; O'Keeffe et al., 2016; Ozuem et al., 2016). Losing a consumer is a serious setback for a firm in terms of its present and future earnings. In addition to losing the benefits discussed above, the firm needs to invest resources in attracting new consumers to replace the ones it has lost, and this incurs expenditure on advertising, promotions and initial discounts. Peters (1987) suggested it can cost five times more to acquire a new consumer than to retain an old one. Consequently, retaining an established current consumer base is much more attractive and viable than searching for new consumers.

Product characteristics, such as innovation in product contexts with a large number of available alternatives and a short inter-purchase frequency, are likely to affect the exploratory tendencies of brand switching proponents (Hoyer & Ridgway, 1984). Exploratory tendencies are likely to be influenced by product involvement, perceived risk, brand loyalty, perceived brand differentiation/similarity, hedonism (or pleasure) and strength of preference (Hoyer & Ridgway, 1984; Van Trijp et al., 1996). When individuals are highly involved with a product and loyal to a brand, their propensity to switch is likely to be lower (Sloot et al., 2005).

Individuals who are involved with a product have "a narrow latitude acceptance", thus they are unlikely to be persuaded to switch. Similarly, according to Sloot et al. (2005), loyal consumers are less likely to switch to another brand. Persuasion to switch may be manifested in the form of sales promotions, such as offers and discounts, which have been found to encourage switching across various product contexts (Kahn & Louie, 1990).

Further, the perceived level of risk is key and individuals are typically most concerned with losses resulting from their purchases (Mitchell, 1999). High perceived risk leads to avoidance tendencies and behaviours (e.g., commitment to a brand, repeat purchase behaviour) as consumers are "more often motivated to avoid mistakes than to maximize utility in purchasing" (Mitchell, 1999, p. 163). Further, perceived similarity between brands within a product class indicates that individuals are likely to exhibit switching tendencies, such as alternating between familiar brands within a product class (Hoyer & Ridgway, 1984).

Hedonism may also encourage switching within specific categories of products (Van Trijp et al., 1996). Hedonism is associated with the enjoyment or pleasure that an individual derives from specific products (Griffin et al., 2000). Consumers are more intrinsically motivated by products that are associated with affective (hedonic) sensations (Hirschman & Holbrook, 1982); thus, the repeat consumption of such products is likely to elicit switching tendencies (Van Trijp et al., 1996).

Market disruptions are the major cause of brand switching. Market disruptions are major events occurring in a market that threaten customer–brand relationships (Appiah et al., 2016; Fournier, 1998). Disruption is defined as a situation where markets cease to function in a regular manner. This is typically characterized by rapid and large market declines. For instance, disruptions in financial markets are caused by a glut of sellers willing to trade at any price, combined with the near or total absence of buyers at a particular time. In these circumstances, prices can decline precipitously (Shapiro, 2010).

In the financial markets, disruptions can result from both physical threats to the stock exchange or unusual trading. According to a report by Shapiro (2010), concerns over the financial situation in Greece and uncertainty concerning elections in the UK, among other things, constrained the financial market of that time with implications for trading.

Brand Switching from Social Mobility Perspective

Current advances in choice modelling and social identity theory indicate that brand switching also serves sociopsychological purposes apart from functional utility maximization (Rao et al., 2000; Tajfel & Turner, 1979). Per the theory, consumers develop their identity from affiliations with social groups. Their membership of those groups is valued as they feel distinguished from those who are outside the in-group. Lam et al. (2010) stated that when a social identity is perceived in a negative manner, members belonging to the in-group will probably respond by resorting to the following strategic options: social mobility, social creativity and social change.

Social mobility is defined as a consumer's attempt to leave or dissociate himself or herself from a particular group. A typical instance is given of a consumer who decides to move out of a lower status group to one of a higher status (Lam et al., 2010). Social creativity refers to a person's attempt to "seek positive distinctiveness for the in-group by redefining or altering the elements of the comparative situation" (Tajfel & Turner, 1979, p. 43). An instance is when a business school which is not performing well academically compared to another school in the same category, may seek to align and compare itself with another business school over which it has superiority in another dimension (Elsbach & Kramer, 1996). Finally, social change is direct competition with the out-group to recover higher status. From a marketing perspective, social change can be instigated either by competitors or by consumers who identify with a specific brand. Market disruptions initiated by competitors (e.g., innovative brands) can be perceived as attempts to initiate social change between competitors to vie for favour among customers. Some customers may perceive a new brand (a luxury brand, in this context) as possessing a more attractive identity than the incumbent's identity. From the customer's perspective, brand identifiers in some cases proactively cultivate negative word of mouth, especially of brands that they do not identify with, after being exposed to comparative advertising. Based on social identity theory, it can be argued that customers may switch to a new brand for self-enhancement purposes and to maximize sociopsychological utility (e.g., symbolic benefits) rather than for reasons associated with functional utility (e.g., functional benefits).

Conclusions and Managerial Implications

This chapter has substantial managerial implications. First, our exploration of both attitudinal loyalty and behavioural loyalty offers more managerial insights than an examination of either type of loyalty independently. For example, it can be deduced that users of luxury smartphones repurchase specific brands that carry meaning for them, as opposed to just offering product utility. Drawing from the above, it can be argued that particular luxury smartphones that possess distinctive identities have the potential to win the attention of consumers and, ultimately, their loyalty.

Accordingly, brand managers should develop and maintain a clear and consistent identity, so that brands can serve as stable references for consumers (Aaker, 1996; Kapferer, 1997). A widely held belief is that a stable brand identity can help firms navigate and adapt to market changes (Collins & Porras, 1994). In practice, and consistent with this principle, companies seek to stabilize the identity of their brands over time.

These insights will help managers plan their marketing programmes more effectively.

Furthermore, attitudinal loyalty provides more insight into the possible reasons why a customer demonstrates behavioural loyalty. For example, a customer may be driven by functional attributes, quality attributes or simply by price. Attitudinal loyalty measures will help brand managers understand: (1) why, and for what reasons, customers purchase their brands as well as those of their competitors; and (2) the strengths and vulnerabilities of their brands.

The theory of disruptive innovation introduced by Christensen (2013) offers an explanation for the displacement of industry leaders by smaller competitors, which are almost always new entrants (Bower & Christensen, 1995; Christensen, 2013). Disruptive innovation is an innovation that helps create a new market and eventually goes on to disrupt an existing market (Ozuem et al., 2008). The term is used in business and technology literature to describe innovations that improve products or services in ways that markets do not expect; first by designing for a different set of consumers in the new market, and later by lowering prices in the existing market.

According to McGrath and Cliffe (2011), the explanatory power of this theory comes from the notion that industry incumbents and new entrants follow different technology trajectories. Industry leaders tend to focus on sustaining innovations that continuously improve their flagship products and increase their overall performance in attributes that are perceived as being important for their existing customer base. Over time, the performance increase achieved through sustaining innovations begins to overshoot the needs of the best customers who pay the most, whereas the new entrants' disruptive products become good enough to meet the needs of consumers.

REFERENCES

Aaker, D. A. (1996). Measuring brand equity across products and markets. *California Management Review, 38*(3), 102–120.

Ahn, J., Park, J. K., & Hyun, H. (2018). Luxury product to service brand extension and brand equity transfer. *Journal of Retailing and Consumer Services, 42,* 22–28.

Albert, N., & Merunka, D. (2013). The role of brand love in consumer-brand relationships. *Journal of Consumer Marketing, 30,* 258–266.

Appiah, D. (2014). *Building brand loyalty: Identity theory perspective*. Institute of Economic Research (ISBN: 1-932917-12-8).

Appiah, D., & Ozuem, W. (2018a). Resistance to brand switching in the smartphone industry. In N. Ray (Ed.), *Managing diversity, innovation and Infrastructure in digital business*. IGI Global.

Appiah, D., & Ozuem, W. (2018b). Issues with the importance of branding, brand personality and symbolic meaning of brands in the Smartphone Industry. In Z. Zhang (Ed.) *Global information diffusion and management in contemporary society*. IGI Global.

Appiah, D., & Ozuem, W. (2019). *Brand switching: Background to contestable customer–brand relationships*. Global Business and Technology Association.

Appiah, D., Ozuem, W., & Howell, K. E. (2016). *Towards a sustainable brand loyalty: Attitudinal loyalty perspective*. Global Business and Technology Association (ISBN: 978-9951-582-11-7).

Appiah, D., Ozuem, W., & Howell, K. E. (2017). Brand switching in the smartphone industry: A preliminary study. In *Global Business and Technology Association Conference*, Vienna, Austria.

Appiah, D., Ozuem, W., & Howell, K. E. (2019a). Disruptive technology in the smartphone industry: Identity theory perspective. In W. Ozuem & G. Bowen (Eds.), *Leveraging computer-mediated marketing environment*. IGI Global.

Appiah, D., Ozuem, W., Howell, K. E., & Lancaster, G. (2019b). Building resistance to brand switching during disruptions in a competitive market. *Journal of Retailing & Consumer Services, 50*(9), 249–257.

Aurier, P., & Lanauze, G. (2010). Impacts of perceived brand relationship orientation on attitudinal loyalty: An application to strong brands in the packaged goods sector. *European Journal of Marketing, 46*(11–12), 1602–1627.

Ball, D., & Tasaki, L. H. (1992). The role and measurement of attachment in consumer behavior. *Journal of Consumer Psychology, 1*(2), 155–172.

Belk, R. W. (1988). Possessions and the extended self. *Journal of Consumer Research, 15*(2), 139–168. https://doi.org/10.1086/209154.

Bennett, R., & Rundle-Thiele, S. (2002). A comparison of attitudinal loyalty measurement approaches. *Journal of Brand Management, 9,* 193–209.

Berné, C., Múgica, J. M., & Yagüe, M. J. (2001). The effect of variety-seeking on customer retention in services. *Journal of Retailing and Consumer Services, 8,* 335–345.

Berthon, P., Pitt, L., Parent, M., & Berthon, J.-P. (2009). Aesthetics and ephemerality: Observing and preserving the luxury brand. *California Management Review, 52*(1), 45–66. https://doi.org/10.1525/cmr.2009.52.1.45.

Biedenbach, G., Bengtsson, M., & Marell, A. (2015). Brand equity, satisfaction, and switching costs: An examination of effects in the business-to-business setting. *Marketing Intelligence & Planning, 33*(2), 164–178.

Bird, M., Channon, C., & Ehrenberg, A. (1970). Brand image and brand usage. *Journal of Marketing Research, 7,* 307–314.

Bower, J. L., & Christensen, C. M. (1995). Disruptive technologies: Catching the wave. *Harvard Business Review, 73*(1), 43–53.

Bradley, J., Barbier, J., & Handler, D. (2016). Embracing the Internet of things to capture your share of $14.4 trillion. Available at: http://www.cisco.com/web/about/ac79/docs/innov/IoE_Economy.pdf. Accessed March 14, 2016.

Brakus, J. J., Schmitt, B. H., & Zarantonello, L. (2009). Brand experience: What is it? How is it measured? Does it affect loyalty? *Journal of Marketing, 73,* 52–68.

Christensen, C. M. (2013). *The innovators dilemma: When new technologies cause great firms to fail.* Harvard Business School Press.

Collins J. C., & Porras J. L. (1994). *Built to last: Successful habits of visionary companies.* Harper Collins.

Crouch, G. I., Perdue, R. R., Timmermans, H. J. P., & Uysal, M. (2004). *Consumer psychology of tourism, hospitality and leisure* (pp. 275–277). CABI.

Day, G. S. (1969). A two-dimensional concept of brand loyalty. *Journal of Advertising Research, 9,* 29–35.

Deutsch, M., & Gerard, H. B. (1955). A study of normative and informational social influences upon individual judgment. *The Journal of Abnormal and Social Psychology, 51*(3), 629–636. https://doi.org/10.1037/h0046408.

Dick, A., & Basu, K. (1994). Customer loyalty: Towards an integrated conceptual framework. *Journal of the Academy of Marketing Science, 22,* 99–113.

Dimitriades, Z. S. (2006). Customer satisfaction, loyalty and commitment in service organisations: Some evidence from Greece. *Management Research News, 29*(12), 782–800.

Elsbach, K. D., & Kramer, M. K. (1996). Members' responses to organizational identity threats: Encountering and countering the business week rankings. *Administrative Science Quarterly, 41*(3), 442–476.

Fournier, S. (1998). Consumers and their brands: Developing relationship theory in consumer research. *Journal of Consumer Research, 24*(3), 343–373.

Giovanisa, A. N., & Athanasopouloub, P. (2018). Consumer-brand relationships and brand loyalty in technology-mediated services. *Journal of Retailing and Consumer Services, 40*(1), 287–294.

Giovannini, S., Xu, Y., & Thomas, J. (2015). Luxury fashion consumption and Generation Y consumers: Self, brand consciousness, and consumption motivations. *Journal of Fashion Marketing and Management, 19*(1), 22–40. https://doi.org/10.1108/jfmm-08-2013-0096.

Gremler, D. D., & Brown, S. W. (1996). Service loyalty; its nature, importance and implications. In B. Edvardsson, S. W. Brown, R. Johnston, & E. Scheuing (Eds.), *QUIS V: Advancing service quality: A global perspective* (pp. 171–181). ISQA.

Griffin, M., Babin, B. J., & Modianos, D. (2000). Shopping values of Russian consumers: The impact of habituation in a developing economy. *Journal of Retailing, 76*, 33–52.

Hallowell, R. (1996). The relationships of customer satisfaction, customer loyalty, and profitability: An empirical study. *International Journal of Service Industry Management, 7*(4), 27–42.

Hirschman, E. C., & Holbrook, M. B. (1982). Hedonic consumption: Emerging concepts, methods and propositions. *The Journal of Marketing, 46*, 92–101.

Hofmeyr, J., & Rice, B. (2000). *Commitment-led marketing.* Wiley.

Homburg, C., & Giering, A. (2001). Personal characteristics as moderators of the relationship between customer satisfaction and loyalty—An empirical analysis. *Psychology and Marketing, 18*(1), 43–66.

Hoyer, W. D., & Ridgway, N. M. (1984). Variety seeking as an explanation for exploratory behaviour: A theoretical model. In T. C. Kinnear (Ed.), *Advances in consumer research* (Vol. 11, pp. 114–119). Association for Consumer Research.

Hudders, L. (2012). Why the devil wears Prada: Consumers' purchase motives for luxuries. *Journal of Brand Management, 19*, 609–622.

Itami, H., & Roehl, W. T. (1987). *Mobilizing invisible assets.* Harvard University Press.

Jacoby, J. (1971). A model of multi-brand loyalty. *Journal of Advertising Research, 11*(3), 25–31.

Jacoby, J., & Kyner, D. B. (1973). Brand loyalty vs. repeat purchasing behaviour. *Journal of Marketing Research, 10*, 1–9.

Jenkins, R. (2004). *Social identity* (2nd ed.). Routledge.

Jung, J., Hun, H., & Oh, M. (2017). Travellers switching behaviour in the airline industry from the perspective of the push-pull-mooring framework. *Journal of Tourism Management, 59*, 139–153.

Kahn, B. E., & Louie, T. A. (1990). Effects of retraction of price promotions on brand choice behaviour for variety-seeking and last-purchase loyal consumers. *Journal of Marketing Research, 27*, 279–289.

Kapferer, J. N. (1997). *Strategic brand management: Creating and sustaining brand equity long term.* Kogan Page Ltd.

Kaplan, M. F., & Miller, C. E. (1987). Group decision making and normative versus informational influence: Effects of type of issue and assigned decision rule. *Journal of Personality and Social Psychology, 53*(2), 306–313. https://doi.org/10.1037/0022-3514.53.2.306.

Karikari, S., Osei-Frimpong, K., & Owusu-Frimpong, N. (2017). Evaluating individual level antecedents and consequences of social media use in Ghana. *Technological Forecasting and Social Change, 123*, 68–79. https://doi.org/10.1016/j.techfore.2017.06.023.

Keller, K. L. (2009). Managing the growth trade off: Challenges and opportunities in luxury branding. *Journal of Brand Management, 16*(5–6), 290–301. https://doi.org/10.1057/bm.2008.47.

Kumar, V., & Shah, D. (2004). Building and sustaining profitable customer loyalty for 21st century. *Journal of Retailing, 80,* 317–330.

Kuusik, A., & Varblane, U. (2009). How to avoid customers leaving: The case of the Estonian telecommunication industry. *Baltic Journal of Management, 4,* 66–79.

Lam, S. K., Ahearn, M., Hu, Y., & Schillewaert, N. (2010). Resistance to brand switching when a radically new brand is introduced: A social identity theory perspective. *Journal of Marketing, 74*(6), 128–146.

Lee, J. W. (2009). Relationship between consumer personality and brand personality as self-concept: From the case of Korean automobile brands. *Academy of Marketing Studies Journal, 13*(1), 25–44.

Liu, T. C., Wu, L. W., & Hung, C. T. (2007). The effects of inertia and switching barriers on satisfaction-retention relationship: A case of financial service industries. *Journal of Management, 24,* 671–687.

Matzler, K., Strobl, A., Thurner, N., & Füller, J. (2015). Switching experience, customer satisfaction, and switching costs in the ICT industry. *Journal of Service Management, 26*(1), 117–136. https://doi.org/10.1108/JOSM-04-2014-0101.

McGrath, R. G., & Cliffe, S. (2011, January–February). When your business model is in trouble. *Harvard Business Review, 89,* 96–98.

Melumad, S., & Pham, M. T. (2020). The smartphone as a pacifying technology. *Journal of Consumer Research, 47*(2), 237–255. https://doi.org/10.1093/jcr/ucaa005.

Miller, K. W., & Mills, M. K. (2012). Contributing clarity by examining brand luxury in the fashion market. *Journal of Business Research, 65*(10), 1471–1479. https://doi.org/10.1016/jjbusres.2011.10.013.

Mitchell, V.-W. (1999). Consumer perceived risk: Conceptualisations and models. *European Journal of Marketing, 33,* 163–195.

Nam, J., Ekinci, Y., & Whyatt, G. (2011). Brand equity, brand loyalty and consumer satisfaction. *Annals of Tourism Research, 38*(3), 1009–1030.

O'Keeffe, A., Ozuem, W., & Lancaster, G. (2016). Leadership marketing: An exploratory study. *Journal of Strategic Marketing, 24*(5), 418–443.

Okonkwo, U. (2009). Sustaining the luxury brand on the Internet. *Journal of Brand Management, 16*(5–6), 302–310. https://doi.org/10.1057/bm.2009.2.

Oliver, R. L. (1997). *Satisfaction: A behavioural perspective on the consumer.* Irwin/McGraw-Hill.

Oliver, R. L. (1999). Whence consumer loyalty? *Journal of Marketing, 63*(October), 33–44.

Osei-Frimpong, K., & McLean, G. (2018). Examining online social brand engagement: A social presence theory perspective. *Technological Forecasting and Social Change, 128C,* 10–21.

Ozuem, W., Howell, K. E., & Lancaster, G. (2008). Communicating in the new interactive marketplace. *European Journal of Marketing, 42*(9–10), 1059–1083.

Ozuem, W., Thomas, T., & Lancaster, G. (2016). The Influence of customer loyalty on small island economies: An empirical and exploratory study. *J. Strateg. Mark, 24*(6), 447–469.

Peters, T. (1987). *Thriving on Chaos.* Alfred A. Knopf.

PR Newswire. (2015, December 7). Secure spaces incorporated with Fantome Arcane luxury smartphones. *PR Newswire US.* Available at: http://search.ebs cohost.com/login.aspx.

Rao, H., Davis, F. G., & Ward, A. (2000). Embeddedness, social identity and mobility: Why firms leave the NASDAQ and join the New York Stock Exchange. *Administrative Science Quarterly, 45*(2), 268–292.

Ringberg, T., & Gupta, S. F. (2003). The importance of understanding the symbolic world of customers in asymmetric business-to-business relationships. *Journal of Business and Industrial Marketing, 18,* 607–626.

Risselada, H., Verhoef, P. C., & Bijmolt, T. H. A. (2014). Dynamic effects of social influence and direct marketing on the adoption of high-technology products. *Journal of Marketing, 78,* 52–68.

Romaniuk, J., & Huang, A. (2020). Understanding consumer perceptions of luxury brands. *International Journal of Market Research, 62*(5), 546–560.

Romaniuk, J., Bogomolova, S., & Dall'Olmo Riley, F. (2012). Brand image and brand usage: Is a forty-year-old empirical generalization still useful? *Journal of Advertising Research, 52,* 243–251.

Roos, I. (1999). Switching processes in customer relationships. *Journal of Service Research, 2,* 376–393.

Sadeghi, M. A., Mollahosseini, A., & Forgh, M. (2014). A study on the effect of product quality on behavioral and attitudinal loyalty: A case study of SME companies. *Management Science Letters, 4,* 1647–1650.

Seiders, K., & Tigert, D. J. (1997). Impact of market entry and competitive structure on store switching/store loyalty. *International Review of Retail, Distribution & Consumer Research, 7*(3), 227–247.

Shankar, V., Smith, A. K., & Rangaswamy, A. (2003). Customer satisfaction and loyalty in online and offline environments. *International Journal of Research in Marketing, 20*(2), 153–175.

Shapiro L. M. (2010). *Severe market disruption on 6th May, 2010: Congressional testimony.* Diane Publishing Co.

Sloot, L. M., Verhoef, P. C., & Franses, P. H. (2005). The impact of brand equity and the hedonic level of products on consumer stock-out reactions. *Journal of Retailing, 81,* 15–34.

Smith, A. (2013). *Smartphone ownership.* Pew Research Center.

Tajfel, H., & Turner, J. C. (1979). The social identity theory of inter-group behaviour. In S. Worchel, & W. G. Austin (Eds.), *Psychology of intergroup relations.* Nelson-Hall.

Tynan, C., McKechnie, S., & Chhuon, C. (2010). Co-creating value for luxury brands. *Journal of Business Research, 63*(11), 1156–1163. https://doi.org/10.1016/j.jbusres.2009.10.012.

Uncles, M. D., & Laurent, G. (1997). Editorial: Special issue on loyalty. *International Journal of Research in Marketing, 14,* 399–404.

Van Trijp, H. C. M., Hoyer, W. D., & Inman, J. J. (1996). Why switch? Product category-level explanations for true variety-seeking behaviour. *Journal of Marketing Research, 33,* 281–292.

Vickers, J. S., & Renand, F. (2003). The marketing of luxury goods: an exploratory study—Three conceptual dimensions. *The Marketing Review, 3*(4), 459–478. https://doi.org/10.1362/146934703771910071.

Digital Marketing in Luxury Fashion: From Crisis to Strength

Aster Mekonnen and Liz Larner

INTRODUCTION

Although it is too early to measure the total financial loss of the fashion sector as a result of Covid-19, the pandemic has certainly shaken some key aspects of the luxury industry. While some brands will emerge from the crisis stronger, others will struggle to preserve the integrity of their business (Achille & Zipser, 2020). This will partially depend on how brands respond to short-term need whilst simultaneously planning for a long-term sustainable strategy. Covid-19 is an unprecedented event resulting in one of the biggest economic contraction since World War II (Grech, 2020; He & Harris, 2020; Mazzoleni et al., 2020). The pandemic represents one of the most significant environmental changes in the modern marketing history, which could potentially have a profound

A. Mekonnen (✉)
UAL: London College of Fashion, London, UK

L. Larner
University of Salford, Salford, UK

impact on corporate social responsivity (CSR), consumer ethics, and the basic marketing philosophy (He & Harris, 2020). It has affected every sector of the economy, however due to its discretionary nature, fashion is particularly vulnerable. The average market capitalisation of apparel, fashion and luxury players dropped almost 40% between the start of January and the end of March 2020, which is a much steeper decline than that of the overall stock market (BOF and McKinsey & Company, 2020).

Businesses in the twenty-first century are hugely reliant on the internet to support the growth of their organisations. Whether one should integrate internet technology as part of their business plan is no longer questionable, but rather a matter of how it may be most effectively deployed (Porter, 2001). Digitisation is gaining a prominent position within the marketing mix (Mitterfellner, 2019). The growth of and investment in digital marketing has been exponential. Fashion has been reported to be the largest B2C eCommerce market segment with its global size estimated at US$528.1 billion in 2019 and expected to grow further in the future (Statista.com, 2020). As the internet presents a unique opportunity for brands to strengthen their competitiveness as well as build on their customers experience it is evident that most industries have changed their approach and marketing strategies. The internet presents the ultimate interactive and integrative communications system (Schultz, 1996). It has been a game-changer and going online effectively means brands can go global. For customers that are cash rich but time poor the internet is an alternative channel that could fulfil their desire. The fashion communication landscape has evolved.

One of the most significant contributions of the internet is that of value-added marketing, adding value to the consumer experience by allowing marketers to give them additional information as well as providing accessible services. The concept of 'value' is widely discussed from different perspectives. For the consumer value can be more complex, linked to diverse factors such as the products functional worth, its price and/or the symbolic meaning it holds (Dahl, 2018). Historically, there was resistance from some luxury fashion brands to embark on utilizing the internet for marketing purposes because they felt that e-commerce was not a very luxurious experience. In particular with some luxury heritage brands, there is a misconception that heritage is interchangeable with history rather than representative of the emotional response originally developed in customers (Morley & McMahon, 2011). This has inevitably led to the idea of heritage as static history inhibiting innovation to a degree. Luxury is about the experience, not just the product providing the consumer with a sense of enhanced status or identity through feelings of authenticity, exclusivity, culture and or quality. The internet has presented the industry with a valuable tool to successfully to enhance consumers' relationship with the brand, by involving them in the 'experience', 'personality' and associated lifestyle of the brand. Consumers' needs are evolving rapidly. Contemporary consumers have a greater expectation to engage in a conversation with brands, to express their evolving needs but also to have a shared dialogue. The Covid-19 pandemic, has required more consumers, traditional and contemporary to engage with brands in a digital environment as access to many traditional environments has been restricted. Additionally, during the pandemic we have also seen an unprecedented societal situational and contextual changes, which have had a significant impact on consumer ethical decision. Pre pandemic we saw the growth of environmental concerns, elevated by 'Extinction Rebellion'. Some organizations and individuals within the fashion industry was impacted by #MeToo. Particularly Black Lives Matter gained significant momentum during the pandemic. All of these are likely to continue in the long run, post pandemic, with the change in focus of self to society shifting (Rogers & Cosgrove, 2020). It is argued that "Pre pandemic *consumer centric brand strategy* is now *society centric strategy*. Further, against this new backdrop there are the 4C's of the modern planet community, content, curation and collaboration" (Andjelic, 2020).

In the face of today's rapidly changing environment, with the advent of a technology revolution and the customers' decision-making processes changing, organisations need to take digital integration seriously (Retail Weeks Report, 2014). Companies which master the process of digital integration are 2.5 times more likely to convert their customers (Bughin, 2013). In 2020, the pandemic has forced organisations to adopt to technology rapidly. Satya Nadella's—Microsoft's CEO, holds the view that the crisis has actually brought forward the adoption of a wide range of technologies by two years (Waters, 2020).

Luxury fashion brands who are not fully integrating digital marketing tools to engage their customers risk being left behind. More brands are exploring on how they can do it better rather than shying away from it (Ortved, 2011). Consumer behaviour and expectation in relation to fashion coupled with the level of engagement that social media is able to provide has made this area of innovation in the internet a focal point in several studies relating to fashion marketing (Kim & Ko, 2012; Ortved, 2011; Phan, 2011). Social media which allows and encourages user-generated content such as creating and sharing texts, pictures or videos, and comment on existing content has empowered customers giving them the platform to engage with brands, consequently enhancing their expectation and perception of their brands. Moreover, the luxury industry is continuously expanding, reaching out to and targeting a larger consumer base—while Generation X(Gen X) currently tops the list of luxury consumers it is anticipated that millennials(Gen Y) and Gen Z will account for 45% of the global personal luxury goods market by 2025. With the Gen Y and Gen Z luxury industry are able to easily create a point of contact through the use of social media platforms (Kapferer & Valette-Florence, 2016). Understanding the role that digital plays in these different generations is going to be key to the longevity of luxury fashion brands.

This chapter intends to provide an outlook on the current role of digital marketing in luxury fashion brands and highlight the significance of integrating digital marketing as a key component to drive success and sustainable growth. Mainly through digital connectivity and interaction with customers at a time of such unprecedented crisis. The remainder of the chapter is organised under three key areas: (1) Digital marketing—encompassing the technology behind it and associated digital marketing strategy with the significance of social media highlighted (2) Luxury fashion and digital transformation and (3) Looking at key strategies for luxury fashion at a time of crisis which includes setting objectives, being customer focused and recognising the importance of social media.

Digital Marketing

Aghaei et al. (2012) describes the four generations of the web as follows: Web 1.0 as a web of information connections, Web 2.0 as a web of people connections, Web 3.0 as a web of knowledge connections and Web 4.0 as a web of intelligence connections (the future). Web 5.0 will be about the (emotional) interaction between humans. The internet has grown from strength to strength since its innovation phase 1964–1974 (creation of the fundamental building blocks), through the institutionalisation phase 1975–1995 (when large intuitions were provided funding and legitimisation), up to today's commercialisation phase 1995–present (private corporations take over, expand the backbone of the internet and local services) (Laudon & Travis, 2013). By July 2020 4.57 billion people were active internet users, 4.17 billion unique mobile internet users, 3.96 active social media users and 3.91 active mobile social media users (Clement, 2020). Today, the web provides a tremendous opportunity to reach customers directly. In 2018 it was estimated that global spending on digital marketing will be approaching 100 billion. Top digital activities key to marketing success are the operation of a corporate website, social marketing and digital advertising. Social media is undoubtedly gaining in prominence, with over 86% of internet users now active on social media.

Advances in technology and the evolution of marketing are inseparable. The printing press, radio, television and now the internet are all examples of major breakthroughs in technology that also advanced the field of marketing. Technology has the ability to open up new markets and to radically change existing ones. The rapidness of changes in technology makes it necessary to continuously study consumer behaviour. As soon as one thinks that they may have a grasp on what their archetypal consumer wants, those wants will have changed. In the developed world, the digital revolution is changing the way we choose and buy our products and services. People are now going online on a daily basis to fulfil needs such as banking, shopping, recreation and communication. The role of digital technology in consumers lives has in itself changed from what was once exceptional to now in many cases being utility. Some marketing principles never change, companies must meet the needs of their customers; their need is now access in a digital environment, which is further fuelled by digitally enabled social networking, more commonly known as social media.

The Technology Behind Digital Marketing

The terms internet marketing, e-marketing and digital marketing are often used interchangeably. However, e-marketing is sometimes considered to have a broader scope than internet marketing since it refers to digital media such as web, e-mail and wireless media, but also includes management of digital customer data and electronic customer relationship management systems (E-CRM systems). The term 'digital marketing' was first used in the 1990s and was then described as the marketing of products or services using digital channels to reach consumers (Dorie, 2012). The key objective being to promote brands through various forms of digital media. This implies the use of traditional approaches through a digital medium. Digital marketing now is not a separate activity digital marketing is now simply marketing and the technology is driving shifts in approaches to all aspects of marketing. To help clarify these alternative terminologies and definitions, in collaboration with the Institute of Digital Marketing, Chaffey et al. (2006) proposed an all-encompassing explanation of digital marketing, describing it as an activity that involves the application of technologies which form online channels to market; that's web, e-mail, databases, plus mobile/wireless and digital TV.

The digital age as we know it now began with the internet and the Web 1.0 platforms of the early 1990s. This was a rather static world in which users could get the information they desired but it could not be shared on the web. There was no such thing as interaction, as the only activity was reading of content. In 1993, we saw the entrance of the first clickable banner ad and by the next year online magazine Hotwired had begun to purchase huge numbers of banner ads. This was the first step towards shifting the market into a new digital age.

Web 1.0 then slowly progressed into Web 2.0. This is not a new version of Web 1.0; it is about enhancing how people use technology. People were no longer passively taking in information, but instead the internet became a sort of super-highway where users could directly interact with both other users and businesses, the collaborative potential enabling users to share, interact and communicate via rich media content such as Facebook, Instagram, YouTube, FaceTime, Skype and many more. In the early 2000s, supported by the capabilities of broadband and fibre optics, numerous networks and social platforms were developed. This finally enabled Web 2.0 to become truly social. Social media has now become a thriving entity. There is more to come, from the transition of the digital world towards evolutionary Web tools, shifting from the Web of Communication (Web 2.0) towards the Web of Thought (Web 5.0)—The evolution increases opportunities for organisations as well as providing enhanced forms of communication and immersive virtual experiences for users (Fig. 9.1). Immersive virtual experiences are already being used in luxury fashion, the move from live to virtual fashion shows during the pandemic has driven further innovation.

In the 2000s and the 2010s, as digital marketing continued to get more sophisticated, it became recognised as an effective technology to enable and foster a relationship with more concisely targeted consumers. With this came the need to formulate a strategy specifically tailored to meet the demands of the internet audience. Digital marketing has

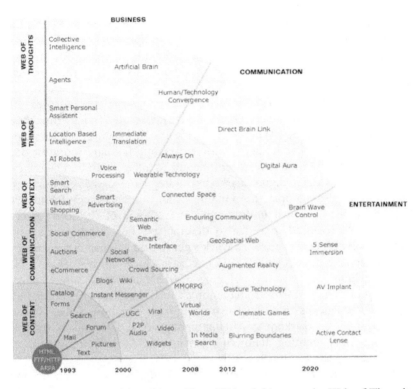

Fig. 9.1 The web of expansion—From Web of things to the Web of Thought (*Source* www.Trendone.com)

changed astoundingly since its conception in the early 1990s and will continue to change.

Digital Marketing Strategy

Stabilizing the business during the crisis is crucial but management must not lose sight of the longer-term considerations when strategizing for the future. Although the term 'strategy' has been used in many different contexts, they are all synonymous in being described as the means to achieve a goal. One simple definition is that it is "a plan of action designed to achieve a long-term or overall aim" (Strauss & Frost, 2014, p. 72). In comparison to traditional strategy, e-business strategy is described as "the deployment of enterprise resources to capitalise on technologies for reaching specified objectives that ultimately improve performance and create sustainable competitive advantage" (Strauss & Frost, 2014). This is inclusive of information technology components such as the internet, digital data, databases, etc.

There are several tools that have been developed or adapted by marketers in their effort to integrate digital marketing strategy into their overall business strategy. When considering the formulation of a strategic plan suitable for online luxury fashion marketing, first and foremost one has to examine the unique features inherent to luxury brands. The review of generic and specific digital marketing strategies, as well as current best practice, can also support the building of an online strategy for luxury fashion brands as it will undoubtedly unveil some of the most essential elements required in order to develop a robust digital marketing strategy. Chaffey et al.'s and Chadwick's generic digital marketing strategy development process (2006, 2012); Chaffey and Smith's 'SOSTAC© Planning Framework for E-Marketing' (2013); and Strauss and Frost's 'E-Marketing Plan' (2014) being amongst such theories. The foundation of these strategies is traditional marketing with common elements such as—assessing the marketplace; defining objectives; selecting a strategic approach; implementing actions or activities; and measuring results or performance (being comparable).

Digital Marketing Strategy with Social Media in Focus—When using social media, setting a clear goal when building a digital marketing and PR plan is important (Scott, 2011). Here, the emphasis is on a buyer orientated focus in the context of the organisational goals and organisations learning as much as they can about their buyers and segment them into groups identified by 'buyers' persona'. This should be the first and single most important step that an organisation needs to take in creating a digital marketing plan. Further, other components such as tactics for the implementation and measurement of the marketing effort and success need to be included in the overall planning. Dahl (2018) pointed out that when planning a social media marketing campaign, the broad stages of the planning process are similar to those for traditional marketing campaigns which include key stages such as analysis, objective setting, strategy decision, details and evaluation.

Luxury consumers are highly social in the digital sense with 80% using social media on monthly basis, 50% being weekly and 25% being daily users. Moreover, they are not passive users, two thirds actively generate varied content on regular basis. This is partly enabled by the accessibility of social media on several applications such as mobile devices, tablets, and computers (Lamberton & Stephen, 2016; Richardson et al., 2016). Utilising social media effectively allows brands to keep up to date with current issues their consumers may be involved in (Arrigo, 2018). Moreover, it provides brands an additional channel to communicate with their consumers as well as enhancing the brand experience through additional information provision (Saravanakumar and SuganthaLakshmi, 2012; Stokinger & Ozuem, 2014).

What is clear from the review is that the digital marketing strategy must support and be integrated with the overall business and marketing plans. The review has also shown that there is no single common approach to building a digital marketing strategy, nor should there be one. But there are essential elements that every marketing strategy must have. This should include, but not be exclusive to, setting digital goals or objectives; analysing the situation; knowing one's customer; setting the strategy and tactics by which to execute it; and having a control mechanism for evaluating performance. To the same effect, one must design a strategy or plan that is well structured and comprehensive in the context of the specified sector.

To explore the issues from the review and current situation in the context of luxury fashion further, this chapter refers to the views of leaders and consultants that are closely involved with the sector globally and locally—Marketing, PR and Management consultants and a Board director. The participants were able to share their views via interviews and focus group discussion. Considering that the UK is one of the top fashion markets in the world and the crisis is a global unprecedented event, the findings are relevant to a wider audience. The UK has been one of the leading fashion retail destinations of the world, at the forefront of fashion innovation (Retail Week, 2014).

Luxury Fashion and Digital Transformation

As with most industry's fashion retail has undergone a major change as a result of innovation which has transformed customers shopping behaviour and their engagements with brand. In light of the intense rivalry that exists in the fashion industry digital integration has given retailers and brands the platform and opportunity to differentiate their offering and gain competitive advantage. A new shopping era which encompasses omni-channel, multichannel and cross-channel has emerged. For many companies, this crisis has been a catalyst for developing and executing an online and omni-channel strategy (Achille & Zipser, 2020).

Whilst luxury brands take up a relatively small share of the fashion market, its impact in terms of sales, influence and leading change in the sector is high. It has seen significant growth since 2013. It was reported that the British luxury sector has grown by 49% in the four years from 2013 to 2017 (Wightman-Stone, 2019). The effect of innovation on fashion marketing of luxury brands in today's digitally enabled and empowered era is an area that needs further exploration. Luxury shoppers are among the most digitally connected of any consumer segment (Timms, 2015). For the average luxury shopper digital experience is a necessity. Yet some brands have shown resistance in embracing digital integration fully (Deloitte, 2016). Hindered by the belief that digital can in no way replicate the in-store exclusive experience, brands such as Channel have been slow to adopt digital marketing. This is possibly due to the added fear of losing brand positioning by breaking with traditions (Okonkwo, 2010). On the other hand, the likes of Burberry have demonstrated that harnessing digital could not only revive a declining profit but can potentially be used to reach new target. Moreover, when targeting new groups, it is important to recognise different generations exhibit varied knowledge and association with the role of digital technology. With social media in particular, as the Marketing Consultant working with luxury brands explained:

> ...With millennials, they know of a time before social media existed, it had novelty and was exciting. For Gen Z it's a utility, it has always been there and it is a core part of their interactions but it doesn't hold the value it does to previous generations. What we've seen with Covid-19 to some extent is all generations relying much more on the digital world, so it has started to become much more of a utility to us all. (Marketing Consultant)

There are five key customer touch points that luxury brands must strive to excel in digital marketing. These are the physical store (preferably located in the city or travel hubs); the person to person interaction option; an established online search; knowledgeable sales people and a well-developed brand website (Remy et al., 2015). Further, to achieve success online luxury brands must try to (1) Redefine what a truly excellent and distinctive luxury experience should be through innovation (2)

Ensure their distinctiveness in the five key customer touch points and (3) Radically rethink their consumer engagement strategy. The above report also indicated the growing importance of social media.

Ko and Megehee's (2012) seminal work in a special issue on fashion of luxury brand highlighted four key issues which significant in the sector: luxury consumer behaviour; luxury status or values; luxury brand management; and luxury brand counterfeiting. In this special issue where the authors reviewed 15 articles, the section on brand management clearly shows the importance of utilising and managing innovation, particularly the social media activities as this is an area that is gaining prominence.

The focus group conducted for this study highlights that it is a transformational period. Understanding the crisis management required following the Covid-19 pandemic; change in consumers' behaviour and value; and recognising the role and reliance on digital across generations is imperative. The excerpt below, further corroborates the points raised above.

> ...We're in a period of transformation and nobody really knows the full impact of that and everyone is looking for what the new business model looks like. We've seen transformation in the way buyers usually buy new seasons, the traditional fashion weeks were taken online, even with some opening up, buyers are more scheduling one to one appointment. (Board Director)

With luxury consumers' being fully digital with raising and evolving expectations, the challenge for luxury fashion brands is high. The online market is anticipated to grow, with 75% of all luxury sales being influenced by digital and expected to go up to 100% by 2025 (Remy et al., 2015). Thus, luxury brands have no choice but to embrace the digital era and become omni-channel. This will inevitably require them to rethink how they should implement both their customer experience and their consumer engagement strategy.

KEY STRATEGIES FOR LUXURY FASHION

Digital became the primary mode of interaction during the Covid-19 crisis. How brands respond at a time of crisis will determine their future. With luxury fashion brands, given the nature of engagement that customer traditionally had, which was predominantly in-store, the challenge is to determine the extent to which marketers were using the internet to enhance consumers experience, improve market positioning as well as keep up with evolving customer need.

Even after stores begin to re-open, companies should be cognisant that the digital step change during the pandemic is an acceleration of innovation. This change demands that companies change their mindset and begin to operate like pure digital organisations: rather than asking what benefits online can offer offline channels, they should ask how their brick-and-mortar presence can support e-commerce sales (BOF and McKinsey & Company, 2020). Digital plan should be prioritised. Concurring with the view above the Board Director of fashion remarked:

> For luxury fashion, people are and will definitely be buying less. This means brands are having to consider what the new business model is. We're seeing growth in areas such as rental, peer to peer and even brands buying back their products on sites to sell themselves. (Board Director)

The remainder of this section is organised under the three key areas which could support the planning of digital marketing strategy for luxury brands at a time of crisis—setting digital inclusive objectives, implementing a customer focused strategy and recognising the importance of social media.

Setting Objectives

In the post-pandemic era, consolidation of the luxury market will only intensify. The goal or objective desired from the digital channel needs to be clearly identified. It is important that organisations build on their overarching objectives. As such, luxury fashion brands should follow the same ethos, as it is an extension of the channel or means by which the organisation reaches existing and new customers. One challenge that luxury brands face in the advent of digital integration is maintaining exclusivity while also avoiding ubiquity.

To create fitting digital marketing objectives for luxury fashion brands, the core value related to the luxury brand under consideration must be re-examined. Society-centric customers are emerging (Andjelic, 2020). Brands need to consider how this can be incorporated with or achieved through digital integration. Brands should consider platforms as a way of preserving their reach and fulfilment capability as for consumers, the rapid pivot to digital will continue long after the immediate crisis (BOF and McKinsey & Company, 2020).

In the past it has been suggested that luxury brands must tell a story that either involves their own history or that they have developed to encourage emotional connection with customers (Kapferer & Bastien, 2009). Heritage brands can potentially have an advantage over competition since there is an increased credibility and feelings of trust because over time the brand has opportunities to build strong 'brand stature' based on consumers' knowledge and familiarity with the brand (Keller, 2009). While heritage is a valuable tool for luxury brands, it runs the risk of being viewed as static history which could in turn impede its ability to redefine and strengthen its brand in current marketplaces such as that driven by innovation. Some key values articulated at the discussion is authenticity and storytelling. Digital marketing is essential in storytelling, a point of difference, it enables brands to engage consumers with their brand proposition. It was pointed out that, *"previously marketing communications was storytelling and with traditional media you can control that conversation but it's a bit of a one-way conversation."* Further, linking it to social media it was highlighted that, *"with social media there's a dialogue, brands can't control the order in which the story unfolds but they are in control of their own story within that conversation. To make that an impactful or meaningful conversation brands need authentic content."* (Marketing Consultant)

A study by user-generated content marketing platform, DeGruttola (2017) revealed that 86% of consumers think authenticity is key when deciding which brands to like and support. Yet, 57% of consumers think that less than half of the brands create authentic content.

An organisation has to ensure that its core value is conveyed to the digital arena, without losing its panache. Ideally the strategy should focus on complementing rather than replicating the offline experience. Objectives informed and led by knowledge of the brands current core values as well as customers evolving expectation, should be one of the key drivers in planning strategy.

Customer Focused Strategy

Consumers' behaviour is changing, in the past luxury was only available to small group of consumers but in recent year the luxury market has expanded serving a wider target. While 'old luxury' focuses on key characteristics derived from features such as status and prestige, the new luxury consumer value the experience of luxury embodied in the goods and services they buy (Danzinger, 2005). For instance, ethical dimension as part of the decision-making process is one value that has been noted recently (Andjelic, 2020).

> Luxury brands that succeed understand their target audiences and we're seeing the transformation as audiences of the more traditional brands are changing. (Management Consultant)

This new aspirational consumer can choose to buy 'up' or 'down', but still requires the prestige and emotional relationship luxury provides (Morley & McMahon, 2011). Understanding these changes and the new boundaries is important to meet the challenges presented and to take advantage of the many opportunities that the digital revolution has provided the luxury market. For instance, the use of social media has paved the way for brands to co-create with their consumers (Arrigo, 2018; Hollebeek et al., 2014). Further, customers are now expecting authenticity, the sector is in a transition phase—"*much from a corporate perspective has been driven by the bottom line. We're starting to see the triple bottom line being used. Brands are recognising the importance of environmental and sustainable issues which could be key to their survival.*" (Board Director)

With digitisation, the main focus should be to create an online experience for customers that is just as exclusive as the process of buying a luxury good instore. As the number of customers shopping online increases luxury fashion brands should pay even more attention on retention strategies since this is likely to increase profit and possibly the market share. To enable success brands need to invest in building appropriate content to serve customers. Recent data on 'Enabling the good life' by sustainablebrands.com (2020) indicates that: 80% of people say they are loyal to businesses that help them achieve the Good Life; 76% believe making a difference in the lives of others is necessary for living the good life; and 89% of consumers believe purpose is demonstrated through how the company benefits the society (and environment). These customers want to see action brands take that could contribute to their loyalty, they expect brands to share their impact through all touchpoints. During Covid-19 pandemic, due to the lockdown and other restrictions-imposed consumers have cultivated some habits, particularly relating to increasingly salient role of the ethical dimension in their decision making. Some of these habits will likely stick or even fundamentally shift towards more responsible and prosocial consumption (He & Harris 2020). Pre-pandemic consumer-centric brand strategy is now society-centric strategy, with the 4C's as the new backdrop of the modern planet: community, content, curation and collaboration (Andjelic, 2020). In the discussion, the Marketing Consultant working with luxury brands explained that *"The other aspect of this is the authenticity of the content that brands can then share... perception of lifestyle is important. Customers care or want to be seen to care about issues that matter. It'll become the core ingredient to the 'feel good factor' of buying luxury brands"* (Marketing Consultant). In agreement with the above the PR Consultant added:

> Picking up on the feel-good factor, consumers have always wanted to feel good about their purchases whether that's craftmanship, atelier etc. and feel good factor is also now coming from engagement in social issues. (PR Consultant)

Importance of Social Media

The growing importance of social media is reflected by the rise of invest-ment in this area. Brands and in particular luxury brands should have a clear understanding of the role of social media in enhancing customer experience. An investigation on the impact of social media marketing activities on customer equity, in the case of luxury fashion brand, iden-tifies five constructs of perceived social media activities—entertainment, interaction, trendiness, customisation and word of mouth (Kim & Ko, 2012). This study also elicited that social media marketing activities posi-tively affect value equity, relationship equity and brand equity. In support of the above Park and Youn-Kyung (2015) have also found a positive relationship between social media activity and brand loyalty.

In recent years social media's role in raising awareness and enabling users to share values and opinions on a wide range of issues has elevated its importance further. Social media has been transformational. For example, consumers not only expect the organisation to exhibit some cooperate social responsibility, and participate in current issues be it political or envi-ronmental, they expect to see this being shared via social media platforms. As pointed out during the discussion:

> ... Consumer consciousness is possible due to social media, digital world and the platform for communications that this provides. If they didn't exist there wouldn't be global perspective on issues, influencing change for social good and greater social consciousness. (Management Consultant)

Brands must differentiate and set short term as well as long term objectives—conversation needs to be managed and maintained for continuity. This is supported by the discussion participants view on how "*social media's success can be measured in reach and views, but key is engagement .... those that do it well, do it authentically.*" Further, it was pointed out that once an organisation has engaged in an issue, "*the key for them is how they continue to live by that value.*" (Management Consultant)

High consumer trust in a luxury brand based on social media is likely to have a significantly positive impact on their purchase intention, in particular consumers level of trust is increased when they are able to interact with the brand and other consumers on the social media platform (Benson et al., 2019; Kim & Ko, 2010).

> As we know WOM is most effective and most trustworthy and that the role social media plays, whether it's a friend or an influencer you trust, Gen Z take their cues from there. (PR Consultant)

Investment in social media should be thought through carefully. Like any other business strategy, it should be a long-term strategy integrated with the overall business strategy. Its value is clearly visible in relation to how it has been utilised amidst the Covid-19 crisis. Building consumers engagement through social selling and virtual shows is picking momentum. Luxury firms need to develop a clear understanding of what social media could do for them, and define a clear strategy to improve customers' experience and perceptions of their brands on social media (Phan et al., 2011).

Discussions with the group has also shown that action/strategy taken need to be considered at varying levels, "*... one of those is around the familiarity the regular, frequent communications so that you are familiar, known and trusted e.g. regular stories, presence*" and another level could be "*... less frequent bigger hits that have impact, the content that gets shared and takes a brand viral*" (Marketing Consultant). Further, it was pointed out that these actions could be planned or unplanned. Additionally, the 'Marketing Consultant commented that "*Trust doesn't come from volume* *trust comes from source of the information. Brands are learning how to build and establish trust really well and others aren't. Ultimately that will impact on their survival."*

CONCLUSION

Knowledge of established generic strategies for implementing digital marketing may be useful in setting the foundation for luxury fashion brands. However, one has to be aware that specific objectives will need to be aligned with the core values sought from luxury fashion brands and driven by the changing need of the consumer. Luxury brands have historically been very cautious about digital integration. Yet, luxury e-commerce has been gaining traction, with over 4.57 billion people being active internet users, 4.17 billion unique mobile internet users, 3.96 active social media users and 3.91 active mobile social media users (Clement, 2020). Luxury fashion brands who are not fully integrating digital marketing tools to engage their customers risk being left behind. More brands are exploring on how they can do it better rather than shying away from it (Ortved, 2011). Since the start of the pandemic we are seeing change that was in progress being accelerated. Organisations have been forced to adopt to technology rapidly.

World Health Organisation has predicted that the current circumstances surrounding the Covid-19 pandemic are like to stay until at least 2022 (Hayes et al., 2020). Further, in the post-pandemic era, consolidation of the luxury market will only intensify. As Remy et al.'s (2015) report has pointed out currently there is a 14€ billion online market which is anticipated to grow up to 70€ billion by 2025. Furthermore over 75% of all luxury sales today are influenced by digital and this too is expected to go up to 100% by 2025. Thus, luxury brands have no choice but to embrace the digital era and become omni-channel. This will inevitably require them to rethink how they should implement both their customer experience and their consumer engagement strategy.

During the pandemic survival may be a priority. Nonetheless, with the recognition of the significance of digitisation, looking ahead intending to turn crisis into strength is also paramount. In agreement the discussion group participants have stated that *"the luxury brands that will survive and thrive are those that are most advanced and yet adaptable."*

Brands need to consider a long-term strategy that incorporates digital when setting objectives. A customer focused strategy that understands consumers changing value and underlying behaviour must be a key driver. Further, the impact that social media is making must be recognised and utilised to maximise opportunities for sustainable growth. The discussion group participants also pointed out that "*authenticity in sustainability, diversity and inclusion are increasingly key in luxury and those who don't engage will be replaced.*"

With growing interest of luxury fashion brands in providing luxurious value to customers, using social media appears predominant in attracting new customers as well as retaining existing ones. There is growing interest in the use of experiential—digital marketing as a corporate communication strategy in encouraging sales and as a tool for competitive differentiation. As the role of information communication technology in the fashion industry is rapidly growing more and more retailers are now beginning to acknowledge the importance of developing a strategy that combines an online and in-store retail experience, allowing consumers to develop brand loyalty.

REFERENCES

Achille, A., & Zipser, D. (2020). *A perspective for the luxury-goods industry during and after coronavirus.* McKinsey & Company Report.

Aghaei, S., Nematbakhsh, A. N., & Farsani, H. K., (2012). Evolution of the World Wide Web: From Web 1.0 to Web 4.0. *International Journal of Web & Semantic Technology (IJWesT), 3*(1), 1–10.

Andjelic, A. (2020). *The business of aspiration: How social, cultural, and environmental capital changes.* Routledge.

Arrigo, E. (2018). Social media marketing in luxury brands: A systematic literature review and implications for management research. *Management Research Review, 41*(06), 657–679.

Benson, V., Ezingeard, J. N., & Hand, C. (2019). An empirical study of purchase behaviour on social platforms: The role of risk, beliefs and characteristics. *Information Technology and People, 32*(04), 876–896.

Bughin, J. (2013). Brand success in the era of digital Darwinism. *Journal of Brand Strategy, 2*(4), 355–365.

Business of Fashion—BOF and McKinsey & Company Report. (2020). The State of Fashion 2020 Coronavirus update.

Chaffey, D., Ellis-Chadwick, F., Johnson, K., & Mayer, R. (2006). *Internet marketing strategy, implementation and practice* (3rd ed.). Prentice Hall FT.

Chaffey, D., Ellis-Chadwick, F., Johnson, K., & Mayer, R. (2012). *Internet marketing strategy, implementation and practice* (5th ed.). Prentice Hall FT.

Chaffey, D., & Smith, P. R. (2013). *EMarketing excellence planning and optimizing your digital marketing* (4th ed.). Routledge.

Clement, J., & Statista Digital Market Outlook. (2020). *Worldwide digital population as of July 2020.* https://www.statista.com/. Accessed July 8, 2020.

Dahl, S. (2018). *Social media marketing—Theories & applications* (2nd ed.). Sage.

Danziger, P. N. (2005). *Let them eat cake; marketing luxury to the masses—As well as the classes.* Dearborn Trade Publishing.

DeGruttola, M. (2017). *Consumer content report: Influence in the digital age.* https://stackla.com/resources/press-releases/stackla-survey-finds-authentic ity-drives-brand-affinity-and-consumer-created-content-influences-purchases/.

Deloitte. (2016). Global powers of luxury goods 2016—Disciplined innovation.

Dorie, C. (2012). The end of the expert: Why no one in marketing knows what they are doing. *News Archive.* Retrieved November 11, 2013 from http://www.forbes.com.

'Enabling the good life' by sustainablebrands.com. (2020). https://insights.sus tainablebrands.com/full-report/.

Grech, V. (2020, May). Unknown unknowns—COVID-19 and potential global mortality. *Early Human Development, 144.* https://doi.org/10.1016/j.earlhu mdev.2020.105026.

Hayes, G., Stephens, M., & Global Health Security Team. (2020). Coronavirus can be over in under two years, says WHO chief. *The Telegraph.* https://www.telegraph.co.uk/global-health/science-and-disease/coronavirus-news-covid-19-cases-deaths-lockdown-uk-quarantine/. Accessed September 2020.

He, H., & Harris, L. (2020). The impact of Covid-19 pandemic on corporate social responsibility and marketing philosophy. *Journal of Business Research, 116,* 176–182.

Hollebeek, L. D., Glynn, M. S., & Brodie, R. J. (2014). Consumer brand engagement in social media: Conceptualisation, scale development and validation. *Journal of Interactive Marketing, 28*(02), 149–165.

Husted, S. W., & Whitehouse, F. R. (2002). Cause-related marketing via the World Wide Web: A relationship marketing strategy. *Journal of Nonprofit & Public Sector Marketing, 10*(1), 3–22.

Kapferer, J., & Bastien, V. (2009). The specificity of luxury management: Turning marketing upside down. *Brand Management, 16,* 311–322.

Kapferer, J. N., & Valette-Florence, P. (2016). Beyond rarity: The paths of luxury desire. How luxury brands grow yet remain desirable. *Journal of Product and Brand Management, 25*(02), 120–133.

Keller, K. L. (2009). Managing the growth trade off: Challenges and opportunities in luxury branding. *Brand Management, 15*(5–6), 290–301.

Kim, A.J., & Ko, E. (2010). Impacts of luxury fashion brand's social media marketing on customer relationship and purchase intention. *Journal of Global Fashion Marketing, 1*(03), 164–171.

Kim, A. J., & Ko, E. (2012). Do social media marketing activities enhance customer equity? An empirical study of luxury fashion brand. *Journal of Business Research, 65*(10), 1480–1486.

Ko, E., & Megehee, C. M. (2012). Fashion marketing of luxury brands: Recent research issues and contributions. *Journal of Business Research, 65*(10), 1395–1398.

Lamberton, C., & Stephen, A. T. (2016). A thematic exploration of digital, social media, and mobile marketing: Research evolution from 2000 to 2015 and an agenda for future inquiry. *Journal of Marketing, 80*(6), 146–172.

Laudon, K., & Travis, C. (2013). *E-Commerce 2013: Global edition* (9th ed.). Pearson Education.

Mazzoleni, S., Tuchetti, G., & Ambrosino, N. (2020, April 11). *The COVID-19 outbreak: From "black swan" to global challenges and opportunities.* Pulmonology. https://doi.org/10.1016/j.pulmoe.2020.03.002 [Epub ahead of print].

Mitterfellner, O. (2019). *Fashion marketing and communication: Theory and practice across the fashion industry (mastering fashion management).* Routledge.

Morley, J., & McMahon, K. (2011). Innovation, interaction, and inclusion: Heritage luxury brands in collusion with the consumer. In S. Ebel & O. Assouly (Ed.), *Proceedings of the 13th Annual Conference for the International Foundation of Fashion Technology Institutes (IFFTI) Fashion & Luxury: Between Heritage & Innovation,* pp. 1–22.

Okonkwo, U. (2010). *Luxury online: Styles, systems, strategies.* Palgrave Macmillan.

Ortved, J. (2011, September 12). Is digital killing the luxury brand? *Adweek.* http://www.adweek.com/.

Park, H., & Youn-Kyung, K. (2015). The role of benefits of brand community within social network sites. *Journal of Global Fashion Marketing, 6*(2), 75–86.

Porter, M. E. (2001). Strategy and the Internet. *Harvard Business Review, 79*(3), 62–78.

Phan, M. (2011). Do social media enhance consumer's perception and purchase intentions of luxury fashion brands? *The Journal for Decision Makers, 36*(1), 81–84.

Phan, M., Thomas, R., & Heine, K. (2011). Social media and luxury brand management: The case of Burberry. *Journal of Global Fashion Marketing, 2*(4), 213–222.

Remy, N., Catena. M., & Durand-Servoingt, B. (2015). *Digital inside: Get wired for the ultimate luxury experience* (McKinsey Report).

Retail Week's Report. (2014). The future of fashion retailing in a digital age—Land Securities Retail.

Richardson, P. S., Choong, P., & Parker, M. (2016). Social media marketing: Theory and research propositions. *Journal of Marketing Development and Competitiveness, 10*(02), 24–34.

Rogers, K., & Cosgrove, A. (2020, April 16). *Future Consumer Index: How COVID-19 is changing consumer behaviors.* https://www.ey.com/. Accessed July 2020.

Saravanakumar, M., & SuganthaLakshmi, T. (2012). Social media marketing. *Life Science Journal, 9*(04), 4444–4451.

Schultz, D. E. (1996, December 18). *Integration and the Internet.* Marketing News, No. 12.

Scott, D. M. (2011). *The new rules of marketing & PR.* Wiley.

Strauss, J., & Frost, R. (2014). *E-marketing* (6th ed.). Pearson Education Limited.

Statista Digital Market Outlook. (2020). *Fashion eCommerce report 2020.* https://www.statista.com/. Accessed July 2020.

Stokinger, E., & Ozuem, W. (2014). Social media and customer retention: Implications for the luxury beauty industry. In *Computer-mediated marketing strategies: Social media and online brand communities* (pp. 200–222). IGI Global.

Timms, M. (2015). *Digital: The one fashion luxury brands can't keep up with.* http://www.theneweconomy.com/.

Waters, R. (2020, May 1). Lockdown has brought the digital future forward—But will we slip back? *Financial Times* www.ft.com. Accessed July 2020.

Wightman-Stone, D. (2019). *British luxury sector has grown 49 percent in four years.* https://fashionunited.uk/news/business/. Accessed July 2020.

CHAPTER 10

The Effect of Social EWOM on Consumers' Behaviour Patterns in the Fashion Sector

Donata Tania Vergura, Beatrice Luceri, and Cristina Zerbini

INTRODUCTION

Word of mouth (WOM) communication is a strategic marketing tool for building relationships with consumers, generating awareness and interest in products, and influencing consumers' purchase behaviour (e.g., Chu & Kim, 2011; Lee et al., 2012). It has been defined as an "oral, person to person communication between a receiver and a communicator whom the receiver perceives as non-commercial, concerning a brand, a product or a service" (Arndt, 1967, p. 3). WOM can involve information and advice seeking when making a purchase (opinion-seeking) or the generation of information and advice by influencers, namely individuals who are able to affect the purchasing decisions of others through their opinions (opinion-giving).

As the world became digital, more and more people went online and started to exchange product information electronically (eWOM), thus influencing other peers' preferences and experiences (Cheung & Thadani,

D. T. Vergura (✉) · B. Luceri · C. Zerbini
University of Parma, Parma, Italy

© The Author(s), under exclusive license to Springer Nature   221
Switzerland AG 2021
W. Ozuem and S. Ranfagni (eds.), *The Art of Digital Marketing for Fashion and Luxury Brands*,
https://doi.org/10.1007/978-3-030-70324-0_10

2010; Huang et al., 2011; Kietzmann & Canhoto, 2013; Ozuem et al., 2008). eWOM can be defined as "the positive or negative statement made by potential, actual, or former customers about a product or a company, which is made available to a multitude of people and institutions via the Internet" (Hennig-Thurau et al., 2004, p. 39). More precisely, there are three types of eWOM: opinion-seeking, opinion-giving and the sharing of third-party information (opinion-passing) (Flynn et al., 1996; Sun et al., 2006). These types of eWOM involve roles which do not have a clear distinction as each person can do all three; there is, though, one factor that is common to these three types, and that is of being based on user-generated content (UGC), namely on consumers' online information generation, distribution and retrieval. As the source of information is perceived natural, genuine and honest, other consumers are led to consider its contents as trustworthy (e.g., Doh & Hwang, 2009; Hornik et al., 2015). Therefore, and similarly to WOM, eWOM emerges as a key driver in the buying process; it has a greater impact on customers' purchasing decisions than other communication channels (e.g., Goldsmith & Horovitz, 2006; Lee et al., 2012). That is the reason why eWOM attracts the attention of scholars and practitioners in marketing; past literature has investigated the impact of eWOM on sales (e.g., Abubakar et al., 2017; Bulut & Karabulut, 2018; Goh et al., 2013; Gu et al., 2012; King et al., 2014; Zhu et al., 2020), the effect of positive or negative online comments/posts/reviews (e.g., Hornik et al., 2015; Hu & Kim, 2018; Yang et al., 2015), and the best strategy to induce consumers' positive eWOM (e.g., Erkan & Evans, 2016; Reimer & Benkenstein, 2016; Yen & Tang, 2019).

In the plethora of Web 2.0 online communication channels, social networks (SNs) stand out because they enhance the information sharing process by allowing consumers to chat in real time with each other; for instance, through the creation of microblogging WOM that increases the speed of data exchange (Hennig-Thurau et al., 2015). The high levels of self-disclosure and social presence of SNs have enabled users to connect with other users by exchanging information, opinions and thoughts about products and brands (Chu & Kim, 2011). Accordingly, they are the perfect tool for eWOM as consumers freely create and share brand-related information in their favourite SNs composed by friends, classmates, colleagues and other acquaintances (Chu & Kim, 2011). This participation in online communities may positively or negatively impact on brand reputation/image and, thus, contribute to the process of branding co-creation (Kamboj et al., 2018). From their side, firms push to increase their presence on SNs (See-To & Ho, 2014) and develop online customer relationship management strategies aimed at engaging consumers and connecting them with brands (Azar et al., 2016; Chang et al., 2017). Among these, those that operate in the fashion sector have recognized the power of eWOM and turned towards marketing communication using social media in order to seize the opportunities of new communication models and survive the challenges of heated competition. This translates into a growing need to investigate consumers' engagement in SNs communication during the product evaluation and purchase process.

Fashion products are particularly apt when studying social media usage as new style trends spread through network effects (Ananda et al., 2019; Easley & Kleinberg, 2010). When they are successfully adopted by a large number of people, they shape the perceived value of the product for other users, either positively or negatively. Moreover, fashion products are often used to build and communicate personal and group identities (Ahuvia, 2005; Wolny & Mueller, 2013). This feature, together with the fact that they can be very expensive, can lead to fashion products being classified as high-involvement goods. This has profound implications for peer-to-peer communications as it has been highlighted that high-involvement goods attract a significant amount of UGC and conversations online (Gu et al., 2012). Social media users often share style-related information with their peers with the expectations of receiving feedback on their stylistic choices and, in particular, on the social value of these choices (Lin et al., 2012). In light of this evidence, a better understanding of what motivates consumers to engage in social eWOM during fashion products' evaluation process and how brands can encourage this engagement is undoubtedly of interest for both academics and practitioners. Although eWOM has received a lot of attention in the academic literature, a deep investigation into the influence of online products' reviews through SNs on consumer's decision-making processes is still needed. Through empirical research built on an online survey with a sample of 230 consumers, this chapter contributes to the literature on the spread of eWOM across SNs and its impact on purchase intention. More specifically, focusing on the fashion context, it investigates the effect of (a) involvement with SNs, (b) social cues, (c) accessibility and (d) informative value of reviews on SNs on social eWOM (opinion-seeking) and, contextually, the importance of eWOM in the pre-purchase decision.

THEORETICAL FRAMEWORK AND CONCEPTUAL MODEL

The study described in this chapter adopted the stimulus-organism-response (S-O-R) model to investigate the determinants of social eWOM, focusing on opinion-seeking and its impact on the intention to buy the reviewed products. This model was developed by Mehrabian and Russell (1974) in the context of environmental psychology. Subsequently, it was applied in many areas of consumer behaviour with the aim of explaining the decision-making process (e.g., Chang et al., 2011; Chebat & Michon, 2003; Eroglu et al., 2001, 2003; Kang & Sohaib, 2015; Kim & Lennon, 2013; Ozuem et al., 2017; Rose et al., 2012). Some of the most recent applications are in the context of online consumer experience (e.g., Emir et al., 2016; Eroglu et al., 2003; Fang, 2014; Islam & Rahman, 2017; Kamboj et al., 2018; Mollen & Wilson, 2010; Qiao et al., 2019; Rose et al., 2012; Yan et al., 2018; Zhu et al., 2020). The S-O-R model postulates that Stimuli from the environment influence individuals' internal reactions (Organism), which in turn lead to some behavioural Responses (Donovan & Rositer, 1982). With reference to consumers' behaviour, the literature conceptualized stimuli as environmental inputs, including marketing mix variables (e.g., atmosphere, accessibility, social cues, customer service, information), which affect the attitudinal response. The organism element involves affective and cognitive reactions of individuals, which influence their final behaviour (e.g., Bagozzi, 1986; Bagozzi et al., 1999; Eroglu et al., 2001; Fiore, 2002; Frow & Payne, 2007; Zhang et al., 2014). It is usually operationalized in terms of perception, experience, evaluation and habits. The outcome in the S-O-R paradigm is the behavioural response, which can be classified as either approach or avoidance (Mehrabian & Russell, 1974). Approach behaviours include all positive actions that might be directed towards a particular setting (e.g., positive communications, intention to purchase or to act), whereas avoidance behaviours reflect the opposite responses, such as negative communications and no intention to purchase.

In order to suit the research objectives of the study, five antecedent variables were proposed as external stimuli (S) capable of influencing social eWOM: (1) involvement with SNs, (2) perceived accessibility of reviews, (3) informative value, (4) homophily and (5) social influence. The selection was made according to the relevant literature and to their expected relevance in the context under investigation. The habit of reading reviews of fashion products on SNs took the role of the organism dimension (O) in the S-O-R model. Meanwhile, the final response (R) is the intention to purchase the reviewed products.

The first focal antecedent is involvement with SNs, measured in terms of time spent in reading and/or posting on SNs. Alhidari et al. (2015) found a significant effect of SNs involvement on consumers' propensity to share their opinion on SNs (opinion-giving). Starting with this evidence, the research aimed to investigate the influence of such a variable on the opinion-seeking dimension of eWOM. A higher involvement with SNs should lead to greater familiarity with social environments and, therefore, should strengthen a consumer's habit of reading fashion products reviews published by other users.

The second set of variables pertained to an individual's evaluation of the accessibility and informativeness of other users' reviews on SNs. Accessibility is the ease of using and understanding the use of SNs to collect information on fashion products, while informativeness represents the perceived value (convenience and usefulness) of reviews on SNs as a source of fashion products information. According to the technology acceptance model, the perceived ease of use and the perceived usefulness of a technology predict individuals' attitude towards accepting it (Davis, 1989). Equally, it is supposed that the perceived ease of use and informativeness of reviews on SNs positively influence the degree of openness towards the reviews and the willingness to read them.

The last set of variables pertains to social cues, measured in terms of homophily and normative social influence. Homophily is defined as the degree to which individuals who interact with one another are congruent or similar in certain attributes (Rogers & Bhowmik, 1970), while normative social influence refers to "the influence to conform to the expectations of another person or group" (Deutsch & Gerard, 1955, p. 629). Prior research has suggested that homophiles tend to share information with one another (e.g., Rogers & Bhowmik, 1970). However, literature on social media has produced mixed results. Mainolfi and Vergura (2019) found a positive effect of homophily on opinion-giving through fashion blogs, while Kim et al. (2018) showed that homophily significantly influences attitude towards eWOM information. By contrast, Chu and Kim (2011) highlighted that information deriving from a socially similar source decreases the degree of involvement with eWOM, for both opinion-seeking and opinion-passing. Whereas susceptibility to social influence was found to have a positive impact on all the three dimensions of eWOM (Chu & Kim, 2011). In order to shed light on the relationship pathways between these variables with reference to fashion products, the present study aimed to test the effect of perceived homophily with SNs' contacts and normative social influence on social eWOM adoption.

The last relation investigated is that between the organism dimension (habit of reading product reviews on SNs) and the behavioural response (intention to purchase the suggested products) conceptualized in the S-O-R model. Torres et al. (2018) found a significant effect of acceptance of eWOM information on consumers' purchase intention, while Alhidari et al. (2015) highlighted that consumers' propensity to share their opinion on SNs is positively related to the intention to purchase products reviewed on SNs. Similarly, Vahdati and Mousavi Nejad (2016) and López and Sicilia (2014) confirmed that eWOM, defined as opinion-seeking and opinion-giving, had a positive effect on purchase intention. In light of this evidence, a significant impact of eWOM adoption on fashion products purchase intention has been assumed.

The proposed structural model is shown in Fig. 10.1.

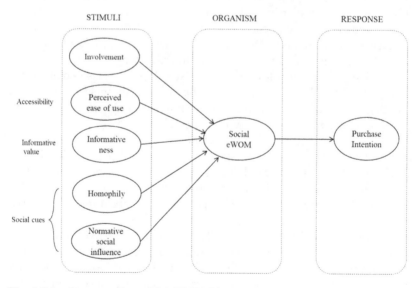

Fig. 10.1 Conceptual model (*eWOM* Electronic word of mouth)

Empirical Research

Data Collection

An online self-administered questionnaire was filled in by a sample of 230 Italian people. All participants were informed that the study was on a voluntary basis and that information provided would be kept confidential. The respondents were first asked about their SNs usage (type and involvement), followed by homophily, perceived ease of use, perceived usefulness and engagement in social eWOM, which were operationalized as opinion seeking, normative social influence and purchase intentions. Finally, demographic information was collected. The items of the questionnaire were adapted from previous research, with some amendments made to fit the context of the present research.

Involvement was assessed using the Alhidari et al. (2015) 7-item scale (see Table 10.1). Homophily was measured through the four items proposed by Kusumasondjaja (2015), while the 8-item scale by Bearden et al. (1989) was used for detecting normative social influence. The items for perceived ease of use were adapted from Glover and Benbasat (2010). The concept of informativeness was assessed using the three items proposed by Taylor et al. (2011). The susceptibility to online product reviews scale by Bambauer-Sachse and Mangold (2011) was used for the measurement of social eWOM adoption (opinion-seeking) . Finally, the scale for purchase intentions was derived from Mikalef et al. (2013). All items were measured on a 7-point anchored scale (from "completely disagree" to "completely agree").

Structural equation modelling with maximum likelihood method was employed for the analysis of the measurement model and of the conceptual model. Data analysis was performed using the IBM SPSS statistical software (SPSS Inc, Chicago, IL; release 25.0) and the LISREL software (release 8.80).

Sample Characteristics

The sample was represented by 70% women and 30% men, with a mean age of 32 (min = 18; max = 63). The respondents were well-educated: 54% had graduated or post-graduated and 38% completed high school; the remaining 8% had left school after the primary or secondary level. Out of the sample, 64% were single, 31% were married or cohabiting and

Table 10.1 Measurement scales and reliability indices

Variables	Items (1 = completely disagree; 7 = completely agree)	CR	AVE	Cronbach's alpha
SNs involvement (Alhidari et al., 2015)	I spend more than 3 hours per day on social networks I update my profile regularly on social networks I post updates of my activities on social networks I comment on my friends' activity, updates and posts I like to get news and other information on social networks I am proud to tell people that I am on social networks Social networks have become part of my daily routine	0.86	0.52	0.86
Informativeness (Taylor et al., 2011)	SNs are a valuable source of fashion products information SNs are a convenient source of fashion products information SNs help keep me up to date on fashion products	0.93	0.83	0.93

Variables	Items (1 = completely disagree; 7 = completely agree)	CR	AVE	Cronbach's alpha
Perceived ease of use (Glover & Benbasat, 2010)	Collecting information on fashion products through SNs is easy to do Learning to collect information on fashion products through SNs is easy The use of SNs to collect information on fashion products is understandable When I collect information on fashion products through SNs, it is easy to do what I want to do It is easy to become skilful in finding information on fashion products through SNs	0.96	0.85	0.97
Homophily (Kusumasondjaja, 2015)	The interests of my contacts on SNs are similar to mine On the SNs, I find ideas similar to mine I share similar tastes with my contacts on SNs I found similarity in likes/dislikes with my contacts on SNs	0.93	0.77	0.94

(continued)

Table 10.1 (continued)

Variables	Items (1 = completely disagree; 7 = completely agree)	CR	AVE	Cronbach's alpha
Normative social influence (Bearden et al., 1989)	I rarely purchase the latest fashion styles until I am sure my friends approve of them	0.95	0.71	0.95
	It is important that others like the fashion products and brands I buy			
	When buying fashion products, I generally purchase those brands that I think others will approve of			
	If other people can see me using a fashion product, I often purchase the brand they expect me to buy			
	I like to know what fashion brands and products make good impressions on others			
	I achieve a sense of belonging by purchasing the same fashion products and brands that others purchase			
	If I want to be like someone, I often try to buy the same fashion products that they buy			
	I often identify with other people by purchasing the same fashion products they purchase			
Social eWOM (Bambauer-Sachse & Mangold, 2011)	I often read other consumers' reviews to gather information about fashion products	0.93	0.76	0.92
	I often read other consumers' reviews to make sure I buy the right fashion product			
	I often read other consumers' reviews to know what fashion products make a good impression on others			
	I often read other consumers' reviews to have confidence in my fashion products' buying decision			

Variables	Items (1 = completely disagree; 7 = completely agree)	CR	AVE	Cronbach's alpha
Purchase intention (Mikalef et al., 2013)	I buy the fashion products reviewed on SNs In the future, I will buy the fashion products suggested by other consumers on SNs My future fashion products purchases will be based on the information I found in SNs I will continue to use reviews on SNs in the future to guide my fashion products purchasing	0.95	0.83	0.95

AVE average variance extracted, CR composite reliability, eWOM electronic word of mouth, SN social network

5% were widowed or divorced. The three most used SNs were Instagram, Facebook and YouTube, followed by Twitter and LinkedIn.

Research Results

As the skew and kurtosis statistics showed that the normality assumption was violated ($\chi^2 = 2533.935$, $p < 0.001$), the model was estimated using the Satorra–Bentler method (Satorra & Bentler, 1994). The fit indices indicated an acceptable overall fit of the measurement model to the data: Satorra–Bentler scaled $\chi^2 = 942.160$, df $= 539$, $p = 0.000$, comparative fit index (CFI) $= 0.986$, root mean square error of approximation (RMSEA) $= 0.057$, non-normed fit index (NNFI) $= 0.984$ and standardized root mean square residual (SRMR) $= 0.049$.

Convergent and discriminant validity were evaluated through the strength and significance of the loadings, the composite reliability (CR), the average variance extracted (AVE) and the Cronbach's alpha (Bagozzi & Heatherton, 1994; Cronbach, 1951). All items loaded strongly and significantly on the hypothesized latent variables, ranging from 0.671 to 0.931. All constructs exceeded the recommended cut-off points for the adequacy of 0.70 for CR (Steenkamp & Van Trijp, 1991) and 0.50 for AVE (Fornell & Larcker, 1981). Finally, the data met Fornell and Larcker's (1981) criterion: the average variance explained by each latent variable was greater than any of the squared correlations involving the variable, suggesting that discriminant validity was achieved. Cronbach's alphas were also used to confirm the scales' internal consistency. The index was very high for each construct, ranging from 0.92 to 0.97.

The results indicated an acceptable fit for the proposed model (Satorra–Bentler scaled $\chi^2 = 950.853$, df $= 544$, $p = 0.000$, CFI $= 0.985$, RMSEA $= 0.057$, NNFI $= 0.984$ and SRMR $= 0.051$). The model explained 57% of variance for social eWOM and 70% for purchase intention. The significant parameters estimates are reported in Fig. 10.2. The analysis of the path coefficients showed that accessibility of fashion products' reviews exerted a significant influence on social eWOM: a higher perceived ease of use of reviews on SNs translates to a greater habit of reading reviews of fashion products ($\beta = 0.397$, $p < 0.05$). By contrast, involvement with SNs and informativeness of fashion products reviews did not have a significant impact on social eWOM adoption. Turning to social cues, both homophily and normative social influence significantly increased the habit of opinion-seeking ($\beta = 0.188$, $p < 0.05$; $\beta = 0.307$,

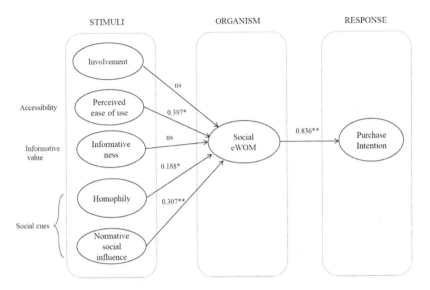

Fig. 10.2 Structural model with standardized coefficients (*eWOM* Electronic word of mouth, *ns* not significant, *p <0.05, **p <0.01)

$p < 0.01$). Finally, a strong relationship emerged between social eWOM and purchase intention ($\beta = 0.836$, $p < 0.01$). Reading fashion products reviews on SNs positively influences a consumer's decision-making process, increasing the intention to purchase those products.

DISCUSSION AND IMPLICATIONS

The major aim of the study was to investigate the factors that can predict consumers' engagement in social eWOM, defined as opinion-seeking, and the impact of engaging in social eWOM on the intention to buy the reviewed product, focusing on fashion products. In the face of the increasing connectivity among SNs users, social eWOM—that is the sharing of content regarding brands/products/venues via online SNs—has also grown. Its pervasiveness and capability to affect users' perceptions of companies and of their products make it a key driver in the buying decision process. Accordingly, both academics and practitioners are interested in exploring consumers' engagement in social eWOM and understanding how to encourage the spread and influence of eWOM.

The research goals were achieved by adopting the S-O-R framework. Results showed that accessibility of reviews on SNs, perceived similarity with the SNs' contacts and susceptibility to social influence positively impact social eWOM adoption. By contrast, involvement with SNs and the informative value of reviews do not translate to a greater habit of reading reviews of fashion products. Finally, the stronger this habit, the greater the intention to purchase the reviewed products.

The study enriches the literature on online products' reviews and provides companies some guidance for the understanding of the role of social eWOM in influencing consumer behaviour.

At the theoretical level, it demonstrates that the S-O-R model is an adequate framework to investigate the decision-making process in the context of social eWOM. Specifically, social cues and perceived ease of use of reviews on SNs represent the environmental inputs that affect the consumers' involvement in opinion-seeking, which in turn influences the intention to purchase the reviewed fashion products.

From a managerial perspective, understanding the role of social eWOM in the consumer–product relationship helps companies to effectively incorporate SNs as an integral and significant part of their marketing communication mix. This is particularly relevant in the fashion industry because peer influence is of great importance. Market trends are created less by established fashion magazines or designers and more by opinion formers who have the power to shape the perception of brands' image and value (Ozuem et al., 2016; Wolny & Mueller, 2013). The findings of the study encourage practitioners to take into consideration the social relationship variables that affect consumers' eWOM behaviours. Community-based ties play a decisive role in creating a persuasive process driven by homophily and normative peer-to-peer influence. The tendencies to be connected to other SN users and to seek social approval appear as significant influencing factors within the process of opinion-seeking and creating purchase intentions. To take advantage of this influence path, companies should employ analytics data to select the more powerful reviews according to the similarity between opinion-giver and opinion-seeker profiles. In this perspective, offering users the ability to autonomously filter reviews according to their preferred parameters would enable the achievement of more effective results. The ease of use of SN channels also stands out as important in the propensity to read reviews. In this perspective, anything that simplifies the move from reading the product review on a social media page to purchasing it on the sales website or through shoppable posts is fit for purpose. By contrast, involvement in SNs does not emerge as a relevant driver in improving consumers' propensity towards social eWOM, at least with reference to the opinion-seeking dimension. This means that familiarity with SNs is not important in persuading users to seek and rely on non-commercial communication in SNs. Even individuals who do not spend much time in posting and updating on SNs have the habit of reading product reviews on this type of social media. This speaks volumes about the current importance of SNs as a source of product and services information. Through eWOM, brands can reach a very large sample of consumers made up of regular and non-regular users of SNs who can both be effectively influenced by other users' content.

Conclusion

In recent years, SNs have gained notable popularity in consumers' information searches and subsequent purchase decisions. From their side, companies and brands have quickly embraced this communication media in order to reap the benefits of direct engagement with customers and peer influence. Indeed, social media platforms are one of the main online channels through which users exchange information and opinions about products and brands. This made social eWOM a key driver in the consumer decision-making process, which can influence products' and brands' image, reputation and equity (e.g., Casaló et al., 2007; Chae & Ko, 2016; Gummerus et al., 2012; Kamboj et al., 2018).

This study aimed at investigating consumers' engagement in social eWOM—measured as search for information—on fashion products. These products were chosen because their consumption is influenced by symbols and images, and often serves to communicate personal and group identities (Ahuvia, 2005; Altuna et al., 2013; Wolny & Mueller, 2013). As SNs are vehicles for self-expression, they are appropriate tools for communicating information about the fashion shopping experience and, in this way, affirming identity and social belonging.

The results confirmed the basic role of eWOM in influencing the purchasing decision-making process and highlighted two main drivers of consumers' habit of reading fashion products reviews on SNs: accessibility and social cues. This means that marketers who want to encourage consumers' engagement in social interaction and induce positive eWOM have to take into consideration the key role of perceived similarity among users and of the seeking of social approval. At the same time, the easy accessibility of reviews is equally relevant. This is an important aspect not only for social networking service providers, who should ensure the ease and understandability of the use of SNs to collect product information, but also for companies and brands, which can facilitate the path from reading the product review to purchasing.

The results of this study are a stepping stone towards future research. Although eWOM emerged as a key resource in influencing and forming behavioural intentions, future research could investigate whether familiarity/involvement with the product/brand might influence the persuasion capability of eWOM and moderate the effect of the stimuli. Moreover, the study focused on the recipient perspective (opinion-seeking) ; however, analysis of the information sender perspective is also valuable (opinion-spreading). Finally, a comparison between different SNs would be opportune in order to explore any differences in the peer influence dynamics.

REFERENCES

Abubakar, A. M., Ilkan, M., Al-Tal, R. M., & Eluwole, K. K. (2017). eWOM, revisit intention, destination trust and gender. *Journal of Hospitality and Tourism Management, 31*, 220–227.

Ahuvia, A. C. (2005). Beyond the extended self: Loved objects and consumers' identity narratives. *Journal of Consumer Research, 32*(6), 171–184.

Alhidari, A., Iyer, P., & Paswan, A. (2015). Personal level antecedents of eWOM and purchase intention on social networking sites. *Journal of Customer Behaviour, 14*(2), 107–125.

Altuna, O. K., Siğirci, Ö., & Arslan, F. M. (2013). Segmenting women fashion magazine readers based on reasons of buying, fashion involvement and age: A study in the Turkish market. *Journal of Global Fashion Marketing, 4*(3), 175–192.

Ananda, A. S., Hernández-García, Á., Acquila-Natale, E., & Lamberti, L. (2019). What makes fashion consumers "click"? Generation of eWoM engagement in social media. *Asia Pacific Journal of Marketing and Logistics, 31*(2), 398–418.

Arndt J. (1967). Word of mouth advertising: A review of the literature. *Advertising research foundation.*

Azar, S. L., Machado, J. C., Vacas-de-Carvalho, L., & Mendes, A. (2016). Motivations to interact with brands on Facebook-towards a typology of consumer–brand interactions. *Journal of Brand Management, 23*(2), 153–178.

Bagozzi, R. P. (1986). *Principles of marketing management.* Science Research Associates.

Bagozzi, R. P., & Heatherton, T. F. (1994). A general approach to representing multifaceted personality constructs: Application to state selfesteem. *Structural Equation Modeling: A Multidisciplinary Journal, 1*(1), 35–67.

Bagozzi, R. P., Gopinath, M., & Nyer, P. U. (1999). The role of emotions in marketing. *Journal of the Academy of Marketing Science, 27*(2), 184–206.

Bambauer-Sachse, S., & Mangold, S. (2011). Brand equity dilution through negative online word-of-mouth communication. *Journal of Retailing and Consumer Services, 18*(1), 38–45.

Bearden, W. O., Netemeyer, R. G., & Teel, J. E. (1989). Measurement of consumer susceptibility to interpersonal influence. *Journal of Consumer Research, 15*(4), 473–481.

Bulut, Z. A., & Karabulut, A. N. (2018). Examining the role of two aspects of eWOM in online repurchase intention: An integrated trust–loyalty perspective. *Journal of Consumer Behaviour, 17*(4), 407–417.

Casaló, L., Flavian, C., & Guinaliu, M. (2007). The impact of participation in virtual brand communities on consumer trust and loyalty: The case of free software. *Online Information Review, 31*(6), 775–792.

Chae, H., & Ko, E. (2016). Customer social participation in the social networking services and its impact upon the customer equity of global fashion brands. *Journal of Business Research, 69*(9), 3804–3812.

Chang, H. J., Eckman, M., & Yan, R. N. (2011). Application of the Stimulus-Organism-Response model to the retail environment: The role of hedonic motivation in impulse buying behaviour. *The International Review of Retail, Distribution and Consumer Research, 21*(3), 233–249.

Chang, S. E., Liu, A. Y., & Shen, W. C. (2017). User trust in social networking services: A comparison of Facebook and LinkedIn. *Computers in Human Behavior, 69,* 207–217.

Chebat, J., & Michon, R. (2003). Impact of ambient odors on mall shoppers' emotions, cognition and spending: A test of competitive causal theories. *Journal of Business Research, 56*(7), 529–539.

Cheung C. M. K., & Thadani D. R. (2010). The state of electronic word-of-mouth research: A literature analysis—Paper 151. *PACIS 2010*, pp. 1580–1587.

Chu, S. C., & Kim, Y. (2011). Determinants of consumer engagement in electronic word-of-mouth (eWOM) in social networking sites. *International Journal of Advertising, 30*(1), 47–75.

Cronbach, L. J. (1951). Coefficient alpha and the internal structure of tests. *Psychometrika, 16*(3), 297–334.

Davis, F. D. (1989). Perceived usefulness, perceived ease of use, and user acceptance of information technology. *MIS Quarterly, 13*(3), 319–340.

Deutsch, M., & Gerard, H. B. (1955). A study of normative and informational influence upon individual judgment. *Journal of Abnormal and Social Psychology, 51*(3), 629–636.

Doh, S. J., & Hwang, J. S. (2009). How consumers evaluate eWOM (electronic word-of-mouth) messages. *Cyber Psychology & Behavior, 12*(2), 193–197.

Donovan, R. J., & Rositer, J. R. (1982). Store atmosphere: An environmental psychology approach. *Journal of Retailing, 58*(1), 34–57.

Easley, D., & Kleinberg, J. (2010), *Networks, crowds, and markets: Reasoning about a highly connected world.* Cambridge University Press.

Emir, A., Halim, H., Hedre, A., Abdullah, D., Azmi, A., & Kamal, S. B. M. (2016). Factors influencing online hotel booking intention: A conceptual framework from stimulus-organism-response perspective. *International Academic Research Journal of Business and Technology, 2*(2), 129–134.

Erkan, I., & Evans, C. (2016). The influence of eWOM in social media on consumers' purchase intentions: An extended approach to information adoption. *Computers in Human Behavior, 61,* 47–55.

Eroglu, S. A., Machleit, K. A., & Davis, L. M. (2001). Atmospheric qualities of online retailing: A conceptual model and implications. *Journal of Business Research, 54*(2), 177–184.

Eroglu, S. A., Machleit, K. A., & Davis, L. M. (2003). Empirical testing of a model of online store atmospherics and shopper responses. *Psychology & Marketing, 20*(2), 139–150.

Fang, Y. H. (2014). Beyond the credibility of electronic word of mouth: Exploring eWOM adoption on social networking sites from affective and curiosity perspectives. *International Journal of Electronic Commerce, 18*(3), 67–102.

Fiore, A. M. (2002). Effects of experiential pleasure from a catalogue environment on approach responses toward fashion apparel. *Journal of Fashion Marketing and Management: an International Journal, 6*(2), 122–133.

Flynn, L. R., Goldsmith, R. E., & Eastman, J. K. (1996). Opinion leaders and opinion seekers: Two new measurement scales. *Journal of the Academy of Marketing Science, 24*(2), 137–147.

Fornell, C., & Larcker, D. F. (1981). Evaluating structural equation models with unobservable variables and measurement error. *Journal of Marketing Research, 18*(1), 39–50.

Frow, P., & Payne, A. (2007). Towards the 'perfect' customer experience. *Journal of Brand Management, 15*(2), 89–101.

Glover, S., & Benbasat, I. (2010). A comprehensive model of perceived risk of e-commerce transactions. *International Journal of Electronic Commerce, 15*(2), 47–78.

Goh, K. Y., Heng, C. S., & Lin, Z. (2013). Social media brand community and consumer behavior: Quantifying the relative impact of user- and marketer-generated content. *Information Systems Research, 24*(1), 88–107.

Goldsmith, R. E., & Horovitz, D. (2006). Measuring motivations for online opinion seeking. *Marketing Science, 23*(4), 545–560.

Gu, B., Park, J., & Konana, P. (2012). Research note-the impact of external word-of-mouth sources on retailer sales of high-involvement products. *Information Systems Research, 23*(1), 182–196.

Gummerus, J., Liljander, V., Weman, E., & Pihlström, M. (2012). Customer engagement in a Facebook brand community. *Management Research Review, 35*(9), 857–877.

Hennig-Thurau, T., Gwinner, K. P., Walsh, G., & Gremler, D. D. (2004). Electronic word-of mouth via consumer-opinion platforms: What motivates consumers to articulate themselves on the internet? *Journal of Interactive Marketing, 18*(1), 38–52.

Hennig-Thurau, T., Wiertz, C., & Feldhaus, F. (2015). Does Twitter matter? The impact of microblogging word of mouth on consumers' adoption of new movies. *Journal of the Academy of Marketing Science, 43*(3), 375–394.

Hornik, J., Satchi, R. S., Cesareo, L., & Pastore, A. (2015). Information dissemination via electronic word-of-mouth: Good news travels fast, bad news travels faster! *Computers in Human Behavior, 45,* 273–280.

Hu, Y., & Kim, H. J. (2018). Positive and negative eWOM motivations and hotel customers' eWOM behavior: Does personality matter? *International Journal of Hospitality Management, 75,* 27–37.

Huang, M., Cai, F., Tsang, A. S. L., & Zhou, N. (2011). Making your online voice loud: The critical role of WOM information. *European Journal of Marketing, 45*(7/8), 1277–1297.

Islam, J. U., & Rahman, Z. (2017). The impact of online brand community characteristics on customer engagement: An application of Stimulus-Organism-Response paradigm. *Telematics and Informatics, 34*(4), 96–109.

Kamboj, S., Sarmah, B., Gupta, S., & Dwivedi, Y. (2018). Examining branding co-creation in brand communities on social media: Applying the paradigm of Stimulus-Organism-Response. *International Journal of Information Management, 39,* 169–185.

Kang, K., & Sohaib, O. (2015). Individual level culture influence on online consumer iTrust aspects towards purchase intention across cultures: A SOR model. *International Journal of Electronic Business, 12*(2), 141–161.

Kietzmann, J., & Canhoto, A. (2013). Bittersweet! Understanding and managing electronic word of mouth. *Journal of Public Affairs, 13*(2), 146–159.

Kim, J., & Lennon, S. J. (2013). Effects of reputation and website quality on online consumers' emotion, perceived risk and purchase intention: Based on the stimulus-organism-response model. *Journal of Research in Interactive Marketing, 7*(1), 33–56.

Kim, S., Kandampully, J., & Bilgihan, A. (2018). The influence of eWOM communications: An application of online social network framework. *Computers in Human Behavior, 80,* 243–254.

King, R. A., Racherla, P., & Bush, V. D. (2014). What we know and don't know about online word-of-mouth: A review and synthesis of the literature. *Journal of Interactive Marketing, 28*(3), 167–183.

Kusumasondjaja, S. (2015). Information quality, homophily, and risk propensity: Consumer responses to online hotel reviews. *Journal of Economic, Business and Accountancy Ventura, 18*(2), 241–252.

Lee, D., Kim, H. S., & Kim, J. K. (2012). The role of self-construal in consumers' electronic word of mouth (eWOM) in social networking sites: A social cognitive approach. *Computers in Human Behavior, 28*(3), 1054–1062.

Lin, T. M. Y., Lu, K., & Wu, J. (2012). The effects of visual information in eWOM communication. *Journal of Research in Interactive Marketing, 6*(1), 7–26.

López, M., & Sicilia, M. (2014). eWOM as source of influence: The impact of participation in eWOM and perceived source trustworthiness on decision making. *Journal of Interactive Advertising, 14*(2), 86–97.

Mainolfi, G., & Vergura, D. T. (2019). The role of fashion blogger credibility, homophily and engagement on followers' intentions to buy fashion products: Results of a binational study. In *Proceedings of the Global Fashion Management Conference,* Paris, 11–14 July 2019.

Mehrabian, A., & Russell, J. A. (1974). *An approach to environmental psychology.* MIT Press.

Mikalef, P., Giannakos, M., & Adamantia, P. (2013). Shopping and word-of-mouth intentions on social media. *Journal of Theoretical and Applied Electronic Commerce Research, 8*(1), 17–34.

Mollen, A., & Wilson, H. (2010). Engagement, telepresence and interactivity in online consumer experience: Reconciling scholastic and managerial perspectives. *Journal of Business Research, 63*(9), 919–925.

Ozuem, W., Howell, K. E., & Lancaster, G. (2008). Communicating in the new interactive marketspace. *European Journal of Marketing, 42*(9–10), 1059–1083.

Ozuem, W., Patel, A., Howell, K. E., & Lancaster, G. (2017). An exploration of customers' response to online service recovery initiatives. *International Journal of Market Research, 59*(1), 97–116.

Ozuem, W., Thomas, T., & Lancaster, G. (2016). The influence of customer loyalty on small island economies: an empirical and exploratory study. *Journal of Strategic Marketing, 24*(6), 447–469.

Qiao, L., Song, M., & Wang, N. (2019). Virtual brand community experience, identification, and electronic word-of-mouth. *Journal of Computer Information Systems*, 1–14.

Reimer, T., & Benkenstein, M. (2016). Altruistic eWOM marketing: More than an alternative to monetary incentives. *Journal of Retailing and Consumer Services, 31*, 323–333.

Rogers, E. M., & Bhowmik, D. K. (1970). Homophily–heterophily: Relational concepts for communication research. *Public Opinion Quarterly, 34*(4), 523–538.

Rose, S., Clark, M., Samouel, P., & Hair, N. (2012). Online customer experience in e-retailing: An empirical model of antecedents and outcomes. *Journal of Retailing, 88*(2), 308–322.

Satorra, A., & Bentler, P. M. (1994). Corrections to test statistics and standard errors in covariance structural analysis. In A. Von Eye & C. C. Clogg (Eds.) *Latent variables analysis: Applications for developmental research* (pp. 399–419). Sage.

See-To, E. W., & Ho, K. K. (2014). Value co-creation and purchase intention in social network sites: The role of electronic Word-of-Mouth and trust—A theoretical analysis. *Computers in Human Behavior, 31*, 182–189.

Steenkamp, J. E. M., & Van Trijp, H. C. M. (1991). The use of LISREL in validating marketing constructs. *International Journal of Research in Marketing, 8*(4), 283–299.

Sun, T., Seounmi, Y., Guohua, W., & Mana, K. (2006). Online word-of-mouth (or mouse): An exploration of its antecedents and consequences. *Journal of Computer-Mediated Communication, 11*, 1104–1127.

Taylor, D. G., Lewin, J. E., & Strutton, D. (2011). Friends, fans, and followers: Do ads work on social networks? How gender and age shape receptivity. *Journal of Advertising Research, 51*(1), 258–275.

Torres, J. A. S., Moro, M. L. S., & Irurita, A. A. (2018). Impact of gender on the acceptance of electronic word-of-mouth (eWOM) information in Spain. *Contaduría Y Administración, 63*(4), 1–19.

Vahdati, H., & Mousavi Nejad, S. H. (2016). Brand personality toward customer purchase intention: The intermediate role of electronic word-of-mouth and brand equity. *Asian Academy of Management Journal, 21*(2), 1–26.

Wolny, J., & Mueller, C. (2013). Analysis of fashion consumers' motives to engage in electronic word-of-mouth communication through social media platforms. *Journal of Marketing Management, 29*(5–6), 562–583.

Yan, X., Shah, A. M., Zhai, L., Khan, S., & Shah, S. A. A. (2018). Impact of mobile electronic word of mouth (EWOM) on consumers purchase intentions in the fast-causal restaurant industry in Indonesia. In *Proceedings of the 51st Hawaii International Conference on System Sciences*.

Yang, K., Li, X., Kim, H., & Kim, Y. H. (2015). Social shopping website quality attributes increasing consumer participation, positive eWOM, and co-shopping: The reciprocating role of participation. *Journal of Retailing and Consumer Services, 24*, 1–9.

Yen, C. L. A., & Tang, C. H. H. (2019). The effects of hotel attribute performance on electronic word-of-mouth (eWOM) behaviors. *International Journal of Hospitality Management, 76*, 9–18.

Zhang, H., Lu, Y., Gupta, S., & Zhao, L. (2014). What motivates customers to participate in social commerce? The impact of technological environments and virtual customer experiences. *Information & Management, 51*(8), 1017–1030.

Zhu, L., Li, H., Wang, F. K., He, W., & Tian, Z. (2020). How online reviews affect purchase intention: A new model based on the stimulus-organism-response (SOR) framework. *Aslib Journal of Information Management.*

RECOMMENDED FURTHER READING

Batra, R., Homer, P. M., & Kahle, L. R. (2001). Values, susceptibility to normative influence, and attribute importance weights: A nomological analysis. *Journal of Consumer Psychology, 11*(2), 115–128.

Kudeshia, C., & Kumar, A. (2017). Social eWOM: Does it affect the brand attitude and purchase intention of brands? *Management Research Review, 40*(3), 310–330.

Lee, E. J., & Shin, S. Y. (2014). When do consumers buy online product reviews? Effects of review quality, product type, and reviewer's photo. *Computers in Human Behavior, 31*(1), 356–366.

Park, D. H., Lee, J., & Han, I. (2007). The effect of on-line consumer reviews on consumer purchasing intention: The moderating role of involvement. *International Journal of Electronic Commerce, 11*(4), 125–148.

Zainal, N. T. A., Harun, A., & Lily, J. (2017). Examining the mediating effect of attitude towards electronic words-of mouth (eWOM) on the relation between the trust in eWOM source and intention to follow eWOM among Malaysian travellers. *Asia Pacific Management Review, 22*(1), 35–44.

CHAPTER 11

Online Service Failure and Recovery Strategies: Examining the Influences of User-Generated Content

Samuel Ayertey, Silvia Ranfagni, and Sebastian Okafor

INTRODUCTION AND BACKGROUND

The rapid rise of the internet, latest technology and smartphones has brought new paradigms to retailing, such that many luxury and fashion retailers engage in online retailing. According to *The Independent* (Graham, 2020), the revenues of the online fashion retailer Asos, which broke through £1 billion in the last four months of 2019, were lifted by a record Black Friday, whereas other retailers were hit hard by the rise of online shopping, resulting in the disappearance of several well-known

S. Ayertey (✉)
University of Plymouth, Plymouth, UK

S. Ranfagni
University of Florence, Florence, Italy

S. Okafor
University of Cumbria, Cumbria, UK

© The Author(s), under exclusive license to Springer Nature   243
Switzerland AG 2021
W. Ozuem and S. Ranfagni (eds.), *The Art of Digital Marketing for Fashion and Luxury Brands*,
https://doi.org/10.1007/978-3-030-70324-0_11

UK high street brands (McGleenon, 2020). Okonkwo (2010) stated that the internet is by far the most effective marketing tool that will propel fashion and luxury businesses forward in the next decade. The internet has become essential to strengthen brand image, break into unconquered areas, achieve the culmination of a series of customer experiences and exemplify overall value. Consequently, the potential for profit online is huge.

The finest customer service is a critical component of the marketing mix to keep customers repurchasing. The proliferation of the internet together with its subgroups has generated a host of opportunities as well as several complexities and challenges, particularly regarding shoppers' expectations of service quality, and service failure (key terms, such as service failure, are defined at the end of this chapter) and recovery (Ozuem et al., 2017).

Depending on the degree of missing knowledge involved, product ambiguity may be an integral aspect of customer decision making in online shopping. Ayertey et al. (2019) argued that this may reflect the need that luxury and fashion customers have to see a product before deciding to purchase it. As a result, fashion brands are constantly at risk of online service failure (Luo et al., 2012). In addition, digital marketing scholars indicated that the online environment presents a higher risk of service failure than the offline environment (Liu & Ji, 2019, Zhu et al., 2013). Given that consumers do not have the ability to evaluate products based on product quality and so on, online returns are expected to hit £5.6 billion by 2023. This phenomenon has hit fashion and luxury brands the hardest because of the importance of fit to online pure plays (Hughes, 2018). Consequently, many customers continue to experience service breakdowns.

Academics and practitioners continually warn about the damaging consequences of service failures for the development of successful and profitable customer relationships (Azemi et al., 2019; Cambra-Fierro et al., 2015). However, despite recognising the benefits of limiting the number of unsatisfactory situations, customer complaints as a result of service failures continue to be the norm, rather than the exception, in most businesses (Zhu et al., 2013). Although there has been extensive research regarding service failure and recovery, we have much to learn. Consider these findings from the sixth annual "Consumer Action Monitor report" of 2019 (Ombudsman Services, 2019) which reported that customer complaints are rising sharply. It further stated that the average number of complaints per person in the UK for 2019 was 4.2 (compared to 2.5 last year) and, despite the rise, many consumers are still not getting what they want from the complaints process. In addition, the report revealed that of the total active complaints in 2019, retail continues to receive the most complaints, both in the online and offline areas (Ombudsman Services, 2019). The report stated that many complaints remain passive in nature with millennials, in particular, sharing their displeasure on social media or with friends and family rather than with the business (Ombudsman Services, 2019). Consequently, companies often struggle to accurately gauge customer frustration or to handle service deficiencies effectively (Harun et al., 2018).

One of the ways consumers interact via social media is through user-generated content (UGC); UGC is media content created by members of the general public, it includes any form of online content created, initiated, circulated and consumed by users (Daugherty et al., 2008). Because social media enables consumers to actively gather information and share opinions, consumers are no longer passive recipients of product information but active generators and distributors of such information in a range of forms (e.g., videos, text, audio). Thus, consumers are able to influence other consumers' consumption activities on a level not previously seen (Accenture, 2015; Ozuem et al., 2008).

The UK Ombudsman Services "Consumer Action Monitor report" showed that the growth in customer appetite for grievances is not balanced by organisational responses to manage such grievances (Ombudsman Services, 2019). Therefore, at the heart of this issue is the need for a clearer insight into customer expectations of organisational restoration efforts. Service recovery in general is a topic that has received a great deal of attention from academics as well as practitioners. Researchers have explored customers' preferred timing of recovery and compensation (Kim & Ulgado, 2012), customers' attitudes towards excessive recovery efforts (Noone, 2012), the impact of various demographic characteristics on recovery preferences (Chung-Herrera et al., 2010) and even the differences between customer involvement in preferences for service recovery (Bambauer-Sachse & Rabeson, 2015) among others. Silber et al. (2009) conducted a study of service failures and recoveries in restaurants; their results suggest that customers tend to forgive technical failures if recovery attempts are made. However, customers may not completely forgive service problems, even when there are subsequent recovery attempts. It appears that various failures require different recovery actions and that, even then, the outcomes may not be favourable, which could lead to negative word of mouth (Weitzl & Hutzinger, 2017). Although extensively studied, these issues are often addressed in discrete streams of research, hindering a comprehensive understanding of the subject matter. In addition, anecdotal reports indicate that companies are experimenting with different recovery approaches and, in particular, are adapting offline recovery methods to new technological tapestries (Azemi et al., 2019).

The authors of this chapter argue that in addition to considering customers' perceptions of service failure and recovery, which separates the service provider from the customer (e.g., Ringberg et al., 2007; Choi & Choi, 2014), customers' interactions with the service provider must also be considered. Furthermore, scholars and practitioners of online failure recovery approaches stress that the digitalised environment no longer permits the isolation of the recovery process in the offline setting (Gruber et al., 2015). Ozuem et al. (2017) also affirmed that the popularity of the online environment has shifted the individualist failure and recovery position of customers to a strategic alliance with providers. Therefore, the challenge is to deal with heterogeneous customers who may respond differently to different complaints handling efforts.

Social influence theory (SIT) proposed that an individual's attitudes, beliefs, and subsequent actions or behaviours are influenced by referent others intentionally or unintentionally (Kelman, 1958). SIT has recently attracted the attention of service failure researchers (such as Schaefers & Schamari, 2016; Sridhar & Srinivasan, 2012) who showed that a customer's attitudes, beliefs and actions can be shaped by UGC and this can have an effect on their perception of a company's recovery efforts.

Extending SIT to explain users' UGC would be a valuable contribution to research. Drawing on SIT, the underlying aim of this chapter is to explore the behaviour of fashion customers in relation to online UGC, and their attitudes towards a firm's response after a negative service experience, which to date is an under researched area, as well as to establish a proper "fit" between a service failure and the recovery effort.

The first part of the chapter discusses the theoretical context, the fashion industry, and service failure and recovery. The second part of the chapter considers strategies to recover difficult online service failures and concludes with a discussion on the implications of the study as well as offering solutions and some conclusions for both marketing professionals and academics.

THEORETICAL CONTEXT

The term social media refers to a group of internet-based applications where UGC can be exchanged, shared and rated (Fox et al., 2018; Israeli et al., 2017). Within the fashion industry, UGC is created in the form of visual imagery on social media networks, such as Instagram. Millennials commonly create photos as a form of UGC (Ana & Istudor, 2019). Kwahk and Ge (2012) stated that many shoppers harness social media and UGC to make key purchase decisions and to acquire information about a brand, product or service. They added that social media interactions can also be a tool to develop fashion trends, which can lead to online purchases.

Before social media became prevalent, communications between managers and customers about customers' unsatisfactory experiences were shared predominantly with the vendor or staff, family and friends, among others. Nowadays, the reality is that such communications can be shared with the general public through various social media platforms (e.g., Facebook, Twitter); some customers use this approach to seek resolution when their service interaction with a business falls short of their expectations (Causon, 2015; Schaefers & Schamari, 2016). Thus, it is important to understand customers' post-service failure postings on social media platforms, since they may be a big influencer on prospective customers who review the content.

The spectacular growth of social media enabled customers to change their roles from passive observers to active participants who create UGC to communicate by electronic word of mouth (eWOM) (Kim & Johnson, 2016; Ozuem et al., 2016). Previously, business marketers were able to influence the opinions of consumers (Viswanathan et al., 2018), but today's consumers influence other consumers as they can interact without the constraints of geographical boundaries. EWOM through UGC contains information, opinions and consumption experiences that can be shared without limits of space and time. In recent years, however, fashion companies have been struggling to maintain a balance in terms of control and in handling the new generations of empowered consumers (Montecchi & Nobbs, 2017). Nevertheless, social media marketing activities enable fashion retailers to gain a powerful insight into consumers' perceptions (Ana & Istudor, 2019).

UGC takes shape when previous buyers share their own experiences online, which allows others, including companies, to read about their experiences. UGC on review websites (Ayeh et al., 2013) is perceived as credible and a rich source of online information, because customers who share their experiences in UGC generally do not seek direct commercial benefits from promoting or discrediting a product (Lee, 2017). It is also argued that online consumers believe users will not only speak about the good sides of a product but also about the negative sides (Fox et al., 2018). A study conducted by Ayeh et al. (2013) showed that customers' eWOM in UGC is undoubtedly one of the most important factors that influence consumers' attitudes, behaviours and decision-making processes, such as purchase intentions or decisions in regards to hotel room bookings, flight tickets and fashion brands. Sparks and Browning (2011) identified eWOM factors that influence consumers' intention to purchase: valence, framing and easy-to-process information of the reviews. Valence can be predominantly positive or negative, that is, it can be an expression of descriptions that are, respectively, pleasant and novel or unpleasant and denigrating (Anderson, 1998). Framing is the manner in which information is presented (Donovan & Jalleh, 1999): research demonstrated that information received first has a greater impact on the impression formed than information coming later (Pennington, 2012). Positive and negative framing can result from information that is positively or negatively valenced (Levin et al., 1998). Easy-to-process information, such as numerical and star ratings, acts as a shortcut in making evaluations and developing judgements (Van Schaik & Ling, 2009). All these factors can contribute to reducing potential consumer uncertainty associated with purchasing decisions, thereby influencing trust in certain products and services: they serve as a means to verify whether expectations stemming from a company's promises find confirmation in consumers' online reviews.

Today, marketers have assisted in a real powershift from the organisation to the consumer. Consumers are now in control of a series of variables which were previously managed by managers (Zhang et al., 2016). It is argued that consumers tend to demand proof of trust and authenticity over quality, fit, aesthetics, realistic representation and so on for fashion brands because they have limited access to evaluate the products before they actually experience them (McKinsey & Company, 2019a).

Existing research also observed that social influence is a crucial factor behind the purchasing decisions that UGC is able to foster (Floyd et al., 2014). In this regard, Wang and Zhang (2012) showed that people's buying decisions are influenced by views shared by their friends. This is called referent power and describes a situation in which people like to identify with popular views held by their friends.

The current discussion of UGC and its relation to buying decisions indicates that the optimum approach to studying this relation is a SIT approach. The central theme of this approach is that an individual's attitudes, beliefs and subsequent actions or behaviours are influenced by referent others through three processes: compliance, identification and internalisation (Kelman, 1958), which are often represented by subjective norm, social identity and group norm, respectively (Shen et al., 2011). SIT was developed and modified by Dholakia et al. (2004). Their model contains two factors which are social identity (identification) and group norms (internalisation). Dholakia et al.'s (2004) social influence model does not contain normative social influence (i.e., subjective norm), which is seen as less significant in their studies. However, subjective norms are significant in the current study because of their role in influencing consumers' purchase behaviours (Kashif et al., 2018; Ozuem et al., 2017). Previous researchers argued that compliance (subjective norms) is a fundamental factor that is associated with developing normative social influence (Kashif et al., 2018). These researchers further suggested that normative social influence has a direct relationship with the conformity and trust dimensions of consumers' purchase-related behaviour. Normative social influence also plays a significant part in the development of purchase intentions through an increase in the individual's trust and benevolence (Nolan et al., 2008). This chapter is innovative because it explores the value and antecedents of UGC and SIT in relation to service failure and recovery strategies in the fashion industry within the setting of online social media.

THE FASHION INDUSTRY

Notably, over the last two decades, the fashion industry has evolved considerably. The demand side is defined by the uncertainty of fashion consumption, with a diversity of quality, price and innovativeness and different consumers' different requirements (Bhardwaj & Fairhurst, 2010). Due to the internet, fashion is everywhere. Every year, the online market grows in both prominence and technological complexity (Donnell et al., 2012). With fashion surpassing sectors such as books, CDs, DVDs and travel in terms of sales, the UK online fashion market is expected to increase and to be worth £29 billion by 2022 (Mintel, 2017). There is, therefore, a promising business prospect for fashion retailers that are focused on optimising the communication of their products to their target audience in a way that meets or exceeds their shopping expectations. A recent study showed that most UK customers shopped for fashion two or three times in a three-month period (Amed & Berg, 2019). Fashion remains an important part of how people define themselves and others and, as such, it is always a powerful tool of influence. Studies revealed that we are more likely to trust and even obey orders from people dressed in suits or uniforms (Sabanoglu, 2020). Helal and Ozuem (2018) under-scored that people try to speak, behave or dress individually in a way that is noticeable and meaningful but that resides simultaneously within the context of their putative group's standards. Overall, the UK fashion industry is of great importance to the UK economy in terms of trade, employment, investment and revenue. Despite the current economic growth, fashion products have short product lifecycles and huge differ-entiation combined with fast shifts in demand and lengthy supply systems (Statista, 2017).

Some academics and practitioners question whether the model of fast fashion can still be sustainable (Fletcher, 2010; Pookulangara & Shephard, 2013). The emphasis on shortened lead times can be justi-fied by certain social and environmental impacts; the vast majority of clothing ends up in landfills, with only 20% of clothes being collected for reuse or recycling at present. The latest figures show that each year 235 million clothing items are sent to landfill in the UK (BBC News, 2019). Two-thirds of customers expect luxury and fashion retailers to be more sustainable and accountable than non-luxury retailers, according to a report by McKinsey & Company (2019b). In addition, the vast majority of these customers (85%) added that they were more bothered about issues of climate change and sustainability than they were a year ago. Fashion retailing has to face new environmental challenges.

Fashion presents itself as a complex industry (Mollá-Descals et al., 2012) that includes several types of companies that are differentiated in terms of strategic positioning, commercialisation of products and brand strategies (see for instance, designer retailers and multibrand retailers). Despite sector complexity, fashion retailers have been recognised as being among the most important international companies (De Angelis et al., 2017), especially with the emergence of fashion retailer super-brands such as Gap Inc. and Gucci. This is the reason (Fraser, 2019), as Jackson and

Shaw (2006) explained, why London Fashion Week (LFW) is a significant event. Extensively documented as one of the "big four" international fashion festivals, it is a vivacious showcase for the UK's industry and talent. Moreover, this event has taken the social media world by storm. In this regard, a study conducted by The Luxury Channel (2020) indicated the magnitude of attention the fashion industry gains from social media. For example, in 2016, stories on the official LFW generated 503,404 mentions of #LFW on Twitter during LFW in September (up 44% since 2015). With the advent of social media, the fashion industry has been vigorously undertaking innovative marketing strategies which continue to influence consumers' attitudes towards brands as well as creating brand equity (Godey et al., 2015).

By the end of 2020, consumer access to fashion brands on social media sites is expected to reach more than one billion users. Additional analyses found younger age groups, 18–34 years, are especially involved in researching products online via social networks as well as for updates on high-end fashion, whereas previous generations reported less percentage of average time spent on social media sites (Globalwebindex, 2020). Being the leading users of social media, the millennial generation outnumbers all age groups. An underlying reason why millennials use social media is to stay connected to real-time events. Brands, consequently, use interactive technologies to reach millennials directly (Helal & Ozuem, 2018; Valentine & Powers, 2013). Millennials actively contribute, share, search for and consume content on social media (Globalwebindex, 2020). Extensive current literature explored social media, but few studies have examined the functioning of social media in the fashion industry, especially in relation to millennials. Helal and Ozuem (2018) accentuated the fact that fashion brands are aware of their power to accumulate followers across social media platforms, which has the potential for content dissemination among millennial communities.

Social media has filtered into the fashion industry because active consumers use social media to interact with brands throughout different phases of a product's lifecycle. Social media integration constitutes granting customers a margin to receive and, above all, contribute to communication about a brand (Ayertey et al., 2019). Prominent luxury brands are embracing social media to increase the credibility of their marketing and to foster close relationships with their customers. For example, the traditional British luxury brand Burberry successfully utilised social media in their marketing campaigns, which were developed to transform the brand identity to innovation (Milnes, 2015). Additionally, Olenski (2017) noted that media outlets have often highlighted the value of user-generated branded content. *Forbes* magazine (Olenski, 2017) recommended that companies "take proactive steps to stimulate the creation of UGC".

Researchers (Tsai & Men, 2013) who have investigated the reasons why users contribute and create brand-related content have identified personal identity, integration and social interaction as major motivations. Many users upload pictures displaying brands in order to express their connection to a brand's image and popularity as well as their inclusion in the social group that uses the brand (Mayrhofer et al., 2020). Fashion continues to be an important angle for ideas.

A crucial disadvantage of online fashion retailing is the lack of tactility and experience a consumer can have with a product prior to purchase. Moreover, no human interactions with store personnel can be made, and visual merchandising is not easily accomplished. In the traditional business setting, consumers could evaluate the quality of products by looking, touching and feeling the products. However, these traditional ways of searching for more information are not available online. Therefore, product uncertainty may be a particularly important dimension in a consumer's online purchasing decision, depending on the degree of incomplete information associated with the product. This uncertainty has been considered a major barrier to online transactions (Luo et al., 2012).

It is widely accepted in the literature that the key to retailing is to understand one's customers (Grewal et al., 2017). In a time of unprecedented retail change and turbulence where customers are constantly adapting their consumption behaviour (Donnell et al., 2012), understanding customer needs and wants has become a matter of survival for fashion retailers of all sizes. New technology and the rise of social media have created more channels through which to complain and greater ease of access. No more calling the company, conflicting options and spending hours on hold while being handed over from representative to representative. Customers can make a complaint online within minutes. An example of this situation is a UK customer's complaint about H&M's "ridiculous" sizing that went viral (Pham, 2017). At every store, sizing is diverse and until you go into the dressing room and try the clothing on yourself, you never really know precisely how something fits. A customer who was usually a size 12, tried on a size 12 dress at H&M but it was far too small, she then tried a size 14 and then a size 16, both were still too small, when she asked for a size 18 she was told it was out of stock. In revenge, the customer posted a witheringly scornful complaint about the clothing company on Facebook. Furthermore, she not only condemned the retail company for its "ridiculous" sizing, but also criticised the store for the emotional distress it could cause to customers who were uncertain about their true size. Her post received more than 3000 likes and 300 shares, which suggests that people worldwide are now aware of H&M's unreliable sizing. This is just an instance of how social media can turn local events into global news. Once negative word of mouth is spread online (e.g., Facebook), users build on each other's comments and the involved company may lose control over the conversation.

From a company's point of view, this is one of the worst ways that customers can complain (Grégoire et al., 2015). Sivakumar et al. (2014) argued that when disgruntled customers air their grievances anonymously, it prevents providers from being able to conceptualise the failure and the customer's expectations of recovery. Stratemeyer et al. (2014) stated that approximately 90–95% of customers, rather than complain about a situation involving a service failure, will simply not return to the service provider. With these findings, service employees can find it problematic to identify disappointment unless the customer "offers" a recognisable sign (Ozuem et al., 2017). Indeed, a company is responsible for returning consumers to a happy state in spite of "self-service" when shopping online (Ayertey & Howell, 2019). This chapter argues that service recovery is a key strategy that can be utilised to help increase customer satisfaction, regardless of the industry setting. Consequently, it is worth exploring how a company can communicate with customers and what recovery strategy it should provide in the event of service failure.

Service Failure and Service Recovery

Service failure is defined as a private service performance that falls below the expectation of one or a few customer(s) (Smith et al., 1999). The notions of service failure and service recovery are almost inseparable (Tax et al., 1998). Some researchers, such as Lastner et al. (2016) and Liu and Ji (2019), argued that hesitating to fix service deficiencies could be costly for service providers and lead to customer displeasure. Consequently, when service failures inevitably occur, providers implement recovery strategies, such as apologising, offering compensation or allowing customers to voice their concerns (Wu et al., 2020). A service recovery is defined as all the actions a firm can take to redress the grievances or loss caused by a service failure.

Service recovery is useful to counteract the negative effects that negative eWOM can generate after a service failure. Verhagen et al. (2013) demonstrated that negative eWOM can have two effects: it reduces a consumer's repatronage intention, that is the intention to buy from the same provider in the future; and, at the same time, it increases a consumer's intention to switch to a competitor. Chevalier and Mayzlin (2006) reported a negative correlation between negative eWOM and sales, evidence that "an incremental negative review is more powerful in decreasing book sales than an incremental positive review is in increasing sales" (p. 346). Sen and Lerman (2007) demonstrated that negative valence impacts differently on different products: it is higher for utilitarian products than for hedonistic ones. In the former, reviews reflect product-related motivations and are the result of cognitive-driven, instrumental and goal-oriented judgements, whereas in the latter, they reflect personal emotions that emerge from affective and sensory experiences of aesthetic or sensorial pleasure.

However, the recovery strategies companies adopt do not always lead to desired outcomes in terms of repatronage intentions, reduced negative eWOM or reconciliation. Furthermore, Harrison-Walker (2019) affirmed that companies that implement recovery strategies are not giving customers what they want, leaving 60% of customers unsatisfied. Zhou et al. (2013) argued that it is the customer who can best determine whether recovery efforts are successful. The authors further pointed out that customer satisfaction is a good measurement of the effectiveness of service recovery efforts. In other words, it is crucial that the recovery actions that the company undertakes should be perceived by the complaining consumers. These actions must generate a perceived justice, which is considered the basis of the effectiveness of service recovery strategies. Perceived justice has been used as a multidimensional construct that includes distributive justice, procedural justice, interactional justice (Homburg & Fürst, 2005) and informational justice (Liao, 2007). Distributive justice concerns the perceived fairness of the complaint outcome (i.e., service provider's apology and compensation) as a reward that can redistribute esteem in exchange relationships. Procedural justice reflects the perceived fairness of the complaint handling process. Prompt answers to consumers' complaints can be seen as a recovery effort that satisfies a need for procedural justice. Interactional justice refers to the perceived fairness of the behaviour that employees exhibit towards complainants. When service personnel are empathic, show interest in the problem and are honest when interacting with customers, then interactional justice can be satisfied. Lastly, informational justice concerns the adequacy of information and communication provided. It is satisfied, when, for example, the service providers are well informed and candid in communication. The better the company is able to generate perceived justice, the more likely a state of equity is restored to the relationship.

Today, the ubiquity of internet access through, for example, smartphones, enables customers to vocalise their dissatisfaction very quickly after a negative service experience. This poses continuous new challenges for the management of negative UGC. UGC-based social media enable individuals to represent their self-selected styles on social webs and have initiated a new mode of consumer–brand communication and engagement (Kenesei & Bali, 2020). For instance, Harris et al. (2006) contended that service recovery strategies, such as an apology, through online interfaces seem less effective than when done offline. Such epistemological orientations restrict the possibilities of adopting online environments. How firms should provide recovery strategies and respond to negative UGC online is another challenging topic waiting for research. Failure recovery literature has traditionally described customer satisfaction as a customer's perception that the recovery process was fair (Gelbrich et al., 2016; Wang et al., 2011). This view is also echoed by Ayertey and Howell (2019), that the understanding of service failure comes down to an individual's expectations of the recovery. While the literature has been enhanced by research into service failure and recovery in online retail (e.g., Azemi et al., 2019; Holloway & Beatty, 2003), financial services (e.g., De Matos et al., 2013; Maxham & Netemeyer, 2002), restaurant/dining/hotel services (e.g., Park et al., 2014; Siu et al., 2013) and airlines (Migacz et al., 2018; Nikbin et al., 2016), the findings have always been inconclusive and associated with unsatisfactory practical utilisation of recovery strategies. As such there is still an unsolved puzzle in the extant research and an additional contribution is essential for it to be understood.

A thorough review of the literature shows that a customer–provider experience of the service failure and recovery approach can be presented in five phases: (1) service failure happens, (2) service recovery expectations are developed, (3) recovery strategy is given, (4) recovery evaluations are created, and (5) customers are interested in post-recovery behaviour

(Gohary et al., 2016; Migacz et al., 2018; Mohd-Any et al., 2019). While customer perception is substantially linked to specific phases of the process (Grewal et al., 2017), dominant definitions in the literature are struggling to describe online customers' failure and recovery experiences, and the extent to which the recovery process needs to be explored, so that it is satisfactorily deciphered, remains unresolved. Mohr et al. (2006) stressed that understanding the customer is about appreciating the above stages. Customers' experiences are related to their particular backgrounds and other descriptive factors.

Almost all of the previous research was developed using context-free generalisations and ontological positivist affirmation. Positivist approaches give limited clarifications of the specific antecedents and process phases associated with service recovery, and view consumer behaviour and reactions as predictable (Lai & Chou, 2015). The literature has concentrated on the customer's point of view and descriptions of the realities faced by customers in the context of service failures and recovery (Choi & Choi, 2014). This would suggest that service failure and recovery strategies are linked as iterative experiences. In addition, the customer's experience during service failure and recovery is anticipated. Accordingly, Miller et al. (2000) showed that some literature on service failure and recovery strategies attempts to attribute expectations of customers in service failures and recovery as objective facts. That being said, the literature points to a number of conflicting and contradictory results, which suggests that customers are heterogeneous and need to be managed subjectively (Azemi & Ozuem, 2016; Cambra-Fierro et al., 2015). Subjectivity contributes to different realities, which are continuously co-created as qualitative researchers clarify (Howell, 2016).

The existing literature on service failures and recovery strategies emphasises the benefits of service recovery, which has been the focus of research. Researchers such as Rust and Oliver (2000) and Cambra-Fierro et al. (2015), however, warn that the outcome of acceptable recovery may be detrimental to the provider of the service. They showed that from a relativist realism position, customers differ and they recommended a common contextual method for service failures and recovery approaches that are specific to customers. In a complex world, and particularly in hypermedia computer-mediated environments, Wiktor (2016) suggested that the world wide web inspires and encourages customers to gain insights and act on extremely individual orientation methods. Furthermore, providers' observations of customers in relation to the recovery of service failures are influenced by the combined experience of the customer and the provider of service.

This chapter suggests that service failure, recovery expectation and evaluation, and post-recovery behaviour are developed through interaction with other social factors, including the provider of the service and other customers. This means that a customer continually accepts new information generated through interactions that complements and/or replaces existing information, such as subconscious motives. This approach considers an online service failure and recovery strategy to be a shared experience between the customer and the service provider, which addresses the research problem. In this approach, customers are regarded as heterogeneous. This chapter presents a comprehensive and contextual conceptualisation of the phenomenon as opposed to the earlier research undertaken by Ringberg et al. (2007), which distinguished the features of customers before service failure happened. Online fashion customers are volatile and there is a strong risk that unexpected online consumer actions could harm a business's finances and reputation.

STRATEGIES TO RECOVER ONLINE SERVICE FAILURES

The multidimensional nature of social media provides great opportunities for service failure recovery (Grégoire et al., 2015). However, a growing consensus across academics and practitioners is that if inappropriate service recovery is provided, social media can pose immense risks to the marketer (Daugherty & Hoffman, 2014). The risk is associated with the speed with which customers' complaints can go viral and the lack of control businesses have over the flow of information (Cox, 2018). In this context, Hajli and Sims (2015) suggested that social media has transferred power from the marketer to the consumers, because one negative feedback or criticism of a brand from a customer is visible to a large audience through social media and review websites. The literature emphasises a persistent online consumer–company relationship that starts long before the service failure happens, rather than one that emerges with the occurrence of the incident. Cox (2018) suggested that if a company communicates online repeatedly, then social media enables both reach and engagement stances, with the former referring to the provider knowing the customer's recovery requirements and the latter referring to a customer's voluntary involvement in the recovery process. Additionally, Grégoire et al. (2015) associated recovery decision making with customers' heterogeneity. They argued that customers differ and suggested that the timing of a customer's engagement in online communication/complaint is associated with the individual's service failure perception and recovery expectation and evaluation. This is in line with the ongoing debate in the literature on offline service failure and recovery strategy (Ringberg et al., 2007; Schoefer & Diamantopoulos, 2009). The epistemological orientation, which undermines customers' individuality, overestimates the comfort of recovery decision making that social media provides.

The literature on offline failure recovery has named customers' voluntary involvement as a co-creation recovery strategy (Bagherzadeh et al., 2020; Dong et al., 2008). In analysing service recovery strategies, the concept of co-creation strategy has received limited attention from online recovery strategy scholars. However, the omnidimensional nature of social media provides great opportunities for online co-creation. The customer does not always convey a recovery recommendation through an online message, yet the message itself is an important source to understand the customer's recovery expectations. Dong et al. (2008, p. 126) defined co-creation as "the degree to which the customer is involved in taking actions to respond to a service failure". Co-creation recovery strategies appear to be more successful than firm recoveries, which in turn are more effective than customer recoveries, particularly in co-created services. Such strategies have led to higher satisfaction, better recovery time management, enhanced repurchase intentions and greater intention to co-create in the future (Bagherzadeh et al., 2020).

The literature on online service recovery has been specifically developed across non-financial recovery strategies, such as acknowledgement, apology, empower the front line, explanation and quick response (Chaffey & Smith, 2017; Harrison-Walker, 2019). Thus, the success of an online recovery strategy is greatly attributed to the service provider's response speed (Pang et al., 2014). Essentially, engagement in conversation with the customer (Chaffey & Smith, 2017) immediately after he/she uploads the complaint shortens the pre-recovery phase. In a recent study in 2018, Clutch surveyed 532 social media users to find out what they expected from companies on social media in the event of a service failure (Cox, 2018). According to the findings, 76% of people expect brands to respond to comments on social media more quickly, 90% of millennials expect brands to respond within a day or less, and 45% would view a brand more positively if it responded to negative comments on social media (Cox, 2018). This indicates that consumers and millennials expect businesses to address or keep up in an age of instant comments, views and communication by responding, acknowledging and contacting the person as quickly as possible. Time is of the essence. The faster the firm responds to the problem, then the better the message the firm sends to customers about the value it places on pleasing its customers. Today, many organisations have representatives that communicate with online customers in real time. Gu and Ye (2014) referred to this activity as online management response. Their study examined online management responses in hotel reviews. According to them, "on average, 23% of customer reviews receive online management responses" (pp. 573–574), the majority of the reviews that received responses were those that went against the company (p. 574). This indicates that company representatives have a tendency to approach dissatisfied customers more than those with better evaluations. This isolation may generate frustration among the latter group. The aforementioned risk is highly possible considering Gu and Ye's (2014) proclamation that 40% of customers read other customers' online reviews prior to posting theirs (p. 574). This highlights that social media is an open source to everyone, and the company is subject to monitoring. However, if the company manages the online communication well, the articulated information may be a well-embedded source for strategic decisions. Instagram is the obvious social media choice for customers of fashion brands (O'Connor, 2018). O'Connor (2018) discussed two dominant fashion brands, Gucci and Prada, who made use of public figures in fashion, namely, Chiara Ferragni, employed by Gucci, and Arielle Noa Charnas, employed by Prada, to meet and engage with a multitude of target audiences. This indicates that influencers can, therefore, be used to establish successful online recovery strategies.

Conclusions and Managerial Implications

The implications for managers are significant, particularly for promoting the never-ending new collections, seasons, runways and campaigns that define fashion businesses. This chapter suggests that because service failure may influence customers' post-recovery attitude and behaviour on social media platforms, finding effective recovery strategies for online fashion customers, especially millennials, is important to improve customers' experiences. As explained by researchers on offline service failure (Ringberg et al., 2007; Schoefer & Diamantopoulos, 2009), customers are highly heterogeneous and unpredictable in recovery evaluations, and a structured approach leads to contradictory research findings and unsatisfactory recovery cases. Thus, a qualitative approach to customers may provide an enlarged explanation of customers' perceptions of online service failure and recovery platforms for fashion brands. Such an epistemological approach seems to have been excluded by many scholars of online service recovery. The literature on offline service failure and recovery strategy indicates the "limited understanding of customers" to be the main indicator of unsuccessful recoveries (Ringberg et al., 2007). Following this line of thought, if fashion retailers leverage social media properly, they will be a step closer to overcoming the key recovery challenges posed by negative UGC. Living and growing up in a digital world gives instant gratification, expression and responses. Sherman (2018) suggested that when millennials take that mindset to the world as a consumer, their mindset does not really change. This chapter delivers substantial indicators for managers in the fashion industry. Anticipating needs for recovery, compensation, apology, confirmatory rapid response to customers and following up have been acknowledged as effective recovery strategies in order to increase consumer satisfaction (Grégoire et al., 2015; Pang et al., 2014). Helal and Ozuem (2018) warned that the expectations and behaviours of the millennial generation have a vast influence on other generations. The findings advise that businesses should have in place practical recovery strategies that they may implement in order to resolve service failures. Expecting employees to be naturals at service recovery is unrealistic. Consequently, it is essential that managers should train employees to respond to disappointed consumers with a recovery strategy in a way that expresses sincere regret for the service failure, as opposed to generic recovery efforts. Such an approach may enhance and enable the process of managerial decision making involving communication choices aimed at strengthening relationships with customers.

Key Terms and Definitions

User-generated content	Content generated by users, for example, messages, videos and written

	reviews that are related to a product or service in some way.
Service failure	Service failure is service performance or a product that does not meet the expectations of a customer.
Recovery strategy	The actions taken by a service provider to overcome a customer's displeasure caused by a service failure, that is, to transform the displeasure of the customer into satisfaction.
Social media	A collection of various social platforms and channels which enables users to connect and engage with other users and content online.
Fashion industry	A global enterprise that involves the production, retail and consumption of clothing.
Social influence theory	Proposes that an individual's attitudes, beliefs or behaviour can be influenced by others through compliance, internalisation or identification.
Electronic word of mouth (eWOM)	Favourable and unfavourable online comments made by social media participants, especially millennials, about a brand, product or organisation.

Acknowledgements Special acknowledgment is given to Professor Wilson Ozuem for his consultation in the research process for this chapter.

References

Accenture. (2015). *Digital business era: Stretch your boundaries* [Online]. https://www.accenture.com/t20151117T010853__w__/nlen/_acnmedia/Accenture/Conversion-Assets/Microsites/Documents11/AccentureTechnology-Vision-2015.pdf. Accessed 10 August 2020.

Amed, I., & Berg, A. (2019). *The state of fashion 2019* [Online]. https://www.mckinsey.com/~/media/McKinsey/Industries/Retail/Our%20Insights/

The%20State%20of%20Fashion%202019%20A%20year%20of%20awakening/ The-State-of-Fashion-2019-final.ashx. Accessed 30 June 2020.

Ana, M. I., & Istudor, L. G. (2019). The role of social media and user-generated-content in millennials' travel behaviour. *Management Dynamics in the Knowledge Economy, 7*(1), 87–104.

Anderson, E. W. (1998). Customer satisfaction and word of mouth. *Journal of Service Research, 1*(1), 5–17.

Ayeh, J. K., Au, N., & Law, R. (2013). "Do we believe in TripAdvisor?" Examining credibility perceptions and online travelers' attitude toward using user-generated content. *Journal of Travel Research, 52*(4), 437–452.

Ayertey, S., & Howell, K. (2019). Service failure and recovery strategy in computer-mediated marketing environments (CMMEs). In W. Ozuem & G. Bowen (Eds.), *Leveraging computer-mediated marketing environments* (pp. 173–192). IGI Global.

Ayertey, S., Bowen, G., & Banor, M. A. (2019). Online service failure and recovery strategies: Creative insights and strategies. In W. Ozuem, Y. Azemi, & E. Patten (Eds.), *Harnessing omni-channel marketing strategies for fashion and luxury brands* (pp. 337–360). Brown Walker Press.

Azemi, Y., & Ozuem, W. (2016). Online service failure and recovery strategy: The mediating role of social media. In W. Ozuem & G. Bowen (Eds.), *Competitive social media marketing strategies* (pp. 112–135). IGI Global.

Azemi, Y., Ozuem, W., & Lancaster, G. (2019). Service failure and recovery strategies in the Balkans: An exploratory study. *Qualitative Market Research: An International Journal, 22*(3), 472–496.

Bagherzadeh, R., Rawal, M., Wei, S., & Torres, J. L. S. (2020). The journey from customer participation in service failure to co-creation in service recovery. *Journal of Retailing and Consumer Services, 54.*

Bambauer-Sachse, S., & Rabeson, L. (2015). Determining adequate tangible compensation in service recovery processes for developed and developing countries: The role of severity and responsibility. *Journal of Retailing and Consumer Services, 22*(c), 117–127.

BBC News. (2019). *Fast fashion: How to make clothes last longer and save the planet* [Online]. https://www.bbc.co.uk/news/newsbeat-47292087. Accessed 20 July 2020.

Bhardwaj, V., & Fairhurst, A. (2010). Fast fashion: Response to changes in the fashion industry. *The International Review of Retail, Distribution and Consumer Research, 20*(1), 165–173.

Cambra-Fierro, J., Melero, I., & Sese, F. J. (2015). Managing complaints to improve customer profitability. *Journal of Retailing, 91*(1), 109–124.

Causon, J. (2015). *Customer complaints made via social media on the rise— The Guardian,* May 21 [Online]. https://www.theguardian.com/media-network/2015/may/21/customer-complaints-social-media-rise. Accessed 13 July 2020.

Chaffey, D., & Smith, P. R. (2017). *Digital marketing excellence: Planning, optimizing and integrating online marketing* (5th ed.). Routledge.

Chevalier, J. A., & Mayzlin, D. (2006). The effect of word of mouth on sales: Online book reviews. *Journal of Marketing Research, 43*(3), 345–354.

Choi, B., & Choi, B. J. (2014). The effects of perceived service recovery justice on customer affection, loyalty, and word-of-mouth. *European Journal of Marketing, 48*(1–2), 108–131.

Chung-Herrera, B. G., Gonzalez, G. R., & Hoffman, K. D. (2010). When demographic differences exist: An analysis of service failure and recovery among diverse participants. *Journal of Services Marketing, 24*(2), 128–141.

Cox, T. A. (2018). *How social media is transforming PR and the consumer-business relationship* [Online]. https://clutch.co/pr-firms/resources/how-social-media-transforming-pr-consumer-business-relationship. Accessed 9 September 2020.

Daugherty, T., Eastin, M. S., & Bright, L. (2008). Exploring consumer motivations for creating user-generated content. *Journal of Interactive Advertising, 8*(2), 16–25.

Daugherty, T., & Hoffman, E. (2014). eWOM and the importance of capturing consumer attention within social media. *Journal of Marketing Communications, 20*(1–2), 82–102.

De Angelis, M., Adıgüzel, F., & Amatulli, C. (2017). The role of design similarity in consumers' evaluation of new green products: An investigation of luxury fashion brands. *Journal of Cleaner Production, 141*, 1515–1527.

De Matos, C. A., Henrique, J. L., & de Rosa, F. (2013). Customer reactions to service failure and recovery in the banking industry: The influence of switching costs. *Journal of Services Marketing, 27*(7), 526–538.

Dholakia, U. M., Bagozzi, R. P., & Pearo, L. K. (2004). A social influence model of consumer participation in network-and small-group-based virtual communities. *International Journal of Research in Marketing, 21*(3), 241–263.

Dong, B., Evans, K. R., & Zou, S. (2008). The effects of customer participation in co-created service recovery. *Journal of the Academy of Marketing Science, 36*(1), 123–137.

Donnell, L., Hutchinson, K., & Reid, A. (2012). Fashion retailing in the new economy: The case of SMEs. *International Journal of Retail & Distribution Management, 40*(12), 906–919.

Donovan, R. J., & Jalleh, G. (1999). Positively versus negatively framed product attributes: The influence of involvement. *Psychology & Marketing, 16*(7), 613–630.

Fletcher, K. (2010). Slow fashion: An invitation for systems change. *Fashion Practice, 2*(2), 259–265.

Floyd, K., Freling, R., Alhoqail, S., Cho, H. Y., & Freling, T. (2014). How online product reviews affect retail sales: A meta-analysis. *Journal of Retailing, 90*(2), 217–232.

Fox, A. K., Bacile, T. J., Nakhata, C., & Weible, A. (2018). Selfie-marketing: Exploring narcissism and self-concept in visual user-generated content on social media. *Journal of Consumer Marketing, 35*(1), 11–21.

Fraser, H. (2019). *London fashion week: Brexit, protest and a new femininity* [Online]. https://edition.cnn.com/style/article/london-fashion-week-highli ghts-autumn-winter-2019/index.html. Accessed 20 July 2020.

Gelbrich, K., Gäthke, J., & Grégoire, Y. (2016). How a firm's best versus normal customers react to compensation after a service failure. *Journal of Business Research, 69*(10), 4331–4339.

Globalwebindex. (2020). *Social media marketing trends in 2020* [Online]. https://www.globalwebindex.com/reports/social. Accessed 20 August 2020.

Godey, B., Manthiou, A., Pederzoli, D., Rokka, J., Aiello, G., Donvito, R., & Singh, R. (2015, June). Luxury brands social media marketing efforts: Influence on brand equity and consumers' behaviour. In *Proceedings of the 2015 global fashion management conference at Florence* (p. 68).

Gohary, A., Hamzelu, B., Pourazizi, L., & Hanzaee, K. H. (2016). Understanding effects of co-creation on cognitive, affective and behavioral evaluations in service recovery: An ethnocultural analysis. *Journal of Retailing and Consumer Services, 31*, 182–198.

Graham, A. (2020). Asos hails £1bn sales in final four months of decade after record Black Friday [Online]. *The Independent*. 23 January 2020. https://www.independent.co.uk/news/business/news/asos-sales-rev enue-record-black-friday-a9298676.html. Accessed 1 July 2020.

Grégoire, Y., Salle, A., & Tripp, T. M. (2015). Managing social media crises with your customers: The good, the bad, and the ugly. *Business Horizons, 58*(2), 173–182.

Grewal, D., Roggeveen, A. L., Sisodia, R., & Nordfält, J. (2017). Enhancing customer engagement through consciousness. *Journal of Retailing, 93*(1), 55–64.

Gruber, D. A., Smerek, R. E., Thomas-Hunt, M. C., & James, E. H. (2015). The real-time power of Twitter: Crisis management and leadership in an age of social media. *Business Horizons, 58*(2), 163–172.

Gu, B., & Ye, Q. (2014). First step in social media: Measuring the influence of online management responses on customer satisfaction. *Production and Operations Management, 23*(4), 570–582.

Hajli, N., & Sims, J. (2015). Social commerce: The transfer of power from sellers to buyers. *Technological Forecasting and Social Change, 94*, 350–358.

Harris, K. E., Grewal, D., Mohr, L. A., & Bernhardt, K. L. (2006). Consumer responses to service recovery strategies: The moderating role of online versus offline environment. *Journal of Business Research, 59*(4), 425–431.

Harrison-Walker, L. J. (2019). The critical role of customer forgiveness in successful service recovery. *Journal of Business Research, 95,* 376–391.

Harun, A., Rokonuzzaman, M., Prybutok, G., & Prybutok, V. R. (2018). How to influence consumer mindset: A perspective from service recovery. *Journal of Retailing and Consumer Services, 42,* 65–77.

Helal, G., & Ozuem, W. (2018). Social identity matters: Social media and brand perceptions in the fashion apparel and accessories industries. In W. Ozuem & Y. Azemi (Eds.), *Digital marketing strategies for fashion and luxury brands* (pp. 326–361). IGI Global.

Holloway, B. B., & Beatty, S. E. (2003). Service failure in online retailing: A recovery opportunity. *Journal of Service Research, 6*(1), 92–105.

Homburg, C., & Fürst, A. (2005). How organizational complaint handling drives customer loyalty: An analysis of the mechanistic and the organic approach. *Journal of Marketing, 69*(3), 95–114.

Howell, K. E. (2016). Paradigm of inquiry: Critical theory and constructivism. In K. E. Howell & K. Sorour (Eds.), *Corporate governance in Africa: Assessing implementation and ethical perspectives* (pp. 29–46). Springer.

Hughes, H. (2018). *Online returns to reach 5.6 billion pounds by 2023, fashion hit hardest* [Online]. https://fashionunited.uk/news/retail/online-returns-to-reach-5-6-billion-pounds-by-2023/2018121740591. Accessed 9 July 2020.

Israeli, A. A., Lee, S., & Karpinski, A. C. (2017). Investigating the dynamics and the content of customers' social media reporting after a restaurant service failure. *Journal of Hospitality Marketing & Management, 26*(6), 606–626.

Jackson, T., & Shaw, D. (2006). *The fashion handbook.* Routledge.

Kashif, M., Zarkada, A., & Ramayah, T. (2018). The impact of attitude, subjective norms, and perceived behavioural control on managers' intentions to behave ethically. *Total Quality Management & Business Excellence, 29*(5–6), 481–501.

Kelman, H. C. (1958). Compliance, identification, and internalization: Three processes of attitude change. *Journal of Conflict Resolution, 2*(1), 51–60.

Kenesei, Z., & Bali, Z. (2020). Overcompensation as a service recovery strategy: The financial aspect of customers' extra effort. *Service Business, 14*(2), 187–216.

Kim, A. J., & Johnson, K. K. (2016). Power of consumers using social media: Examining the influences of brand-related user-generated content on Facebook. *Computers in Human Behaviour, 58,* 98–108.

Kim, N., & Ulgado, F. M. (2012). The effect of on-the-spot versus delayed compensation: The moderating role of failure severity. *Journal of Services Marketing, 26*(3), 158–167.

Kwahk, K. Y., & Ge, X. (2012). The effects of social media on e-commerce: A perspective of social impact theory. In *2012 45th Hawaii international conference on system sciences* (pp. 1814–1823). IEEE.

Lai, M. C., & Chou, F. S. (2015). The relationships among involvement level, service failure, service recovery disconfirmation and customer lifetime value. *Journal of Economics, Business and Management, 3*(4), 452–457.

Lastner, M. M., Folse, J. A. G., Mangus, S. M., & Fennell, P. (2016). The road to recovery: Overcoming service failures through positive emotions. *Journal of Business Research, 69*(10), 4278–4286.

Lee, I. (2017). A study of the effect of social shopping deals on online reviews. *Industrial Management & Data Systems, 117*(10), 2227–2240.

Levin, I. P., Schneider, S. L., & Gaeth, G. J. (1998). All frames are not created equal: A typology and critical analysis of framing effects. *Organizational Behavior and Human Decision Processes, 76*(2), 149–188.

Liao, H. (2007). Do it right this time: The role of employee service recovery performance in customer-perceived justice and customer loyalty after service failures. *Journal of Applied Psychology, 92*(2), 475.

Liu, W., & Ji, R. (2019). Do hotel responses matter? A comprehensive perspective on investigating online reviews. *Information Resources Management Journal (IRMJ), 32*(3), 70–89.

Luo, J., Ba, S., & Zhang, H. (2012). The effectiveness of online shopping characteristics and well-designed websites on satisfaction. *MIS Quarterly, 36*(4), 1131–1144.

Maxham, J. G., III, & Netemeyer, R. G. (2002). Modeling customer perceptions of complaint handling over time: The effects of perceived justice on satisfaction and intent. *Journal of Retailing, 78*(4), 239–252.

Mayrhofer, M., Matthes, J., Einwiller, S., & Naderer, B. (2020). User generated content presenting brands on social media increases young adults' purchase intention. *International Journal of Advertising, 39*(1), 166–186.

McGleenon, B. (2020). *IKEA store closure: Superstore shuts in UK for first time in 33 years—352 jobs at risk* [Online]. https://www.express.co.uk/news/uk/1237648/IKEA-store-closure-Coventry-latest-Sweden-home-store-job-risk. Accessed 4 July 2020.

McKinsey & Company. (2019a). *Fashion's new must-have: Sustainable sourcing at scale* [Online]. https://www.mckinsey.com/industries/retail/our-insights/fashions-new-must-have-sustainable-sourcing-at-scale. Accessed 2 September 2020.

McKinsey & Company. (2019b). *What radical transparency could mean for the fashion industry* [Online]. https://www.mckinsey.com/industries/retail/

our-insights/what-radical-transparency-could-mean-for-the-fashion-industry. Accessed 28 August 2020.

Migacz, S. J., Zou, S., & Petrick, J. F. (2018). The "Terminal" effects of service failure on airlines: Examining service recovery with justice theory. *Journal of Travel Research, 57*(1), 83–98.

Miller, J. L., Craighead, C. W., & Karwan, K. R. (2000). Service recovery: A framework and empirical investigation. *Journal of Operations Management, 18*(4), 387–400.

Milnes, H (2015). *How Burberry became the top digital luxury brand* [Online]. https://digiday.com/marketing/burberry-became-top-digital-luxury-brand/. Accessed 11 August 2020.

Mintel. (2017). *Brits hung up on online fashion: Online sales of clothing, fashion accessories and footwear grow by 17% in 2017* [Online]. https://www.min tel.com/press-centre/fashion/uk-online-sales-of-clothing-fashion-accessories-and-footwear-grow-by-17-in-2017. Accessed 10 August 2020.

Mohd-Any, A. A., Mutum, D. S., Ghazali, E. M., & Mohamed-Zulkifli, L. (2019). To fly or not to fly? An empirical study of trust, post-recovery satisfaction and loyalty of Malaysia Airlines passengers. *Journal of Service Theory and Practice, 29*(5/6), 661–690.

Mohr, L. A., Harris, K. E., & Bernhardt, K. L. (2006). Online service failure, consumer attributions and expectations. *Journal of Services Marketing, 20*(7), 453–458.

Mollá-Descals, A., Lorenzo-Romero, C., Mondéjar-Jiménez, J. A., & Fayos-Gardó, T. (2012). An overview about fashion retailing sector: UK versus Spain. *International Business & Economics Research Journal (IBER), 11*(13), 1439–1446.

Montecchi, M., & Nobbs, K. (2017). Let it go: Consumer empowerment and user-generated content—An exploratory study of contemporary fashion marketing practices in the digital age. In A. Vecchi (Ed.), *Advanced fashion technology and operations management* (pp. 294–317). IGI Global.

Nikbin, D., Hyun, S. S., Iranmanesh, M., Maghsoudi, A., & Jeong, C. (2016). Airline travelers' causal attribution of service failure and its impact on trust and loyalty formation: The moderating role of corporate social responsibility. *Asia Pacific Journal of Tourism Research, 21*(4), 355–374.

Nolan, J. M., Schultz, P. W., Cialdini, R. B., Goldstein, N. J., & Griskevicius, V. (2008). Normative social influence is underdetected. *Personality and Social Psychology Bulletin, 34*(7), 913–923.

Noone, B. M. (2012). Overcompensating for severe service failure: Perceived fairness and effect on negative word-of-mouth intent. *Journal of Services Marketing, 26*(5), 342–351.

O'Connor, T. (2018). *5 ways brands can stand out on social media* [Online]. https://www.businessoffashion.com/articles/fashion-tech/5-ways-brands-can-stand-out-on-social-media. Accessed 10 September 2020.

Okonkwo, U. (2010). *Luxury online: Styles, systems, strategies.* Palgrave Macmillan.

Olenski, S. (2017). *4 ways brands should use native advertising in 2017* [Online]. https://www.forbes.com/sites/steveolenski/2017/02/16/4-ways-brands-should-use-native-advertising-in-2017/#21ba4fd41c4c. Accessed 2 September 2020.

Ombudsman Services. (2019, March). *Consumer action monitor report* [Online]. https://www.ombudsman-services.org/about-us/annual-reports/consumer-action-monitor-report-2019. Accessed 13 August 2020.

Ozuem, W., Howell, K. E., & Lancaster, G. (2008). Communicating in the new interactive marketspace. *European Journal of Marketing, 42*(9/10), 1059–1083.

Ozuem, W., Patel, A., Howell, K. E., & Lancaster, G. (2017). An exploration of customers' response to online service recovery initiatives. *International Journal of Market Research, 59*(1), 97–116.

Ozuem, W., Thomas, T., & Lancaster, G. (2016). The influence of customer loyalty on small island economies: An empirical and exploratory study. *Journal of Strategic Marketing, 24*(6), 447–469.

Pang, A., Hasan, N. B. B. A., & Chong, A. C. Y. (2014). Negotiating crises in the social media environment. *Corporate Communications: An International Journal, 19*(1), 96–118.

Park, S. G., Kim, K., & O'Neill, M. (2014). Complaint behaviour intentions and expectation of service recovery in individualistic and collectivistic cultures. *International Journal of Culture, Tourism and Hospitality Research, 8*(3), 255–271.

Pennington, D. C. (2012). *Social cognition.* Routledge.

Pham, J. (2017). *This customer's complaint of H&M's "Ridiculous" sizing is going viral* [Online]. https://stylecaster.com/hm-customer-complaint-ridiculous-sizing/. Accessed 11 August 2020.

Pookulangara, S., & Shephard, A. (2013). Slow fashion movement: Understanding consumer perceptions—An exploratory study. *Journal of Retailing and Consumer Services, 20*(2), 200–206.

Ringberg, T., Odekerken-Schröder, G., & Christensen, G. L. (2007). A cultural models approach to service recovery. *Journal of Marketing, 71*(3), 194–214.

Rust, R. T., & Oliver, R. L. (2000). Should we delight the customer? *Journal of the Academy of Marketing Science, 28*(1), 86–94.

Sabanoglu, T. (2020). *Online clothing market in the UK—Statistics & facts* [Online]. https://www.statista.com/topics/5499/online-clothing-market-in-the-uk/. Accessed 16 August 2020.

Schaefers, T., & Schamari, J. (2016). Service recovery via social media: The social influence effects of virtual presence. *Journal of Service Research, 19*(2), 192–208.

Schoefer, K., & Diamantopoulos, A. (2009). A typology of consumers' emotional response styles during service recovery encounters. *British Journal of Management, 20*(3), 292–308.

Sen, S., & Lerman, D. (2007). Why are you telling me this? An examination into negative consumer reviews on the web. *Journal of Interactive Marketing, 21*(4), 76–94.

Shen, A. X., Cheung, C. M., Lee, M. K., & Chen, H. (2011). How social influence affects we-intention to use instant messaging: The moderating effect of usage experience. *Information Systems Frontiers, 13*(2), 157–169.

Sherman, J. (2018). *Does your company listen carefully, consistently and responsively? PR and customer service need social media* [Online]. https://www.shermancm.com/does-your-company-listen-carefully-consistently-and-responsively-heres-how-pr-and-customer-service-need-social-media/. Accessed 9 September 2020.

Silber, I., Israeli, A., Bustin, A., & Zvi, O. B. (2009). Recovery strategies for service failures: The case of restaurants. *Journal of Hospitality Marketing & Management, 18*(7), 730–740.

Siu, N. Y. M., Zhang, T. J. F., & Yau, C. Y. J. (2013). The roles of justice and customer satisfaction in customer retention: A lesson from service recovery. *Journal of Business Ethics, 114*(4), 675–686.

Sivakumar, K., Li, M., & Dong, B. (2014). Service quality: The impact of frequency, timing, proximity, and sequence of failures and delights. *Journal of Marketing, 78*(1), 41–58.

Smith, A. K., Bolton, R. N., & Wagner, J. (1999). A model of customer satisfaction with service encounters involving failure and recovery. *Journal of Marketing Research, 36*(3), 356–372.

Sparks, B. A., & Browning, V. (2011). The impact of online reviews on hotel booking intentions and perception of trust. *Tourism Management, 32*(6), 1310–1323.

Sridhar, S., & Srinivasan, R. (2012). Social influence effects in online product ratings. *Journal of Marketing, 76*(5), 70–88.

Statista. (2017). *Size of selected global apparel markets in 2017* [Online]. https://www.statista.com/statistics/279735/global-apparel-market-size-by-region/. Accessed 22 October 2020.

Stratemeyer, A. W., Geringer, S. D., & Canton, A. (2014). An exploratory investigation of the effects of service failures and recovery efforts on customer satisfaction. *American Journal of Management, 14*(3), 20.

Tax, S. S., Brown, S. W., & Chandrashekaran, M. (1998). Customer evaluations of service complaint experiences: Implications for relationship marketing. *Journal of Marketing, 62*(2), 60–76.

The Luxury Channel. (2020). *London fashion week—facts and figures* [Online]. https://theluxurychannel.com/magazine/london-fashion-week-facts-and-figures/. Accessed 23 August 2020.

Tsai, W. H. S., & Men, L. R. (2013). Motivations and antecedents of consumer engagement with brand pages on social networking sites. *Journal of Interactive Advertising, 13*(2), 76–87.

Valentine, D., & Powers, T. (2013). Generation Y values and lifestyle segments. *Journal of Consumer Marketing, 30*(7), 597–606.

Van Schaik, P., & Ling, J. (2009). The role of context in perceptions of the aesthetics of web pages over time. *International Journal of Human-Computer Studies, 67*(1), 79–89.

Verhagen, T., Nauta, A., & Feldberg, F. (2013). Negative online word-of-mouth: Behavioral indicator or emotional release? *Computers in Human Behavior, 29*(4), 1430–1440.

Viswanathan, V., Tillmanns, S., Krafft, M., & Asselmann, D. (2018). Understanding the quality–quantity conundrum of customer referral programs: Effects of contribution margin, extraversion, and opinion leadership. *Journal of the Academy of Marketing Science, 46*(6), 1108–1132.

Wang, C., & Zhang, P. (2012). The evolution of social commerce: The people, management, technology, and information dimensions. *Communications of the Association for Information Systems, 31*(1), 5.

Wang, Y. S., Wu, S. C., Lin, H. H., & Wang, Y. Y. (2011). The relationship of service failure severity, service recovery justice and perceived switching costs with customer loyalty in the context of e-tailing. *International Journal of Information Management, 31*(4), 350–359.

Weitzl, W., & Hutzinger, C. (2017). The effects of marketer-and advocate-initiated online service recovery responses on silent bystanders. *Journal of Business Research, 80,* 164–175.

Wiktor, J. W. (2016). Marketing communication in hypermedia computer-mediated environments vs the paradigm of a network society. *International Journal of Business and Globalisation, 17*(3), 287–298.

Wu, X., Du, S., & Sun, Y. (2020). E-tailing service recovery and customer satisfaction and loyalty: Does perceived distributive justice matter? *Social Behaviour and Personality: An International Journal, 48*(5), 1–15.

Zhang, X., Yu, Y., Li, H., & Lin, Z. (2016). Sentimental interplay between structured and unstructured user-generated contents: An empirical study on online hotel reviews. *Online Information Review, 40*(1), 119–145.

Zhou, Y., Huang, M., Tsang, A. S., & Zhou, N. (2013). Recovery strategy for group service failures: The interaction effects between recovery modes and recovery dimensions. *European Journal of Marketing, 47*(8), 1133.

Zhu, Z., Nakata, C., Sivakumar, K., & Grewal, D. (2013). Fix it or leave it? Customer recovery from self-service technology failures. *Journal of Retailing, 89*(1), 15–29.

CHAPTER 12

Building a Sustainable Brand Image in Luxury Fashion Companies

Monica Faraoni

INTRODUCTION AND OVERVIEW

Building a sustainable brand image for a luxury fashion company is a very complex and difficult marketing process involving the entire company, but, above all, it is marketing and communication strategies. Many researchers (e.g., Beckham & Voyer, 2014; Ozuem et al., 2017; Torelli et al., 2012) have pointed out that the values associated with luxury and the values associated with sustainability can be considered antithetical. Luxury is associated with "ostentation, excessive consumption, over-production, indulgence and personal pleasure" (Atwal et al., 2019, p. 3), while sustainability is associated with values such as altruism, sobriety, moderation and morality (Amatulli et al., 2017; Naderi & Strutton, 2015). Authors underlined the existence of an inevitable contradiction between luxury and sustainability (Achabou & Dekhili, 2013; Janssen et al., 2014; Kapferer & Michaut, 2014). More specifically, luxury has been the subject of criticism and has often been accused of being

M. Faraoni (✉)
University of Florence, Florence, Italy

W. Ozuem and S. Ranfagni (eds.), *The Art of Digital Marketing for Fashion and Luxury Brands*,
https://doi.org/10.1007/978-3-030-70324-0_12

behind—if not at odds—with the prerogatives of sustainable development. These criticisms, described by Kapferer (2015), have several aspects. The first concerns the way in which luxury is synonymous with the waste of resources for the pleasure of the so-called "happy few". The second involves the concern of sustainability for social equity: due to its high visibility, the luxury sector enhances social inequality to a much greater extent than other sectors. It encourages irrational purchases as consumers make choices that are based not on functionality but, rather, on the uniqueness of the product. Consumers prefer luxury because of its non-ordinariness, the quality associated with the country of origin, the artisanry that distinguishes it, the one-to-one assistance offered by exclusive shops, and the elegance and status that luxury confers on those who buy it. The third aspect of the critique can be ascribed to the fact that luxury means "excess", which is criticized by sustainability activists who promote a contrasting ethic based on mindfulness, self-control (Wei et al., 2021) and frugality (Roiland, 2016) and whose purpose is to ensure prosperity for future generations. In short, it might seem that luxury, given its visibility and the symbolic power that derives from it, conflicts with the principles of sustainable development.

Another field of research examined consumer perceptions of the luxury–sustainability relation. Dekhili et al. (2019) indicated that sustainability product information negatively impacts the perceived quality of luxury products, while Achabou and Dekhili (2013) found that sustainable luxury products are not associated with prestige. Several studies on luxury brand image and sustainability (Achabou & Dekhili, 2013; Rolling & Sadachar, 2018; Voyer & Beckham, 2014) reported there was a dissonance or negative perceptions of "recycling" in relation to luxury, possibly because characteristics of luxury (e.g. rarity and prestige) were not associated with "recycling". This poses a challenge for luxury brands attempting to appeal to consumers searching for sustainable products.

Therefore, building a sustainable brand image is a major challenge for companies in this sector. To achieve this goal, they need to enhance consumer brand knowledge (Aaker, 2003; Keller, 2003; Supphellen, 2000) around the concept of sustainability by producing effective communication able to build the right brand associations in terms of attributes, benefits and attitudes (Keller, 1998). In fact, consumer brand knowledge can be represented as the brand associations in a consumer's mind which are synthesized into meanings they assign to the brand

(Keller, 1993, p. 3). On the other hand, thanks to its brand communication, a company defines its brand identity as "a unique set of brand associations implying a promise to customers and includes a core or extended identity" (Ghodeswar, 2008, p. 5); it expresses all the distinctive traits, benefits and values capable of differentiating a brand (Roy & Banerjee, 2008). The more the brand identity and brand image emerging from brand associations are aligned (Malär et al., 2012), the more consumer brand knowledge reflects brand communication (Gensler et al., 2013; Ozuem et al., 2008) and the higher a company's brand equity will be (Nandan, 2005).

In this chapter we try to understand whether sustainability is a relevant attribute of the Ferragamo (a luxury brand) consumer image. In particular, we try to answer to the following question: Are the project and the commitment communicated by the company on sustainability issues (sustainable brand identity) correctly perceived by consumers (sustainable brand image)? The subjects of our analysis are social media in general and brand communities in particular. Consumers talk about their brand experiences in blogs, forums and social networks because they are social spaces where they can exchange their perceptions of the brands they interact with (Ramaswamy & Ozcan, 2016). Their online brand narratives can turn into fast word of mouth as the social media used to convey them are visible, ubiquitous and available in real time (Hennig-Thurau et al., 2010). By using a social media dataset we obtain interesting results. In the following sections we present some theoretical issues about the relationship between sustainability and luxury fashion brand image. We then describe the case of the luxury brand Salvatore Ferragamo. A methodological section provides information on the research analysis. This is followed by a results section. The final section discusses managerial implications and future research directions.

Theoretical Context

Luxury and Sustainability

Despite the substantial literature that views luxury and sustainability as two antithetical concepts, recent studies provide a new interpretation of this relationship that is becoming far more complementary than antithetical. Bendell and Kleanthous (2007) pointed out that a paradigm shift is taking place in the luxury sector. In particular, while there is no single definition of luxury, at the same time there are characteristics that unite luxury products and brands. Among these we can identify high quality, rarity (Lochard & Murat, 2011) (which derives from precious and difficult to find raw materials), exclusivity, artisanry and durability (Carcano, 2013). It is precisely these characteristics that reduce the apparent gap between luxury and sustainability. In fact, "luxury" and "sustainability", especially in their environmental dimension, converge in the characteristics of "durability" and "rarity", constituting possible bridges between the two (Guercini & Ranfagni, 2013, p. 80). The essence of true luxury is that of selling rare, high-quality products characterized by good taste and elegance. The "rarity" of resources is another element that unites sustainability and luxury. Luxury is dependent on resources and obsessed with their sustainability (Han et al., 2016; Janssen et al., 2014; Kapferer, 2015): the demand for luxury products is limited by their price, which represents a way to protect the future of resources and, consequently, the luxury sectors based on these resources. Small volumes of luxury production are not a threat to the planet whereas mass production is. Finally, "durability" is at the heart of both sustainable development and luxury. Luxury is a business built on lasting value with a long-term perspective (Godart & Seong, 2014) contrary to the fast fashion market for example, which is based on mass production, or the technology market, which has its roots in planned obsolescence. The association between luxury and timelessness (Venkatesh et al., 2010)—or the fact that luxury is not trendy but durable—suggests many synergies with sustainability. Finally, some researchers, such as Janssen et al. (2014), considered the scarcity of luxury products, premium prices that limit consumption, selective distribution channels and limited editions, as limits that indirectly protect natural resources, thus contributing to more reasonable and responsible consumption. In the light of these considerations, we propose a graphic elaboration (Fig. 12.1) which highlights common "luxury" and "sustainability" meanings.

Sustainability therefore becomes an important part of a marketing branding strategy for luxury fashion brands. To appeal to the expectations of consumers more sensitive to a brand's sustainability narrative, a luxury brand image can differentiate its strategy to provide a competitive advantage (Carcano, 2013; Karaosman et al., 2018). Several directions have been adopted by companies. Many luxury brands are developing new sustainable business practices (Campos Franco et al., 2019), while other brands try to strengthen the connotations of the prestige of a luxury

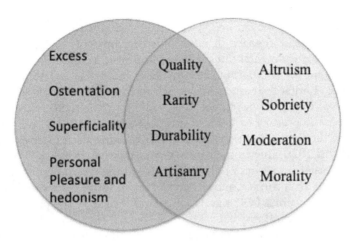

Fig. 12.1 Common "luxury" and "sustainability" meanings

good by increasing the exclusivity of the brand and its perceived value; in this latter case, sustainability is an additional attribute to the pre-existing range of luxury products, "instrumental" to a brand image reinforcement or to build a new brand image reputation (Noh & Johnson, 2019). This is the idea inspiring the recent initiatives on diversity and inclusion of Tommy Hilfiger, Diesel, Calvin Klein and Adidas (Ostillio & Antonucci, 2020). In other cases, sustainability can be conceived to be an original source of luxury. This is what seems to emerge in the context of production and supply chain management, such as the appeal of a particularly valuable production process or recycled raw material (Cimatti et al., 2017; Guercini & Ranfagni, 2013; Karaosman et al., 2018). In this type of experience, the sustainable resource generates an exclusive asset. Whatever the direction used, and communicated to the market, its effectiveness depends on the actual perception of the consumer.

The Consumer Perspective

From a consumer perspective, several studies aimed to identify the reasons why consumers are disinterested in sustainability when making luxury purchases. According to Davies et al. (2012), consumers do not want to "be disturbed" when they make a luxury purchase, especially when they are willing to enhance the dimension of pleasure coming from the purchase itself. Moreover, luxury consumers are often unaware of which brands are actively engaged in sustainable development. Therefore, if the sustainable luxury mental category does not exist, it cannot influence the process (Kapferer & Michaut, 2020). There could also be an intentional ignorance (Ehrich & Irwin, 2005) in which consumers deliberately avoid any type of negative information that could dissuade them from buying their favourite product or brand (Carrigan & Attalla, 2001), or a perception that the luxury industry has a low environmental impact (Kapferer & Michaut, 2020) due to the sporadicity of their purchases, a hypothesis also supported by Davies et al. (2012). Finally, some consumers believe that there is an intrinsic contradiction between luxury and sustainability (Voyer & Beckham, 2014) that is sometimes fuelled by the phenomenon of *perceived greenwashing* (Beckham & Voyer, 2014), or the recognition, by consumers, of a corporate communication that conveys positive but false information regarding the environmental practices and/or the environmental benefits of the products marketed (Parguel et al., 2011). If a brand deceives its customers through greenwashing, these practices may involve negative word of mouth that discourages other consumers from purchasing the company's products (Chen et al., 2014; Leonidou & Skarmeas, 2017). Therefore, greenwashing not only increases the scepticism of those who perceive it, but also of many other consumers, especially nowadays, when information spreads at an exponential speed due to the massive presence and influence of social media (Lim et al., 2013). In fact, Zhang et al. (2018) affirmed that a decrease in consumers' perception of greenwashing may correspond to an increase in purchase intention.

By contrast, consumers sensitive to the sustainability/ethics of luxury products and brands are actively engaged in researching the most sustainable luxury brands and are eager to know the degree of sustainability of the luxury products they buy (Kapferer & Michaut, 2020). They could also boycott a brand if it were guilty of incorrect behaviour in terms of sustainability. A recent stream of research considers how the scope of ethical consumption can be broadened in the luxury sector (Osburg et al., 2020). Some authors in this field highlighted the important role that social media can play in promoting ethical and sustainable luxury (Leban et al., 2020; Septianto et al., 2020), while Bartikowski et al. (2020) explored the important but under-researched area of nationalist appeals for ethical luxury goods and services by investigating Chinese luxury products. Among the reasons for a high sensitivity to the ethics of luxury brands and products, Kapferer and Michaut (2020) identified several factors: the high price of luxury which should imply the inclusion of sustainability; the expectations raised by the storytelling of luxury brands that are not expected to have any defects and, consequently, be consistent with ethical and sustainable aspects; the fact that luxury brands describe themselves as the highest quality, a term whose meaning is evolving quickly, and which has recently included sustainability issues; and the social image that the luxury purchase projects on those who make the purchase, especially if the brand and sustainable products are known among the population. Thus, having a *Gucci Rain Forest* bag spreads a message of caring for the planet as well as wealth. This latter motivation is what Griskevicius et al. (2010) called "green conspicuousness". This self-image motivation does not work when the sustainable brand is not sufficiently known by consumers and its prices are consequently not perceived. Sustainable luxury must first and foremost be luxurious. Griskevicius et al. (2010) investigated the reasons behind the success of "green" products based on the link between altruistic acts and status. In fact, starting from well-established theories in the literature, such as that of "expense reporting", they stated that altruism can signal not only the fact that a person is pro-social but also their status in society in terms of time availability, energy, money or other resources that allow them to afford to purchase products that do not negatively impact the environment.

In terms of consumer behaviour, research suggests that consumers adopt different approaches to gain sustainable credentials. In some cases they choose to consume less according to the "consumer citizenship" rules (Gabriel & Lang, 2006), while in other cases they refine their product choices towards recycled or vintage (Ryding et al., 2018) or second-hand luxury products (Kessous & Valette-Florence, 2019; Turunen et al., 2020). This pathway allows the experience of luxury to be transferred between owners without negative impacts, and it can result in deeper meanings and closer relationships with purchases. Finally, intergenerational considerations are also important, that is, understanding the differences in perception of sustainable luxury between different generations, such as millennials (Kapferer & Michaut, 2020). In fact, in support of these theories, Veronica Tonini, Ferragamo's Chief Risk Officer and Sustainability Coordinator, stated in an interview with us that:

the new generations of consumers, including millennials and Generation Z, are among the most attentive to sustainability issues. They ask about the origin of the materials, are interested in certifications and ask for more information on the places where the products are produced. Transparency and traceability are important to them; it's not just about fashion, but also about food and all body-care products. The mentality as well as the lifestyle of the new generation is changing irrespective of their country of origin and their culture.

According to Dr Tonini, these consumers have a completely different mentality from that of previous generations and the transparency and traceability of products are among the factors with the greatest impact on their purchasing decisions, as well as on their lifestyle in general.

In conclusion, the transition from "visible consumption" to "conscious consumption" (Achabou & Dekhili, 2013) has led consumers, regardless of their social class, to be concerned about social and environmental issues and to prefer sustainable products in line with their values and principles (Hennigs et al., 2013). However, sustainability is a multidimensional phenomenon and there are many problems related to sustainable development that luxury companies have to face which entail various difficulties in actual implementation (Amatulli et al., 2017). Reconciling the needs of mindfulness, self-control (Wei et al., 2021) and frugality (Roiland, 2016) typical of sustainability, with the multiple dimensions of luxury is anything but easy. Brand communication strategies must be carefully defined to accomplish such a difficult task.

The Salvatore Ferragamo Case and the Research Objective

Salvatore Ferragamo is one of the main players in the fashion and luxury sector at an international level, but its history started from a small workshop in the province of Avellino (Italy) and grew in Florence. The company started as a family business and it has been able to maintain this peculiarity over time in its organizational structure and identity, despite global development. We chose the case of Salvatore Ferragamo for our research for two reasons. First, the Florentine brand has adopted an omnichannel strategy by integrating the digital channel in its distribution and communication strategies with the eCommerce platform, it uses touchpoints in all stores and there are other initiatives aimed at making a more complete and engaging customer shopping experience. Added to this is intense communication activity on social media through short stories about the brand published in formats tailored to each channel. Second, the company has always paid particular attention to social problems and the theme of sustainable development. For the Salvatore Ferragamo Group, investing in sustainable development means respecting the values handed down by the founder and there is a widespread belief that the use of innovative materials, top artisanry, the creation of a bond with the local community, as well as respect for the environment and people are all essential for success. In 2016, Ferragamo launched a section dedicated entirely to corporate responsibility on its website. In 2018, an interactive digital version of the "Corporate Sustainability Report" was published, which offers a user-friendly experience optimized for mobile devices, as well as the video "We are Ferragamo", which describes the main areas of intervention in terms of sustainability. The brand's sustainability initiatives have also been promoted on social channels. Since the day of publication of the "Sustainability 2017 Report" on the Ferragamo LinkedIn page, the profile has received more than 70,000 views, while the video has reached over 120,000 views. Finally, the Salvatore Ferragamo Museum, especially its "Sustainable Thinking" exhibition, is seen as the emblem of this vision whose goal is to deliver a specific concept of a sustainable brand to its customers

The objective of the research concerns the identification of brand associations relating to company communication on the one hand, and user-generated content (UGC) (Bradlow, 2010; Ozuem et al., 2016) on the other. Online brand studies that include analyses of UGC (Burmann & Arnhold, 2009; Burmann, 2010) show how useful UGC is for tracing consumer brand image. Barreda and Bilgihan (2013) defined UGC as "brand virtual image" because UGC includes consumers' comments and reviews in virtual settings. UGC is considered an online form of communication that marketers need to constantly monitor in order to detect any correspondences and discrepancies between consumer brand perceptions and company brand identity (Berni et al., 2020). As already reported, the growth of online platforms has facilitated the creation of social behaviours via the Web, changing the nature of human activities. The exodus of social relations from the real world to the virtual world has meant that online communities made up of people from all parts of the world have been created. This phenomenon allows individuals to share knowledge and promote dialogues among different cultures (Budden et al., 2011).

The management and control of brand associations allows companies to obtain a competitive advantage, since they are able to create value for consumers by helping them in the processing and storing of information, guaranteeing a differentiated positioning and inducing a high inclination to purchase a product or service (Camiciottoli et al., 2014). For this reason, companies seek strong, positive and unique associations to strengthen and increase the value of their brand, especially compared to competitors (Keller, 2003). Through a consistent management of associations, the company can generate brand knowledge among consumers (Keller, 2003). An analysis of the associations therefore allows companies to assess any gaps or discrepancies between the competitive positioning of the brand as planned by the company and that perceived by the consumer. Basically, the brand identity (Ghodeswar, 2008) transmitted by the company and the brand image (Keller, 1993) perceived by the customer need to be aligned (Malär et al., 2012; Ranfagni & Faraoni, 2018) to have a positive impact on brand management and communication performance. This analysis aims to investigate the existence of such alignment in two dimensions: the Ferragamo brand image/identity alignment and the Ferragamo brand sustainable brand image/identity alignment.

The Methodological Approach: Netnography and Text Mining

The research approach we propose for identifying brand associations integrates netnography with text mining. Netnography is a qualitative research method that adapts ethnographic techniques for exploring consumer behaviour in online communities. In contrast to ethnography, in which data are collected during face-to-face encounters, netnography makes use of the computer-mediated discourse produced by participants interacting in virtual settings. As Kozinets (2002) explained, a netnographer observes consumers by investigating the online conversations of consumers based on a research process that includes research planning, data collection and data interpretation steps. Conversely, text mining (Hearst, 1999) is a research technique closely linked to the fields of natural language processing and computational linguistics, which develop and implement computer software programs for the purpose of generating, analysing and manipulating electronically stored texts (Witten, 2005). It allows for extracting new and previously unknown information from textual data, thus offering far more than simple information retrieval (Hearst, 1999). From a procedural point of view, we began the process by identifying sources of company and consumer textual data. For the company, we focused on: (a) sections related to brand history, business strategies and brand description on the corporate website (www.ferrag amo.com); (b) information and corporate communications on the *social media* official pages; (c) interviews with Ferragamo's CEOs and managers in online magazines and non-financial reports. As regards customer textual data sources, we focused on Ferragamo blogs and forums, texts from social media (Facebook, Instagram, Twitter), electronic magazines, online newspapers, and articles by professionals. Specifically, we searched for the presence of online communities, influencers, ambassadors, industry professionals, current or potential consumers, enthusiasts, and so on who expressed opinions on the brand. Such a technological form of communication mediates social interaction, providing a "window" on consumer perceptions in relation to the Ferragamo brand in an authentic interaction setting. The reference timeframe was the period 2018 to 2019.

After reading the computer-mediated communications in online communities, we copied and pasted them in a Word file. By also drawing from the company's data sources, we created another Word file containing company narratives. The total words collected were 52,121 (95 pages) for the company file and 109,020 (151 pages) for the consumer file. The text files contained in the two datasets were then subjected to analytical text mining procedures (Marzá, 2013, Swales & Burke, 2003) by the T-LAB software. T-LAB is an application consisting of a set of linguistic, statistical and graphic tools for text analysis. In the pre-processing phase, T-LAB automatically carries out the processes of corpus normalization, stop-word recognition, segmentation in elementary contexts (ECs), lemmatization, vocabulary construction and keyword selection. For the purposes of our research, we used the "co-occurrence" analysis, which allowed us to verify the word associations within the corpus. The analysis units were lexical units or lemmas (a set of words having the same lexical root and belonging to the same grammatical category, such as verb, adjective, etc.); the context units or elementary contexts (ECs were portions of text into which the corpus is divided represented by sentences or paragraphs. An EC corresponds to a paragraph with a minimum length of 50 characters and a maximum length of 1000 characters. We then subjected all the textual data to a co-occurrence analysis. More specifically, for the consumer and company files, the software identified how many times a lemma co-occurred first with the target lemma "Ferragamo" and then with the lemma "sustainable". Since co-occurrences are used as a proxy of similarity (Netzer et al., 2012), the resulting co-occurrences were considered expressions of company and consumer brand associations. Tables 12.1 and 12.2 report the outputs for the lemma "Ferragamo"; Tables 12.3 and 12.4 report the outputs for the lemma "Sustainable". Tables 12.1 to 12.4 serve as a clarification and in-depth analysis of the associations relating to the competitive positioning of the brand perceived by the consumer.

Results: Similarities and Discrepancies Between the Perceived Image and the Conveyed Identity

Results can be divided into two sections: (1) results on the Ferragamo brand identity/brand image alignment, and (2) results on the Ferragamo sustainable brand identity/image alignment.

1. *Ferragamo brand identity/image alignment.* Theories on brand identity/image alignment propose that a lack of alignment makes communication ineffective in creating brand value (Berni et al., 2020; Ranfagni & Faraoni, 2018). By analysing and interpreting the results from the online sources, we can see how in some respects the identity conveyed by Ferragamo coincides with the perceived image, while for others, the two are further apart. The circumstances in which the perceived image fully matches that conveyed are the mentions and contexts in which the words "create", "experimentation", "craftmanship", "material" and "techniques" appear. On the corporate side, it emerges that the most widespread keywords associated with the brand are not the same as those with which the consumer recognizes and immediately distinguishes the company. This result indicates a communication strategy adopted by the company that is not very effective. Corporate identity and consumer perceptions are both based on the idea that the brand distinguishes itself through "creative fashion products, fruit of artisan experimentation with new techniques and unusual materials". In terms of dissimilarities, a peculiarity concerns the word "quality". In the corporate communication, "quality" is one of the most important

Table 12.1 Company brand identity

Lemma B	COEFF	C.E.(B)	C.E.(AB)	CHI^2
Salvatore	0.656	34	32	27.54
Group	0.415	14	13	8.692
Maison	0.365	13	11	4.822
Ferruccio	0.338	8	8	6.176
Years	0.319	14	10	1.523
Time	0.316	7	7	5.826
Footwear	0.302	10	8	2.541
Shoe	0.288	11	8	1.37
Brand	0.279	9	7	1.867
Create	0.276	12	8	5.826
Museum	0.271	7	6	2.657
Experimentation	0.267	5	5	4.092
Quality	0.267	5	5	4.092
Corporate	0.254	8	6	1.252
Founder	0.254	8	6	1.252
Techniques	0.254	8	6	5.826
Creation	0.244	6	5	5.826
Material	0.244	6	5	4.822
Representation	0.244	6	5	1.911
Achieve	0.244	6	5	1.911
Find	0.244	6	5	1.911
Family	0.239	9	6	6.716
Craftmanship	0.239	4	4	6.716
Believe	0.239	4	4	3.247
Young	0.239	4	4	3.247
Italian	0.239	4	4	6.716
History	0.239	4	4	5.826
Sustainable	0.208	18	7	4.092

Lemma A–lexical unit selected (Ferragamo)
Lemma B–lexical unit associated with lemma A (Ferragamo)
Coeff.–lemma spread within the text. The higher the coefficient, the more widespread the lemma
CE(B)–number of elementary contexts (EC) in which each associated lemma is present (B)
CE(AB)–number of elementary contexts (EC) in which the lemmas A and B are associated (co-occurrences)
CHI^2–statistical significance of co-occurrences

and widespread terms that characterize the brand identity. This aspect is not perceived by online consumers or, rather, based on the data collected it could be assumed that while they do perceive quality products, this attribute does not immediately fall into the

Table 12.2   Consumer brand image

Lemma B	COEFF	C.E.(B)	C.E.(AB)	CHI^2
Salvatore	0.735	36	35	81.118
Museum	0.419	13	12	21.669
Exhibition	0.386	18	13	13.388
Sustainable	0.38	11	10	17.276
Thinking	0.359	10	9	15.126
Material	0.351	29	15	5.105
Firenze	0.342	11	9	12.237
Experimentation	0.312	8	7	10.931
Ferruccio	0.309	6	6	12.297
Sustainability	0.307	43	16	0.342
Creative	0.291	12	8	6.324
Our	0.279	10	7	6.312
Create	0.267	18	9	2.429
Artisan	0.267	8	6	6.455
Path	0.267	8	6	6.455
Research	0.267	8	6	6.455
Foundation	0.252	4	4	8.109
Accessory	0.252	4	4	8.109
Techniques	0.238	7	5	4.692
Recent	0.238	7	5	4.692
Historical	0.238	7	5	4.692
Fashion	0.228	44	12	1.003
Explore	0.225	5	4	4.983
Models	0.225	5	4	4.983
Footwear	0.223	8	5	3.152
Craftmanship	0.223	8	5	4.983
Skin	0.218	12	6	1.564
Founder	0.208	18	7	0.258

Lemma A–lexical unit selected (Ferragamo)
Lemma B–lexical unit associated with lemma A (Ferragamo)
Coeff.–lemma spread within the text. The higher the coefficient, the more widespread the lemma
CE(B)–number of elementary contexts (EC) in which each associated lemma is present (B)
CE(AB)–number of elementary contexts (EC) in which the lemmas A and B are associated (co-occurrences)
CHI^2–statistical significance of co-occurrences

brand image. Similarly, from a user's perspective, very little is said about the "country of origin", as opposed to what happens on the corporate side. Another gap concerns the term "family" and

Table 12.3 Corporate brand identity related to the "sustainable" lemma

Lemma B	COEFF	C.E.(B)	C.E.(AB)	CHI²
Towards	0.507	5	3	29.157
Museum	0.445	18	5	19.565
Commitment	0.378	4	2	15.41
Market	0.378	4	2	15.41
Strategy	0.378	4	2	15.41
Guide	0.338	5	2	11.659
Brand	0.286	7	2	7.402
Family	0.286	7	2	7.402
History	0.267	8	2	6.085
Material	0.21	13	2	2.628
Artist	0.189	4	1	2.942
Believe	0.189	4	1	2.942
Designer	0.189	4	1	2.942
Generation	0.189	4	1	2.942
Take	0.189	4	1	2.942
Soon	0.189	4	1	2.942
Responsability	0.189	4	1	2.942
Social	0.189	4	1	2.942
Value	0.189	4	1	2.942
Behavior	0.169	5	1	2.043
Growth	0.169	5	1	2.043
Offer	0.169	5	1	2.043
Product	0.169	5	1	2.043
Relationship	0.169	5	1	2.043
Technique	0.169	5	1	2.043

Lemma A–lexical unit selected (sustainable)
Lemma B–lexical unit associated with lemma A (sustainable)
Coeff.–lemma spread within the text. The higher the coefficient, the more widespread the lemma
CE(B)–number of elementary contexts (EC) in which each associated lemma is present (B)
CE(AB)–number of elementary contexts (EC) in which the lemmas A and B are associated (co-occurrences)
CHI²–statistical significance of co-occurrences

"history". The family plays a central role not only in the organizational sphere but also in that of Ferragamo's brand identity communication. This does not emerge on the consumer side.

2. *Ferragamo sustainable brand identity/image alignment.* Regarding the concept of "sustainability", there appear to be some important issues in theory and practice. From a theoretical point of view, we can confirm the literature that proposes that the relationship

Table 12.4 Consumer brand identity related to the "sustainable" lemma

Lemma B	COEFF	C.E.(B)	C.E.(AB)	CHI²
Museum	0.539	18	15	41.249
Exhibition	0.44	12	10	26.562
Goal	0.386	10	8	19.539
Theme	0.374	6	6	20.9
Environment	0.356	9	7	16.153
Quality	0.322	11	7	11.006
Fashion	0.322	44	14	2.606
Made_in_Italy	0.311	6	5	12.843
Social	0.311	6	5	12.843
Ferragamo	0.307	63	16	0.342
World	0.305	4	4	13.782
Challenge	0.305	4	4	13.782
Craftmanship	0.273	5	4	9.503
Rare	0.273	5	4	9.503
Engagement	0.267	16	7	4.321
Group	0.254	13	6	4.291
Guide	0.249	6	4	6.738
National	0.249	6	4	6.738
Company	0.249	6	4	6.738
Behavior	0.245	14	6	3.425
Project	0.241	10	5	4.406
Future	0.241	10	5	4.406
Line	0.236	15	6	2.711
Development	0.231	7	4	4.841
Engage	0.231	7	4	4.841

Lemma A–lexical unit selected (sustainable)
Lemma B–lexical unit associated with lemma A (sustainable)
Coeff.–lemma spread within the text. The higher the coefficient, the more widespread the lemma
CE(B)–number of elementary contexts (EC) in which each associated lemma is present (B)
CE(AB)–number of elementary contexts (EC) in which the lemmas A and B are associated (co-occurrences)
CHI²–statistical significance of co-occurrences

between luxury and sustainability is becoming far more complementary than antithetical (Carcano, 2013; Guercini & Ranfagni, 2013; Lochard & Murat, 2011). Luxury and sustainability are able to coexist and find a point of encounter precisely in such values as artisanry, rarity (Han et al., 2016; Janssen et al., 2014; Kapferer, 2015) and quality (see Table 12.4; Fig. 12.1). From a managerial point of view, an interesting aspect that needs to be underlined concerns the mention of the "museum". The museum appears among the most direct associations of both perspectives of analysis, however, the meaning attributed to it differs. The consumer talks about the museum's "Sustainable Thinking" exhibition. In this sense, it can be assumed that for users the museum is the symbol of Salvatore Ferragamo's sustainability and creativity, and the social role of the brand in protecting the environment. On the other hand, the meaning attributed by the company is different. The reference to sustainable exhibition is present, but far more often the museum is approached with terms such as "history", "culture", "art" and "family". This indicates that the meaning attributed to the term "museum" relates more to cultural aspects, as a form of artistic expression, linked to the history of the brand and the family. In other words, the consumer links the brand image in terms of "sustainability" to the specific event of the "Sustainable Thinking" exhibition and to the museum, while the brand's corporate communication of the concept of sustainability is aimed at associating sustainability with culture and family history.

CONCLUSION AND FUTURE OUTLOOK

This work offers a methodological approach to understanding a consumer's knowledge of a brand through brand associations, and the managerial implications are manifold. First, it investigates associations by extracting information from online communities without directly involving the consumer, thanks to the non-intrusive approach of text mining. The availability of unfiltered, spontaneous opinions, without any kind of influence could be useful for assessing the power and reputation of a company brand. Specifically, the analysis aims to verify whether the associations perceived by consumers coincide with the competitive positioning of the brand in the consumer's image.

If the company detects gaps between the identity/image of consumers, it can use this information to define new marketing communication strategies or improve existing ones (Ranfagni & Faraoni, 2018). Online discussions can therefore be very useful, as they reveal the existence of information asymmetries on which the company can intervene. Based on the data obtained, it emerged that only some of the most important associations relating to the image and reputation of Ferragamo coincide; it follows that the marketing communication may not be very effective. The results emerging from our analytical approach can be used to review brand communication and brand strategy. Companies could decide to conduct brand reinforcement and brand revitalization for example. A brand reinforcement strategy (Keller, 2003) strengthens a brand's attributes for increasing brand awareness and brand loyalty, while also fortifying product associations. A revitalization strategy (Keller, 2003) is able to refresh existing brand attributes or identify new ones, thereby generating changes in competitive positioning.

Other research implications concern the consumer image of the luxury brand's sustainability. Despite the countless contradictions existing between luxury and sustainability and the difficult and controversial consumer approach to such products, as widely debated in the literature presented, the results of our work offer interesting insights for discussing the issue. When the brand's sustainability values, ideals and messages are communicated to consumers through offline events, the consumer's brand knowledge building process is such that it overcomes any scepticism. The Salvatore Ferragamo Museum used its "Sustainable Thinking" exhibition as the emblem of the company's sustainability vision and identity, the goal of which is to deliver a specific concept of a sustainable brand linked to family history and culture. What emerges from our results, however, is that the customer image of the company's brand sustainability focuses more on the cultural and artistic value of the exhibition itself, thus demonstrating an appreciation of the event as such, highlighting a gap between the customer image and the identity that the brand wanted to convey with this event. The concept and value of sustainability is therefore linked to the event and not to the brand identity. The managerial implications are that the process of building a sustainable luxury brand takes time and through the production of events that go beyond the traditional consumer scepticism it will be possible to build this identity.

As regards the limitations of this research, we must consider the limited number of corpora collected and the subsequent impossibility of generalizing the results, although an attempt was made to extend the data collection to as large a number of sources as possible. Furthermore, the period of the survey analysis can be seen as a limitation, as the issue of sustainability is very topical and almost all the information from the digital world was focused on it. For this reason, it would be interesting to repeat this analysis in the future with a different timeframe. As regards possible research developments, since the company is an international player, it would be stimulating to expand the study to this level as well. Another direction to follow could be that of conducting a more in-depth quantitative analysis of consumer opinions about sustainability values in general and comparing it with those related to luxury fashion brands.

REFERENCES

Aaker, D. (2003). The power of the branded differentiator. *MIT Sloan Management Review, 45*(1), 83–87.

Achabou, M. A., & Dekhili, S. (2013). Luxury and sustainable development: Is there a match? *Journal of Business Research, 66*(10), 1896–1903.

Amatulli, C., De Angelis, M., Costabile, M., & Guido, G. (2017). *Sustainable luxury brands: Evidence from research and implications for managers. Palgrave advances in luxury*. Palgrave McMillan.

Atwal, G., Bryson, D., & Tavilla, V. (2019). Posting photos of luxury cuisine online: An exploratory study. *British Food Journal, 121*(2), 454–466.

Barreda, A., & Bilgihan, A. (2013). An analysis of user-generated content for hotel experiences. *Journal of Hospitality and Tourism Technology, 4*(3), 263–280.

Bartikowski, B., Fastoso, F., & Gierl, H. (2020). How nationalistic appeals affect foreign luxury brand reputation: A study of ambivalent effects. *Journal of Business Ethics*. https://doi.org/10.1007/s10551-020-04483-8

Beckham, D., & Voyer, B. G. (2014). Can sustainability be luxurious? A mixed-method investigation of implicit and explicit attitudes towards sustainable luxury consumption. *Advances in Consumer Research, 42*, 245–250.

Bendell, J., & Kleanthous, A. (2007). *Deeper luxury: Quality and style when the world matters*. WWF UK.

Berni, R., Nikiforova, N. D., & Ranfagni, S. (2020). An integrated approach to estimate brand association matching and strength in virtual settings. *Journal of Global Fashion Marketing, 11*(2), 117–136.

Bradlow, E. T. (2010). *User-generated content: The "voice of the customer" in the 21st century. Marketing intelligent systems using soft computing*. Springer.

Budden, C. B., Anthony, J. F., Budden, M. C., & Jones, M. A. (2011). Managing the evolution of a revolution: Marketing implications of internet media usage among college students. *College Teaching Methods and Styles Journal, 3*(3), 5–10.

Burmann, C. (2010). A call for 'user-generated branding'. *Journal of Brand Management, 18*(1), 1–4.

Burmann, C., & Arnhold, U. (2009). *User generated branding: State of the art of research*. Lit.

Camiciottoli, B. C., Ranfagni, S., & Guercini, S. (2014). Exploring brand associations: An innovative methodological approach. *European Journal of Marketing, 48*(5–6), 1092–1112.

Campos Franco, J., Hussain, D., & McColl, R. (2019). Luxury fashion and sustainability: Looking good together. *Journal of Business Strategy, 41*(4), 55–61.

Carcano, L. (2013). Strategic management and sustainability in luxury companies: The IWC case. *Journal of Corporate Citizenship, 52*(19): 36–54.

Carrigan, M., & Attalla, A. (2001). The myth of the ethical consumer: Do ethics matter in purchase behavior? *Journal of Consumer Marketing, 18*(7), 560–578.

Chen, Y. S., Lin, C. L., & Chang, C. H. (2014). The influence of greenwash on green word-of-mouth (green WOM): The mediation effects of green perceived quality and green satisfaction. *Quality & Quantity, 48*(5), 2411–2425.

Cimatti, B., Campana, G., & Carluccio, L. (2017). Eco design and sustainable manufacturing in fashion: A case study in the luxury personal accessories industry. *Procedia Manufacturing, 8,* 393–400.

Davies, I. A., Lee, Z., & Ahonhhan, I. (2012). Do consumers care about ethical-luxury? *Journal of Business Ethics, 106*(1), 37–51.

Dekhili, S., Achabou, M. A., & Alharbi, F. (2019). Could sustainability improve the promotion of luxury products? *European Business Review, 31*(4), 488–511.

Ehrich, K. R., & Irwin, J. R. (2005). Willful ignorance in the request for product attribute information. *Journal of Marketing Research, 42*(3), 266–277.

Gabriel, Y., & Lang, T. (2006). *The unmanageable consumer.* Sage.

Gensler, S., Völckner, F., Liu-Thompkins, Y., & Wiertz, C. (2013). Managing brands in the social media environment. *Journal of Interactive Marketing, 27*(4), 242–256.

Ghodeswar, B. M. (2008). Building brand identity in competitive markets: A conceptual model. *Journal of Product & Brand Management, 17*(1), 4–12.

Godart, F., & Seong, S. (2014). Is sustainable luxury fashion possible? In: M. A. Gardetti, & A. L. Torres (Eds.), *Sustainable luxury: Managing social and environmental performance in Iconic brands* (pp. 12–28). Greenleaf.

Griskevicius, V., Tybur, J. M., & Van den Bergh, B. (2010). Going green to be seen: Status, reputation and conspicuous conservation. *Journal of Personality and Social Psychology, 98*(3), 343–355.

Guercini, S., & Ranfagni, S. (2013). Sustainability and luxury: The Italian case of a supply chain based on native wools. *Journal of Corporate Citizenship, 2013*(52), 76–89.

Han, J., Seo, Y., & Ko, E. (2016). Staging luxury experiences for understanding sustainable fashion consumption: A balance theory application. *Journal of Business Research, 74,* 162–167.

Hearst, M. A. (1999, 20–26 June). Untangling text data mining. In *Proceedings of ACL'99: The 37th annual meeting of the association for computational linguistics, University of Maryland.* http://people.ischool.berkeley.edu/~hea rst/papers/acl99.pdf.

Hennig-Thurau, T., Malthouse, E. C., Friege, C., Gensler, S., Lobschat, L., Rangaswamy, A., et al. (2010). The impact of new media on customer relationships. *Journal of Service Research, 13*(3), 311–330.

Hennigs, N., Wiedmann, K. P., Klarmann, C., & Behrens, S. (2013). Sustainability as part of the luxury essence: Delivering value through social and environmental excellence. *Journal of Corporate Citizenship, 52,* 25–35.

Janssen, C., Vanhamme, J., Lindgreen, A., & Lefebvre, C. (2014). The catch-22 of responsible luxury: Effects of luxury product characteristics on consumers' perceptions of fit with corporate social responsibility. *Journal of Business Ethics, 119*(1), 45–57.

Kapferer, J. (2015). *Kapferer on luxury. How luxury brands can grow yet remain rare.* Kogan Page Limited.

Kapferer, J., & Michaut, A. (2014). Is luxury compatible with sustainability? Luxury consumers' viewpoint. *Journal of Brand Management, 21,* 1–22.

Kapferer, J., & Michaut, A. (2020). Are millennials really more sensitive to sustainable luxury? A cross-generational international comparison of sustainability consciousness when buying luxury. *Journal of Brand Management, 27,* 1–13.

Karaosman, H., Perry, P., Brun, A., & Morales-Alonso, G. (2018). Behind the runway: Extending sustainability in luxury fashion supply chains. *Journal of Business Research, 117,* 652–663.

Keller, K. L. (1993). Conceptualizing, measuring, and managing customer-based brand equity. *Journal of Marketing, 57*(1), 1–22.

Keller, K. L. (1998). *Strategic brand management: Building, measuring, and managing brand equity.* Prentice-Hall.

Keller, K. L. (2003). Brand synthesis: The multidimensionality of brand knowledge. *Journal of Consumer Research, 29,* 595–600.

Kessous, A., & Valette-Florence, P. (2019). From Prada to Nada: Consumers and their luxury products: A contrast between second-hand and first-hand luxury products. *Journal of Business Research, 102,* 313–327.

Kozinets, R. V. (2002). The field behind the screen: Using the method of netnography to research market-oriented virtual communities. *Journal of Consumer Research, 39*(1), 61–72.

Leban, M., Thomsen, T. U., von Wallpach, S., & Voyer, B. G. (2020). Constructing personas: How high-net-worth social media influencers reconcile ethicality and living a luxury lifestyle. *Journal of Business Ethics, 169*(1), 1–15. https://doi.org/10.1007/s10551-020-04485-6.

Leonidou, C. N., & Skarmeas, D. (2017). Gray shades of green: Causes and consequences of green skepticism. *Journal of Business Ethics, 144,* 401–415.

Lim, W. M., Ting, D. H., Bonaventure, V. S., Sendiawan, A. P., & Tanusina, P. P. (2013). What happens when consumers realise about green washing? A qualitative investigation. *International Journal of Global Environmental Issues, 13*(1), 14–24.

Lochard, C., & Murat, A. (2011). *Luxe et développement durable: La nouvelle alliance*. Eyrolles.

Malär, L., Nyffenegger, B., Krohmer, H., & Hoyer, W. D. (2012). Implementing an intended brand personality: A dyadic perspective. *Journal of the Academy of Marketing Science, 40*(5), 728–744.

Marzá, N. E. (2013). The formation of the image of top-ranked hotels through real online customer reviews: A corpus-based study of evaluative adjectives as image-formers/providers. *International Journal of English Linguistics, 3*(4).

Naderi, I., & Strutton, D. (2015). I support sustainability but only when doing so reflects fabulously on me: Can green narcissists be cultivated? *Journal of Macromarketing, 35*(1), 70–83.

Nandan, S. (2005). An exploration of the brand identity–brand image linkage: A communications perspective. *Journal of Brand Management, 12*(4), 264–278.

Netzer, O., Feldman, R., Goldenberg, J., & Fresko, M. (2012). Mine your own business: Market-structure surveillance through text mining. *Marketing Science, 31*(3), 521–543.

Noh, M., & Johnson, K. K. P. (2019). Effect of apparel brands' sustainability efforts on consumers' brand loyalty. *Journal of Global Fashion Marketing, 10*(1), 1–17.

Osburg, V., Davies, I., Yoganathan, V., & McLeay, F. (2020). Perspectives, opportunities and tensions in ethical and sustainable luxury: Introduction to the thematic symposium. *Journal of Business Ethics.* https://doi.org/10.1007/s10551-020-04487-4.

Ostillio, M. C., & Antonucci, C. (2020). Tommy adaptive: Diversità e inclusione nel settore moda. *Micro & Macro Marketing, 2,* 419–430.

Ozuem, W., Howell, K. E., & Lancaster, G. (2008). Communicating in the new interactive marketspace. *European Journal of Marketing, 42*(9/10), 1059–1083.

Ozuem, W., Patel, A., Howell, K. E., & Lancaster, G. (2017). An exploration of customers' response to online service recovery initiatives. *International Journal of Market Research, 59*(1), 97–116.

Ozuem, W., Thomas, T., & Lancaster, G. (2016). The influence of customer loyalty on small island economies: An empirical and exploratory study. *Journal of Strategic Marketing, 24*(6), 447–469.

Parguel, B., Benoît-Moreau, F., & Larceneux, F. (2011). How sustainability ratings might deter 'greenwashing': A closer look at ethical corporate communication. *Journal of Business Ethics, 102*(1), 15–28.

Ramaswamy, V., & Ozcan, K. (2016). Brand value co-creation in a digitalized world: An integrative framework and research implications. *International Journal of Research in Marketing, 33*(1), 93–106.

Ranfagni, S., & Faraoni, M. (2018). How to drive brand communication in virtual settings: An analytical approach based on digital data (consumer brand alignment and social engagement). In W. Ozuem, & Y. Azemi (Eds.), *Digital marketing strategies for fashion and luxury brands* (pp. 248–263). IGI Global.

Roiland, D. (2016). Frugality, a positive principle to promote sustainable development. *Journal of Agricultural and Environmental Ethics, 29*(4), 571–585.

Rolling, V., & Sadachar, A. (2018). Are sustainable luxury goods a paradox for millennials? *Social Responsibility Journal, 14*(4), 802–815.

Roy, D., & Banerjee, S. (2008). CARE-ing strategy for integration of brand identity with brand image. *International Journal of Commerce and Management, 17*(1/2), 140–148.

Ryding, D., Henninger, C. E., & Blazquez Cano, M. (Eds.). (2018). *Vintage luxury fashion: Exploring the rise of secondhand clothing trade. Palgrave advances in luxury series.* Palgrave.

Septianto, F., Seo, Y., & Errmann, A. C. (2020). Distinct effects of pride and gratitude appeals on sustainable luxury brands. *Journal of Business Ethics, 169*, 211–224. https://doi.org/10.1007/s10551-020-04487-4.

Supphellen, M. (2000). Understanding core brand equity: Guidelines for in-depth elicitation of brand associations. *International Journal of Market Research, 42*(3), 1–14.

Swales, J. M., & Burke, A. (2003). "It's really fascinating work": Differences in evaluative adjectives across academic registers. *Language and Computers, 46*(1), 1–18.

Torelli, C. J., Basu-Monga, S., & Kaikati, A. (2012). Doing poorly by doing good: Corporate social responsibility and brand concepts. *Journal of Consumer Research, 38*(5), 948–963.

Turunen, L. L. M., Cervellon, M. C., & Carey, L. D. (2020). Selling second-hand luxury: Empowerment and enactment of social roles. *Journal of Business Research, 116*, 474–481.

Venkatesh, A., Joy, A., Sherry, J. F., Jr., & Deschenes, J. (2010). The aesthetics of luxury fashion, body and identify formation. *Journal of Consumer Psychology, 20*, 459–470.

Voyer, B. G., & Beckham, D. (2014). Can sustainability be luxurious? *Advances in Consumer Research Conference Proceedings, 42*, 245–250.

Wei, L., Li, Y., Zeng, X., & Zhu, J. (2021). Mindfulness in ethical consumption: The mediating roles of connectedness to nature and self-control. *International Marketing Review*, 4–41. https://doi.org/10.1108/IMR-01-2019-0023.

Witten, I. H. (2005). Text mining. In M. P. Singh (Ed.), *Practical handbook of internet computing.* Chapman & Hall/CRC Press.

Zhang, L., Li, D., Cao, C., & Huang, S. (2018). The influence of greenwashing perception on green purchasing intentions: The mediating role of green word-of-mouth and moderating role of green concern. *Journal of Cleaner Production, 187,* 740–750.

PART III

Complexities and Possibilities: Tactics and Strategies

Becoming Digital: The Need to Redesign Competences and Skills in the Fashion Industry

Lucia Varra

INTRODUCTION

Technology, which has always been an important driver of change, has in recent years become the most disruptive factor in manufacturing and service industries, as well as in consumer lifestyles. The pervasiveness of technologies in manufacturing industries has given rise to a new approach to business activities which interconnects all the components of the value chain, both mechanical and human; this interconnection results in more efficient, flexible, fast and reliable business processes.

In smart factories, which are based on intelligent technologies combined with new values and new or renewed competences and skills, accurate and fast decisions can be made based on extensive information (big data) derived from the interactions between workers, objects, and machines. This information allows factories to use resources more intelligently, drastically reduce waste, and increase general efficiency, including

L. Varra (✉)
University of Florence, Florence, Italy

© The Author(s), under exclusive license to Springer Nature
Switzerland AG 2021
W. Ozuem and S. Ranfagni (eds.), *The Art of Digital Marketing for Fashion and Luxury Brands*,
https://doi.org/10.1007/978-3-030-70324-0_13

energy efficiency (Guercini & Ranfagni, 2013; Majeed & Rupasinghe, 2017; Ozuem et al., 2008; Tao et al., 2018; Zhong et al., 2017).

The fashion sector, particularly the luxury fashion sector, is an interesting field of study for the transformations underway: it constitutes a laboratory of solutions that reconcile artisanry, authenticity, and product exclusivity with the most innovative industrial technologies. However, it is also a sector that, even more than others, must take advantage of the opportunity to exploit digital technology to create symbiotic relationships with customers and translate new requests into products and processes, including emotional experiences and sustainability. The absence of a rigid separation inside a smart factory between physical and digital components deeply affects both operational and managerial processes and both organisational and interorganisational processes, with strong implications for professional skills, both technical and soft skills.

The problem of skills and competences is at the core of an effective transformation towards the factory of the future. In this factory, smart machines and "augmented operators" are paradigms that exist simultaneously (Longo et al., 2017; Weyer et al., 2015); however, these developments also present challenges that must be overcome, and the ability and vision of managers are fundamental to this process (Longo et al., 2017). At the same time, the need for specialists and newly conceived engineering roles increases (Magone & Mazali, 2016). Therefore, all types of performed tasks – operational, specialist, and managerial – are affected by the required changes to activities and skills. These changes also raise questions about the acquisition, development, and enhancement of skills both within organisations and through the education and university training system. Yet the issue of competences in Industry 4.0 has only recently been addressed, and few previous studies have linked it to the processes and roles that are involved.

This work, beginning with an analysis of the most recent literature on the topic of Industry 4.0, examines the implications of changing required competences within this industry, linking them to the processes of the fashion sector and some key roles within the sector. It also identifies several new roles entering the sector, considering roles and competences in the context of both manufacturing processes and managing processes supporting technology.

Finally, the work investigates the impact the required new skills have on employee management processes in human resource management (HRM) and reflects on the challenges of adapting to these skills at both an organisational level and at a level of education and training.

LITERATURE OVERVIEW

Digital Factory and Digital Fashion: Characteristics and Processes

The transformations in the production and services sector can be traced back to the 4.0 revolution (Hofmann & Rusch, 2017; Zhang et al., 2019; Zhong et al., 2017) which fundamentally changed the technological matrix, including integrated systems, applications of information and communications technology (ICT), and industrial technology; the result was the creation of a digital and intelligent factory that allows faster production driven by information, including information from users, (Zhong et al., 2017; Zhou et al., 2015). The so-called fourth industrial revolution arose from a plan developed by the German government in 2011 that exploited the potential of digital technologies to renew the country's production system (BMBF, 2014; Kagermann et al., 2013). This revolution was based on the concept of cyberphysical systems or (Wu et al., 2017; Zhong et al., 2017), which centre on real-time interaction between people, products, and devices during the production process (Zhou et al., 2015).

In particular, three groups of technologies support the new factory: (1) the internet of things (IoT) (Liu et al., 2017; Kong et al., 2019; Majeed & Rupasinghe, 2017); (2) cloud computing technology (Chen & Lin, 2015; Wan et al., 2013); and (3) big data analytics (Obitko et al., 2013; Silva et al., 2020; Tao et al., 2018).

The IoT allows you to integrate IT with operations technology and is characterised by the pervasive presence of a variety of exchanges that not only put people in perpetual communication with each other but also put people in communication with machines and, crucially, put machines in communication with each other (Wan et al., 2013; Zhou et al., 2015). These exchanges make it easier and more effective to control and monitor processes in companies. The IoT includes radio frequency identification devices, infrared sensors, global positioning systems, laser scanners, and other information sensing devices and objects which communicate and exchange information relating to intelligent identification, location, and tracking (Beltrametti et al., 2017; Zhou et al., 2015).

Cloud computing technology (Hashem et al., 2015; Tao et al., 2014, 2018) refers to the set of technologies aimed at storing, processing, and transmitting data and the set of applications and software that allow users access to the resources they need (applications, programs, and services). Cloud computing technology uses a "software as a service" mode, avoiding companies' investments in IT infrastructures, system maintenance, and upgrades in favour of a dynamic allocation of services, more flexible access and consumption, and the ability to share resources with other subjects (Zhou et al., 2015).

Big data and advanced analysis techniques allow users to quickly obtain valuable information from a variety of sources at various levels to acquire, process, and understand in-depth data and information, as well as to make queries necessary to make complex decisions. In addition to the aforementioned enabling technologies, others exist in Industry 4.0 (Tao et al., 2018; Zhou et al., 2015): advanced manufacturing solutions, such as interconnected and rapidly programmable collaborative robots; augmented reality; cyber security, and so on; and complementary technologies, such as e-commerce systems, geolocation systems, and technologies supporting the in-store customer experience.

The smart factory model affects the fashion industry by ushering in a gradual transformation (Bertola & Teunissen, 2018; Gilchrist, 2016; Hermann et al., 2016; Sun & Zhao, 2017, 2018). This transformation particularly affects the luxury sector as technology provides major contributions to the main critical success factors in the field (Brun, 2017; Brun et al., 2008), including premium quality, exclusivity and brand development, expertise, and timeliness (Brun, 2017; Brun et al., 2008; Freire, 2014; Kapferer & Bastien, 2009, 2012).

This sector has always been susceptible to change due to the volatility of fashion and the companies' ongoing search for positive performance, which has historically been elusive because of the high complexity of the reference environment (De Felice & Petrillo, 2013).

The transformations that fashion companies have undergone in recent decades concern both the supply chain and relations with the market. The fashion supply chain had already undergone an upheaval in the 1980s and 1990s after new low-cost competitors and the need to reduce production costs and increase efficiency led to the strategies of outsourcing and delocalising of some phases of the production processes (Bertola & Teunissen, 2018). The crumbling of the value chain has led to a company's transformation from a pyramidal organisation to a horizontal one, dictated by the lean production of the 1990s, and ultimately to a network organisation with new coordination mechanisms (Cavaliere & Varra, 2020; Mintzberg, 1983; Thompson, 1967) and new leadership styles (Kleefstra, 2019).

In the wake of this transformation, as the emphasis on market relations has increased, knowledge and communication systems have become focused on the search for complicity with consumers. The ability to understand the customer is an asset (Som & Blanckaert, 2015) which is supported by continuously balancing between exploitation and exploration or innovation (Jensen, 2017) to safeguard the mix between identity and renewal, both are valued aspects to consumers of fashion.

Therefore, from the competitive perspective of organisations in advanced sectors, knowledge has become a productive factor, a feature of material processes that is directly integrated with information and its systems of creation and development (Tao et al., 2018). This is a massive difference compared to previous processes where information, although it was always the basis of manufacturing decisions, remained on a separate distinct level from production (Tao et al., 2018). In the artisan era, information was transferred to paper artefacts that incorporated the operators' tacit knowledge (Polanji, 1966), while the limited amount of production data the system generated was transferred to scheduling tools or verbally handed down. In the industrial era, especially the second industrial era, a high amount of data existed, but it was handled on a managerial level where analyses were increasingly accurate and special systems facilitated the creation and development of knowledge, which was then shared within the system. It is only in the information age and with the exponential growth of data that companies can collect, process, and use data to facilitate production and meet customer expectations more economically and effectively (Tao et al., 2018).

All this has contributed to the development in fashion companies of a structured set of activities that exploit digital channels to build lasting, trusting, and two-way relationships with customers and to promote products and services in a personalised way. These activities fall under the name of digital marketing (Kannan & Li, 2017; Ozuem et al., 2017). Digital marketing uses a variety of technologies and devices in both online and mobile contexts to overcome information asymmetry between the consumer and the company (relating to the product search process, expectations, price and quality preferences, judgements, etc.) by creating a high number and variety of contact points with the customer and generating extensive information. Information coming from online platforms, in which customers interact with each other or other companies, as well as platforms in which companies interact with each other, is added to information generated or acquired from direct contacts between company and consumer. Innovative, open platforms are increasingly being developed that allow customers to directly provide requests for products and services, as well as crowdsourcing platforms (Bayus, 2013; Kannan & Li, 2017; Luo & Toubia, 2015) where volunteers and freelance professionals willing to offer their services meet with companies that intend to outsource parts of internal processes, including online communication activities. Therefore, various one-to-one relationships also develop between the company and "the crowd". Recent research has questioned how platforms can keep the crowd engaged in e-commerce interactions or in the process of new product development (Kannan & Li, 2017). Search engines also provide high-quality information on the behaviours of actual and potential customers (Chan et al., 2011; Dinner et al., 2014) that companies increasingly buy, because of the fact that company actions based on lists provided by search engines have been found effective.

Digital marketing activities have an almost immediate impact on the organisation and products of a digital fashion factory. Competitive advantage in digital enterprises comes from the ability to transfer external information into internal products and processes in almost real time. Therefore, digital marketing is a fundamental and transversal support process for the entire value chain of the digital factory. Furthermore, the trend towards product digitalisation, and therefore the transformation of products into services, invites the question of the creation of special virtual products; for example, a virtual outfit for a selfie to be published on social networks requires the creation of a new product or service that agrees with the design policies of real products and services. More generally, product digitisation introduces the problem of freemium products, that is, the definition of choice models to strategically offer a product to the consumer in the free online version and the paid material version (Li et al., 2019). This customer interaction poses the problem of defining the price in real time based on product demand and customer purchasing alternatives, which involves creating pricing models that have yet to be defined and communicating with production and company policies to facilitate the service.

Product design in the digital age requires new design and pricing options and introduces concerning questions about privacy (Kannan & Li,

2017) from both the consumer and company point of view, as well as the possible barriers that can be erected to prevent the sharing of knowledge.

Digital Fashion Processes

Intelligent production compresses the typical processes of a fashion company (such as design, planning, manufacturing, distribution, maintenance, and quality control) to increase effectiveness and efficiency. The variable of time, which significantly impacts both of these elements, refers to: time-to-market or the time between the recognition of a market opportunity and the translation into a product or service on the market; time-to-serve or the time between the acquisition of an order and its delivery; and reaction time or the time it takes a company to adapt its output in response to volatile demand (Christopher et al., 2004).

It is a complex task to examine the literature on the classification of processes in the fashion sector because their level of aggregation and articulation varies (depending on the field of activity and size of the company), and the names studios and companies assign to these processes vary as well. The literature on processes in the fashion industry has largely revolved around two themes: the supply chain and the process of new product development. While the first theme was guided by the need for rationality and efficiency, the second focused on the need for creativity and responsiveness to consumers' changing expectations. Parallel to the development of ICT and, subsequently, intelligent factories, researchers focused attention on knowledge processes, the operational and communication networks that are generated on the market, and the construction of intercompany and intercommunity processes.

Researchers frequently measured processes against the critical success factors for each stage of the supply chain. Brun et al. (2008) considered three macro processes (sourcing, manufacturing and retail) and indicated a company's attention points (e.g., co-design, co-branding, suppliers and localisation) for each. Lin and Piercy (2013) analysed the development process of a new product, distinguishing between conception, creation, commercialisation, and production, drawing from various authors and research on the subject. Their description of the development process covered the following topics: market and trend research, the creation of sources and fabrics, design patterns and samples, review and finalisation of collections, commercialisation and marketing, fashion show and fashion week, sales and marketing, production of fabric, collation of orders, delivery of fabrics, and pre-production samples, patterns and production (Lin & Piercy, 2013).

As already mentioned, the timelines of these processes are increasingly compressed, even when they are spatially distant from each other. The implementation of a new process system in a smart factory is based on six design principles: interoperability, virtualisation, decentralisation, modularity, service orientation, and real-time capability (Hermann et al., 2016; Ozuem et al., 2016).

Due to the characteristics of the product, the fashion industry can benefit from an extensive interpretation of the concept of Industry 4.0 that goes beyond smart manufacturing (Bertola & Teunissen, 2018; Gilchrist, 2016) to include supply networks, sales networks, and consumer networks. This digitised open process can create unprecedented advantages in efficiency, leanness, and speed (Bertola & Teunissen, 2018; Schwab, 2017; Ustundag & Cevikcan, 2017) and overcome the issues of environmental impact and social exclusion (Ashby, 2016; Fratocchi et al., 2014) that the mass production model produced. The rise of modularity and decentralisation (Hermann et al., 2016) virtually recreated new glocal manufacturing districts, which is an ideal system to foster the development of the fashion industry (Becattini, 1998; Bertola & Teunissen, 2018; Buciuni & Finotto, 2016).

Two major challenges arise in the creation of a 4.0 system in the fashion sector: (1) how to preserve artisanal and high-quality "professional" content in a digitised company; and (2) how to update skill adaptation and learning processes which have received less attention than operational processes.

The creation of an integrated digital infrastructure in which objects, machines, and people can communicate is complex, and even a manufacturing model that is "artisanal and advanced" requires organisational reflections (Tao et al., 2018; Vacca, 2015). However, many examples exist of fashion companies that have embarked on digital transformation, although they now appear to have shifted towards downstream processes in contact with the customer or with customer communities, and are more focused on internal automation (Bertola & Teubussen, 2018).

Researchers investigating required skills within a sector must pay attention not only to the creation of the product but also to the entire production system (Piccarozzi et al., 2018; Trstenjak, 2018). This system involves designing a multidisciplinary complex and reimagining new workforce concepts and roles in the process (Mabkhot et al.,

2018); however, the human element of these processes is still frequently overlooked (Jerman et al., 2019).

Skills and Competences in the Digital Fashion Industry

The theme of skills and competences linked to a smart factory is very recent (Imran & Kantola, 2018; Jerman et al., 2018; Pecina & Sladek, 2017). A review on the subject (Jerman et al., 2018), conducted on articles and proceedings in the Web of Science and Scopus databases, counted 43 works specifically concerning the skills of employees. The earliest articles were written in 2012, with an increase in number starting from 2015. In the literature, these articles often focused on sectors other than fashion; therefore, analyses and reflections may be affected by the specific characteristics of specific sectors.

An explanation of the terminology appears necessary. In the literature, the concept of skills does not have a unique meaning (Roberts, 1997; Spencer & Spencer, 1993; Torres et al., 2003) and numerous overlaps exist between concepts. The relationship between skill and competence is not always clear. By skill, we mean a capacity or personal characteristic that, in adequate motivational and contextual conditions, manifests as competence or effective, successful behaviours and performances (Boyatzis, 1982). According to this interpretation, competence is a proven ability to use and finalise knowledge, skills, and abilities; it includes a result (Rowe, 1995) and can be developed (McClelland, 1973), while skill is a more stable element. Therefore, a competence is a skill that has been activated by personal motivations in a job or an organisational context.

Extensive variety exists in the classification of skills and competences (skills vs competences, technical skills vs soft skills, generic skills vs specialist skills, transversal skills vs job-related skills, etc.). An initial macro distinction separates technical skills and soft skills, or technical competences and behavioural competences: technical competences concern knowledge and skills related to the performance of work, while behavioural competences concern relational, cognitive, social, and personal skills, such as motivation, attitudes, abilities, emotional intelligence, and relational intelligence (Hecklau et al., 2017; Grzybowska & Łupicka, 2017; Prifti et al., 2017; Fitsilis et al., 2018).

The existing articles on skills associated with the digital industry are framed against the broader theme of the correlation between technologies and the labour market (Piwowar-Sulej, 2020), which suggests two alternative situations: a negative correlation, which suggests technology destroys traditional workplaces and replaces workers with automation; and a positive correlation, which suggests technology is a lever that can increase skills and therefore offer more job opportunities (Ugur et al., 2018; Piwowar-Sulej, 2018; Whysall et al., 2019). The World Economic Forum (2020) presented the opinions expressed by companies on the technological changes expected in work by 2025: 43% of the companies interviewed planned to reduce the current workforce as a result of automation, 34% planned to expand it as a result of deeper technology integration and new potential for exploiting the value chain, and 41% planned to expand the use of contractors for specialised tasks. Most companies interviewed expected an increase in skills related to critical thinking and analysis, problem solving, and technology use and development.

No comprehensive overview exists of anticipated future competencies for manufacturing processes in smart factory systems (Antosz, 2018; Jerman et al., 2019; Kinkel et al., 2017; Nyikes, 2018), and existing literature presents several methodologies and focuses on different aspects and sectors (Grzybowska & Łupicka, 2017; Hecklau et al., 2017; Prifti et al., 2017). Although some skills can be considered interdisciplinary (Prifti et al., 2017), research has shown that the importance attributed to one factor can change across sectors (Grzybowska & Łupicka, 2017), especially for technical skills, which can vary significantly in their perceived importance (Gehrke et al., 2015). Moreover, it is precisely the technical aspect of competences that has been mostly discussed in the works on digital companies (Sinsel et al., 2017), while fewer articles focused on the areas of soft skills and management skills, which have instead been the subjects of analysis by consulting companies such as Boston Consulting Group (Lorenz et al., 2015), Ares2.0—Confindustria (Bettarini & Tartaglione, 2018), and others (Jerman et al., 2019; Vacek, 2016). Some studies on the skills associated with Industry 4.0 involved keyword analyses of literature contributions (Benešová & Tupa, 2017; Hartmann & Bovenschulte, 2013; Hecklau et al., 2017; Jerman et al., 2018, 2019; Lorenz et al., 2015). Using this methodology, Hecklau et al. (2017) analysed skills in various areas by searching for the keywords "Industry 4.0" or "Digital transformation" combined with "job", "skills", and so on. Their search included all studies that were published before July 2017 and spanned various roles and sectors. The research was based on a database of 2709 enterprise interviews and 90 expert interviews. The competences found covered four areas: methodological competences, or knowledge and skills related to problem solving and successful decision making (analytical competence, complex problem solving, decision making, creativity); social competences, including knowledge, skills, and abilities to communicate and cooperate with other individuals and groups (cooperation and communication, leadership competences); personal competences, or individual values, motivation, and attitudes (willingness to learn, flexibility, and adaptability); and domain-related or specialist competences (digital networks, digital security, coding competence, process understating, interdisciplinary competence). Their research indicated that the most important and necessary competence was social competence (communication and cooperation), followed by coding, complex problem solving, interdisciplinary competence, and other competences.

Following a methodology similar to Hecklau et al.'s (2017), an analysis by Jerman et al. (2018) focused on paper content and four clusters of themes. This analysis indicated: technical competences, including the ability to understand IT security, processes, and analogies of the operations of new technologies; methodological competences, including creativity, research skills, and problem solving; social competences, such as networking skills and the ability to transfer knowledge; and personal competences, such as social responsibility and personal flexibility (Jerman et al., 2018).

The results of Piwowar-Sulej (2020) similarly identified the following types of skills needed for Industry 4.0: social (communication and cooperation), methodological (analytic competence, complex problem solving, and decision making), personnel (willingness to learn), and domain-related skills (digital networks, digital security, coding competence, and process understanding).

Notably, digital skills are transversal; the literature emphasises the importance of skills related to the ability to work with new materials, manage information, and plan and control IT tasks (Bonekamp & Matthias, 2015; Grzybowska & Łupicka, 2017; Jerman et al., 2019).

Some researchers identified necessary skills that are specific to the fashion industry by examining job postings from LinkedIn (Kalbaska & Cantoni, 2019 Ronchetti et al., 2020). The research by Kalbaska and Cantoni (2019), covering 29 countries, including all 28 in the European Union, examined 1427 available digital fashion jobs to determine which major skills were most in demand in the current digital fashion job market; in order, the skills most frequently mentioned in job titles were digital marketing, social media, digital design, graphic design, and e-commerce management. The skills most frequently mentioned within the job descriptions of available jobs were social media, digital marketing, e-commerce, and communication skills, followed by customer service care, customer/user experience, web analytic skills, and experience with luxury fashion. The research highlights how digital fashion roles require both analytical and creative skills as well as knowledge of certain tools, such as social media or paid searches, at the operational level. Kalbaska and Cantoni (2019, p. 133) ultimately found that successful candidates should have a strong attitude as well as a passion for the digital world.

With a similar methodology applied in the same countries, the research by Ronchetti et al. (2020) confirmed, albeit in a different order, the presence of similar requirements in terms of skills. The results, arising from 1397 digital fashion jobs examined in 2020, showed that the most frequent combinations of keywords found in digital fashion job titles appeared to be (in order of frequency) e-commerce, digital marketing, visual associate, product manager, and social media. The most frequent keyword combinations found in the job descriptions of digital fashion job postings were (in order of frequency) social media, customer service/care, commerce, communication skills, digital marketing, team player, and customer experience. Considering both of these studies, the top required competence today in the digital fashion domain appears to be "social media", and the demand for skills in "digital marketing" continues to increase over time.

These new skills required in digital fashion companies may modify the traditional roles of typical activities of the industry, such as product development and creation, marketing development and retailing, and communication planning and management (Bertola et al., 2017), while also creating new positions. The development of new skills in traditional profiles leads to an increase in operational roles, creating an "augmented operator" who can conduct traditional activities by interacting with intangible assets and new digital content (Longo et al., 2017, Weyer et al., 2015).

The most typical jobs in fashion, designer and producer, are also affected by the change (Bertola & Teunissen, 2018; Sun & Zhao, 2017, 2018). Sun and Zhao (2018), through the focus groups method, explored the new skills related to these two roles. Designers perceived themselves (and are perceived in research) as workers who must be experts in many different things, with an increasing need for technical knowledge and a profile between a stylist and an engineer (Sun & Zhao, 2018). They must have the ability to connect in real time with internal and external sources of information and generate emotions in customers connected to the product to satisfy customers' search for an aesthetic experience.

Even the producer, who is typically involved in rational, standardised processes, must adopt a dynamic role, able to quickly make necessary or requested changes. Producers must consider the fact that with the adoption of new technology, their role can be played by anyone, including users who choose their product configurations before testing them out in virtual showcases and dressing rooms. As the fashion industry develops, the producer will be one node of a network (Bertola et al., 2017) with an increasingly communicative role with everyone (Sun & Zhao, 2018). IT designers, programmers, robotics and mechatronics experts, as well as maintenance experts, are new key figures (Jerman et al., 2019) with the ability to collect big data and conduct monitoring activities to detect problems in products or equipment (Lorenz et al., 2015; Nagorny et al., 2017). The role of data analysts, particularly big data analysts, is also fundamental; they possess the ability to use tools to capture, process, and interpret an enormous amount of data (Waterman & Bruening, 2014).

Digital companies will see the development of strategic business units which can grow effectively through the interconnection of strategic plans with operational ones; therefore, intermediate roles with hybrid managerial and creative characteristics will be needed. These roles include brand managers, merchandisers, product managers, and line builders (Bertola et al., 2017; Granger, 2012).

Digitalisation requires the development of skills throughout the system at various levels of job specialisation (Mintzberg, 1983); traditional artisans will coexist in companies and within the same role with hyperspecialised engineers, augmented workers, and advanced craftspeople. These possess different sets of skills that allow unique human attributes, creativity, and manual skills to be in dialogue with technology and digital devices, improving dexterity and productiveness (Bertola & Teunissen, 2018; Bostrom, 2016; Braidotti, 2008).

These changes underscore the importance of continuous learning, which emerges in the form of key skills (Jerman et al., 2019) and benefits from two other skills, teamwork and leadership, which research suggests are also in high demand.

Major changes are needed at all levels, including managerial and entrepreneurial skills. Kruger and Steyn (2020 identified the entrepreneurial skills needed in Industry 4.0. Skills were classified according to several significant dimensions: experience or knowledge of the business, qualification (e.g., branding), strategy, customer focus, and training. They proposed a model that combined business functions with competencies; among these, the main classifications were innovation, creativity, integrated business and technology skills, leadership and communication, and networking and sales. Similar needs exist in small and medium-sized enterprises (SMEs), where 3D printing (3DP) technology is introducing digital content to the following key competences: strategy vision, marketing orientation, operational competence, supply chain management, project management, commercial competence, innovation management, knowledge management, and network competence (Sun & Zhao, 2018).

Managerial skills have also been affected, with the importance of entrepreneurial thinking, decision-making skills, problem solving, profit resolution, and analytical skills emerging in Industry 4.0 (Grzybowska & Łupicka, 2017).

A qualitative survey of 15 managers highlighted the following clusters of skills required for the transition to Industry 4.0 (Díaz et al., 2017): ICT (knowledge of big data, ability to analyse data, and knowledge and management of software and interfaces that support operational management); innovation management (virtual collaboration and openness to change); organisational learning (the ability to develop employee skills and encourage participation in decision making); and environment (ability to develop research with external partners, creativity in designing strategies to introduce new practices). The same research highlighted the shortcomings within organisational leadership in the processes of developing employee skills, capabilities, and improvement: the knowledge and management of software and interfaces that support operations management (resources, people, and production) within ICT; and the ability to adopt new models of work and organisation within innovation management (Díaz Bermúdez & Flores Juárez, 2017, p. 743).

A recent report by Ares2.0 for the fashion sector (Bettarini & Tartaglione, 2018) identified competences in fashion at entrepreneurial, managerial, and workforce levels, offering the following classifications: knowledge (including knowledge of legislation on health and safety, environment, corporate social responsibility, advanced English language, e-skills, marketing, machinery and device remote control); social skills (including teamwork, communication, and networking skills); technical-productive competences (including data analysis and management of complex machinery); problem-solving skills (including creativity, experimentation, verification, and resourcefulness); self-management skills (including time and stress management skills and the ability to work remotely); management skills (including orientation to change and continuous improvement); and entrepreneurial understanding (including innovation and orientation to the customer) (Bettarini & Tartaglione, 2018, p. 19).

The problem of skills calls into question the management and development of the same, that is the HRM processes. The management of skills in Industry 4.0 is particularly concerned with: the measurement of employee performance, based on data collected from private and public sensors (Grzybowska & Łupicka, 2017) the need to have data on employees in real time and to provide them with immediate feedback on the results achieved (Cascio & Montealegre, 2016) and new forms of compensation in line with the new organisation of work. However, because creative and conceptual work is increasingly autonomous and remote, it is difficult to create tools that help to control this work, meaning feedback on results is essential (Grzybowska & Łupicka, 2017). The traditional money-based remuneration approach will also be a critical element: new forms of compensation will be identified and IT systems will help manage individualised total compensation packages for medium and highly skilled employees.

New opportunities for the implementation of IT tools in human resource (HR) processes are also discussed in the relevant literature (e.g., Cascio & Montealegre, 2016; Onik et al., 2018; Piwowar-Sulej, 2020); new techniques will transform HRM from a straightforward service into "smart HRM" with an increasingly strategic role (Piwowar-Sulej, 2020) and more sustainable systems (Varra & Timolo, 2017).

HRM processes and necessary skills depend on several variables: job characteristics, the contextual conditions determining a department's technology level (i.e., the availability and functioning of connections), and workers' qualification levels (i.e., whether workers are low skilled, medium skilled or in creative jobs, or highly skilled specialists and managers) (Piwowar-Sulej, 2020).

As this review indicates, research has investigated all aspects of the digital revolution, including those related to managerial and HRM skills.

However, findings have not previously been consolidated into a model that could be applied to concrete cases within the fashion sector; such a model could measure knowhow and skills, reflect unfulfilled training needs (Fitsilis et al., 2018), and indicate sources of competitive advantage for companies of the fashion sector.

THE PROPOSED MODEL

The summary of the literature shows that:

- The changes that have taken place in organisations because of Industry 4.0 have an important impact on competences, which have recently been the subject of study at all sectors and levels (Fitsilis et al., 2018; Hecklau et al., 2017; Jerman et al., 2018, 2019; Grzybowska & Łupicka, 2017; Piwowar-Sulej, 2020; World Economic Forum, 2020).
- Few studies exist that specifically focus on digital fashion skills; they do not show substantial differences compared to studies focusing on the types of skills deemed necessary in other sectors. However, they confirm that the changes affect all roles: managerial, middle management, specialist, and operational (Bettarini & Tartaglione, 2018; Kalbaska & Cantoni, 2019; Ronchetti et al., 2020).
- Previous studies have considered the transversal nature of skills across all sectors of Industry 4.0 as they relate to some professional positions. Studies have also focused on how these skills affect key positions in the fashion sector, such as designers and producers (Bertola & Teunissen, 2018; Bertola et al., 2017; Bettarini & Tartaglione, 2018; Lorenz et al., 2015; Sun & Zhao, 2018).
- There is no organic model that brings together the processes of the digital fashion industry and the new skills profiles related to traditional or new roles that are changing as a result of technology.

Based on the literary evidence, the proposed model (see Fig. 13.1) incorporates both skills and professional roles into the best-known classifications of processes, including Brun et al. (2008) and Lin and Piercy (2013). The model identifies the necessary skills and competences within the macro-processes of sourcing, manufacturing, and retailing and the sub-processes that characterise them, following the model of Hecklau

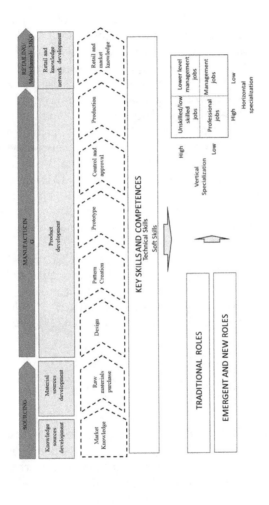

Fig. 13.1 A proposed model of skills and roles in the Industry 4.0 fashion industry

et al. (2017), to create macro-level categories of technical competences and behavioural competences and related sub-divisions. Following the approach of Bettarini and Tartaglione (2018), the skills observations are then related to the content of traditional and new roles in the Industry 4.0 fashion industry. Finally, these transformations are reported in the more general scheme of Mintzberg (1983) on the typology of duties and distinguished according to vertical versus horizontal specialisation.

The future organisation of work will mirror the characteristics of the digital fashion company, that is, an organisation with a high level of knowledge that loosens the boundaries between well-defined activities, functions, and roles in favour of intense but more fluid connections that shorten the traditional value chain (dashed lines in Fig. 13.1). Consequently, work will be characterised by more qualified content at all levels, opportunities for remote work, and hybridisations between work and private life (work porosity) in an organisational system that both incorporates the market and sells assets to the market. Considering these characteristics, it is possible to identify a series of transversal skills for the sector as shown in Table 13.1. These skills will be common to all roles in a fashion company in Industry 4.0. The competences are categorised following the distinctions of Hecklau et al. (2017).

Various specialised technological roles characterise the digital fashion company. Table 13.2 shows several specialists (with related skills) who support the development and application of digital technology in organisations. The roles and skills of digital fashion are described below based on the processes and the innovation level of each role (Tables 13.3, 13.4, 13.5, 13.6, 13.7, 13.8).

Significant Roles and Related Skills in Digital Fashion Processes

Sourcing: Knowledge Source Development and Material Source Development

The macro process includes activities aimed at the market in search of the sources of raw materials, including knowledge. All understanding of market activities is included in this process, which involves market analysis and acquisition of customer trends and expectations through all channels and customer relationship nodes. Therefore the roles and competences related to the macro process will be examined in the "retailing and multi-channel marketing" category in the context of digital marketing activities. Material source development is the process by which raw materials,

Table 13.1   Transversal competences common to all roles in the digital fashion industry

Category of competences	Transversal competences common in the digital fashion industry
Technical competences	Knowledge of health, safety, privacy, cyber security, legislation
	Knowledge of environmental issues; corporate social responsibility
	Marketing knowledge
	Interdisciplinary knowledge
	Digital marketing
	Network social platform
	Digital security
	Coding competence
	Process and product understanding
	Machines and devices understanding
Behavioural competences	
Methodological	Analytical thinking
	Problem solving
	Decision making
	Creativity
	Efficient orientation
	Conflict solving
	Client orientation (internal and external client)
Personal	Flexibility and adaptability
	Willingness to learn
	Resistance to stress
	Sustainable mindset
Social	Communication and cooperation
	Intercultural skills
	Teamworking
	Knowledge sharing
	Leadership

Sources Fitsilis et al. (2018), Grzybowska and Łupicka (2017), Hecklau et al. (2017), Kalbaska and Cantoni, 2019, Leinweber (2013), and Piwowar-Sulej (2020)

fabrics, accessory parts, and so on are sought. This phase is traditionally carried out by the buyer or by textile designers. The globalisation of the market and the virtualisation of the purchases of raw materials mean that the traditional positions related to this process are evolving to require a high mastery of technology, which is essential for intercepting innovations and procurement opportunities for international supply. Digital technology makes it possible to: access all possible information on the

Table 13.2 Roles and competences that support the development of digital technology

Role	Job description	Main technical competences	Main behavioural competences
Industrial data scientist	Extract and prepare data, conduct advanced analyses, apply the results to improve products or production	Ability to understand both production processes and IT systems Programming competences, including the ability to use programming languages	Analytical skills Flexibility. Self-organisational capacity Systemic vision
IT solutions architect	Responsible for the overall design of the system Map business needs based on system requirements and technical requirements Produce the technical specifications, integrating different technologies, platforms, and people	Data management competences Skills and knowledge of enabling and complementary technologies Business processes understanding	Design skills Systemic vision Adaptability
Computer engineer/industrial programmer	Develop the technical solutions identified by the IT solutions architect	Use of major general purpose languages, such as Java, C++ or Python Ability to use specific applications for industrial simulations and general programming of data analysis Ability to program robots and digital devices	Problem solving Analytical skills Design ability

Role	Job description	Main technical competences	Main behavioural competences
Industrial UI (user interface)/UX (user experience) designer	Design and optimise interfaces for the user (UI) and for user experience (UX) Design each screen or page with which a user interacts (UI designer), design the product fruition path (UX designer) Guarantee the correct use of interfaces according to the planned path	Ability to design intuitive dashboards on tablets and mobile phones, machine and robot interfaces, augmented reality applications Ability to optimise the usability of devices	Design skills Customer orientation Systemic vision Flexibility

Table 13.3 An emerging role and related skills in the material source development process

Role	Job description	Main technical competences	Main behavioural competences
E-buyer	Study international supply Monitor trends and performance of countries and suppliers, analyse data in real time and make purchase plans Simulate combinations of international purchases from the perspective of global performance Lead the production team towards raw material changes	Knowledge of international supply markets Mastery of digital tools and e-commerce platforms Language skills (English + emerging countries' languages) Legal knowledge of different international contexts Ability to read global changes in supply and demand Ability to use analytics tools Ability to work on performance indicators	Team management Problem and conflict solving Communication with all parts of the organisation Coordination

sources by which trends are created; develop innovation in terms of materials, fabrics, research, and advanced experiments; and purchase materials virtually. The e-buyer, which is considered an emerging, highly innovative role, represents an evolution of traditional roles (Table 13.3).

Manufacturing

Technology transforms production processes not only in large companies but also in SMEs, which increasingly exploit the opportunities offered by 3DP and related digital technologies to facilitate prototyping, production efficiency, and product customisation. Requiring more limited operational involvement from the designer, 3DP allows users to develop virtual models of products based on generative design algorithms, to modify new or previously inserted models using a digitiser, and to optimise "the placement of the pieces" according to predefined criteria using robotics that reduce operating costs in production by automating and optimising standardised tasks (Sun & Zhao, 2017, 2018). In this way, technology redefines the roles of the designer, patternmaker, and manufacturer and

Table 13.4 Several traditional roles and related skills and competences in the digital manufacturing process

Traditional roles enriched

Role	Job description	Main technical competences	Main behavioural competences
Designer/planner/patternmaker and roles connected with creativity	Design goods that are customisable and in line with the changing demands of the market Improve design processes by making them faster and more actionable throughout the chain Work with digital design machinery Combine new technologies with traditional knowledge	Marketing knowledge and data analysis skills Design skills to develop new collections in line with demand Advanced and constantly updated technical and digital skills Computer competences in the use of computer-aided design and CAM2® programs	Relational skills Teamwork Ability to relate to management and production staff Problem and conflict solving
Repairer and maintenance of industrial machines and plants	Assemble and/or disassemble parts and mechanical components Repair parts or components of machinery or industrial plants by identifying faults and finding effective solutions to solve problems Carry out routine and extraordinary maintenance activities on equipment and systems and carry out checks and revisions on parts and components	Knowledge of mechanics and production techniques Computer and electronic knowledge Technical design skills Knowledge and ability to use machine tools available Ability to interface with various devices Ability to use complex machinery Ability to understand and draw up the technical sheets Ability to evaluate the quality of work	Ability to process and analyse data from a variety of sources Problem solving Systemic vision Adaptability

(continued)

Table 13.4 (continued)

Traditional roles enriched

Role	Job description	Main technical competences	Main behavioural competences
Researcher (on fibres, fabrics, leather, etc.)	Realise studies and solutions for new materials, new textile applications. and the development of digital technologies Combine the knowledge of materials sciences, chemistry, and physics with new engineering and manufacturing technologies to contribute to future innovations	Knowledge of marketing and market trends Chemical-pharmaceutical and physical knowledge Computer and engineering knowledge Knowledge of statistics Ability to collect and interpret empirical data Ability to develop organisational proposals	Ability to investigate alternative solutions Teamwork ability Ability to draw up technical documentation

Table 13.5 Several emerging and new roles and related skills and competences in the digital manufacturing process

Emerging and new roles

Role	Job description	Main technical competences	Main behavioural competences
Systems engineer	Implement structured development processes from conception to implementation up to the commissioning of the system Optimise technological and infrastructural solutions by providing support to management and specialists Collect the needs expressed by the various actors (customers, production units, suppliers) and carry out a project risk analysis Manage the system	Project management Knowledge of IT systems Knowledge of programming languages Understanding of corporate processes and procedures Logical-mathematical skills Ability to jointly process several factors Management of the different interfaces Ability to understand and draft technical documentation	Ability to understand the problems Ability to identify alternative solutions Written and oral technical communication skills Interpersonal skills
Customisation manager	Plan to encourage the production of products in line with the needs of end customers Responsible for conducting product, competition, market trend, and consumer panel analysis Support the purchasing department through the creation and structuring of the collection, ensuring that the range meets market demands	Ability to understand market changes Ability to use tools for analysing consumer preferences Innovation Ability to link between research and production	Ability to work in synergy with different departments Communication skills Problem and conflict solving

(continued)

Table 13.5   (continued)

Emerging and new roles

Role	Job description	Main technical competences	Main behavioural competences
Sustainability manager/risk manager	Ensure that the company operates in conditions of complete legality and ethics, safety, and respect for workers, efficiency and maximum protection of the environment Propose corporate social responsibility policies, exploiting the opportunities of technology Collaborate with designers and managers for the development of sustainable processes and products Ensure contingency plans	Legal-regulatory knowledge of health and safety Business management knowledge Knowledge of environmental sustainability and corporate social responsibility Ability to understand computer, electronic, and production processes. Ability to analyse big data and detect opportunities and problems Ability to prepare reports and projects	Strategic vision, planning, and multitasking control competences Ability to motivate organisational change Relational skills with the whole organisation Ability to communicate with the outside world on social media about sustainability and risk prevention policies

creates new roles. The designer and model maker can increasingly be an independent professional who exists externally rather than being a material part of the company. Table 13.4 presents the new roles according to the level of innovation: traditional roles subject to transformation, emerging roles, and new roles.

Retail and Multichannel Marketing

IT skills are becoming increasingly important in the macro process, as they are necessary to master the new tools of e-commerce and multichannel marketing. The roles that assert themselves in this process are related to digital marketing. They are considered emerging and new roles because they appeared recently and demand for them is growing rapidly. Although these roles are categorised under retail and multichannel marketing processes, in Industry 4.0, they are so frequently associated

Table 13.6 A traditional role and related skills and competences in the retail and multichannel marketing process

Traditional role enriched

Role	Job description	Main technical competences	Main behavioural competences
Online sales clerk	Putting strategies into practice Selling both B2C and B2B types Maintain online platforms where the company's products are marketed Manage orders and purchases and schedules Conduct deliveries Manage online after-sales and customer care services	Commercial and sales knowledge Ability to use new media and ICT Ability to interact with new media Ability to offer customer service Language skills Understanding of processes Knowledge of how to manage orders Bargaining competences Marketing competences Ability to collect, analyse, and interpret data on customers Ability to use IT tools and databases Knowledge of customer data	Empathic skills Cultural skills Relational skills Data and information analysis skills Problem-solving skills

B2B business-to-business, *B2C* business-to-consumer, *ICT* information and communications technology

with all operations that digital marketing skills have become a transversal competence, as indicated in the research mentioned above.

Digital marketers take on very different responsibilities depending on whether they are working as managers or specialists. Specialists frequently possess skills that can constitute specific specialised roles (social marketing expert, search engine optimisation master, etc.). As experts, they often deal with external professionals who collaborate with the company.

The traditional profile of a remote sales employee (including currently required skills) is presented in Table 13.6, while the positions related to multichannel and digital marketing are shown in Table 13.7.

Table 13.7 Several emerging and new roles and related skills and competences in the retail and digital marketing process

Emerging and new roles

Role	Job description	Main technical competences	Main behavioural competences
E-business manager	Study the markets to create an electronic strategic plan for the sale of products and services online Improve data integrity, positioning of online tools and brand exposure Lead the marketing and sales management team using ICT tools to achieve sales goals Provide accurate information and offers to business partners	Knowledge of international markets Advanced marketing knowledge Mastery of digital tools and e-commerce platforms Linguistic knowledge (English + emerging countries) Legal knowledge of the various international contexts Ability to read global changes in supply and demand Ability to use analytics tools Ability to plan a sales strategy	Team management Communication Ability to relate with all parts of the organisatio Coordination Motivation for learning and knowledge transfer
Digital marketing expert Transversal to supply chain processes	Define online marketing strategies and propose online and offline initiatives Take care of online customers Monitor the development of material useful for a marketing strategy (engagement, communication, visual and textual content, marketing strategy, customer and potential)	Marketing knowledge Knowledge of multichannel strategy Ability to use IoT technologies Knowledge of the various customer interface devices Some or all of the competences listed in Table 13.8	Communication skills Empathy Interpersonal skills

ICT information and communications technology, *IoT* internet of things

Table 13.8 Set of skills and competences for specialist roles in the retail and digital marketing process

Competence or specialist role (job description) to support digital marketing	
Social marketing	Select the social networks suitable for promoting the business Publish content on social networks using the most suitable expressive techniques for each publication
Search engine optimisation	Occupy and improve the positioning of the company's website pages within the search engine results Direct the work of copywriters and select external sites with which to collaborate
Customer relationship management	Take care of the systems that keep track of all contacts between company and customer (phone calls, complaints, purchases, etc.) and then allow users to profile guests according to economic importance, level of loyalty, purchasing habits, etc
Copy writer	Curate the contents of the site to optimise its position within search engine results and communicate effectively with visitors to the corporate website
Web editing	Create the contents of the company website while keeping the information provided to customers updated

Table 13.8 lists some skills that may be present in the digital marketing expert, or constitute other specific specialist roles.

A Summary of the Changes to Position Characteristics in the Digital Fashion Industry

The proposed roles and skills in the previous tables highlight how the transformation of the digital fashion industry includes both operational roles and specialist and management roles. To examine these impacts on positions, and the skills required to occupy them, it is useful to consider the classification of jobs created by Mintzberg (1983) according to horizontal and vertical specialisation. Horizontal specialisation measures breadth, or the number and extent of duties required in the position, while vertical specialisation measures depth, or the amount of control employees have over the tasks they perform[1]. Mintzberg identified four types of positions: unskilled/low-skilled jobs, which are characterised by high horizontal and vertical specialisation (few and highly standardised tasks over which workers have no control); specialist or expert/professional positions, which have high horizontal and low vertical specialisation (specific tasks over which workers have a high level of control); middle-management positions, which have low horizontal and high vertical specialisation (many and varied tasks over which workers do not have full control); and other management positions (many varied tasks over which workers have full control).

Unskilled/Low-Skilled Jobs

Operational roles are characterised by gradual position expansion and enrichment with a consequent increase in skills and a strong reduction in their traditionally high levels of horizontal and vertical specialisation. These positions are expanding due to a work organisation that is less and less fragmented and more oriented to the logic of the process; this evolving system asks workers to perform a plurality of operations that are strongly integrated. These operational positions require higher levels of qualification than traditional activities in these roles and, as such, companies are more likely to invest in training to improve operator qualifications. It follows that the nine activities associated with traditionally unskilled jobs require a higher level of decision-making discretion and autonomy (Scheer, 2012); these competences are associated with responsibility and, often, results that must be achieved. Therefore, initially unskilled positions also absorb activities traditionally associated with higher levels of employment, entrusted with not only the programming and control of simple machines but also more advanced coordination roles. A transition from initially or traditionally low-skilled positions to specialist positions or coordination positions (upgrading) is likely. Operators are therefore more educated and digitised, working in teams with engineers, technologists, logisticians, and maintainers (Magone & Mazali, 2016); this collaboration inserts them within knowledge-sharing processes that facilitate further professional development.

Consequently, there is a strong reduction in truly unskilled positions; these positions are increasingly replaced by automation and robotics.

Lower-Level Management Jobs

Lower-level managers are traditionally characterised by a wide range of activities which places them in a position of coordination of processes or at the head of organisational units at an intermediate level. From a quantitative point of view, two scenarios are possible: middle management positions may be reduced following the downward transfer of programming and coordination skills that were traditionally their focus, or these positions may increase as more low-skilled workers become professionalised and must be coordinated (which reduces the extent of control for each middle manager). In any case, these positions will be subject to job enrichment processes, and entrusted with the task of using increasingly sophisticated and innovative tools for programming and controlling activities. Regardless of the scenario, managerial competences will be important for those occupying these positions. These positions are also increasingly likely to require leadership skills or the ability to involve, guide, and support a group.

Professional Jobs

Future digital fashion companies will feature an increasing number of specialist figures. The strong integration between activities means there will be a need for roles capable of in-depth intervention on specific activities and problems, both regarding technology (Table 13.2) and parts of production and managerial processes. Specialists in risks, sustainability, innovative fibres and products, research and development, and HRM processes (online recruiters, etc.), although they may be external, will share business activities and objectives. Therefore, specific technical skills previously associated with middle management (programming and control, marketing, finance, etc.) and soft skills (such as internal and external communication) will be necessary even within increasingly specialised positions.

Management Jobs

Managerial roles will be associated with a rapidly expanding set of skills, particularly skills related to technological principles and tools. New knowledge and skills related to digital techniques will be applied to traditional positions (marketing managers, finance managers, etc.). Necessary

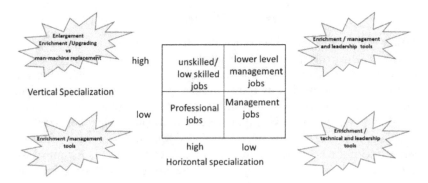

Fig. 13.2 Summary of changes in jobs according to the level of specialisation

competences will include real-time monitoring of information, knowledge related to supervisees and activities, and knowledge decision-making systems that integrate quantitative and qualitative information. HRM tools will also be fundamental due to the widespread and collaborative nature that management will increasingly assume within organisations; rather than only applying to HRM experts, HRM skills and tools will be required of all those who coordinate teams. Figure 13.2 represents a synthesis of these anticipated position changes.

THE IMPACT OF THE DIGITAL FASHION INDUSTRY ON HRM

The new professions present in Industry 4.0 raise the question of skills required in HRM processes. Technology will strongly integrate operations, machinery, and other parts of the physical and digital system, and digitalisation will organise workers into collective units (teams, task forces, etc.) in which workers with different skills will manage integrated nuclei of activities together while probably conducting many activities remotely. These two trends will considerably loosen traditional boss–employee bonds in favour of horizontal relationships of support, self-programming, and control. This situation poses challenges for HRM; it will be necessary to consider the changes caused by technology when reimagining the processes of evaluating, training, and managing employees. Through a survey conducted in focus groups, Piwowar-Sulej (2020) noted that the methods of managing human resources change depending on the type of position, that is, depending on whether employees are low skilled, middle skilled, creative/highly skilled or specialists/managers. The surveyed individuals believed that companies reserve innovative HRM tools and approaches for the most qualified levels. This result, as Piwowar-Sulej hypothesised, is very likely due to access to technology that is not yet widespread in the area under investigation; therefore, it seems likely that context, culture, and level of business skills make a greater difference in the use of HRM techniques and tools than the characteristics of jobs.

Technology impacts HRM in two major ways: how new techniques and tools enter HRM processes and which new skills become required for HR managers.

The sections below explore technology's effect on HRM processes based on recent literature on the subject (Cascio & Montealegre, 2016; Onik et al., 2018; Sivathanu & Pillai, 2018).

Recruitment and Selection

Recruitment and selection could represent an example of how, in contrast to the Piwowar-Sulej (2020) research results, for some activities, technology could apply especially to low-skilled positions. Because less strategic decision making is involved, technology may be most useful in recruiting and selecting unskilled roles (Varra, 2020): predictive techniques can manage the entire process of recruitment, choice, and relative learning (Elfenbein & Sterling, 2018; Varra, 2020). The use of algorithms is important for probing context information, including the data that candidates leave on social media, mobile devices, electronic cards, and so on, and, therefore, for predicting candidates' productivity. Furthermore, the software can adapt information to internal data and incorporate it into their evolution, developing a progressive model of learning that improves prediction (Elfenbein & Sterling, 2018; Varra, 2020). Artificial intelligence can also adequately support the recruitment and selection process of other moderately skilled positions, especially by decreasing the number of candidates when it is too high. For highly qualified figures, automation is limited to the recruitment phase and almost exclusively used to sift through the candidate's previous work experience (Elfenbein & Sterling, 2018). These positions are less compatible with predictive techniques; even in this case, however, ICT techniques (such as expert systems, scenario techniques, and simulations) can facilitate the interpretation of information or the formulation of alternative prefigurations of the decision-making context. These tasks are fundamental for exploring and rethinking problems, even when they do not automatically arrive at a solution.

Technological changes have affected the actual selection phase by changing the required methods of verifying the skills candidates possess. The soft skills component, required in all positions of the digital fashion factory, means that the interview phase cannot be conducted in a summary "to meet" way; rather, it requires specific techniques (assessment centres, in-depth interviews, personality tests) to verify the wide set of skills the literature phase and job postings indicate are needed. It may be useful to conduct necessary tests on candidates, including fact finding, role playing, leaderless discussions, and so on.

Appraisal

Similar considerations must be made for the employee appraisal process. The assessment of human resources will extend to all levels and include different methodologies and a broad portfolio of skills. Much assessment information will come from digital traces left from work—instant or on-demand—alerts triggered by integrated, context-sensitive technologies that track the work of roaming employees. The software manages performance evaluation. Other factors, however, must take on increased weight in the evaluation, namely skills such as self-organisation, teamwork, and internal communication. Like employee selection, appraisal requires HR managers to possess adequate skills and use appropriate techniques and assessment tools (such as assessment centres). Furthermore, the introduction of autonomy and discretion to tasks performed at all levels raises the issue of performance evaluation, particularly when it comes to defining and verifying objectives which in the digital factory are also a coordination mechanism (Mintzberg, 1983; Thompson, 1967) while loosening the hierarchical links within organisational units. The process of defining objectives must increasingly be conducted by those who are within the system. This situation emphasises the importance of participatory leadership styles with ample autonomy left to collaborators, and of evaluation systems that are not only brought to employees' attention and shared but also, in a move toward self-determination, largely entrusted to individuals.

Remuneration

Technology also affects the remuneration process. Modern software can handle pay survey analyses, complex bonus and commission structures, reports, and analyses. Future remuneration will be based on an articulated system that includes specific work production and individual results linked to objectives, productivity, and company results in terms of efficiency, sustainability, and so on.

Increasing weight may be attributed to the variables of remuneration, which will have to both compensate the individual for their contribution to the organisation and create a very high commitment at the base of low top-level systems. It is essential to combine three types of information: information on context (benchmarking of remuneration systems); information on how work is carried out (appraisal system); and information on the personal and professional needs of workers (which can be used to identify effective compensation and incentive systems).

Career

The career system is based on employee-centred career arrangements in recognition that wishes and needs vary throughout an individual's career. Unattached workers can carry out activities anywhere and at any time (Piwowar-Sulej, 2020). Therefore, personalised paths will be designed outside company boundaries that will be supported by the operational and relationship networks created by Industry 4.0. The mobility of resources across innovative structures can increase the development of knowledge and innovation within structures and the transfer of knowledge across the industry system. Therefore, in addition to traditional vertical career paths, the spiral paths and professional paths of deepening knowledge typical of specialist jobs will be important.

Training

The corporate training process is affected by technological change in both the content of employee training and the tools used to complete the training. The transition to the digital fashion industry requires strong training support and internal adaptation of the technical skills necessary to develop, expand, and enrich the roles we have discussed. Training cannot stop at the content of the new technology; it must also develop new ways of approaching and organising activities, considering issues of teamwork, cooperation, orientation to change, and adaptability, while simultaneously focusing on the need to develop sustainable orientations and social responsibility. Training in Industry 4.0 is based on access to immediately available knowledge through new techniques and tools; this transformation requires on-demand development of intellectual skills and abilities through the unlimited supply of teaching materials, virtual reality simulations, asynchronous training, educational games, chat rooms, and knowledge management systems (Piwowar-Sulej, 2020).

Conclusions: The Challenges for Businesses and the Education System

The fourth technological era is gradually transforming the world of manufacturing and services, while also creating closely related social and cultural changes. This transformation affects all processes and all professional roles within companies. The fashion sector, by nature exposed to extremely variable demand and a long-standing trade-off between exclusivity and artisan refinement and the need for efficiency and productivity, can grasp, with new technologies, the possibility of incorporating into internal processes, in almost real time, customers' expectations and purchasing and consumption behaviours; they can then combine these behaviours with the demands of environmental sustainability and the needs of internal organisational rationality. Two issues are particularly critical: the difficulty of making innovations in very small contexts, and the difficulty of adapting traditional roles to incorporate new required qualifications, increased hybridity, and the possibility of acquiring the latest professional skills. These changes cannot occur unless managerial positions incorporate greater technical skills and leadership components to integrate the traditional set of skills and competences with modern ones. Management skills and leadership skills must coexist in all managerial roles. A major managerial process subject to change is that of human resources, which faces challenges both in having to manage employees with more qualified skills and in losing its exclusive role of HRM as automation and other departments take on these tasks. All roles coordinating teams or employees will adopt HRM activities, which means specific relationships must be defined between centre and periphery. As a result, those conducting HRM activities will need to prepare to use technological HRM tools suitable for different contexts and support their effective use by others.

Organisational culture appears to play a fundamental role in all innovation processes (Varra, 2012). Innovation requires a culture of comparison, exchange, and collaboration within and outside the system so that all processes of knowledge development can be activated (Nonaka & Takeuki, 1995) and remain innovative on the market.

A person-centric culture is needed which emphasises the characteristics and contributions of individuals. The enhancement of the person in a high-tech system is mistakenly considered an oxymoron, considering how the technological changes have depersonalised many public and private organisations, yet it is the prerequisite for the creation of digital factories because of the close interconnection between machines, skills, and reasons. Finally, institutions must support organisations in the transition to Industry 4.0 enterprises by creating adequate policies. A system of basic and applied research must be developed and adequately supported to remain competitive at a national level. The systems of education and academic training must adapt to change. Education in technological innovation must be present in all schools. Schools must not only bridge the gaps in the use of technology to support traditional forms of knowledge sharing and delivery, but also create structured and frequent opportunities for experimentation through innovation and applied research laboratories. In particular, management schools must adapt to the updated needs of businesses. It is clear that, especially in countries such as Italy, university programmes are slower to react to the needs of companies in terms of skills: university masters' programs, professional courses, and a wider range of academic offerings must be designed to adequately respond to the rise of digital businesses. It is once again necessary that countries create development plans, following European requests for Innovation 4.0., and implement them with a systemic vision and the involvement of all interested parties.

NOTE

1. Therefore, the positions in which few and very limited tasks are carried out have high levels of horizontal specialisation, while the positions in which workers operate with low decision-making autonomy have high levels of vertical specialisation. At the opposite extreme are positions in which many major tasks are carried out and workers have significant or complete control over these tasks.

References

Antosz, K. (2018). Maintenance—Identification and analysis of the competency gap. Eksploatacja I Niezawodnos. *Maintenance and Reliability, 20*(3), 484–494.

Ashby, A. (2016). From global to local: Reshoring for sustainability. *Operations Management Research, 9*(3/4), 75–88.

Bayus, B. L. (2013). Crowdsourcing new product ideas over time: An analysis of the Dell IdeaStorm community. *Management Science, 59*(1), 226–244.

Becattini, G. (1998). *Distretti industriali e made in Italy.* Bollati Boringhieri.

Beltrametti L., Guarnacci N., Intini N., & La Forgia C. (2017). *La fabbrica connessa. La manifattura italiana (attra)verso Industria 4.0.* Guerini e Associati.

Benešová, A., & Tupa, J. (2017). Requirements for education and qualification of people in Industry 4.0. *Procedia Manufacturing, 11*, 2195–2202.

Bertola, P., Colombi, C., & Vacca, F. (2017). Managing the creative process. In E. Rigaud-Lacresse & F. M. Pini (Eds.), *New luxury management, Palgrave: Creating and managing sustainable value across the organization* (pp. 159–188). MacMillan.

Bertola, P., & Teunissen, J. (2018). Fashion 4.0. Innovating fashion industry through digital transformation. *Research Journal of Textile and Apparel, 22*(4), 352–369.

Bettarini, U., & Tartaglione, C. (2018). Le nuove professioni 4.0 nel sistema moda. https://ares20.it/wp-content/uploads/2018/06/ebook_len uoveprofessioni4.0giugno2018.pdf.

BMBF. (2014). Industrie 4.0-Volks- und betriebswirtschaftliche Faktoren für den Standort Deutschland. https://www.digitaletechnologien.de/DT/Red aktion/DE/Downloads/Publikation/autonomik-40-studie-markttperspekti ven-broschuere.html. Accessed 29 November 2020.

Bonekamp, L., & Matthias, S. (2015). Consequences of Industry 4.0 on human labour and work organization. *Journal of Business and Media Psychology, 6*(1), 33–40.

Bostrom, N. (2016). *Superintelligence: Paths, dangers, strategies.* Oxford University Press.

Boyatzis, R. E. (1982). *The competent manager: A model for effective performance.* John Wiley and Sons.

Braidotti, R. (2008). *The posthuman.* Polity Press.

Brun, A. (2017). Luxury as a construct: An evolutionary perspective. In E. Rigaud-Lacresse & F. M. Pini (Eds.), *Palgrave, advances in luxury* (pp. 1–18). MacMillan.

Brun, A., Caniato, F., Caridi, M., Castelli, C., Miragliotta, G., Ronchi, S., et al. (2008). Logistics and supply chain management in luxury fashion retail:

Empirical investigation of Italian firms. *International Journal of Production Economics, 114,* 554–570.

Buciuni, G., & Finotto, V. (2016). Innovation in global value chains: Co-location of production and development in Italian low-tech industries. *Regional Studies, 50*(12), 2010–2023.

Cascio, W. F., & Montealegre, R. (2016). How technology is changing work and organizations. *Annual Review of Organizational Psychology and Organizational Behavior, 3*(1), 349–375.

Cavaliere, V., & Varra, L. (2020). La gestione delle interdipendenze e il coordinamento. In C. Bonti, V. Cavaliere, & E. Cori (Eds.), *Lineamenti di organizzazione* (pp. 203–233). EGEA.

Chan, T. Y., Wu, C., & Xie, Y. (2011). Measuring the lifetime value of customers acquired from google search advertising. *Marketing Science, 30*(5), 837–850.

Chen, T., & Lin, C. W. (2015). Estimating the simulation workload for factory simulation as a cloud service. *Journal of Intelligent Manufacturing, 28,* 1–19.

Christopher, M., Lowson, R., & Peck, H. (2004). Creating agile supply chains in the fashion Industry. *International Journal of Retail & Distribution Management, 32*(8), 367–376.

De Felice, F., & Petrillo, A. (2013). Key success factors for organizational innovation in the fashion industry. *International Journal of Engineering Business Management, 5,* 1–11.

Díaz Bermúdez, M., & Flores Juárez, B. F. (2017). Competencies to adopt Industry 4.0 for operations management personnel at automotive parts suppliers in Nuevo Leon. In *Proceedings of the international conference on industrial engineering and operations management Bogota, Colombia* (pp. 736–747).

Dinner, I. M., Van Heerde, H. J., & Neslin, S. A. (2014). Driving online and offline sales: The cross-channel effects of traditional, online display, and paid search advertising. *Journal of Marketing Research, 51*(5), 527–545.

Elfenbein, D. W., & Sterling, A. D. (2018). (When) is hiring strategic? Human capital acquisition in the age of algorithms. *Strategy Science, 3*(4), 668–682.

Fitsilis, P., Tsoutsa, P., & Gerogiannis, V. (2018). Industry 4.0: Required personnel. *International Scientific Journal "Industry 4.0", 3*(3), 130–133.

Fratocchi, L., Di Mauro, C., Barbieri, P., Nassimbeni, G., & Zanoni, A. (2014). When manufacturing moves back: Concepts and questions. *Journal of Purchasing and Supply Management, 20*(1), 54–59.

Freire, N. A. (2014). When luxury advertising adds the identitary values of luxury: A semiotic analysis. *Journal of Business Research, 67,* 2666–2675.

Gehrke, L., Rule, D., Bellmann, C., & Siemes, S. (2015). A discussion of qualifications and skills in the factory of the future: A German and American perspective. https://www.academia.edu/26953030/A_Discussion_of_Qua

lifications_and_Skills_in_the_Factory_of_the_Future_A_German_and_Ame rican_Perspective. Accessed 25 November 2020.

Gilchrist, A. (2016). *Industry 4.0: The industrial internet of things*. Apress.

Granger, M. M. (2012). *Fashion: The industry and its careers*. Fairchild Books.

Grzybowska, K., & Łupicka, A. (2017). Key competencies for industry 4.0. *Economics & Management Innovations, 1*(1), 250–253.

Guercini, S., & Ranfagni, S. (2013). Sustainability and luxury: The Italian case of a supply chain based on native wools. *The Journal of Corporate Citizenship, 52,* 76–89.

Hartmann, E., & Bovenschulte, M. (2013). Skills needs analysis for "industry 4.0" based on roadmaps for smart systems. In: SKOLKOVO Moscow School of Management & International Labour Organization (Ed.), *Using technology foresights for identifying future skills needs* (pp. 24–36). Global Workshop Proceedings.

Hashem, I. A. T., Yaqoob, I., Anuar, N. B., Mokhtar, S., Gani, A., & Khan, S. U. (2015). The rise of big data on cloud computing: Review and open research issues. *Information Systems, 47,* 98–115.

Hecklau, F., Orth, R., Kidschun, R., & Kohl, O. (2017). Human resources management: Meta-study—Analysis of future competences in industry 4.0. file:///C:/Users/lucia/Downloads/Human_Resources_Management_Meta-Study_Analysis_of_Future_Competences_in_Industry_4_0%20(1).pdf.

Hermann, M., Pentek, T., & Otto, B. (2016). Design principles for industrie 4.0 scenarios. In *49th Hawaii international conference on system sciences (HICSS)* (pp. 3928–3937).

Hofmann, E., & Rusch, M. (2017). Industry 4.0 and the current status as well as future prospects on logistics. *Computers in Industry, 89,* 23–34.

Imran, F., & Kantola, J. (2018, 21–25 July). Review of industry 4.0 in the light of sociotechnical system theory and competence-based view: A future research agenda for the evolute approach. In *Proceedings of the international conference on applied human factors and ergonomics, Orlando, FL, USA,* (pp. 118–128). Springer.

Jensen K. R. (2017). Global organizational leadership for luxury companies (2017). In E. Rigaud-Lacresse, & F. M. Pini (Eds.), *New luxury management: Creating and managing sustainable value across the organization. Palgrave advances in luxury* (pp. 33–46).

Jerman, A., Bach, M. P., & Aleksić, A. (2019). Transformation towards smart factory system: Examining new job profiles and competencies. *Systems Research and Behavioral Science, 37*(2), 388–402.

Jerman, A., Bach, M. P., & Bertoncelj, A. (2018). A bibliometric and topic analysis on future, competences at smart factories. *Machines, 6*(41), 1–13.

Kagermann, H., Wahlster, W., & Helbig, J. (2013, April). *Recommendations for implementing the strategic initiative industrie 4.0: Final report of the*

Industrie 4.0 Working Group. Munich: Academy of Science and Engineering. http://digital.bib-bvb.de/view/bvb_single/single.jsp?dvs=160664948549 8~98&locale=it_IT&VIEWER_URL=/view/bvb_single/single.jsp?&DEL IVERY_RULE_ID=39&bfe=view/action/singleViewer.do?dvs=&frameId= 1&usePid1=true&usePid2=true. Accessed 29 November 2020.

Kalbaska, N., & Cantoni L. (2019). Digital fashion competences: Market practices and needs. In: R. Rinaldo, & R. Bandinelli (Eds.), Business models and ICT technologies for the fashion supply chain. In *Proceedings of IT4Fashion 2017 and IT4Fashion 2018* (pp. 125–135). Springer.

Kannan, P. K., & Li, H. (2017). Digital marketing: A framework, review and research agenda. *International Journal of Research in Marketing, 34,* 22–45.

Kapferer, J. N., & Bastien, V. (2009). The specificity of luxury management: Turning marketing upside down. *Journal of Brand Management, 16*(5), 311–322.

Kapferer, J. N., & Bastien, V. (2012). *The luxury strategy: Break the rules of marketing to build luxury brands.* Kogan Page.

Kinkel, S., Schemmann, B., & Lichtner, R. (2017). Critical competencies for the innovativeness of value creation champions: Identifying challenges and work-integrated solutions. *Procedia Manufacturing, 9,* 323–330.

Kleefstra, A. (2019). A literature review into leadership styles discussed in the past five years. *Open Journal of Social Sciences, 7,* 180–190.

Kong, X. T. R., Luo, H., Huang, G. Q., & Yang, X. (2019). Industrial wearable system: The human-centric empowering technology in Industry 4.0. *Journal of Intelligent Manufacturing, 30,* 2853–2869.

Kruger, S., & Steyn, A. A. (2020). A conceptual model of entrepreneurial competencies needed to utilise technologies of industry 4.0. *The International Journal of Entrepreneurship and Innovation,* 1–12. https://journals.sagepub. com/doi/pdf/10.1177/1465750320927359. Accessed 29 November 2020.

Leinweber, S. (2013). Etappe 3: Kompetenzmanagement. In M. T. Meifert (Ed.), *Strategische Personalentwicklung - Ein Programm in acht Etappen* (3rd ed., pp. 145–178). Springer Fachmedien.

Li, H., Jain, S., & Kannan, P. K. (2019). Optimal design of free samples for digital products and services. *Journal of Marketing Research, 56*(3), 419–438.

Lin, S., & Piercy, N. (2013). New product development competencies and capabilities: The case of the fashion SME. *Journal of General Management, 38*(2), 61–77.

Liu, M., Ma, J., Lin, L., Ge, M., Wang, Q., & Liu, C. (2017). Intelligent assembly system for mechanical products and key technology based on internet of things. *Journal of Intelligent Manufacturing, 28*(2), 271–299.

Longo, F., Nicoletti, L., & Padovano, A. (2017). Smart operators in industry 4.0: A human-centered approach to enhance operators' capabilities and competencies within the new smart factory context. *Computer and Industrial Engineering, 113*, 144–159.

Lorenz, M., Rüßmann, M., Strack, R., Lueth, K. L., & Bolle, M. (2015). Man and machine in industry 4.0: How will technology transform the industrial workforce through 2025. In BCG (Ed.) https://www.bcg.com/it-it/public ations/2015/technology-business-transformation-engineered-products-infras tructure-man-machine-industry-4.

Luo, L., & Toubia, O. (2015). Improving online idea generation platforms and customizing the task structure on the basis of consumers' domain-specific knowledge. *Journal of Marketing, 79*(5), 100–114.

Mabkhot, M. M., Al-Ahmari, A. M., Salah, B., & Alkhalefah, H. (2018). Requirements of the smart factory system: A survey and perspective. *Machines, 6*(2), 1–22.

Magone, A., & Mazali, T. (2016). *Industria 4.0: Uomini e machine nella fabbrica digitale*. Guerini e Associati Edizioni.

Majeed, M. A. A., & Rupasinghe, T. D. (2017). Internet of things (IoT) embedded future supply chains for industry 4.0: An assessment from an ERP-based fashion apparel and footwear industry. *International Journal of Supply Chain Management, 6*(1), 25–40.

McClelland, D. C. (1973). Testing for competence rather than for intelligence. *American Psychologist, 28*(1), 1–14.

Mintzberg, H. (1983). *La progettazione dell'organizzazione aziendale*. Il Mulino.

Nagorny, K., Lima-Mointeiro, P., Barata, J., & Colombo, A. W. (2017). Big data analysis in smart manufacturing: A review. *International Journal of Communications, Network and System Sciences, 10*(3), 31–58.

Nonaka, I., & Takeuchi, H. (1995). *The knowledge-creating company: How Japanese companies create the dynamics of innovation*. Oxford University Press.

Nyikes, Z. (2018). Contemporary digital competency review. *Interdisciplinary Description of Complex Systems: INDECS, 16*(1), 124–131.

Obitko, M., Jirkovský, V., & Bezdíček, J. (2013). Big data challenges in industrial automation. In V. Mařík, J. L. Martinez Lastra, & P. Skobelev (Eds.) *Applications of Holonic and multi-agent systems* (pp. 305–316). Springer.

Onik, M. M. H., Miraz, M. H., & Kim, C. S. (2018). A recruitment and human resource management technique using Blockchain technology for Industry 4.0. In *Proceedings of the smart cities symposium (SCS-2018)* (pp. 11–16).

Ozuem, W., Howell, K. E., & Lancaster, G. (2008). Communicating in the new interactive marketspace. *European Journal of Marketing, 42*(9/10), 1059–1083.

Ozuem, W., Patel, A., Howell, K. E., & Lancaster, G. (2017). An exploration of customers' response to online service recovery initiatives. *International Journal of Market Research, 59*(1), 97–116.

Ozuem, W., Thomas, T., & Lancaster, G. (2016). The influence of customer loyalty on small island economies: An empirical and exploratory study. *Journal of Strategic Marketing, 24*(6), 447–469.

Pecina, P., & Sladek, P. (2017, 6–8 March). Fourth industrial revolution and technical education. In *Proceedings of the 11th international conference on technology, education and development (INTED), Valencia, Spain* (pp. 2089–2093).

Piccarozzi, M., Aquilani, B., & Gatti, C. (2018). Industry 4.0 in management studies: A systematic literature review. *Sustainability, 10*(10), 3821–3845.

Piwowar-Sulej, K. (2018). Human resources management in the industrial revolution 4.0: General and polish perspective. In *Double-blind peer-reviewed proceedings of the international scientific conference Hradec economic days* (Vol. 8, No. 2, pp. 179–187). https://digilib.uhk.cz/bitstream/handle/20.500.12603/437/Piwowar_HED18_paper_9.pdf?sequence=1&isAllowed=y. Accessed 29 November 2020.

Piwowar-Sulej, K. (2020). Human resource management in the context of industry 4.0. *Scientific Quarterly Organization and Management, 1*(49), 103–113.

Polanji, M. (1966). *The tacit dimension.* Routledge & Kegan Paul.

Prifti, L., Knigge, M., Kienegger, H., & Krcmar, H. (2017). "A competency model for "Industrie 4.0" employees. In J. M. Leimeister, & W. Brenner (Eds.). *Proceedings der 13. Internationalen Tagung Wirtschaftsinformatik (WI 2017)*, St. Gallen, S. (pp. 46–60). https://wi2017.ch/images/wi2017-0262.pdf. Accessed 29 November 2020.

Roberts, G. (1997). *Recruitment and selection: A competency approach.* Chartered Institute of Personnel and Development.

Ronchetti, M., Nobile, T. H., Oliveira, R. A., Kalbaska, N., & Cantoni, L. (2020). *Digital fashion competences: Market practices and needs during COVID19.* https://www.researchgate.net/publication/343259575.

Rowe, C. (1995). Clarifying the use of competence and competency models in recruitment, assessment and staff development. *Industrial and Commercial Training, 27*(11), 12–17.

Scheer, A.-W. (2012). Industrierevolution 4.0 ist mit weitreichenden organisatorischen Konsequenzen verbunden! *Information Management & Consulting, 3*, 10–11.

Schwab, K. (2017). *The fourth industrial revolution.* Crown Business.

Silva, E. S., Hassani, H., & Madsen, D. Ø. (2020). Big Data in fashion: Transforming the retail sector. *Journal of Business Strategy, 41*(4), 21–27.

Sinsel, A., Bangert, C., Stoldt, J., & Buttner, T. (2017). Economic evaluation of the smart ffactory—An approach to the assessment of digitalization in production. *Zeitschrift Für Wirtschaftlichen Fabrikbetrieb, 112*(9), 602–606.

Sivathanu, B., & Pillai, R. (2018). Smart HR 4.0—How industry 4.0 is disrupting HR. *Human Resource Management International Digest, 26*(4), 7–11.

Som, A., & Blanckaert, C. (2015). *The road to luxury: The evolution, markets and strategies of luxury brand management.* John Wiley & Sons.

Spencer, L. M., & Spencer, S. M. (1993). *Competence at work: Models for superior performance.* Wiley.

Sun, L., & Zhao, L. (2017). Envisioning the era of 3D printing: A conceptual model for the fashion industry. *Fashion and Textiles, 4*(25), 2–16.

Sun, L., & Zhao, L. (2018). Technology disruptions: Exploring the changing roles of designers, makers, and users in the fashion industry. *International Journal of Fashion Design, Technology and Education, 11*(3), 362–374.

Tao, F., Cheng, Y., Xu, L. D., Zhang, L., & Li, B. H. (2014). CCIoT-CMfg: Cloud computing and internet of things-based cloud manufacturing service system. *IEEE Transactions on Industrial Informatics, 10*(2), 1435–1442.

Tao, F., Qi, Q., Liu, A., & Kusiak, A. (2018). Data-driven smart manufacturing. *Journal of Manufacturing Systems, 48*, 157–169.

Thompson, J. D. (1967). *Organizations in action.* McGraw-Hill.

Torres, M. V. T., Cardelle-Elawar, M., Mena, M. J. B., & Sanchez, A. M. M. (2003). Social background, gender and self-reported social competence in 11- and 12-year-old Andalusian children. *Electronic Journal of Research in Educational Psychology, 1*(2), 38–56.

Trstenjak, M. (2018). Challenges of human resources management with implementation of industry 4.0. file:///C:/Users/lucia/Downloads/956303.IoTSm_2018_paper_87.pdf. Accessed 29 November 2020.

Ugur, M., Churchill, S. A., & Solomon, E. (2018). Technological innovation and employment in derived labour demand models: A hierarchical meta-regression analysis. *Journal of Economic Surveys, 32*(1), 50–82.

Ustundag, A., & Cevikcan, E. (2017). *Industry 4.0: Managing the digital transformation.* Springer.

Vacca, F. (2015). Artisanal advanced design: Advanced manufacturing processes as a tool to revitalize peculiar Italian (craft)productions. In L. Collina, L. Galluzzo, & A. Meroni (Eds.), *The virtuous circle: Design culture and experimentation* (pp. 703–715). Proceedings of the Cumulus Conference, Milano, McGraw–Hill, Milano.

Vacek, J. (2016). Socio-economic aspects of Industry 4.0. In Proceeding of 4th international conference on innovation management, entrepreneurship and corporate sustainability (IMECS) (pp. 731–741).

Varra, L. (2012). *L'innovazione in azienda: razionalità e creatività nei relativi processi decisionali e organizzativi*. CEDAM.

Varra, L. (2020). Sulla decisione di assunzione: Approcci, contenuti di strategicità e caratteri della scelta. In V. Cavaliere (a cura), *Employability e soft skilldegli studenti universitari. Un modello di analisi del mismatchnella prospettiva manageriale. Implicazioni per l'alta formazionee i career service* (pp. 77–99). Pacini.

Varra, L., & Timolo, M. (2017, 13–15, September). Sustainable human resource management and CSR performance measurement: Sseeking an integration through international standards. In *9th conference on performance measurement and management control- EIASM conference proceedings, Nice, France* (pp. 1–31).

Wan, J., Chen, M., Xia, F., Li, D., & Zhou, K. (2013). From machine-to-machine communications towards cyberphysical systems. *Computer Science and Information Systems, 10*(3), 1105–1128.

Waterman, K. K., & Bruening, P. J. (2014). Big data analytics: Risks and responsibilities. *International Data Privacy Law, 4*(2), 89–95.

Weyer, S., Schmitt, M., Ohmer, M., & Gorecky, D. (2015). Towards industry 4.0—Standardization as the crucial challenge for highly modular, multi-vendor production systems. *IFAC-PapersOnLine, 48*(3), 579–584.

Whysall, Z., Owtram, M., & Brittain, S. (2019). The new talent management challenges of Industry 4.0. *Journal of Management Development, 38*(2), 118–129.

World Economic Forum. (2020). *The future of the job Report 2020*. http://www3.weforum.org/docs/WEF_Future_of_Jobs_2020.pdf. Accessed 29 November 2020.

Wu, D., Liu, X., Hebert, S., Gentzsch, W., & Terpenny, J. (2017). Democratizing digital design and manufacturing using high performance cloud computing: Performance evaluation and benchmarking. *Journal of Manufacturing Systems, 43*, 316–326.

Zhang, J., Ding, G., Zou, Y., Qin, S., & Fu, J. (2019). Review of job shop scheduling research and its new perspectives under Industry 4.0. *Journal of Intelligent Manufacturing, 30*, 1809–1830.

Zhong, R. Y., Xun, X., Klotz, E., & Newman, S. T. (2017). Intelligent manufacturing in the context of industry 4.0: A review. *Engineering, 3*, 616–630.

Zhou, K., Liu, T., & Zhou, L. (2015). Industry 4.0: Towards future industrial opportunities and challenges. In *IEEE, 12th international conference on fuzzy systems and knowledge discovery (FSKD)* (pp. 2147–2152).

CHAPTER 14

Luxury Fashion in the Chinese Marketplace and the New Online Channels: An Emerging Perspective

Serena Rovai and Li Jing

INTRODUCTION

Given the shift from traditional to new operational approaches in the Chinese luxury and fashion marketplace, most luxury fashion brands no longer fear the digital wave and are increasingly focusing on social media marketing (SMM) for product and services' management through daily narratives. SMM activities are a growing area of interest for scholars in luxury fashion marketing because SMMs are a two-way interactive platform for communication and SMM tools may increase customer consciousness and improve luxury brand–customer relationships in the competitive and diversified Chinese luxury fashion marketplace.

S. Rovai (✉)
Excelia Business School, La Rochelle, France

L. Jing
Chongqing University, Chongqing, China

© The Author(s), under exclusive license to Springer Nature 345
Switzerland AG 2021
W. Ozuem and S. Ranfagni (eds.), *The Art of Digital Marketing for Fashion and Luxury Brands*,
https://doi.org/10.1007/978-3-030-70324-0_14

The love Chinese have for luxury has stimulated research in the field (Tsai et al., 2013). The last decade has witnessed an increasing presence of digitalisation in the luxury industry and academia has started to analyse its positive impact on communication as well as on operations and customer relationships with brands (Dacko, 2017; Demirkan & Spohrer, 2014). In the online relationship between consumer and brand, price as well as convenience and product availability have proven to be the key influencing factors, whereas offline, the aesthetic appeal, shopping experience and consumer in-store service were evidenced as the main influencing factors (Liu et al., 2013). Other studies have highlighted that tangibles, physical experiences as well as interactive experiences, must be integrated to better promote and communicate the essence of luxury products in the marketplace and consequently to strengthen their perceived value (Helal & Ozuem 2018; Wu et al., 2015). It has been shown that social media is a fundamental tool for consumer decision making as well as for luxury brand–customer relationship development. Luxury fashion brands have become increasingly present in the Chinese marketplace and lifestyle, and purchasing luxury goods and experiencing a luxury lifestyle have gained unexpected importance and meaning in the Chinese social context. The birth of the Chinese middle class has fuelled the emergence of a highly diversified consumer class with different purchasing attitudes (Cavusgil & Buckley, 2016; Cavusgil & Guercini, 2014; Latham, 2006) and a new way to express their taste, their motivation for purchasing and mode of purchasing luxury fashion (Rambourg, 2014; Rovai, 2016), which has started to disrupt the traditional operations of the luxury and fashion marketplace.

Distinctive aspects of luxury consumer culture have started to emerge in China in the past few years, evidencing new desires and trends for Chinese luxury consumers with respect to luxury brands. In the same way, Chinese luxury brands have entered the Chinese market aspiring to capitalise on the new trend of consumers' increasing "Chinese luxury desire"—even if limited by their lack of specific characteristics of authentic luxury brands, such as heritage, identity and prestige (Chen & Zhang, 2011). With respect to the evolution of the Chinese online consumer market, Jung et al. (2014) evidenced the significant contribution of the internet to the growth in sales of luxury goods in emerging consumer markets. A report from China Internet Network Information Center (2017) indicated that Chinese mobile internet users in China increased to a total of 695.3 million in 2016 and there are approximately 731 million internet users in China, which corresponds to a 53.2% penetration rate. China's luxury marketplace appears to continue to grow despite the challenges associated with international and domestic events. The Chinese luxury and fashion marketplace as well as its shoppers have become fundamental to the survival of the luxury industry in unstable international markets, in particular during the COVID-19 crisis.

The socioeconomic evolution from a centrally planned economy to a market-oriented economy has stimulated Chinese customers to consider luxury fashion brands, which are seen as signs of their newly attained financial accomplishments and acquired social identity (Park et al., 2008). The sociocultural symbolic value of luxury fashion apparel has a key role in adding social status to Chinese shoppers (Adams, 2011). The "new rich" Chinese customers emerged from the new digitally savvy Chinese bourgeoisie, and the increasingly younger chic luxury customers are an exponentially growing segment with an increasing taste for luxury fashion garments. In their appetite for luxury brands, they demonstrate their new status or their need to please themselves and their beloved by converging towards a new digitalised shopping experience, which differs from the experience of other global shoppers. Luxury brands were vigilant about online channels because of their fear of losing their aura of exclusivity (Kapferer, 2014; Okonkwo, 2016) in the marketplace, but the current situation is now totally different. Additional consumers have started to orient themselves towards online purchasing, and luxury brands are increasingly going digital to affirm their brand presence on the net and increase customers' brand awareness (Okonkwo, 2009; Ozuem et al., 2017). If, in the beginning, the online marketplace was not easily considered in relation to exclusivity (Kapferer, 2014), then it is now increasingly assumed that the main issue for luxury fashion brands is no longer the suitability of espousing an online presence but the choice of the most appropriate mode of operations for a specific consumer segment (Okonkwo, 2009). Luxury fashion brands are increasingly positioning themselves in the online marketplace and carefully selecting an appropriate mode of operations in order to have a strategy that suits their brand image (Geerts & Veg-Sala, 2011) and, more specifically, "digitally native" marketplaces, such as the Chinese marketplace (Chen & Zhang, 2011). At present, approximately 80% of international luxury brands have decided to go digital in China following different strategies and related channels. Mobile digital technology has appeared to be particularly relevant to luxury goods firms with mobile sales estimated at 505.74 billion US$ in

2015 (Jing Daily, 2016). Digitalisation continuously contributes not only to the efficiency of operations but also to improved market development and sales growth. A 2015 report by McKinsey Global Institute, *"China's digital transformation: The Internet's impact on productivity and growth"*, highlighted that increased internet applications may boost China's GDP growth from 7 to 22% up to 2025; digitalisation would mean a new way of conceiving business operations for luxury fashion brands in the Chinese marketplace and having a centralised role for the consumer (McKinsey, 2015).

From this perspective, SMM and the channels in the Chinese online marketplace appear to be a critical phenomenon for luxury and fashion that academia has not sufficiently analysed. Consequently, this study, through a theoretical review of studies related to the Chinese online marketplace for luxury and fashion brands and an empirical analysis of the online channels present in the Chinese marketplace, will try to provide an emerging overview of the specificities related to online Chinese luxury fashion channels for future empirical studies in the field. It will focus on a review of the studies related to Chinese consumers' behaviour in the luxury and fashion marketplace and an analysis of the main online channels and their specific characteristics and their unicity.

LITERATURE REVIEW

Luxury Fashion in the Online Marketplace: The Evolution of Customers' Shopping Trends

The last decade has seen an impressive transformation in the retail industry with the entrance of diversified technologies improving customer experience and, at the same time, entertaining and engaging consumers in the online marketplace (Dacko, 2017; Kumar et al., 2014; Willems et al., 2017). The increasing presence of digitalisation has started to be conducive to a juxtaposed context of online and offline retailing, a clear evolution from the initial refusal of luxury fashion to engage in online retail due to the threat of loss of brand identity, exclusivity of the product or the luxury in-store retail experience. The digital footprint has begun to support an integrated model of online and offline retail because of the increasing presence of digital "smart" technologies, such as those related to artificial intelligence, in the customer shopping experience; this sustains a new strategy for luxury fashion brands as well as the reconceptualisation of the customer–brand relationship and the customer shopping experience in the marketplace (Pantano & Timmermans, 2014). In the same way, the evolving presence of the digital trend has modified different aspects of diverse customers' relationships with a brand.

Increased customer–brand interaction: The development of online retailing has certainly improved the customer shopping experience. The online retail model for the new digital marketplace has been able to create an enhanced digital interaction, increased choice and information on products, and specific after sales or before sales customer services: in a context accessible 365 days per year, 24 h a day, for purchasing and information at any internet-accessible geographical location. More specifically, mobile-friendly IT systems offer new retail options to increase personalisation and individual information, and they provide new retail services accessible in a personalised manner on one's own mobile device (Gao & Su, 2017; Pantano & Priporas, 2016).

Unicity in the shopping experience: Luxury and fashion brands have to inspire unicity in the shopping experience and quality, originality and belonging (Yeoman, 2011). Luxury fashion products are defined as not available for everyone but highly desired (Okonkwo, 2009); rarity is one of the main characteristics of a luxury brand (Veblen, 1973) defining its consumption together with exclusivity and uniqueness (Chevalier & Mazzalovo, 2012; Dion & Arnould, 2011). The disruptive and democratic essence of the internet—in its reach to a widespread variety of customer segments—associated with its mode of operations made luxury brands cautious about choosing to go online (Hennings et al., 2012) to avoid jeopardising their image and identity.

Increased brand awareness: Nowadays, the marketplace shows the key changes associated with the perception and operation of luxury online; the availability of new comprehensive information about favoured products in the online marketplace as well as the diverse online transition evidence customers' orientation towards the new luxury fashion shopping experience (Okonkwo, 2010). Nowadays, most luxury fashion shoppers seek information from social media to assist their decision making when purchasing. In the same way, luxury customers' confident perception of social media pages has a positive influence on their online shopping choice of a brand (Annie Jin 2012). Online luxury fashion communication and purchasing have started to contribute to new and disruptive purchasing experiences for luxury fashion shoppers and, at the same time, have contributed to increase awareness of brands, particularly in the new fast-growing economies; e-commerce has led to luxury brand internation-alisation (Guercini & Runfola, 2015) and online experience for luxury fashion shoppers.

Brand value creation for customers: Kaplan and Haenlein (2010) defined social media as a group of internet-based applications that gives the opportunity to exchange user-generated content allowing the diffu-sion of different types of content; the sharing of user-generated content among different communities admiring a brand represents an added value (Muniz & O'Guinn, 2001). The community is considered to contribute to the creation of a meaning for the brand (McAlexander et al., 2002); customer engagement in the brand community differs in its level of engagement and complexity and provides a different added value to the brand (Frow et al., 2015).

Luxury and Fashion and the Chinese Online Marketplace: The Triple D Paradigm

Chen and Zhang (2011) and Jung et al. (2014) evidenced the signifi-cant contribution of the online mode to the continuous purchase growth of luxury fashion goods in emerging consumer markets. In the Chinese market, digitalisation started rivalling and increasingly competing with the traditional luxury approach to retailing, which assigns a key role to the physical store in its diverse forms (Rambourg, 2014). Younger and digitally savvy luxury consumers, the so-called millennials, arising from the new bourgeoisie, who seek social recognition and personal iden-tity acquisition in their luxury purchases (Hennings et al., 2012; Ngai & Cho, 2012; Zhang & Kim, 2013), were shown to significantly rely on SMM platforms to live their luxury experience and to improve their brand consciousness (Rovai, 2018). In the Chinese consumer market, new wealthy and young consumers appeared to be oriented towards new luxury and fashion purchasing habits (Le Monkhouse et al., 2012; Lu, 2011) that were constantly evolving (Lu, 2011), which influenced the luxury and fashion scenario with elements of disruption, democratisation and digitalisation. The new wealthy millennials, emerging from that new bourgeoisie, could be considered responsible for the democratisation of luxury, the disruption of purchasing habits and for assigning a key posi-tion to digitalisation (Rovai, 2016). However, the disruptive orientation that Chinese millennials applied to luxury were not only limited to digital-isation. In the next paragraphs, three main new orientations arising from the millennials' segment in the luxury market will be analysed according to the new paradigm that they will form.

D as Chinese millennial disruption: Digital platforms enable global luxury brands to connect with Chinese luxury clients, in particular with the younger generations. Research has started to evidence the importance of social media among Chinese customers (Kim & Ko, 2012). As a result, a pioneering global luxury player, Burberry, started using social media (Phan et al., 2011); Burberry's action encouraged other luxury brands to adopt social media for communication, for improving the purchasing experience and, generally, for strengthening customer relationships (Cavusgil & Guercini, 2014; Okonkwo, 2010; Rovai, 2018). Chinese customers' shopping mode in luxury is highly specific and unique and still lacks consistency of brand awareness, which challenges retailing strategies (Chevalier & Lu, 2010; Lu, 2011; Zhan & He, 2012), and is a younger (Lu & Pras, 2011) and more conspicuous market than the Western market (Kapferer, 2014; Li et al., 2012; Lu & Pras, 2011; Rovai, 2016). In contrast to most Western markets, the fastest growing—and disrupting—luxury customer segment in the Chinese luxury fashion market has been identified as the younger generation, whose age is between 20 and 30 years, in comparison to the consumers (30–50 years) in developed countries (Hennigs et al., 2012; Li et al., 2012; Ozuem et al., 2016).

D as increased digitalisation: The growth in Chinese customers' online usage has accelerated digitalisation of luxury fashion in China, which undeniably rivals traditional luxury and fashion (Rambourg, 2014) in the marketplace. Young Chinese consumers of luxury seek social recognition and identity in their luxury shopping; they each live their new luxury shopping experiences differently (Ngai & Cho, 2012). The highly digitally savvy young luxury Chinese customers strongly trust online applications to enable them to live their "luxury experience" and make their shopping choices. As a result of the growing awareness of the uniqueness and diversity of the Chinese luxury consumer market, the shopping modes and attitudes of Chinese customers have interested academic researchers. Among other topics, an increasing number of academic researchers analysed the importance of the influence of the luxury industry on Chinese luxury market growth (Cavender & Rein, 2009; Sun et al., 2016; Taylor et al., 2009). Other research studies have focused their interest on Chinese luxury customers' evolving desires and attitudes (Liu, 2016; Lu & Pras, 2011; Rovai, 2016). The Chinese luxury consumer market has witnessed strategic growth and changes in its identity, essence and operation modes as a result of different factors, among which digitalisation and democratisation appear to be the most impactful.

D as Chinese patterns of democratisation: Luxury also shows an increasingly diversified consumers' market, in particular, with the entrance of China's consumers' market. The luxury phenomenon in the Chinese consumer market has evolved in relation to the nature of customers; the rich or emerging middle class have increased their purchasing power and presence in the luxury market, in particular in China, India and the Middle East (Okonkwo, 2010), which has disrupted classical luxury consumer behaviours and broadened the concept of luxury. Despite the fact that global brands set global standards and convey shared symbols (Holt et al., 2004) as well as the myth of cosmopolitanism, which many international consumers appreciate (Strizhacova et al., 2008), brands also seem to represent a type of culture associated with lifestyle, food traditions and fashion choices (Askegaard et al., 2009). Luxury brands have become increasingly present in the Chinese consumer market, and lifestyle and the role of luxury shopping experience have gained unexpected importance and meaning in the Chinese social context. Post-1979 reforms have slowly given rise to private businesses and the birth of a consumer middle class, "the new rich", in China. The surge of the Chinese middle class has been conducive to the rise of a highly heterogeneous consumer class with new ways of showing their taste, their shopping motivations and (Li, 2006; Xu et al., 2018), in particular, a new mode as well as attitudes towards the online marketplace (Latham, 2006; Rambourg, 2014; Rovai, 2016).

Among those studies that investigated the new orientations in luxury fashion shopping for Chinese consumers, there has not been a specific focus on trying to understand the specific channels affecting the Chinese luxury fashion digital shopping experience. Despite the limited research in the field, increasingly, Chinese consumers have shown that they firstly consider fashion garments presented in social media and, in particular, fashion recommended by their relatives or friends. Luxury shopping websites, including business-to-consumer (B2C) and consumer-to-consumer websites, are the websites that sell luxury products. Among these, B2C websites mainly include independent B2C websites that only sell luxury products or have independent channels for luxuries; they are independently responsible for purchase, storage and logistics. Consider if such a situation existed in Mainland China, people could find what they tended to buy on several different online platforms, which would enrich people's purchasing choices and create an extraordinary shopping experience.

In line with the three orientations emerging from the literature related to millennial consumers' impact on the luxury and fashion marketplace, the triple D paradigm (see Fig. 14.1) could be used as a reference for further specific empirical research in the field besides helping in analysing the different channels existing in the luxury and fashion market in the current paper to formulate a research agenda.

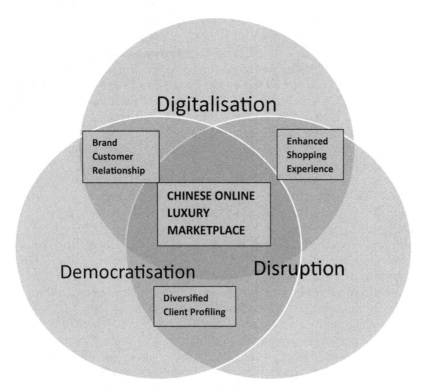

Fig. 14.1 The three D Chinese online luxury marketplace

Luxury and Fashion and the Chinese Marketplace Orientation

Luxury academics (Moore & Birtwistle, 2004; Fionda & Moore, 2009; Kapferer & Bastien, 2012; Moore & Doherty, 2007) showed that brand identity is not the only critical factor in luxury brand recognition and cannot be considered the only key factor ensuring luxury brand identity. "Luxury" usually refers to the main sort of authentic renowned brands (Vigneron & Johnson, 2004). Luxury brands are usually connected with the idea of exclusiveness, unicity and wealth, the accomplishment of nonessential desires (Brun et al., 2008; Dubois & Laurent, 1995), values of very highly quality, and symbols of rarity and prestige, which offer symbolic and emotional values to customers (Tynan et al., 2010). Wiedman et al. (2007) referred to luxury as the physical and psychological attitudes related to the prestige of luxury brands and highlighted the individual and collective dimension of luxury; the importance of that dimension to the sociocultural context was also evidenced, as representative of individual and social identity (Vickers & Renand, 2003). In the past decades, the Chinese luxury and fashion marketplace has accelerated evolution in the modes of luxury consumption as a result of the diversified sociocultural context (Atwal & Williams, 2017; Heilman et al., 2000; Yeonan, 2011).

Luxury consumption has started to be perceived not simply in a classic conspicuous perspective but as a 360 degrees experience, where cities from the most developed to the less developed areas have their place. The main fashion cities and other cities have begun to become filled with luxury and fashion brands that declare their presence from streets to airports, from clinics to hotels (Rambourg, 2014; Rovai, 2014, 2016).

Culture is considered a key influencing factor in relation to the swift change from traditional to fast growing markets; this is particularly the case with the Chinese market (Rovai, 2016), as Chinese consumers differ remarkably from their foreign counterparts (Atsmon & Dixit, 2009; Phau & Prendergast, 2000; Rovai, 2014). With its fast-growing economy and impressive social changes, China has become one of the most attractive markets for luxury brands worldwide. Despite the worldwide economic downturn in 2008, and the slowdown of the past years, China is still a key market for the luxury industry (Jing Daily, 2016). The new wealth segments are eager for luxury brands (Degen, 2009), to show signs of their newly acquired social status through luxury products (Hedrick-Wong, 2008). When purchasing luxury products, therefore, consumers of this generation are more likely to focus on their social needs (Liao & Wang, 2009). The expectation of a high-quality lifestyle has been formed in their growth period; they are thus more ambitious for success and achievement. Influenced by the Western culture that is oriented more towards an individualistic shopping mode, young Chinese customers are orienting themselves towards personal tastes, even if luxury brands also symbolise social and personal status (Hennigs et al., 2012; Zhang & Kim, 2013). However, despite the fast growth in their brand awareness and sophistication, Chinese luxury customers' conceptualisation of luxury is still a conglomerate of contemporary as well as more domestic values (Dong & Tian, 2009; Hung et al., 2007).

Research has evidenced that Chinese shoppers have modified their lifestyle, including relaxation, travelling, shopping, catering and sport, and their shopping habits in the marketplace, with an addiction to luxury products (Chen & Lamberti, 2015). After more than a decade of digital development, Chinese customers are definitely more demanding and attentive in their luxury and fashion purchases modes in the online marketplace as a result of their increasing luxury and fashion knowhow and awareness (Rovai, 2018). Besides being more attentive to the choice and quality of products, they have shown a different attitude in their shopping habits and needs with a higher requirement of safety and convenience in the online marketplace. A specific study evidenced that a website and payment process with a high standard of safety would increase customers' level of trust in the online marketplace (Kim et al., 2009). Specific attention needs to be paid with respect to the level of quality of the service in order to create a satisfying shopping experience in the marketplace.

Some luxury brands have already established their official websites but, nowadays, in China, shopping platforms such as G.Taobao.com, ShangPin.com and JD.com are successfully operating in the luxury market (Jones, 2014). In particular, Jiapin.com and 5Lux.com appear to be the most popular platforms attracting luxury shoppers. Their popularity and success rely on the reliability and authenticity of their offers and they also increase brand awareness, in some cases they achieve this with a specific brand focus through formal agreements with luxury brands. Similar kinds of website include vipshop.com and xiu.com, which seem to be the first to have appeared on the scene; they have an impressive presence of brands and products and mainly focus on sales. By contrast, other shopping channels seem to be more oriented towards an informative positioning; a typical example is represented by YMALL, a website initially providing both lifestyle information and advice as well as luxury products. However, besides brands' websites, vertical or horizontal websites or platforms in the luxury and fashion sectors, an increasing revolution in the online marketplace for fashion brands is represented by the multi-purpose platform WeChat and its mini-programs. In the digitalisation and SMM context, WeChat has a unique and interesting position for luxury brands and SMM customer relations with respect to its structure and evolution. WeChat was created in 2011 as a response to a domestic Chinese SMM platform and it developed from a messaging application to a centralised comprehensive SMM platform gathering approximately 900 million users. It is considered the optimal platform for customer relationship management with specific capabilities of social engagement because of its comprehensive digital ecosystem approach and it is extremely popular with Chinese consumers (Bonhomme, 2017).

In China, most luxury brands have established their official websites as well as WeChat pages, events and mini-programs with the main objective of providing information for visitors and expanding brand images instead of being limited to an online shopping mall. In order to enhance awareness of brand images, many luxury brands initially equipped their official websites with several languages to adapt to different nations, including China, until they developed entire platforms or social media in different languages; WeChat is totally available in Chinese and is dedicated to the Chinese segment, particularly in relation to the consumption modes of younger customers that differ highly from traditional customers' consumption modes (O'Cass & Siahtiri, 2013). In respect to customers' consumption modes, in the past) considered consumer behaviour as a dynamic concept that was significantly influenced by outer factors and inner elements.

DISCUSSION AND CONCLUDING REMARKS FOR A FUTURE RESEARCH AGENDA

The younger generation, seeking to show their characteristics and value orientations through a brand, were each seen to live their new luxury purchasing experiences differently (Ngai & Cho, 2012). As a consequence of their "digital education" and the related familiarity with the digital world, they appeared to rely on online applications to live their "luxury fashion experience" and legitimise the importance of online channels. Young customers seemed to search for data online and compared feedback on brands or garments before finalising their own in-store or online shopping decisions. In addition, after purchasing, most of them expressed their opinions on websites and shared their opinions with their friends.

Consequently, digital luxury branding appears as a necessary measure for luxury brands not only for selling purposes but also in order to better understand the younger luxury customers' needs and motivations to purchase in the Chinese luxury fashion marketplace. The Chinese love affair with luxury has evolved as a result of an increased brand awareness—thanks to digitalisation—as well as sociocultural development and specificities (Dubois et al., 2005; Hennigs et al., 2012). Certainly, research has also increased in the field, however, by reviewing the existing literature in the field, specific research on the Chinese luxury fashion online marketplace and its specificities in the channels appeared to be still limited.

This study has evidenced how in the past years, a growing presence of digitalisation in the luxury and fashion industry has stimulated academia to analyse its positive impact on communication as well as on operations and customer relationships with brands (Dacko, 2017; Demirkan & Spohrer, 2014), without definitely focusing on the diverse online channels present in the marketplace and their impact on luxury and fashion brands. In a fast-growing, but also increasingly demanding and complex, Chinese luxury consumer market—highly diversified in its brand consciousness but highly harmonised in digital orientation—luxury fashion brands engaging in a locally based strategy in the online marketplace can find a key to successfully enter and to acquire a sustainable positioning.

As emphasized by Chu et al. (2013), because of the fast-growing adoption of an online communication and operational approach for luxury fashion, more empirical research is required to examine young customers' behaviours, attitudes and responses to the diverse channels in the online Chinese marketplace. While Western countries have found common non-geographically bounded platforms, the situation appears different and more complex in China due to institutional barriers to the use of Western platforms and media, and the presence of unique Chinese context-related barriers. With the increasing presence and critical importance of the millennial segment in the Chinese consumer market, local online channels provide luxury fashion brands with a privileged way to engage the millennial luxury segment and to strengthen their relationship with the brand that requires more in-depth understanding.

Certainly, future studies will have to go more in-depth in the use of those channels with respect to luxury fashion, and other luxury sectors, to provide appropriate strategies.

REFERENCES

Adams, R. (2011). The utility of prestige: Chinese and American hedonic ratings of prestige goods. *Journal of Global Marketing, 24*(4), 287–304.

Annie Jin, S. (2012). The potential of social media for luxury brand management. *Marketing Intelligence & Planning, 30*(7), 687–699.

Askegaard, S., Kjeldgaard, D., & Arnould, E. J. (2009). Reflexive culture's consequences. In *Beyond Hofstede* (pp. 101–122). Palgrave Macmillan.

Atsmon, Y., & Dixit, V. (2009). Understanding China's wealthy. *McKinsey Quarterly, 4,* 32–33.

Atwal, G., & Williams, A. (2017). Luxury brand marketing—The experience is everything! In *Advances in luxury brand management* (pp. 43–57). Palgrave Macmillan.

Bonhomme, A. (2017). How to get the most from WeChat. *Journal of Digital & Social Media Marketing, 5*(2), 146–152.

Brun, A., Caniato, F., Caridi, M., Castelli, C., Miragliotta, G., Ronchi, S., Sianesi, A., & Spina, G. (2008). Logistics and supply chain management in luxury fashion retail: Empirical investigation of Italian firms. *International Journal of Production Economics, 114*(2), 554–570.

Cavender, B., & Rein, S. (2009). LUXURY GOODS-Still Strong Sellers-China's luxury goods sales may perform well despite bear-market conditions. *China Business Review, 36*(2), 36.

Cavusgil, S. T., & Buckley, P. J. (2016). Interdisciplinary perspectives on the middle class phenomenon in emerging markets. *International Business Review, 3*(25), 621–623.

Cavusgil, T., & Guercini, S. (2014). *Trends in middle class as a driver for strategic marketing*. Mercati e competitività.

Chen, F., & Zhang, Y. (2011, August). Online marketing of luxury goods-take Chinese market as example. In *2011 international conference on management and service science (MASS)*, (pp. 1–4). IEEE.

Chen, S., & Lamberti, L. (2015). Entering the dragon's nest: Exploring Chinese upper-class consumers' perception of luxury. *Qualitative Market Research: An International Journal*.

Chevalier, M., & Lu, P. X. (2010). *Luxury China: Market opportunities and potential*. John Wiley & Sons.

Chevalier, M., & Mazzalovo, G. (2012). *Luxury brand management: A world of privilege* (2e éd.).

China Internet Network Information Center. (2017). The 40th China statistical report on internet development. *Office of the Central Leading Group for Cyberspace Affairs.*

Chu, S. C., Kamal, S., & Kim, Y. (2013). Understanding consumers' responses toward social media advertising and purchase intention toward luxury products. *Journal of Global Fashion Marketing, 4*(3), 158–174.

Dacko, S. G. (2017). Enabling smart retail settings via mobile augmented reality shopping apps. *Technological Forecasting and Social Change, 124,* 243–256.

Degen, R. J. (2009). Opportunity for luxury brands in China. *IUP Journal of Brand Management, 6*(3/4), 75–85.

Demirkan, H., & Spohrer, J. (2014). Developing a framework to improve virtual shopping in digital malls with intelligent self-service systems. *Journal of Retailing and Consumer Services, 21*(5), 860–868.

Dion, D., & Arnould, E. (2011). Retail luxury strategy: Assembling charisma through art and magic. *Journal of Retailing, 87*(4), 502–520.

Dong, L., & Tian, K. (2009). The use of Western brands in asserting Chinese national identity. *The Journal of Consumer Research, 36,* 504–523.

Dubois, B., & Laurent, G. (1995). Luxury possessions and practices: An empirical scale. *ACR European Advances.*

Dubois, B., Czellar, S., & Laurent, G. (2005). Consumer segments based on attitudes toward luxury: empirical evidence from twenty countries. *Marketing letters, 16*(2), 115–128.

Fionda, A. M., & Moore, C. M. (2009). The anatomy of the luxury fashion brand. *Journal of Brand Management, 16*(5–6), 347–363.

Frow, P., Nenonen, S., Payne, A., & Storbacka, K. (2015). Managing co-creation design: A strategic approach to innovation. *British Journal of Management, 26*(3), 463–483.

Gao, F., & Su, X. (2017). Omnichannel retail operations with buy-online-and-pick-up-in-store. *Management Science, 63*(8), 2478–2492.

Geerts, A., & Veg-Sala, N. (2011). Evidence on internet communication management strategies for luxury brands. *Global Journal of Business Research, 5*(5), 81–94.

Guercini, S., & Runfola, A. (2015). Internationalization through e-commerce. The case of multibrand luxury retailers in the fashion industry. In *International marketing in the fast changing world* (pp. 15–31). Emerald Group Publishing Limited.

Hedrick-Wong, Y. (2008). *The future and me: Power of the youth market in Asia.* John Wiley & Sons Incorporated.

Heilman, C. M., Bowman, D., & Wright, G. P. (2000). The evolution of brand preferences and choice behaviors of consumers new to a market. *Journal of Marketing Research, 37*(2), 139–155.

Helal, G., & Ozuem, W. (2018). Social identity matters: Social media and brand perceptions in the fashion apparel and accessories industries. In *Digital marketing strategies for fashion and luxury brands* (pp. 326–361). IGI Global.

Hennigs, N., Wiedmann, K. P., Klarmann, C., Strehlau, S., Godey, B., Pederzoli, D., Neulinger, A., Dave, K., Aiello, G., Donvito, R., & Taro, K. (2012). What is the value of luxury? A cross-cultural consumer perspective. *Psychology & Marketing, 29*(12), 1018–1034.

Holt, D. B., Quelch, J. A., & Taylor, E. L. (2004). How global brands compete. *Harvard Business Review, 82*(9), 68–75.

Hung, K. H., Li, S. Y., & Belk, R. W. (2007). Global understandings: Female readers' perceptions of the new woman in Chinese advertising. *Journal of International Business Studies, 38*(6), 1034–1051.

Jing Daily. *China luxury market predictions for 2017.* 30 December 2016.

Jones, S. (2014). Number of luxury consumers to reach 440 million by 2020: BCG. *Luxury Daily.*

Jung, H., Lee, Y., Kim, H., & Yang, H. (2014). Impacts of country images on luxury fashion brand: Facilitating with the brand resonance model. *Journal of Fashion Marketing and Management, 18*(2), 187–205.

Kapferer, J. N. (2014). The future of luxury: Challenges and opportunities. *Journal of Brand Management, 21*(9), 716–726.

Kapferer, J. N., & Bastien, V. (2012). *The luxury strategy: Break the rules of marketing to build luxury brands.* Kogan Page Publishers.

Kaplan, A. M., & Haenlein, M. (2010). Users of the world, unite! The challenges and opportunities of Social Media. *Business Horizons, 53*(1), 59–68.

Kim, A. J., & Ko, E. (2012). Do social media marketing activities enhance customer equity? An empirical study of luxury fashion brand. *Journal of Business Research, 65*(10), 1480–1486.

Kim, D. J., Ferrin, D. L., & Rao, H. R. (2009). Trust and satisfaction, two stepping stones for successful e-commerce relationships: A longitudinal exploration. *Information Systems Research, 20*(2), 237–257.

Kumar, V., Vimal, B. K., Kumar, R., & Kumar, M. (2014). Determination of soil pH by using digital image processing technique. *Journal of Applied and Natural Science, 6*(1), 14–18.

Latham, K. (2006). Introduction: Consumption and cultural change in contemporary China. In Latham, K., Thompson, S., & Klein, J. A. (Eds.). *Consuming China: Approaches to cultural change in contemporary China* (pp. 1–21). Routledge.

Le Monkhouse, L., Barnes, B. R., & Stephan, U. (2012). The influence of face and group orientation on the perception of luxury goods: A four market study of East Asian consumers. *International Marketing Review, 29*(6), 647–672.

Li, N., Robson, A., & Coates, N. (2013). Chinese consumers' purchasing: Impact of value and affect. *Journal of Fashion Marketing and Management: An International Journal, 17*(4), 486–508.

Liao, J., & Wang, L. (2009). Face as a mediator of the relationship between material value and brand consciousness. *Psychology & Marketing, 26*(11), 987–1001.

Liu, S., Perry, P., Moore, C., & Warnaby, G. (2016). The standardization-localization dilemma of brand communications for luxury fashion retailers' internationalization into China. *Journal of Business Research, 69*(1), 357–364.

Liu, Y., Li, H., & Hu, F. (2013). Website attributes in urging online impulse purchase: An empirical investigation on consumer perceptions. *Decision Support Systems, 55*(3), 829–837.

Lu, P. X. (2011). *Elite China: Luxury consumer behavior in China.* John Wiley & Sons.

Lu, X. P., & Pras, B. (2011). Profiling mass affluent luxury goods consumers in China: A psychographic approach. *Thunderbird International Business Review, 53*(4), 435–455.

McAlexander, J. H., Schouten, J. W., & Koenig, H. F. (2002). Building brand community. *Journal of Marketing, 66*(1), 38–54.

McKinsey & Co. (2015). Digital inside: Get wired for the ultimate luxury experience. https://www.mckinsey.de/sites/mck_files/files/dle-2015-globalreport.pdf.

Moore, C. M., & Birtwistle, G. (2004). The Burberry business model: Creating an international luxury fashion brand. *International Journal of Retail & Distribution Management.*

Moore, C. M., & Doherty, A. M. (2007). The international flagship stores of luxury fashion retailers. In *Fashion Marketing* (pp. 301–320). Routledge.

Muniz, A. M., & O'guinn, T. C. (2001). Brand community. *Journal of Consumer Research, 27*(4), 412–432.

Ngai, J., & Cho, E. (2012). The young luxury consumers in China. *Young Consumers, 13*(3), 255–266.

O'Cass, A., & Siahtiri, V. (2013). In search of status through brands from Western and Asian origins: Examining the changing face of fashion clothing consumption in Chinese young adults. *Journal of Retailing and Consumer Services, 20*(6), 505–515.

Okonkwo, U. (2009). Sustaining the luxury brand on the Internet. *Journal of Brand Management, 16*(5–6), 302–310.

Okonkwo, U. (2010). *Luxury online: Styles, systems, strategies.* Springer.

Okonkwo, U. (2016). *Luxury fashion branding: Trends, tactics, techniques.* Springer.

Ozuem, W., Howell, K. E., & Lancaster, G. (2008). Communicating in the new interactive marketspace. *European Journal of Marketing, 42*(9/10), 1059–1083.

Ozuem, W., Patel, A., Howell, K. E., & Lancaster, G. (2017). An exploration of customers' response to online service recovery initiatives. *International Journal of Market Research, 59*(1), 97–116.

Ozuem, W., Thomas, T., & Lancaster, G. (2016). The influence of customer loyalty on small island economies: An empirical and exploratory study. *Journal of Strategic Marketing, 24*(6), 447–469.

Pantano, E., & Priporas, C. V. (2016). The effect of mobile retailing on consumers' purchasing experiences: A dynamic perspective. *Computers in Human Behavior, 61,* 548–555.

Pantano, E., & Timmermans, H. (2014). What is smart for retailing? *Procedia Environmental Sciences, 22,* 101–107.

Park, H. H., Jeon, J. O., & Kwak, W. (2007). The influence of perceived quality and VMD fitness of fashion brand on brand attitude and purchase intention. *Korean Marketing Management Research, 12*(1), 55–70.

Park, H. J., Rabolt, N. J., & Jeon, K. S. (2008). Purchasing global luxury brands among young Korean consumers. *Journal of Fashion Marketing and Management: An International Journal.*

Phan, M., Thomas, R., & Heine, K. (2011). Social media and luxury brand management: The case of Burberry. *Journal of Global Fashion Marketing, 2*(4), 213–222.

Phau, I., & Prendergast, G. (2000). Consuming luxury brands: The relevance of the 'rarity principle'. *Journal of Brand Management, 8*(2), 122–138.

Rambourg, E. (2014). *The bling dynasty: Why the reign of Chinese luxury shoppers has only just begun.* John Wiley & Sons

Rovai, S. (2014). The evolution of luxury consumption in China. In *Luxury Brands in Emerging Markets* (pp. 130–134). Palgrave Macmillan, London.

Rovai, S. (2016). *Luxury the Chinese way: The emergence of a new competitive scenario.* Springer.

Rovai, S. (2018). Digitalisation, luxury fashion and "Chineseness": The influence of the Chinese context for luxury brands and the online luxury consumers experience. *Journal of Global Fashion Marketing, 9*(2), 116–128.

Strizhakova, Y., Coulter, R. A., & Price, L. L. (2008). Branded products as a passport to global citizenship: Perspectives from developed and developing countries. *Journal of International Marketing, 16*(4), 57–85.

Sun, G., D'Alessandro, S., & Johnson, L. W. (2016). Exploring luxury value perceptions in China: Direct and indirect effects. *International Journal of Market Research, 58*(5), 711–731.

Taylor, G., Gao, L., Norton, M. J., Zhang, Z. M., & To, C. K. M. (2009). Potential niche markets for luxury fashion goods in China. *Journal of Fashion Marketing and Management: An International Journal.*

Tsai, W. S., Yang, Q., & Liu, Y. (2013). Young Chinese consumers' snob and bandwagon luxury consumption preferences. *Journal of International Consumer Marketing, 25*(5), 290–304.

Tynan, C., McKechnie, S., & Chhuon, C. (2010). Co-creating value for luxury brands. *Journal of Business Research, 63*(11), 1156–1163.

Veblen, T. (1973). *The theory of the leisure class* (p. 468646). Houghton Mifflin.

Vickers, J. S., & Renand, F. (2003). The marketing of luxury goods: An exploratory study—Three conceptual dimensions. *The Marketing Review, 3*(4), 459–478.

Vigneron, F., & Johnson, L. W. (2004). Measuring perceptions of brand luxury. *Journal of Brand Management, 11*(6), 484–506.

Wiedmann, K. P., Hennigs, N., & Siebels, A. (2007). Measuring consumers' luxury value perception: A cross-cultural framework. *Academy of Marketing Science Review, 2007,* 1.

Willems, K., Smolders, A., Brengman, M., Luyten, K., & Schöning, J. (2017). The path-to-purchase is paved with digital opportunities: An inventory of shopper-oriented retail technologies. *Technological Forecasting and Social Change, 124,* 228–242.

Wu, M., Chaney, S. S., Chen, I., Nguyen, C. H. S., & Melewar, T. C. (2015). Luxury fashion brands: Factors influencing young female consumers' luxury fashion purchasing in Taiwan. *Qualitative Market Research, 183,* 298–319.

Xu, Y., Chi, T., & Su, J. (Eds.). (2018). *Chinese consumers and the fashion market.* Springer.

Yeoman, I. (2011). The changing behaviours of luxury consumption. *Journal of Revenue and Pricing Management, 10*(1), 47–50.

Zhan, L., & He, Y. (2012). Understanding luxury consumption in China: Consumer perceptions of best-known brands. *Journal of Business Research, 65*(10), 1452–1460.

Zhang, B., & Kim, J. H. (2013). Luxury fashion consumption in China: Factors affecting attitude and purchase intent. *Journal of Retailing and Consumer Services, 20*(1), 68–79.

CHAPTER 15

Managing Online Touchpoints for a Consistent Customer Experience: Cases from Fashion Retailing

Giada Salvietti, Marco Ieva, and Cristina Ziliani

INTRODUCTION

The topic of Customer Experience has been studied and researched in marketing since the 1980s. However, today, due to the increasing complexity of the customer journey and the growing importance of any interaction occurring between consumers and companies (Lemon & Verhoef, 2016), academics are updating and extending the definition of Customer Experience, while practitioners are working to redesign and improve the Customer Experience.

In the first part of this chapter, the focus will be on the concept of Online Customer Experience and its characteristics. Online Customer Experience will be analysed in comparison with In-store Customer Experience, in order to bring out differences and similarities. The second part will focus on the various possible touchpoints which allow consumers

G. Salvietti (✉) · M. Ieva · C. Ziliani
University of Parma, Parma, Italy

© The Author(s), under exclusive license to Springer Nature
Switzerland AG 2021
W. Ozuem and S. Ranfagni (eds.), *The Art of Digital Marketing for Fashion and Luxury Brands*,
https://doi.org/10.1007/978-3-030-70324-0_15

365

to encounter a given brand throughout the customer journey. Besides providing a definition and discussing classifications of touchpoints, the second part of the chapter will also show which touchpoints can be key to reaching loyal customers and contributing to the development of Customer Loyalty, which is the final goal of managing the Customer Experience (Homburg et al., 2017; Ozuem et al., 2016).

The third and fourth parts of the chapter will examine the luxury market and how its peculiarities present challenges to providing a satisfying Customer Experience. Eighteen cases will be presented, to show how luxury and fashion companies are driving their offline and online channels towards an efficient integration of technologies and experiences. The cases—listed in Table 15.1—are based on academic literature and secondary data (company websites, press releases, etc.). As a conclusion, considerations about future challenges for the sector will be shared.

Table 15.1 Fashion and luxury companies delivering an omnichannel customer experience

Company name	Country of origin	Type of company	Sector
Adidas	Germany	Manufacturer	Fashion
Astley Clarke	United Kingdom	Manufacturer	Luxury
Balenciaga	Spain	Manufacturer	Luxury
Burberry	United Kingdom	Manufacturer	Luxury
Carlings	Norway	Manufacturer	Fashion
Chanel	France	Manufacturer	Luxury
Dior	France	Manufacturer	Luxury
Farfetch	United Kingdom & Portugal	Manufacturer	Luxury
Hermès	France	Manufacturer	Luxury
L'Oreal	France	Manufacturer	Beauty
Nordstrom	United States	Pure retailer	Fashion
Nyx	Canada	Manufacturer	Beauty
Sephora	France	Manufacturer	Beauty
Target	United States	Pure retailer	Fashion
Tommy Hilfiger	United States	Manufacturer	Luxury
TOMS	United States	Manufacturer	Fashion
YOOX	Italy	Pure retailer	Luxury
Zara	Spain	Manufacturer	Fashion

Online Versus in-Store Customer Experience: Theoretical Background

What Is the Customer Experience?

Customer Experience is "the internal and subjective response customers have to any direct or indirect contact with a company" (Meyer & Schwager, 2007, p. 2). In its general conceptualization, Customer Experience includes the cognitive, emotional, physical, sensorial, and social dimensions that characterize any interaction occurring directly or indirectly between consumers and companies across the pre-purchase, purchase and post-purchase stages of the customer journey (De Keyser et al., 2015; Lemon & Verhoef, 2016).

On the basis of this definition, Customer Experience represents a subjective perception of the consumer interaction with the different points of contact, namely touchpoints, of a given brand or company. Customer Experience occurs at different levels, as it involves different aspects of customers themselves: their cognitive, affective, social, sensorial and behavioural dimensions. Companies can manage these dimensions to deliver an effective Customer Experience that can lead to long-term Customer Loyalty (Homburg et al., 2017). Finally, Customer Experience occurs at different stages of the customer journey: during the information search, at the purchase stage and after the purchase. It is thus a dynamic process, changing over time, which requires ongoing evaluation from the company.

The complexity of Customer Experience is also related to its environment. It might in fact be expected that Experience occurring in the online environment will show different characteristics and touchpoints from those that characterize the experience in a physical store (Ziliani & Ieva, 2020). It is worthwhile to highlight and compare the key elements that characterize the Online and the In-store Customer Experience. This will allow us to better clarify how consumers live the interactions in offline and online environments, and how companies can improve the Experience delivered.

Online Customer Experience: Theoretical Framework

Online Customer Experience (OCE) occurs through the different stimuli that consumers encounter in the online environment (Rose et al., 2012)

These stimuli can be in different forms, including text-based information, images, videos, or audio, and they can be delivered through a website, a search page, or a social media app, etc. Exposure and subsequent processing of these stimuli constitute the OCE. Building on the work of Gentile et al. (2007), Rose et al. (2012, p. 309) find that the OCE is a "psychological state manifested as a subjective response" to an online encounter. This subjective response occurs along the cognitive and affective dimensions and contributes to shaping an impression in memory (Rose et al., 2012). In this respect, the cognitive component of the OCE has to do with the thinking and conscious mental processes that occur when the subject is exposed to the online stimuli. The affective component of the OCE involves the feelings, the emotions and the moods that are triggered within the online environment. Rose et al. (2012) also find that the affective dimension of the Customer Experience can influence the Cognitive dimension too, and this finding points to the importance of designing online apps or websites that have the potential to leverage affective states, not only cognitive processing.

It is important to highlight the difference between OCE and User Experience, similar concepts which are sometimes confused. User experience has to do with how a user interacts with a specific product, website, or app (Morgan, 2017). It is very important to analyse the user experience with a given site or application as it gives directions as to how the specific online touchpoint can be designed or re-designed to satisfy consumer needs. There are different ways to measure the User Experience with a website, such as the abandonment rate, error rate, and clicks to completion. User Experience is an important element that can influence OCE. OCE is also a broader concept, as it refers to all the different ongoing interactions that a customer has with a brand in the online environment. This chapter will focus specifically on OCE, and includes cases where the delivery of a great user experience leads to positive OCE.

Effective OCE can lead to positive consequences for consumers: multiple studies have found that a positive OCE can increase Customer Satisfaction (Martin et al., 2015; Rose et al., 2012), Trust (Bilgihan et al., 2016) Repurchase Intention, Positive Word of Mouth (e.g. Bilgihan et al., 2016; Singh & Söderlund, 2020) and in turn Customer Loyalty (Pandey & Chawla, 2018). On the other hand, negative OCE can lead to Dissatisfaction and Negative Word of Mouth (Barari et al., 2020).

It is also essential to identify the key drivers of a positive OCE that can support better management of Customer Experience online. Different drivers of the OCE have been found (Bilgihan et al., 2016; Martin et al., 2015; Rose et al., 2012), namely Information Processing, Perceived Ease of Use, Perceived Usefulness, Perceived Benefits, Perceived Control, Skill, Trust Propensity, Perceived Risk and Enjoyment. For an extensive review of these, see Rose et al. (2012).

The in-Store Customer Experience: Key Theoretical Elements

As well as OCE, academics have also studied the key characteristics of the In-Store Customer Experience in the context of retailing (Bustamante & Rubio, 2017). The In-Store Customer Experience is the Experience deriving from the interactions occurring between customers and the different components of the retail mix, for example price experience and promotion experience. The main difference between In-Store and Online Customer Experience is that In-Store experience takes place in a physical environment and involves interactions with employees or with other customers in person. The In-Store Customer Experience entails the cognitive, emotional, social and physical responses to a service occurring during a customer shopping visit to a physical store (Bustamante & Rubio, 2017). The social dimension is related to the relationships between the individual's ideal, the "self", and the other people in the store: the interactions with other customers or with the store associates are an essential element of the Experience in the store. The cognitive dimension is related to the processes that transform interactions into thoughts and reflections. It relates to mental activity triggered by encountering products, services, etc. The affective dimension is related to positive and negative emotions arising in the store. Lastly, the physical dimensions involve physiological responses to the interaction with the physical environment of the store.

The consequences of the In-Store Customer Experience are similar to those of OCE: a successful In-Store Customer Experience drives higher Customer Satisfaction and higher Store Loyalty (Bustamante & Rubio, 2017; Ozuem et al., 2017).

AN EFFECTIVE CUSTOMER
JOURNEY ACROSS TOUCHPOINTS

Definition of Touchpoints in the Customer Journey

All types of interaction between consumers and brands along the customer journey have today become increasingly important for academics and practitioners, and the concept of touchpoint has become more widely used. A touchpoint can be defined as any verbal or non-verbal incident that any individual perceives and attributes to a firm or a brand (Duncan & Moriarty, 2006). Touchpoints are thus any direct or indirect encounters with a firm (Lemon & Verhoef, 2016). They include TV advertisements, the store, the mobile app, and even peer observation, for example, watching another person making a purchase or using a product, can be considered as a touchpoint (Baxendale et al., 2015).

Few studies provide indications on how to define touchpoints. One approach could be to discard those encountered by a low number of subjects, but sometimes even the less frequently encountered touchpoints are influential in driving purchase behaviour. Moreover, the type and the importance of touchpoints might vary according to the context or sector. For instance, loyalty programmes and promotional flyers might be especially important for supermarket retail, while special events and influencers might be more important in luxury retailing.

To handle this growing variety of touchpoints, academics and experts have attempted to classify touchpoints according to different features. Lemon & Verhoef (2016) classify touchpoints according to the entity managing them: brand-owned, partner-owned, customer-owned and social/external. Brand-owned touchpoints are those under the control of the company, and include, for example, a loyalty programme or the staff of a store owned and managed directly by the company. Partner-owned touchpoints are touchpoints whose management is shared between the company and a partner, such as a different company, for example in coalition loyalty programmes, or a service provider, for example a digital agency running social media communications of the company. In this case, coordination between partners is very important in designing and managing touchpoints consistently with the brand image and in line with all the other touchpoints of the company. Customer-owned touchpoints are those points of contact that are not under the control of the company but which are entirely owned by the customers. This category includes the mode of payment, chosen freely by customers among different options, and user-generated content, which can enhance the awareness of certain products or services, or even challenge company reputation. Finally, there are the social/external touchpoints, for instance customer reviews of products or services. This type of touchpoint has expanded since the rise of online infomediaries such as Booking.com or TripAdvisor and review platforms such as TrustPilot. This category also includes experts or influencers who independently review a given product or service and, as noted above, peer observation.

A novel approach to touchpoints is proposed by De Keyser et al. (2020) in a framework called TCQ (Touchpoints, Context, Qualities). The TCQ framework considers three aspects:

- control, i.e. whether the touchpoint is under or outside the control of the company
- nature, i.e. whether the touchpoint is human, digital or physical
- stage, i.e. the phase of the customer journey (pre-purchase, purchase, or post-purchase) when consumers encounter a given touchpoint.

This classification in fact summarises the different aspects reviewed above. Companies are thus advised to develop a touchpoint overview by listing all the different touchpoints, and for each one identifying the level of control, nature and stage(s) of the customer journey (De Keyser et al., 2020).

Review of Studies on Touchpoint Importance

In order to understand the importance of touchpoints in business-to-consumer (B2C) settings, academics and practitioners have attempted to measure how consumers interact with touchpoints along three dimensions, i.e. reach, frequency and positivity. Reach has to do with the relevance of the touchpoint in the customer journey. High reach means that a high number of consumers encounter the touchpoint on their journey, and that it has the potential to positively (or negatively) influence a high number of consumers.

In a study which reveals the ongoing complexity of the customer journey, Herhausen et al. (2019) develop a segmentation across different product categories, with different segments of consumers encountering touchpoints. The five segments are consumers who:

- encounter few online touchpoints ("pragmatic online shoppers")
- encounter a high number of online touchpoints ("extensive online shoppers")
- encounter a high number of online and offline touchpoints ("multiple touchpoint shoppers").
- use online touchpoints for information research and the store for purchasing ("online-to-offline")
- focus only on the physical store ("store-focused shoppers").

Frequency of exposure is similar to reach, but provides additional information: it measures how many times consumers encounter a given touchpoint. There can be touchpoints with high reach, as well as touchpoints with low reach, that are encountered by consumers with varying frequency in a given time period.

Frequency of exposure to touchpoints is positively related to loyalty intentions: studies have found that consumers who encounter a firm across many touchpoints more frequently over time display higher loyalty intentions, specifically, higher relationship commitment and positive word of mouth (Ieva & Ziliani, 2018a, 2018b).

Finally, positivity of touchpoints is also considered in evaluating their importance. Touchpoint positivity represents the valence of the affective response to a given touchpoint. The previous section explained the importance of affect for Customer Experience in online and offline environments. Academics have also studied the role of affective response to a given touchpoint and have found that the consumer's affective response has the potential to influence brand consideration and loyalty intentions (Baxendale et al., 2015; Ieva & Ziliani, 2018b; Ou & Verhoef, 2017). Findings on touchpoint reach, frequency and positivity in the B2C setting support the view that touchpoints differ in their relationship with consumer attitudes, such as loyalty intentions. The strength of these relationships appears to vary according to the context and the touchpoints encountered in that given setting.

Focus on Online Touchpoints

As described in previous sections, the TCM framework focuses on the nature of touchpoints. As far as this nature is concerned, it is clear that online touchpoints have dramatically increased their presence in the customer journey compared with human and physical touchpoints. It is probably impossible to list all the different types of online touchpoints, as there are frequent innovations, but a provisional list includes websites, mobile apps, email marketing, online advertising, search results, pages/profiles on social networks, online influencers, blogs, live chats, price comparison websites, online intermediaries, and virtual assistants. The list gives a preliminary indication of differences in terms of reach, positivity and frequency between online touchpoints in different sectors. Attitude towards digital touchpoints has also been found to differ (Hallikainen et al., 2019). Specifically, Hallikainen et al. (2019) identify anti-digital consumers, or people who are averse to digital touchpoints, as opposed to digital enthusiasts, or consumers who want to try new online touchpoints as soon as they are available.

This growing variety of online touchpoints has been classified by Straker et al. (2015), who divide them into four types: functional touchpoints, social touchpoints, corporate touchpoints and community touchpoints. This classification is based on the goal of each touchpoint. Functional touchpoints have the goal of providing diversion, functionality and interaction. Social touchpoints aim to allow interaction among users. Corporate touchpoints aim to obtain customer feedback and include FAQ pages, customer feedback forms, and the like. Community touchpoints aim to build a sense of belonging among the users and are focused on developing a social identity for the brand. This category includes, for instance, brand communities and blogs.

In short, studies on online touchpoints across different settings provide the following insights:

- social media and word of mouth have been found to reach heavy brand users (Romaniuk et al., 2013);
- mobile apps have been found to have a positive relationship with loyalty intentions in terms of reach, frequency and positivity. They in fact appear to reach more loyal than "average" customers, more frequently, and to elicit a more positive response in affective terms (Ieva & Ziliani, 2018b);

– the importance of online touchpoints tends to vary significantly depending on the sector and degree of consumer adoption of online services. For instance, the role of online touchpoints, such as the website and the mobile app, appears to be more important in banking than in grocery retailing (Ziliani & Ieva, 2018).

The Role of Online Touchpoints in Delivering an Effective in-Store Customer Experience: Cases from Fashion and Luxury Brands

Omnichannel Customer Experience and the Luxury Sector: The Strategic Importance of the Store

Managing Customer Experience, both offline and online, has become an imperative for companies in many sectors, given the influence it exerts on brand perception, consumer engagement and customer loyalty, in the short and long run alike. For each purchase process, consumers are increasingly relying on multiple touchpoints throughout their customer journey, and online touchpoints appear to be the most widespread. This section and the following section describe a range of online touchpoints with specific reference to their practical usefulness in guiding consumer choices and enriching Customer Experience, in-store and in marketspaces.

Today, in fact, customers expect consistent, integrated service and experience, regardless of the channel used (Piotrowicz & Cuthbertson, 2014). In this respect, Channel Integration is a key requirement for offering a seamless Customer Experience, and appears to be the main challenge in the shift from multichannel to omnichannel retailing. Channel Integration, defined as "the degree to which a firm coordinates the objectives, design, and deployment of its channels to create synergies for the firm and offer particular benefits to its consumers" (Cao & Li, 2015, p. 200), can provide customers with more choice in their shopping process, and can empower customers by reducing uncertainty and confusion, allowing them to take better shopping decisions (Zhang et al., 2018). Channel Integration requires companies to deal with the digital transformation challenges and issues, and may bring the need to redesign traditional assets and strategies.

This is even more significant for companies in the fashion and luxury sector, since luxury itself embodies the "Experience" concept (Atwal & Williams, 2017). It is paramount in fact for luxury brands to be perceived as "*exclusive*" by their customers, and critically this entails the design of new and satisfying experiences (Kapferer, 2015).These experiences should be fully coherent with the brand's distinguished values – such as its signature, its story and its heritage (Ricca & Robins, 2012). The role of the store as a critical place to shape experience is clear (Dion & Borraz, 2015).

Flagship stores have always been perceived as one of the strongest assets of fashion and luxury brands, as a "*manifestation of the brand's identity*" (Manlow & Nobbs, 2013, p. 50). As these authors point out, every design element of the store should recall or embody the brand: the architecture, the décor, the merchandise display, as well as the cues that constitutes the store atmospherics, such as music, perfumes and smells, etc. (Turley & Milliman, 2000). Stores function as mediators, connecting customers with luxury brands on an emotional level through the differentiating experiences offered, all evoking the elegance and quality of the product and the uniqueness of the brand (Hagtvedt & Patrick, 2009).

The focus on flagship stores as the brand's physical representation and embodiment (Berthon et al., 2009) is in fact believed to be one of the main reasons why luxury companies have been relatively slow in adopting e-commerce websites. As described in previous sections, the In-Store Experience is multidimensional and complex, and has been perceived by companies as too difficult to be translated and transferred into an online environment. Clothing, the main product category in fashion and luxury, has moreover traditionally been regarded as high involvement, needing to be seen, felt, touched and tried on before purchase. These perceptions have in fact been even stronger in the fast-fashion segment, where business is built on the customer's repeated visits to the store in a short period of time (Blázquez, 2014).

But despite this initial reluctance, and despite initial uncertainty stemming from companies' limited experience with digital touchpoints, as reported by Heine and Berghaus (2014), many brands have reacted successfully. They have quickly adapted their businesses to integrate digital technologies in a distinctive manner as well as competitively. Omnichannel has been defined as "*one of the most significant innovations in the fashion industry*" (Lynch & Barnes, 2020, p. 4), since consumers are highly involved in each stage of the purchase and rely on multiple channels for their various needs emerging during the shopping journey. Nowadays, technologies have allowed luxury companies to deliver enhanced Customer Experiences, and effectively integrate the online and offline dimensions, thus qualifying themselves as part of the in-store experience itself, and contributing to updating and developing the role of the store (Blázquez, 2014).

In a retail environment moving towards Omnichannel and constantly subject to innovation, the store has however remained the cornerstone of company strategies for many firms. Firstly, from a logistics perspective, it is a primary node for online-to-offline and offline-to-online interactions, allowing companies to offer new services nudging customers towards the seamless use of multiple channels (e.g. click-and-collect; cross-channel promotions). From an experiential perspective, the store can enhance the customers' emotional involvement through the integration of technologies in the store atmosphere, thus contributing to their experience by entertaining them and at the same time meeting their expectations (Savastano et al., 2016).

The aim of both academics and practitioners is, thus, to explore and identify the best design configurations that allow stores to integrate storytelling and brand identity, fluidity and experimentation, and to identify social sharing spaces and micro-spaces for digital technologies, and thus define the "store of the future" (Alexander & Cano, 2020).

Channel Integration: Services and Technologies to Deliver Omnichannel Experience

Channel Integration, as we noted above, can help in following and guiding the consumer through the various channels, while at the same time increasing levels of consumer satisfaction through the creation of distinctive and fluid experiences (Cao & Li, 2015). Sound Channel Integration practices repay retailer commitment by reducing the risk of cannibalization between physical store, website and mobile channel (Herhausen et al., 2015; Ozuem et al., 2008). It is true that Channel Integration entails a substantial investment in technology, both on the consumer side and on the management side, as it is based on reading, analyzing and matching the thousands of data generated by each customer in each channel used. The technical and operational requirements have impacted significantly on the management of the traditional Channel integration practices, such as BOPS (Buy-Online-Pickup-in-Store) and returns. Both require an efficient data management system, able to match customer-related information with the company's internal data on warehousing and logistics. These services directly address practical and empirical needs expressed by omnichannel customers, but they actually contribute to the shopping experience as a whole, by simplifying certain phases of the wider process and allowing consumers to be more easily entertained and retained (Schramm-Klein et al., 2011).

Rosenblum & Kilcourse (2013) identify the in-store technology most widely implemented in an omnichannel strategy as follows: interactive kiosks and interactive totems, interactive screens and showcases, virtual fitting rooms, digital signage, location-based services and beacon technologies, RFID technology, NFC and QR-code, tablet and personal digital assistant, mobile POS, augmented reality and Google Glass.

The implementation of *interactive kiosks and totems* allows customers to be autonomous in looking for product information: interaction with these tools is usually simple and immediate. The assistance provided includes sharing the selected product's datasheet to compare alternatives, completing a purchase order and verifying product availability through stock visibility (Vakulenko et al., 2018). Alongside this virtual assistance, technology can be used to strengthen the effectiveness of the sales force: store managers and shop assistants can be equipped with *tablets and portable devices* that support them in instantly recalling all information required by customers, at the same time improving internal data and inventory management (Bodhani, 2012).

Digital signage, interactive screens and *showcases,* and *QR Codes* are used to deliver additional information in the form of dynamic content to enrich the customer's knowledge of the product and the brand, thus enhancing their awareness (El Azhari & Bennett, 2015). A similar role is played by *beacon technologies*, which interact with the customers' mobile devices during their in-store visit through a Wi-Fi connection and Bluetooth systems. Beacons can enrich the experience by sending profiled and personalized messages, such as a welcome to customers, or offering special promotions to create interest in certain products and incentivize impulse purchases. (Savastano et al., 2016).

Finally, *smart mirrors and virtual fitting rooms* deserve a mention as the most recent cues being tried out by fashion and luxury companies. *Augmented reality (AR)* and *RFID technologies* make it possible to scan the customer's body or face to make product try-on easier and more entertaining. These devices moreover usually incorporate connection with social media, providing an additional service that satisfies fashion customers' need for social approval (Bodhani, 2012).

Case Studies: Shaping Technologies for the Brand's Purposes

Companies operating in the fashion and luxury industry have by now embraced technological change and applied in-store technologies to pursue the creation of unique experiences, while simultaneously enhancing the brand's distinctive features. Each of the companies we discuss below has been successful in tailoring and combining technologies adopted to reflect their own image and meet their most important aims.

For **Burberry**, bringing digital into its retail outlets meant enhancing the In-Store Customer Experience with unique and engaging content. The brand invested in this technological improvement of its stores while simultaneously proceeding to completely redesign its online channels. Each Burberry store is equipped with digital signage and screens, showing exclusive video content about the brand, its symbols and attributes, and live streaming events, to stimulate customers' awareness and positive associations of the products with exciting vibes.

The content is created in the London headquarters and is broadcast from there to Burberry stores all over the world. The house has also strengthened its link with its English heritage, by paying special attention to its Regent Street flagship store. This was the first to test the "Burberry Retail Theater"; an innovative live show concept that allows in-store customers to live the catwalk experience and atmosphere, while benefiting from early access to the new collections.

The latest Burberry project for 2020 is intended to bring store design to a higher level: in July 2020, the company launched a new environment called the "social store", in Shenzen, China. The store was custom-designed for the Chinese tech-savvy customers in partnership with Tencent. It allows visitors to unlock exclusive content from the WeChat app while visiting the store, and share each step with their social communities. Every room, including the cafeteria, is designed as a separate environment for customers to explore and to experience, and is dominated by a distinctive element representative of the brand (e.g. colours, patterns, monograms, products). Customers can thus experience an innovative narrative, which rather than simply providing information about the brand pushes them towards discovery and interpretation.

Luxury brand strength is built not only on quality and trust, but also on relevance and differentiation (Keller, 2009). *Storytelling* is a powerful tool to relate to customers through an emotional connection, and can either be developed from the brand's history, successes and activities or specifically tailored to appeal to the brand's target (Kapferer & Bastien, 2017). Virtual reality is acknowledged to be particularly effective in digital storytelling (Van Laer et al., 2019).

The shoe brand **TOMS** uses virtual reality to increase awareness of the social giving campaigns that represent the heart of its business. Since 2006, this inclusive and sustainable brand has been noted for its "One for One" business model, based on the idea that every purchase is beneficial not only to the purchaser but also to the world. For each pair of shoes purchased, a new pair is given to a child in need during Giving Trips to more than 70 countries organized by TOMS.

In 2015, TOMS opted to further stress the significance of the donations powered by consumers' purchase decisions, and to give customers a stronger perception of their impact. VR headsets were installed in a dedicated corner of TOMS flagship stores. Customers are invited to sit in a VR-powered chair to live in first-person the experience of a giving trip, in which they are able to personally hand over a pair of new shoes to a young child living in a remote village in Peru. The VR experience lasts around 4 min, but is tailored to be immersive and thus emotional and emphatic, strengthening the affective dimension of the In-Store Customer Experience. The VR feature was first tried out in the California store, and then replicated in 30 TOMS retail stores and other department store corners around the globe. A year later, to celebrate the first 10 years of the company, another new virtual giving experience was released through a partnership with AT&T, generating as much publicity as customer satisfaction.

Other companies are interpreting the in-store digital experience as a way to manage and ensure the fluidity of the customers' purchase process, which generates additional value by anticipating their needs. Sometimes, this process requires retailers to rethink their products, and offer new processes integrating additional or different touchpoints.

In 2018, fashion retailer **Nordstrom** redesigned its Buy-Online-Pickup-In-Store (BOPS) service in order to diminish waiting times for customers along each phase of the process, keeping in constant touch with them through smartphone. Customers can access the service through the mobile app and are presented with different possibilities. BOPS has been integrated with the "curbside pickup" option, which is new in fashion retail but appeals to many US consumers. When the order is confirmed, the customer receives an email showing the service phone number. The customer calls or texts the service 10 min before arriving at the store to collect the order, which is thus presented straight on arrival. It is also possible to request a complimentary gift wrap kit.

Nordstrom has also introduced the "Reserve Online, Try-On In Store" service, allowing customers to select and reserve items via the app. This requires complete transparency concerning product availability data. Customers are notified via text message when their order is ready, which reduces waiting times. When arriving at the store, they are directed to a dedicated dressing room containing their items to be tried on. This process is designed to reduce every possible source of customer discomfort, particularly waiting times and queues, and was perfected after a long-term pilot test in six Washington stores. Customers proved immediately favorable to the initiative, and the company reports that more than 80% used the service multiple times after the first trial.

Product availability is in fact a key consideration for many retailers, and is represented with different technologies reflecting brands' style and customers' preferred channels. **Adidas** presents its products through an in-store 3D catalogue that can be accessed through the virtual wall displays. The device is interactive, so that customers can examine products just as they can in real life. The actual purchase is carried out with the help of sales assistants through their tablets, which avoids queues at cash counters. Customers can pay immediately, or request the product to be home delivered (Aubrey & Judge, 2012). Since 2017, **Target** has powered its stores with beacon systems which use Bluetooth technology to connect with the customers' mobile app. Target is known for its Target Run newsfeed service, which uses the two most popular features in the brand app, namely lists and maps. Target Run guides and supports users throughout their visit to the store, making it easier for them to find the items they want to purchase, check the in-store inventory and store-exclusive promotions in real time, and find interesting content based on their location (e.g. trending items on social media like Pinterest).

The latest trend in retail, however, is *augmented reality* (AR) , technology that enhances real world objects, such as products or in-store furniture, with computer-generated, multisensory information. AR allows companies to deliver more powerful and engaging experiences, appealing to those customers who desire personalization and social interactions in their shopping routines.

Farfetch boutiques in London are an example of modern and digitally enhanced stores. In 2017, the company implemented a sign-in station that allows the customer to check into the store and use new devices such as RFID-enabled clothing racks, which detect the products browsed by the customer, and digital mirrors that can recall wishlists and put together items of different sizes and colours. **Dior**, **Balenciaga** and **Tommy Hilfiger** have developed VR/AR headsets in the line of Google glasses, which give customers immersive access to exclusive content from their catwalk shows, such as backstage footage, which would not otherwise be shared. Fast fashion too has trid out these technologies: **Zara** had applied Augmented Reality to 120 of its worldwide stores by April 2018, creating dedicated spaces for customers to explore using their smartphones. The Zara campaign focused mainly on integrating AR with outfit displays and window displays, which would appear as empty to the naked eye and reveal their content when framed via the Zara app in a smartphone camera. Mannequins were replaced with AR replicas of fashion models, showing off to customers, posing and moving for 7–12 s, in 12 different environments. AR thus improved and enhanced the cognitive and physical dimensions of the In-Store Customer Experience for users of the Zara app.

Delivering Customer Experience in the Digital Environment: Best Practices in Luxury and Fashion Retailing

Digital Technologies as Drivers of Change in Luxury Markets: Emerging Trends and Challenges

The in-store move towards digital integration described above is making necessary the evolution of online channels and marketspaces. According to the 2019 Luxury Goods Market Study by Bain & Company, retail online channels account for 12% of the whole market, having grown 22% in one year. Moreover, 75% of purchases were influenced by the online channel, and more than 20% of purchases were digitally enabled. The personal luxury goods market reported a big increase in online purchases, especially in the accessory, beauty and "hard luxury" categories.

Amongst online channels, brand-owned website performance has risen faster than e-tailer website performance. The secondhand market for luxury goods has also grown, due to an increase in the number of specialized online platforms (D'Arpizio et al., 2019), which often partner with the fashion houses themselves. Examples are Burberry and The RealReal and Urban Outfitters and the rental service Nuuly.

These impressive results reward the commitment of many companies to developing online channels, but "going digital" has brought many challenges which continue to impact on the evolution of the sector.

The study by Chandon et al. (2016) noted that digital has disrupted the tight control which luxury companies once held over their brands and products. Moreover, the openness and the accessibility ensured by online marketspaces appear in some way to conflict with the "dream value" of luxury goods (Dubois & Paternault, 1995). Although IT allow companies to share their brand values and information about heritage and quality, they make it more difficult to ensure the traditional one-to-one, confidential relationships with customers they were used to. Luxury companies perceive a loss of control over their image, and an alteration in the power balance, due to the intervention of new influential actors in their interactions with customers (Lee & Watkins, 2016).

Wider access to luxury also raises new issues affecting the exclusivity usually surrounding a brand because of its rarity. Digital channels are open-access, so companies now need to learn how to manage content in order to segment their customers and deliver dedicated and exclusive services to their top clients, allowing them to maintain their superior status. This issue is intertwined with "cultural" aspects of fashion and luxury, and closely linked to its codes and symbols. Leading companies are finding themselves facing the task of educating new segments of consumers which have emerged from the expansion of the sector in new countries and towards the younger generations (Chandon et al., 2016). It seems that Millennials, the current generation of digital natives, are one of the biggest challenges for luxury companies, as their vision and perception of the brands and products, and the way they approach the purchase process itself, differ enormously from those of other customer segments (Taplin, 2019).

The challenge for companies today is thus to communicate the brand experience to different target groups simultaneously. On one hand, they must reach new targets, trying not to be perceived as outdated; on the other hand, they must avoid alienating existing target groups (Klein et al., 2016). Online engagement needs to be redefined in order to appeal to new customers as well as traditional segments.

Designing an Exclusive Digital Marketspace: Online Communication Through IT Technologies

Nowadays, companies have at their disposal a wide range of digital technologies and touchpoints they can exploit to manage their online presence. Each has a different impact on the audience and appeals to certain targets (Heine, 2010).

Heine and Berghaus (2014) list the most important digital touchpoints that fashion and luxury companies should manage, or at least monitor: brand website, direct mailing, online advertising, brand communities, social campaigns, phone and tablet apps, and e-commerce.

The luxury *brand website* is a priority to invest in, since it is usually the first source customers use when looking for brand information. Customers consult brand websites for insight into brand vision and history, and expect to be quickly immersed in the brand's atmosphere through both content and aesthetics (Riley & Lacroix, 2003). The website should therefore offer as many interesting contributions as possible. Smaller sites may include only a few sections to present products, distinctive features and values, and awards or press articles, while larger ones may be structured as a digital hub, including sub-brands, dedicated pages for iconic products, and may even incorporate brand communities and blogs (Díaz et al., 2016).

User Experience is of extreme importance in luxury retailing, and digital native customers require an immediate comprehension of the platform they interact with, linear and smooth processes, and engaging layouts. It has been shown that the design of the brand website can significantly affect customer perceptions by evoking a strong sense of luxury (Mu et al., 2020).

These considerations also hold for the design of e-commerce websites and digital apps.

In fashion and luxury, *e-commerce* was considered a threat for many years: and concerns have often been voiced over channel cannibalization with the brand's own stores, the spread of counterfeit goods, loss of control over third party retailers, and grey markets, due to the opening of consumer-to-consumer platforms. However, many companies have succeeded in keeping control over their products and brands online. Firstly, in developing their own branded e-commerce websites, most fashion houses have given customers the same feeling of exclusivity they would perceive in-store, paired with appropriate services and terms of sale.

For example, the luxury jewellery brand **Astley Clarke** has connected its e-commerce with an extensive personal shopper service to assist its customers (Heine & Berghaus, 2014). As for independent retailers, the marketspace is dominated by a few specialized companies that have been able to develop their own recognizable brands, very distinct from mass-market online retail. Examples include Farfetch, MyTheresa, and LuisaViaRoma. These retailers operate worldwide, and compete on product range and access to exclusive fashion collections, as well as delivery and return services. They run differentiated loyalty programs, and follow a highly technological experiential approach (Balasyan & Casais, 2018).

Phone and tablet apps are used by fashion houses for a dual purpose. On one hand, they facilitate customer purchases by granting quick and direct access to products and carts. On the other hand, they help to create customer engagement by offering complementary information to enrich customer experience. The challenge for marketing is thus to acquire detailed knowledge of customer profiles, identify what is important to customers, and present relevant content that is also consistent with brand identity. **Hermès'** app "Silk Knots" has become a case study: the brand is teaching its customers how to wear tie and scarf accessories, starting from the basics and going up to presenting fashionable styles that change every season, and thus leveraging the cognitive dimension of the OCE. By sharing interesting content, Hermès is also enhancing its customers' trust and presenting itself to the market as a recognized and reliable source (Heine & Berghaus, 2014).

So in an omnichannel perspective, apps can be used to integrate and connect online touchpoints, and sometimes online and offline channels, while embracing all the features of the brand, in order to enrich the customer's experience. Increasing app usage matches the constant increase in the use of mobile devices in customers' daily routines, and customers are constantly connected both with the brand and other customers.

Direct mailing is still used by fashion and luxury companies, mainly to deliver exclusive promotions or access to limited content, or to drawing customers in-store or to the brand website. *Online advertising* and *social campaigns,* on the other hand are useful for building brand awareness (Godey et al., 2016) Regarding social campaigns, given the importance of social recognition in fashion and luxury, companies need to monitor their reference brand communities, whether private and brand-initiated or public and customer-initiated. Brand communities are a unique opportunity for companies to observe authentic consumer behavior, gain specific insight into preferences and perceptions, and capture critical cues or anticipate dissatisfaction (Muniz & O'Guinn, 2001). In-house brand communities can be an even more valuable asset, as in these companies have the strongest hold over their members and can initiate co-creation processes through activities and contests.

Last but not least, other new technologies, such as *VR* and *AR*, are enriching digital channels and touchpoints and rapidly expanding their range.

Many fashion companies today use AR to make their apps and social campaigns more attractive, or to create interactions between their online channels and stores. In 2019, it was found that certain luxury brands also use AR in their physical products and in digital-only collections that exist only virtually. The historic Scandinavian brand **Carlings**, for example, released a digitally enhanced t-shirt, "Last Statement" that appears as a white shirt in "real life" but whose design can be changed using Instagram AR filters.

In short, "digital luxury marketing is one act of balance between technological innovation and gadgets, and substantial authenticity and usefulness" (Heine & Berghaus, 2014, p. 231), and today companies are competing by carefully incorporating digital assets into their brands.

Best Practice for Online Experience Management

Effective OCE requires companies to manage all dimensions that influence purchase decisions. Companies need to work on verbal and visual design elements to capture consumers' interest, to connect with them, and to develop a long-term relationship built on trust (Bleier et al., 2019). The fashion and luxury sector offers interesting case studies, since many companies have invested considerable cognitive and financial resources in creating unique experiences (Corbellini & Saviolo, 2014), including through collaborations with top hi-tech specialists. The key to success is to communicate the brand's values in an innovative way, anticipating trends or transforming mass fads into distinctive experiences through a proper integration of digital touchpoints.

The **Chanel** website is a good example of a digital hub in the luxury sector. The website structure is linear, user-friendly and covers the main areas of interest, linking micro-pages for the various product categories.

The design elements are consistent with Chanel style, simple and elegant, of significant impact and enriched with visual elements, and the structure thus contributes to enhancing the cognitive dimension of the OCE. Chanel also provides interesting insights into its heritage in a dedicated blog, accessible from the section "Chanel Inside". Here the customer is presented with a series of short videos that narrate the company's history in various fields in a lively manner. A wide range of insights are offered; episodes in the life of Gabrielle Chanel, the atmosphere of the early years of the firm, and contemporary celebrities, as well as the history of the most iconic products, and the brand's symbols and colours. This sophisticated blog can be considered an online brand museum.

Customers can often become part of iconic and historic luxury brands. While Chanel links its history to celebrities like Marilyn Monroe, **Burberry** in fact involves their current customers as part of the brand itself. The social campaign Burberry Love, which contributed to the creation of the brand's in-house community, aimed to increase engagement in its leading product, the classic trench coat. The campaign was built around an emotional approach; it invited consumers "to be part of Burberry's story" (Straker & Wrigley, 2016), thus enhancing the affective dimension of the OCE. The approach is also reflected in the brand's website, which hosts on its first page customers pictured wearing their own trench coats. These photographs are submitted through the brand community forum and periodically selected by the company.

Other retailers reinforce the e-commerce website by introducing new features and services. In 2019, **Sephora** launched an updated version of their e-commerce and informed customers of additional services. When they start the purchase process, a progress bar appears, which allows them to select or request free shipping, free gifts, samples, etc. **Nyx** connects its e-commerce with social media, delivering "social proof" information and messaging while customers are shopping. While selecting a product or a product category, users are informed in real time of other customers' reviews and opinions, and of best-selling products or products trending on social media.

Moreover, both Sephora and Nyx incorporate augmented reality into their ecommerce websites, with the aim of reproducing the try-on and consultancy services that usually take place in-store. Many other beauty and personal care companies do this too. **L'Oreal**'s investment in the AR company Modiface allows it to offer both virtual makeup and hair colour try-ons, as well as a digital skin diagnostic service. Like a real-life beautician, the software detects signs of ageing from customers' pictures of their faces, and suggests specific product routines for their skin. Clearly, such services can strengthen consumer loyalty, as the company suggests products that can become part of the customer's daily routine, and a relationship of trust can be built up over time. Sometimes, these try-on programs also let customers take pictures of themselves, so as to share their choices on social media and contribute to creating social buzz around the brand or the product.

This type of innovation necessitates creative and effective communication strategies as well as efficient management strategies. Communication is critical when companies are focusing on actively promoting core products or exclusive collections. **YOOX**'s 2017 cooperation with Google is an excellent example of a pop-modern and engaging social media campaign. YOOX in fact reinterprets the idea of "luxury desirability" with its new "Now or Never!" format. The campaign is conducted through a series of short YouTube video commercials: each video shows a 3D cartoon-like scenario and features a product from a selection of prestige clothing and accessories, integrated in real time by a rendering platform. The call-to-action invites the user to "save" the product by buying it in the next 15 s; otherwise, after the deadline, the item will be destroyed. The innovation of this campaign is that the "threat" is real: every product is a unique piece, so the customer will really be unable to find it, and see the video, ever again, and the opportunity will be lost forever. The campaign is notable for its originality, and particularly for the company's expertise in using big data and profiling metrics. Each individual user can in fact visualize the products he or she has searched for online and/or kept on a wishlist. Making full use of technology for marketing in fact includes exploiting its full potential to gain more complete knowledge of what the customer wants, which, as the case of YOOX shows, is vital for creating engaging OCEs.

FUTURE CHALLENGES IN MANAGING
CUSTOMER EXPERIENCE FOR LUXURY BRANDS

Investing in the design of effective Customer Experience should be a priority for every company on the market today, as it is acknowledged that a meaningful customer journey is a precondition for future loyalty. This is somewhat revolutionary in marketing management, as companies are required to rethink the experience they offer their customers as well as the internal processes that support and contribute to its success. Customer Experience Management (CEM) is thus the framework of reference to designing and managing effective customer experiences in a proactive rather than a reactive approach (Homburg et al., 2017). The final goal of CEM is achieving long-term customer loyalty by designing and continually renewing touchpoint journeys (Homburg et al., 2017). CEM involves three main dimensions: cultural mindset, strategic direction and capabilities. These three elements entail cultural orientation of the company towards customer experience, the development of a strategy to design the experience, and the firm's capabilities to continuously adjust and re-design Customer Experience by managing the different touchpoints along the customer journey. Kuehnl et al. (2019) find that companies should focus on the aspects of the customer journey that consumers value the most, namely thematic cohesion, consistency, and context sensitivity of touchpoints. Moreover, the experience must always make reference to the brand and embody its values. Although enriched with many attributes, the customer journey must convey a consistent and coherent brand image, keeping its brand personality and meaning.

The pressing need to be present at multiple touchpoints while maintaining brand consistency through different marketspaces is complementary to communicating the important features and attributes that characterize the customer experience, and, consequently, the brand. This challenge is coupled with the issue of identifying the most important touchpoints to communicate the identity of the brand and to drive customer loyalty. The mobile app for example has been found to have a positive relationship with customer loyalty (Ieva & Ziliani 2018a, 2018b; Ozuem et al., 2008) as it is likely that using a mobile app increases interaction and engagement with the brand, thus driving loyalty in the long run. However, the reach of the mobile app, or the number of active users, is currently very low compared to other digital touchpoints, such as websites or online advertising. The presence of brands on social media and the activities of influencers might also play a key role in driving engagement in order to build a base of loyal fans of the brand and in shifting online traffic towards the company website. It is also reasonable to expect that new digital touchpoints, such as chatbots, will be aligned to the identity of the brand in how they communicate with customers and in their appearance. Assigning a specific role to each digital touchpoint along the online customer journey is the key to designing customer experience consistent with brand identity and which drives customer loyalty and sales.

The issue of brand consistency is of concern for companies operating in many sectors, but is particularly important in the luxury sector, because it calls into question the very concept of "luxury" itself. In academic circles, this challenge is known as "the Internet Dilemma" (Baker et al., 2018). Luxury brands are in fact torn between maintaining their brand image, associated with exclusivity and rarity, and being exposed on the open online marketspace (Mu et al., 2020). The difficulties in embracing this new digital environment weigh differently according to whether the luxury brand is already perceived by customers as accessible, intermediate or inaccessible (De Barnier et al., 2012).

The challenge of the democratization of luxury has led some Ultra-High-Net-Worth luxury companies to support consumer counter-movements, such as *"silent luxury"*, which emphasizes extrinsic product qualities, like authenticity, sustainability and craftsmanship, as "true" quality (McKinsey, 2020).

Finally, note that new and digital native brands have started to emerge alongside top and iconic brands. Such brands operate only in the online marketspace, and compete by offering their own interpretation of luxury in the modern world and by following a direct-to-consumer model. Eager to build relationships with their customers, they start connecting with potential customers on social media sometimes even before the launch of the product. These companies focus strongly on the online customer journey, as this is their market, and tend to target generations Y and Z. Other luxury brands have noticed this new business model, and attracted by their vision and technological skills are trying to connect or cooperate with the new brands. This trend would be interesting to monitor, as integrating different interpretations of the "luxury" concept and business models has today become a serious challenge even for traditional market leaders.

References

Alexander, B., & Cano, M. B. (2020). Store of the future: Towards a (re) invention and (re) imagination of physical store space in an omnichannel context. *Journal of Retailing and Consumer Services, 55.*

Atwal, G., & Williams, A. (2017). Luxury brand marketing—The experience is everything!. In *Advances in luxury brand management* (pp. 43–57). Palgrave Macmillan.

Aubrey, C., & Judge, D. (2012). Re-imagine retail: Why store innovation is key to a brand's growth in the 'new normal', digitally-connected and transparent world. *Journal of Brand Strategy, 1*(1), 31–39.

Baker, J., Ashill, N., Amer, N., & Diab, E. (2018). The internet dilemma: An exploratory study of luxury firms' usage of internet-based technologies. *Journal of Retailing and Consumer Services, 41*, 37–47.

Balasyan, I., & Casais, B. (2018). Keeping exclusivity in an E-commerce environment: The case of Farfetch. com and the market of luxury clothes. *International Journal of Marketing, Communication and New Media,* (4).

Barari, M., Ross, M., & Surachartkumtonkun, J. (2020). Negative and positive customer shopping experience in an online context. *Journal of Retailing and Consumer Services, 53.*

Baxendale, S., Macdonald, E. K., & Wilson, H. N. (2015). The impact of different touchpoints on brand consideration. *Journal of Retailing, 91*(2), 235–253.

Berthon, P., Pitt, L., Parent, M., & Berthon, J.-P. (2009). Aesthetics and ephemerality: Observing and preserving the luxury brand. *California Management Review, 52*(1), 45–66.

Bilgihan, A., Kandampully, J., & Zhang, T. C. (2016). Towards a unified customer experience in online shopping environments. *International Journal of Quality and Service Sciences.*

Blázquez, M. (2014). Fashion shopping in multichannel retail: The role of technology in enhancing the customer experience. *International Journal of Electronic Commerce, 18*(4), 97–116.

Bleier, A., Harmeling, C. M., & Palmatier, R. W. (2019). Creating effective online customer experiences. *Journal of Marketing, 83*(2), 98–119.

Bodhani, A. (2012). Shops offer the e-tail experience. *Engineering & Technology, 7*(5), 46–49.

Bustamante, J. C., & Rubio, N. (2017). Measuring customer experience in physical retail environments. *Journal of Service Management.*

Cao, L., & Li, L. (2015). The impact of cross-channel integration on retailers' sales growth. *Journal of Retailing, 91*(2), 198–216.

Chandon, J. L., Laurent, G., & Valette-Florence, P. (2016). Pursuing the concept of luxury: Introduction to the JBR Special Issue on "Luxury Marketing from Tradition to Innovation". *Journal of Business Research, 69*(1), 299–303.

Corbellini, E., & Saviolo, S. (2014). *Managing fashion and luxury companies.* Etas.

D'Arpizio, C., Levato, F., Prete, F., Del Fabbro, E., & De Montgolfier, J. (2019). *The future of luxury: A look into tomorrow to understand today.* Bain and Company.

De Barnier, V., Falcy, S., & Valette-Florence, P. (2012). Do consumers perceive three levels of luxury? A comparison of accessible, intermediate and inaccessible luxury brands. *Journal of Brand Management, 19*(7), 623–636.

De Keyser, A., Lemon, K. N., Klaus, P., & Keiningham, T. L. (2015). A framework for understanding and managing the customer experience. *Marketing Science Institute Working Paper Series, 85*(1), 15–121.

De Keyser, A., Verleye, K., Lemon, K. N., Keiningham, T. L., & Klaus, P. (2020). Moving the customer experience field forward: Introducing the touchpoints, context, qualities (TCQ) nomenclature. *Journal of Service Research,* 1094670520928390.

Díaz, E., Martín-Consuegra, D., & Estelami, H. (2016). A persuasive-based latent class segmentation analysis of luxury brand websites. *Electronic Commerce Research, 16*(3), 401–424.

Dion, D., & Borraz, S. (2015). Managing heritage brands: A study of the sacralization of heritage stores in the luxury industry. *Journal of Retailing and Consumer Services, 22,* 77–84.

Dubois, B., & Paternault, C. (1995). Observations: Understanding the world of international luxury brands: The "dream formula". *Journal of Advertising Research.*

Duncan, T., & Moriarty, S. (2006). How integrated marketing communication's 'touchpoints' can operationalize the service-dominant logic. *The Service-Dominant Logic of Marketing: Dialog, Debate, and Directions, 21*(1), 236–249.

El Azhari, J., Bennett, D. (2015). Omni-channel customer experience: An investigation into the use of digital technology in physical stores and its impact on the consumer's decision-making process. In *AEDEM international conference* (pp. 1–13).

Fog, K., Budtz, C., & Yakaboylu, B. (2005). *Storytelling.* Springer.

Gao, F., & Su, X. (2017). Omnichannel retail operations with buy-online-and-pick-up-in-store. *Management Science, 63*(8), 2478–2492.

Gentile, C., Spiller, N., & Noci, G. (2007). How to sustain the customer experience: An overview of experience components that co-create value with the customer. *European Management Journal, 25*(5), 395–410.

Godey, B., Manthiou, A., Pederzoli, D., Rokka, J., Aiello, G., Donvito, R., & Singh, R. (2016). Social media marketing efforts of luxury brands: Influence on brand equity and consumer behavior. *Journal of Business Research, 69*(12), 5833–5841.

Hagtvedt, H., & Patrick, V. M. (2009). The broad embrace of luxury: Hedonic potential as a driver of brand extendibility. *Journal of Consumer Psychology, 19*(4), 608–618.

Hallikainen, H., Alamäki, A., & Laukkanen, T. (2019). Individual preferences of digital touchpoints: A latent class analysis. *Journal of Retailing and Consumer Services.*

Heine, K. (2010). The personality of luxury fashion brands. *Journal of Global Fashion Marketing, 1*(3), 154–163.

Heine, K., & Berghaus, B. (2014). Luxury goes digital: How to tackle the digital luxury brand–consumer touchpoints. *Journal of Global Fashion Marketing, 5*(3), 223–234.

Herhausen, D., Binder, J., Schoegel, M., & Herrmann, A. (2015). Integrating bricks with clicks: Retailer-level and channel-level outcomes of online–offline channel integration. *Journal of Retailing, 91*(2), 309–325.

Herhausen, D., Kleinlercher, K., Verhoef, P. C., Emrich, O., & Rudolph, T. (2019). Loyalty formation for different customer journey segments. *Journal of Retailing, 95*(3), 9–29.

Homburg, C., Jozić, D., & Kuehnl, C. (2017). Customer experience management: Toward implementing an evolving marketing concept. *Journal of the Academy of Marketing Science, 45*(3), 377–401.

Ieva, M., & Ziliani, C. (2018a). Mapping touchpoint exposure in retailing: Implications for developing an omnichannel customer experience. *International Journal of Retail and Distribution Management, 46*(3), 304–322.

Ieva, M., & Ziliani, C. (2018b). The role of customer experience touchpoints in driving loyalty intentions in services. *TQM Journal, 30*(5), 444–457.

Kapferer, J. N. (2015). *Kapferer on luxury: How luxury brands can grow yet remain rare.* Kogan Page Publishers.

Kapferer, J. N., & Bastien, V. (2017). The specificity of luxury management: Turning marketing upside down. In *Advances in Luxury Brand Management* (pp. 65–84). Palgrave Macmillan.

Keller, K. L. (2009). Building strong brands in a modern marketing communications environment. *Journal of Marketing Communications, 15*(2–3), 139–155.

Klein, J. F., Falk, T., Esch, F. R., & Gloukhovtsev, A. (2016). Linking pop-up brand stores to brand experience and word of mouth: The case of luxury retail. *Journal of Business Research, 69*(12), 5761–5767.

Kuehnl, C., Jozic, D., & Homburg, C. (2019). Effective customer journey design: Consumers' conception, measurement, and consequences. *Journal of the Academy of Marketing Science, 47*(3), 551–568.

Lee, J. E., & Watkins, B. (2016). YouTube vloggers' influence on consumer luxury brand perceptions and intentions. *Journal of Business Research, 69*(12), 5753–5760.

Lemon, K. N., & Verhoef, P. C. (2016). Understanding customer experience throughout the customer journey. *Journal of Marketing, 80*(6), 69–96.

Lynch, S., & Barnes, L. (2020). Omnichannel fashion retailing: Examining the customer decision-making journey. *Journal of Fashion Marketing and Management: An International Journal.*

Manlow, V., & Nobbs, K. (2013). Form and function of luxury flagships. *Journal of Fashion Marketing and Management: An International Journal.*

Martin, J., Mortimer, G., & Andrews, L. (2015). Re-examining online customer experience to include purchase frequency and perceived risk. *Journal of Retailing and Consumer Services, 25,* 81–95.

McKinsey. (2020). *Scatta l'ora del silent luxury.* https://www.mckinsey.it/idee/mckinsey-scatta-lora-del-silent-luxury.

Meyer, C., & Schwager, A. (2007). Understanding customer experience. *Harvard Business Review, 85*(2), 116.

Morgan, B. (2017). The difference between customer experience and user experience. *Forbes.* https://www.forbes.com/sites/blakemorgan/2017/01/18/the-difference-between-customer-experience-and-user-experience-2/#2cf f935416a6.

Mu, W., Lennon, S. J., & Liu, W. (2020). Top online luxury apparel and accessories retailers: What are they doing right? *Fashion and Textiles, 7*(1), 1–17.

Muniz, A. M., & O'guinn, T. C. (2001). Brand community. *Journal of Consumer Research, 27*(4), 412–432.

Ou, Y. C., & Verhoef, P. C. (2017). The impact of positive and negative emotions on loyalty intentions and their interactions with customer equity drivers. *Journal of Business Research, 80,* 106–115.

Ozuem, W., Howell, K. E., & Lancaster, G. (2008). Communicating in the new interactive marketspace. *European Journal of Marketing, 42*(9/10), 1059–1083.

Ozuem, W., Patel, A., Howell, K. E., & Lancaster, G. (2017). An exploration of customers' response to online service recovery initiatives. *International Journal of Market Research, 59*(1), 97–116.

Ozuem, W., Thomas, T., & Lancaster, G. (2016). The influence of customer loyalty on small island economies: An empirical and exploratory study. *Journal of Strategic Marketing, 24*(6), 447–469.

Pandey, S., & Chawla, D. (2018). Online customer experience (OCE) in clothing e-retail. *International Journal of Retail & Distribution Management.*

Piotrowicz, W., & Cuthbertson, R. (2014). Introduction to the special issue information technology in retail: Toward omnichannel retailing. *International Journal of Electronic Commerce, 18*(4), 5–16.

Ricca, M., & Robins, R. (2012). *Meta-luxury: Brands and the culture of excellence.* Springer.

Riley, F. D. O., & Lacroix, C. (2003). Luxury branding on the internet: Lost opportunity or impossibility? *Marketing Intelligence & Planning.*

Romaniuk, J., Beal, V., & Uncles, M. (2013). Achieving reach in a multimedia environment: How a marketer's first step provides the direction for the second. *Journal of Advertising Research, 53*(2), 221–230.

Rose, S., Clark, M., Samouel, P., & Hair, N. (2012). Online customer experience in e-retailing: An empirical model of antecedents and outcomes. *Journal of Retailing, 88*(2), 308–322.

Rosenblum, P., & Kilcourse, B. (2013). Omni-channel 2013: The long road to adoption. *Benchmark Report, RSR Research, Miami.*

Savastano, M., Barnabei, R., & Ricotta, F. (2016, January). Going online while purchasing offline: An explorative analysis of omnichannel shopping behaviour in retail settings. In *Proceedings of the international marketing trends conference* (pp. 21–23).

Schramm-Klein, H., Wagner, G., Steinmann, S., & Morschett, D. (2011). Cross-channel integration—Is it valued by customers? *The International Review of Retail, Distribution and Consumer Research, 21*(5), 501–511.

Singh, R., & Söderlund, M. (2020). Extending the experience construct: An examination of online grocery shopping. *European Journal of Marketing.*

Straker, K., & Wrigley, C. (2016). Designing an emotional strategy: Strengthening digital channel engagements. *Business Horizons, 59*(3), 339–346.

Straker, K., Wrigley, C., & Rosemann, M. (2015). Typologies and touchpoints: Designing multi-channel digital strategies. *Journal of Research in Interactive Marketing.*

Taplin, I. M. (2019). *The evolution of luxury.* Routledge.

Turley, L. W., & Milliman, R. E. (2000). Atmospheric effects on shopping behavior: A review of the experimental evidence. *Journal of Business Research, 49*(2), 193–211.

Vakulenko, Y., Hellström, D., & Oghazi, P. (2018). Customer value in self-service kiosks: A systematic literature review. *International Journal of Retail & Distribution Management.*

Van Laer, T., Feiereisen, S., & Visconti, L. M. (2019). Storytelling in the digital era: A meta-analysis of relevant moderators of the narrative transportation effect. *Journal of Business Research, 96,* 135–146.

Zhang, M., Ren, C., Wang, G. A., & He, Z. (2018). The impact of channel integration on consumer responses in omni-channel retailing: The mediating effect of consumer empowerment. *Electronic Commerce Research and Applications, 28,* 181–193.

Ziliani, C., & Ieva, M. (2018). The role of touchpoints in driving loyalty: Implications for omnichannel retailing. *Micro & Macro Marketing, 27*(3), 375–396.

Ziliani, C., & Ieva, M. (2020). *Loyalty management: From loyalty programs to omnichannel customer experiences.* Routledge.

CHAPTER 16

Leveraging EWOM on Service Failure Recovery Strategy: An Insight into the Brand Perspective

Silvia Ranfagni and Wilson Ozuem

INTRODUCTION

The fashion industry is changing, with new markets, new ways to reach them, and new power for fashion consumers. Fashion consumers are no longer passive actors in the market since they interact with companies and tell other consumers about their brand experiences through social media, co-creating brand value (Athwal et al., 2018). By producing user-generated content (UGC), they can share information, opinions, and feelings, fostering electronic word of mouth (eWOM) as a key source of information about products and services (Cantallops & Salvi, 2014; Ozuem et al., 2008). Thanks to its persuasive influence, eWOM can have

S. Ranfagni (✉)
Department of Economics and Business, University of Florence, Florence, Italy

W. Ozuem
Institute of Business, Industry and Leadership,
University of Cumbria, Lancaster, UK

© The Author(s), under exclusive license to Springer Nature
Switzerland AG 2021
W. Ozuem and S. Ranfagni (eds.), *The Art of Digital Marketing for
Fashion and Luxury Brands*,
https://doi.org/10.1007/978-3-030-70324-0_16

an impact on consumer behaviour. Its influence depends on different factors, such as the valence, framing, and credibility of online messages, amongst which, negative valence mediates consumers' choices the most. EWOM frequently occurs after a consumer has experienced service failure. Regardless of the reasons for negative eWOM, providers must manage adequate recovery strategies, which will only be effective if the recovery actions are perceived by the complaining consumers. Providers, therefore, have to produce a perceived justice. Consumers can be co-creators of this perceived justice. In this chapter we investigate the relationships between UGC, negative eWOM, and service failure and recovery strategies. Understanding them is increasingly more important in the fashion industry, where recent events (e.g., COVID-19) have intensified online sales and increased the likelihood that companies will have to resolve online service failure issues (de Kerviler & Rodriguez, 2019). The value they produce for the customer is also increasingly dependent on how they handle these situations. The analysis we make in this chapter is interpreted through the filter of the brand. The brand is an entity that moves on the market, and it is not just any sort of entity. It is something that consumers know about, and it is something they relate to. Brands populate the fashion industry (Park et al., 2018). In drafting a chapter on useful issues for fashion companies, after a first section in which we investigate the relationship between UGC, negative eWOM, and service failure and recovery strategies, we then explore how this relationship develops around the brand (i.e., when service failure gives rise to negative brand experiences). The brand is therefore at the centre of our discussion. The analysis, although carried out from a theoretical point of view, offers insights into the fashion industry. These insights are explained in the conclusion section.

EWOM Fostered by UGC, and Service Failure and Recovery Strategies

Consumers receive communication but also send communication. They talk about products or services, which fuels eWOM and can lead companies to review their communication strategies. EWOM after a service failure requires the implementation of a recovery strategy. We are going to illustrate the effect that eWOM fostered by UGC can have on consumers and on the company in terms of recovery activities after a service failure.

UGC and EWOM

Today, social media encourage internet users to produce UGC, which is material created and uploaded to the internet by non-professionals (Presi et al., 2014). UGC contains information, opinions, and consumption experiences that can be shared without limits of space and time: UGC can be created and explored anywhere and at any time. Playing a role in generating marketing information, consumers as internet users are no longer passive users of marketer-provided information (Berthon et al., 2008). By means of UGC, they drive eWOM, which is "informal communications directed at consumers though Internet-based technology related to the usage or characteristics of particular goods and services, or their sellers" (Litvin et al., 2008, p. 461). Since eWOM is characterized by rapid interaction and has an extensive reach, it is a key source of information about products and services (Cantallops & Salvi, 2014) that has the potential to influence consumers' information searches and their buying decisions (Zheng et al., 2009). Consumers believe in the informational value of eWOM: they think that the information that other consumers circulate has greater credibility than marketer-generated information (Bickart & Schindler, 2001). Since eWOM comes from a source that is perceived to be similar to the receiver, it exerts persuasive influence on the receiver and creates empathy, which facilitates the sharing of issues related to personal experiences (Deighton et al. 1989).

EWOM and Consumers' Intention to Purchase

For businesses, an intriguing issue to explore is how eWOM can have an impact on consumers' intention to purchase, in other words, how some online reviews are perceived as useful in orienting decisions on whether or not to buy or use the reviewed product or service (Babić Rosario et al., 2016; Cheung et al., 2008). Some studies investigated the *factors* that influence the perceived usefulness of eWOM. Sparks and Browning (2011) identified valence, framing, and easy-to-process information as factors that influence the perceived usefulness of reviews. Valence can be predominantly positive or negative, that is, it can be an expression of descriptions that are pleasant and novel or unpleasant and denigrating, respectively (Hajli, 2019). Framing is the manner in which information is presented: researches demonstrated that information received first has a greater impact on the impression formed than information coming later (Pennington, 2000), and positive and negative framing can result from information that is positively or negatively valenced (Levin, 1987). Easy-to-process information, such as numerical and star ratings, acts as a shortcut in making evaluations and developing judgements (Van Schaik & Ling, 2009). All these factors can contribute to reducing the uncertainty associated with potential consumers' purchasing decisions, thereby influencing trust in products and services; they serve as a means to verify whether expectations stemming from a company's promises find confirmation in consumers' online reviews (Akman & Mishra, 2017).

However, trust in products and services can also be mediated by information quantity (Babić-Rosario et al., 2020) and information quality. Like product ranking, information quantity acts as a peripheral cue in evaluating products or services (Gupta & Harris, 2010), by virtue of the fact that the more conversations there are about them, the more they are perceived as popular and thus, the more sales people expect they can achieve on the market (Godes & Mayzlin, 2004). Information quality is conceptualized as a composite construct (Filieri & McLeay, 2014), it includes information completeness, timeliness, accuracy, relevancy, understandability and value addition; these are all recognized as central cues in a consumer's information processing and become predictors of a consumer's purchase intention, particularly in high-involvement situations (Hsu et al., 2017; Park et al., 2007).

Other predictors of purchase intentions include credibility and conformity of the eWOM: both lead to online reviews being seen as useful. Credibility is generated by the extent to which the reviewer is perceived as expert in the area of concern, and by the extent to which the reviewer is trusted by the individuals receiving the information (Freedman et al., 1981). A source's credibility can have an impact on product evaluations regardless of the content of the message (Buda & Zhang, 2000) and the impact is stronger on uninvolved recipients than on involved recipients. According to Forman et al. (2008), in online communities, a reviewer's disclosure of identity information that can be used by consumers to supplement or replace product information in making purchase decisions has a similar impact to credibility of source. These decisions may result from a striving for conformity (Tsao et al., 2015). Conformity is understood as the tendency in thought and behaviour to gain group approval and meet group expectations (Bearden et al., 1989). Conformity leads consumers to make choices that align with eWOM messages that have higher consensus, that is those that express a high degree of agreement between two or more users regarding a product and its performance (Doh & Hwang, 2009; Ozuem et al., 2017).

EWOM and Service Failure

Among the different factors that influence the perceived usefulness of eWOM messages, *the valence of reviews* is the one which consumers use more than others in heuristic information processing as the basis of their purchase decisions. Used as a proxy for underlying product quality (Allard et al., 2020; Liu, 2006), the valence, if it is negative, has more of an impact than positive valence on consumers' intentions (Chatterjee, 2001; Kordrostami et al., 2020). Moreover, as some studies demonstrated, consumers are more attracted by negative reviews than by positive ones, and negative reviews are also more easily generated, which shows that customers are much more interested in sharing negative experiences than satisfied consumers are motivated to write and talk about their positive experiences (Cantallops & Salvi, 2014). Negative online reviews produce negative eWOM that includes among its main sources the experiences of service failure.

Service failure occurs when the delivered service does not meet customers' expectations (Oliver, 1980). It is often related to slow services and bad packaging or failure to respond to the customer (Kelley et al., 1993). Generally speaking, a technical service failure refers to the tangible aspects of what the consumer receives, whereas a functional service failure is a process failure that emerges from the customer's perception of the various interactions during the service encounter. Understanding *what leads consumers to trigger a negative eWOM* after a service failure is an issue of crucial importance for providers (Zheng et al., 2009). Consumers may use negative eWOM for themselves to make their dissatisfaction known and obtain a possible solution (Thøgersen et al., 2009). However, consumers may also give voice to negative experiences to prevent others from enduring similar bad experiences (Litvin et al., 2008); they are driven, then, by altruistic motivations that enrich the wealth of knowledge that the internet makes available to its users. When the service failure that they have experienced is extremely negative, consumers may react by posting negative reviews to do some harm to the firm or just to reduce tension, frustration and anger (Presi et al., 2014).

Whereas negative emotions feed negative eWOM, positive emotions reduce the chance that consumers will disclose their negative experiences (Nyer, 1997). Individuals who disclose their negative experiences and who have a positive and flattering view of themselves, may have, as Presi et al. (2014) highlighted, self-enhancement motivations that induce active participation in social networks to increase their capacity to attract attention. Put simply, individuals rate a product negatively in expectation of a reward they may receive from the company. The company engages them, then, to manipulate online information concerning their products and services (Dellarocas, 2006; Yusuf et al., 2018). The motivation behind negative eWOM is in this case purely economic. According to Shin et al. (2014), prevention-focused consumers who communicate about a negative experience online are focused on obligations and develop behaviours based on vigilance to stay away from a negative state. In contrast, promotion-focused consumers are focused on their aspirations and adopt behaviours aimed at moving towards a positive end status. Shin et al. (2014) also demonstrated that consumers who have experienced a service failure and find only positive online reviews of the provider, react by giving voice to negative eWOM.

The Effects of Negative EWOM

Negative eWOM resulting from experience of service failure has to be managed by providers with specific recovery strategies, given the effects which may otherwise ensue. Negative eWOM can lead to a failure to attract customers, thereby resulting in a *loss of revenue* (Campbell, 2014; Kim et al., 2018). As Verhagen et al. (2013) demonstrated, negative eWOM has a twofold effect: it reduces the consumer's repatronage intention, that is the intention to buy from the same provider in the future, and, at the same time, it increases the intention to switch to a competitor. Chevalier and Mayzlin (2006) reported a negative correlation between negative eWOM and sales, with evidence that "an incremental negative review is more powerful in decreasing book sales than an incremental positive review is in increasing sales" (p. 346). The more negative the review, the more it can contribute to a decrease in sales; however, Liu (2006) combined analysis of negative reviews of movies with that of the volume of movies and found that the volume more than the valence explained the variation in box office revenues. Sen and Lerman (2007) demonstrated that negative valence impacts differently on different products: it is higher in utilitarian products than in hedonistic ones. In the former, reviews reflected product-related motivations and were the result of cognitive-driven, instrumental, and goal-oriented judgements, whereas in the latter, they reflected personal emotions that emerged from affective and sensory experiences of aesthetic or sensorial pleasure. As some scholars (Doh & Hwang, 2009) highlighted, what influences consumers are not single reviews but rather patterns of multiple reviews and, in particular, sets of clearly negative or positive balanced reviews. Although consumers believe that compared to negative reviews, positive reviews decrease the possibility of purchase failure (Cheung, Lee, et al., 2009), sets of positive reviews disorient users and arouse suspicion that information has been manipulated. A firm can, in fact, post online reviews anonymously praising its own product, offer rewards to consumers who start favourable conversations about them or, once influential community members have been identified, persuade them to write positive reviews (Dellarocas, 2006). It follows that consumers can be more positively influenced by a set of clearly positive balanced reviews, if the set of positive reviews is wrapped in negative reviews, just as consumers can be negatively influenced by a set of clearly negative balanced reviews, if the set of negative reviews is wrapped in positive ones (Purnawirawan et al., 2012).

Service Failure and Recovery Strategies

Negative eWOM after a service failure requires *a service recovery strategy*; this includes all the efforts made by the service provider to turn customer dissatisfaction into satisfaction and thereby retain them. Implementing successful service recovery produces positive consequences. Studies demonstrate that consumers who have their service failure satisfactorily corrected, show intention to spread positive information about their experience (Choi & Choi, 2014; Lee et al., 2009). Others illustrate that effective complaint handling favours a customer's repurchase intentions (Spreng et al., 1995) as well as trust and a loyal relationship (Barakat et al., 2015; Harris et al., 2006). In addition to generating customer satisfaction that is higher than it was prior to the failure, it avoids increasing dissatisfaction during and after the recovery process (Ozuem & Azemi, 2018). In order for such consequences to materialize, it is crucial that the recovery actions that the company undertakes should be perceived by complaining consumers (Azemi et al., 2019). These actions must generate a perceived justice, which is considered the basis of the effectiveness of service recovery strategies.

Perceived justice has been used as a multidimensional construct that includes distributive justice, procedural justice, interactional justice (Homburg & Fürst, 2005), and informational justice (Liao, 2007). Distributive justice concerns the perceived fairness of complaint outcome (i.e., service provider's apology and compensation) as a reward that can redistribute esteem in exchange relationships. Procedural justice reflects the perceived fairness of the complaint handling process. A speedy answer given to consumers' complaints can be seen as a recovery effort that satisfies a need for procedural justice. Interactional justice refers to the perceived fairness of the behaviour that employees exhibit towards complainants. When service personnel are empathic, show interest in the problem, and are honest when interacting with customers, interactional justice can be satisfied. Lastly, informational justice concerns the adequacy of information and communication provided. It is satisfied, when, for example, the service providers are well informed and candid in communication. The better the company is able to generate perceived justice, the more likely a state of equity is restored to the relationship.

Consumers evaluate their experiences by assessing the balance between what they have received and what they expected to receive (Folkes, 1984; Ozuem et al., 2017). High service failure severity and, thus, high perceived intensity of a service problem (Weun et al., 2004) can reduce the force of recovery actions in aligning customers' perceptions with expectations. This can be justified by the fact that as service failure increases, customers perceive that there is a greater discrepancy between the loss from failure and the gain from the recovery. As a consequence, the value of the recovery strategy declines. However, if a consumer's satisfaction falls, despite recovery actions, when the service severity is high, at the same time, it can increase when the consumer is involved in the recovery strategies. Consumers can co-create a service recovery: through joint collaboration with the company (service provider), customers not only participate in the recovery actions designed to answer the service failure (Dong et al., 2008), but also create value that helps reduce their negative experience (Roggeveen et al., 2012). Co-creation occurs when customers believe they have the ability to shape outcomes; that is, when they believe they are able to contribute to the perceived justice and thus restore an equity in the customer–company relationship. Wei et al. (2019) demonstrated that co-created recovery efforts can yield favourable customer perceptions of the firm's competence and ethicalness, which increases customer willingness to co-create in the future; they also pointed out, however, that when co-creation tasks are perceived as intense (e.g., effortful, time-consuming, demanding), they lead to negative customer perceptions of the firm's competence and ethicalness, which can directly undermine customer willingness to co-create in the future. Arsenovic et al. (2019) stressed that service recovery strategies can be interpreted not only as a co-creation experience, but also as a collaborative experience where multiple actors (e.g., friends, family, the service provider's employees) interact across multiple encounters in finding a solution to service failure. They argued that when actors collaborate and integrate their resources (knowledge), they not only understand more easily whether the service experience is favourable, but also manage to maintain a certain level of control over the service process.

Brand-Related EWOM, Service Failure, and Recovery Strategies

The relationships between eWOM, service failure, and recovery strategies can be read through the entity of brand. We focus on negative brand-related eWOM after a service failure, highlighting how the relationship between brand and consumer can have an impact on the reactions consumers have after a service failure and on the recovery strategies a provider can adopt.

Brand-Related EWOM and UGC

Today, brands are becoming a part of the eWOM exchange of information. In fact, UGC includes brand-related subject matter (Smith et al., 2012; Swaminathan et al., 2020) and, thus, facts, opinions, and experiences shared among consumers about brands or products. As brand-related UGC assumes the form of online reviews and appears in social networking sites, it functions as eWOM messages driving product awareness and influencing consumers' purchase decisions. Brand-related eWOM can easily and quickly reach a global audience that shares similar interests in the brand (Christodoulides et al., 2012). In addition, brand-related eWOM can have the power to influence this audience: generated by sources embedded in personal networks, it is considered to be a trustworthy information source (Corrigan, 2013). The influence it exerts derives from positive and negative online reviews. Both affect consumers' attitudes to a brand: positive online reviews encourage purchase intentions (Kudeshia & Kumar, 2017; Ozuem et al., 2016), whereas negative online reviews can discourage them (Lee et al., 2009).

Brand-Related EWOM and Consumers' Intention to Purchase

The *valence* of an online review is a factor that many scholars identify as a precursor of brand purchasing decisions. Research shows, however, that there are other factors that play a role in the evaluation of online reviews of a brand. After all, a brand is something more than a simple product or service. Defined as "a name, term, sign, symbol or design or combination that is intended to identify the goods and services of one seller or group of sellers and to differentiate them from those of competitors" (Kotler, 1991, p. 442), a brand triggers sensations, feelings, and cognitive and behavioural responses in consumers. The perceived valence of brand-related eWOM can be filtered by factors relating to the relation between the brand and the consumer. One of these factors is an *existing brand attitude*. The impact of online reviews on consumer behaviour can depend on individual cognitive processes that are biased by prior dispositions towards the brand, a process known as "biased assimilation" (Lord et al., 1979). This impact diminishes for strong brands. As Ho-Dac et al. (2013) showed, brand strength moderates the influence of online reviews on purchase behaviour: while online reviews can have a strong impact on weak brands, they do not significantly impact the performance of a strong brand. Mafael et al. (2016) pointed out that, due to brand dispersion (Luo et al., 2013), the brand polarization of strong brands can be investigated and, thus, their relationships with consumers who have a positive attitude towards the brand and consumers who have a negative attitude towards the brand. Furthermore, they showed that consumers who perceive positive (negative) arguments in online reviews to be more (less) persuasive have a positive (negative) attitude towards the brand. Perceived persuasiveness, in turn, influences behavioural intentions and acts as a mediator on the relationship between attitude and behavioural intentions. The impact eWOM has on consumers depends on a predefined consumer brand evaluation (Low & Lamb, 2000), on *emotions* that emerge from words used in online messages (Berger & Milkman, 2012; Heath et al., 2001), and on the relationships between senders and receivers (Mittal et al., 2008). The emotions that the eWOM evokes play an important role (Herhausen et al., 2019). Indeed, it is not so much the valence of the message itself as its emotional valence that can influence consumers. Positive or negative emotions expressed in the content of brand-related online reviews (Nabi, 2003) trigger different levels of psychological arousal and inner activation in consumers (Smith & Ellsworth, 1985). Anger, anxiety, and sadness are possible negative emotions that can be felt in processing eWOM messages, but while anger and anxiety are characterized by states of heightened activation, sadness is characterized by deactivation (Barrett & Russell 1999). The combination of emotional valence (positive and negative) and arousal (high and low) produce different reactions in consumers in terms of brand attitude and in behaviours. These reactions also reflect the *bond* that connects those who post and write online messages and those who read them. A message from a close friend or a family member is less likely to be perceived as having a persuasive intention (Buda & Zhang, 2000) and a high level of uncertainty and risk (Cheung, Luo, et al., 2009) than a message from a stranger. Because of the related credibility and trustworthiness, strong ties favour the sharing of sensitive information (Rapp et al., 2013) and are more influential than weak ties in a consumer's decision making. Weak ties are more likely to facilitate information flow in distinct networks. Strong ties also involve more frequent interactions (Burt, 1987) and, for this reason, in addition to generating reciprocal influence, they increase imitative behaviour within networks (McFarland et al., 2008).

Brand-Related EWOM and Service Failure

Negative eWOM messages reduce purchase intentions more than positive eWOM messages increase them. Negative eWOM is a central issue in brand-related eWOM studies (Hansen et al., 2018; Li et al., 2019). One of its main causes is service failure, that is a service performance which is perceived by consumers as being below their expectations (Bell & Zemke, 1987). Services, together with product and performance, are brand-related stimuli that companies adopt in producing brand experience (Brakus et al., 2009); when they disappoint expectations, negative attributions are likely to be directed towards a brand as an effect of a negatively perceived brand experience (Wakefield & Wakefield, 2018). Negative brand experiences, can cause a variety of customer reactions, including dissatisfaction and defection, which have detrimental effects on a brand's profitability (Zeelenberg & Pieters, 2004). Consumers vent their feelings and adopt complaining behaviours that range from private complaining via traditional complaint channels to online complaints. Today, an increasing number of consumers, in addition to voicing their discontent via their social networking sites, express dissatisfaction publicly on platforms like Facebook brand pages (Harrigan et al., 2018).

The *motivations* that lead consumers to generate negative eWOM after a brand-related service failure may be varied. According to McGraw et al. (2015), some consumers use negative eWOM simply to warn and entertain others by means of humorous complaints. Humour is powerful: on the one hand, it can make praise seem more negative (by making an expression of satisfaction seem wrong in a certain way), on the other hand, it can make complaints seem more positive (by making an expression of dissatisfaction seem acceptable). Blodgett et al. (1995) showed that consumers describe negative experiences to try to find out how to ask for a refund, exchange, or repair. They might seek comfort from others (Yi & Baumgartner, 2004) or ask for advice from friends or acquaintances who have had similar experiences (Georgiou & Stavrinides, 2008). Social support together with venting feelings (Ward & Ostrom, 2006), revenge aimed at damaging the brand, and the need to boost self-worth, act as forces that motivate consumers to spread online negative reviews after a brand-related service failure. As Wakefield and Wakefield (2018) demonstrated, creating negative eWOM messages generates tension and *anxiety* in consumers when the creation of negative messages conflicts with their online impression management goals, which are based on self-enhancement and rendering a positive portrait of themselves online.

However, consumers may also decide not to create eWOM messages, to not share opinions and feelings following a brand-related service failure: they restrict themselves to thinking without acting. In doing so, they may focus on the causes (Lazarus & Folkman, 1987) by examining the problem systematically (rational thinking) or they may focus on the opportunities to learn from the negative experience (Johnson & Rapp, 2010) by perceiving the reasons for service failure as uncontrollable and unpredictable (positive thinking). It can also not be excluded that consumers decide to adopt passive behaviour (avoidance) distancing themselves from the problem (Strizhakova et al., 2012) to restore their emotional balance. The reaction that consumers have after a service failure experience depends on their *brand commitment*, that is on their mental and affective bonding with the brand (De Wulf et al., 2001; Mattila, 2004).

Consumers may feel the desire for revenge: the need to punish and cause harm to the brand for damages suffered (Grégoire & Fisher, 2006).

This desire, as shown by Weitzl and Hutzinger (2019), is higher in committed online complainants than in uncommitted ones. The same is true, according to Weitzl and Hutzinger (2019), of the desire for reparation. Complainants' willingness to rebalance their relationships with the brand by seeking redress and problem resolution is higher in committed online complainants than in uncommitted complainants (Grégoire & Fisher, 2008). Negative eWOM messages, posted because of the various feelings (desires) experienced by users, can receive support from customers in a short time and ignite an online firestorm (Pfeffer et al., 2014). The extent to which other customers approve of and share negative eWOM determines its virality and firestorm potential (Tellis et al., 2020). This implies that brand-related eWOM evaluations are shared through a social transmission process, like an emotional contagion (Berger, 2014). Within a brand community, the virality of negative eWOM is higher when the intensity of high-arousal emotion words in negative eWOM is high, and when the social ties and the perceived similarity between the sender and the receiver are strong (Herhausen et al., 2019).

Brand-Related Service Failure: Its Effects and Recovery Strategies

A crucial goal for companies is to develop appropriate service failure recovery strategies with the aim of reducing the consequences that negative eWOM (or a contagion) can cause. Negative eWOM impacts negatively on *brand attitude*, reducing, as Beneke et al. (2015) demonstrated, brand trust, brand affect, and purchase intentions. A lower purchase intention for a brand following negative eWOM may be due to *brand equity dilution*. In fact, as Bambauer-Sachse and Mangold (2011) highlighted, a constructive processing of information can result in a revision of brand evaluation (Loken & Roedder John, 1993) through the weakening of. consumers' perceptions of a brand's additional value at the base of a consumer-based brand equity (Keller, 1993).

A recovery strategy must guide the company in the productive handling of consumers' complaints by identifying actions that can be implemented to resolve the problems they have with brand-related services (Gronroos, 1990). According to Bhandari and Rodgers (2018), a *"brand feedback"*, that is a company-written response to consumer feedback in an eWOM setting, represents a brand's attempt to reinforce the validity of a brand promise and reinstate potential lost trust with customers as a precondition for purchase intention. If, however, as Bhandari and Rodgers (2018) argued, brand feedback creates post-purchase complications for consumers dealing with customer service and suspicions that the brand's responses might be an attempt on the part of the brand to hold on to them, it may heuristically reduce purchase intentions independently of the positive effect of brand trust.

Despite this, Bougoure et al. (2016) showed that a service failure recovery strategy impacts on *brand credibility*, that is on the believability of an organization's intention at a particular time (Erdem & Swait, 2004). Brand credibility comprises two components: trustworthiness and expertise. Bougoure et al. (2016) claimed that customer satisfaction arising from effective complaints handling by a brand is likely to result in an increased perception of the trustworthiness of the brand. If satisfied with the outcome of a complaint, consumers believe that a brand is willing to deliver its brand promise at that time and in the future. They develop a perceived justice after the service failure (Homburg & Fürst, 2005; Liao, 2007) and a state of equity is restored in their relationship with the brand. Complaint handling, when properly carried out, also leads consumers to cultivate repeated transactions with the company (Gummesson, 1995).

As Buttle (2001) and other researchers (MacInnis & Folkes, 2017; Sabermajidi et al., 2019) argued, a recovery strategy offers an opportunity for developing *customer loyalty*. Buttle (2001) built on the results of the research of Zeithaml et al. (1996), that is, that customers whose problems have been resolved satisfactorily express greater loyalty intentions and a willingness to pay more than those with unsolved problems, but also that these intentions are not as great as those of customers who have not experienced service problems. Buttle claimed that they remain loyal if the perceived value they receive from the brand is relatively greater than that of competitors. In developing a service failure recovery strategy, brand reputation is an element to be considered.

Understood as the consumer's perception of service quality associated with the brand name, *brand reputation* moderates the relationship between failure severity and reactions in terms of consumer behaviour (Balaji et al., 2018): when consumers experience high service failure in a highly reputed brand, they evaluate the negative experience as a novel and extraordinary event that would not happen again in the future and continue to exhibit behavioural intentions. A similar effect can result from *customer-based brand equity*, understood as the strength of a brand in customers' minds, which is based on perceived quality, brand awareness, brand associations, and other brand assets (Aaker, 1991). In this connection, Brady et al. (2008) demonstrated that customers who experience service failures are more likely to forgive them if they were caused by high equity brands rather than by low equity brands. Similar to brand reputation and consumer-based brand equity, *brand attachment* can minimize the effects that service failures produce in consumers. Defined as "the strength of the bond connecting the brand with the self" (Park et al., 2010, p. 2), brand attachment regulates customers' negative emotions, especially when consumers attribute service failure to a controllable cause, increasing customer behaviour like word of mouth and loyalty intentions (Torres et al., 2020).

A service failure recovery can be *co-created* with complaining consumers and, thus, can result from a customer's "ability to shape or personalize the content of the recovery through joint collaboration with the service provider" (Roggeveen et al., 2012, p. 722). Hazée et al. (2017) highlighted that co-creating a service recovery makes customers believe they receive the most favourable solution to the brand-related service failure, which, in turn, influences satisfaction with service recovery and repurchase intentions. They stressed, however, that a co-created service recovery is recommended more for companies with a low level of consumer-based brand equity than for companies with high levels of consumer-based brand equity. In the former, higher risk and lower quality perceptions associated with low brand equity arouse in consumers the fear that a favourable outcome during a service recovery cannot be reached; consequently, they prefer to collaborate with the service provider in order to maintain control and to ensure that the provider finds the best solution. In the latter, high brand equity conveys quality signals that can reduce a customer's uncertainty; as a result, consumers do not need to monitor the provider's actions, as they are more likely to believe that the service provider is acting to find the best solution.

In handling complaints, companies can use "empathy" or "explanations" to respond to consumers (Wang & Chaudhry, 2018). To express empathy as a spontaneous response (Hoffman, 1977), a firm might sympathize (e.g., "we realize that you are not happy with our service") or shift to a positive outlook (e.g., "we hope that your experience with our brand will be better in the future") or they may apologize (Davidson, 2003). Alternatively, companies can provide substantial explanations that enhance the perception of response quality and efforts among consumers. Herhausen et al. (2019) claimed that empathic responses are more prone to capturing the attention of consumers who have experienced low-arousal emotions, whereas explanation is better to mitigate the failure for consumers who have experienced high-arousal emotions. Companies can decide to adopt disengagement by suggesting a change of communication channel (e.g., "please contact our customer service office"), by offering compensation (Boshoff, 1997; Mattila & Patterson, 2004) or, as a last resort, by choosing avoidance and nonresponse (Sheppes et al., 2011). This last option is the poorest that can be adopted to regulate negative eWOM.

Conclusions

Several reflections which could be useful for fashion companies emerge from what has been investigated in the chapter. Through UGC, people talk about the brand. The brand can become the protagonist of the stories that consumers tell on social media when they talk either well or badly about a brand. The negative valence of the eWOM they generate does not necessarily influence the purchasing decisions of those who read online reviews. The influence of eWOM is low if the brand is strong and has a high reputation and high customer-based brand equity. People who have a positive attitude towards the brand will not change their opinion after reading negative arguments in online reviews. This means that to create barriers against negative eWOM, fashion brands need to invest in becoming strong and in creating a consumer value that is distinguishable from the one created by their competitors. Sometimes this is not enough. In fact, it turns out that certain emotions that eWOM conveys have the power to fuel feelings that impact the relationship between consumer and brand, even if it has existed for some time. Similarly, the eWOM generated by some people, such as close friends or family members, can have a positive or negative effect on this relationship. It is, above all, negative brand experiences that generate negative eWOM. Among these experiences are those generated by service failures. The reaction that the consumer has after a service failure in terms of generating negative eWOM is influenced by their brand commitment (i.e., their mental and affective bonding with the brand). The higher this is, the greater the likelihood that the consumer will create eWOM to express a desire for revenge against the brand or a desire for compensation. Despite the mixed effects that brand commitment generates, it can help reduce the tensions that certain service failures produce. However, negative eWOM after a service failure can be detrimental to the company. It can have a negative impact on brand trust, brand effect, and purchase intention. It is important that fashion companies protect themselves against all these possible consequences. It follows that the implementation of recovery strategies is essential. They can result in brand feedback: a company's written answer to the consumer or actions aimed at enhancing brand credibility in order to generate perceived justice and restore a state of equity in the consumer's relationship with the brand. Acting in this way can nurture customer loyalty: if problems are solved for consumers, they show a willingness to pay more for that brand. It is easier to manage service failure in the case of high brand reputation and high customer-based brand equity: in these cases, consumers who experience service failure are likely to forgive the brand. The strength of the brand and its relationships with consumers protect against service failures. If properly managed, service failures become a way to make the brand even stronger. This generates a self-sustaining mechanism of brand value, which we believe is one of the main challenges that many luxury fashion brands need to address today.

REFERENCES

Aaker, D. A. (1991). *Managing brand equity*. Free Press.

Akman, I., & Mishra, A. (2017). Factors influencing consumer intention in social commerce adoption. *Information Technology and People, 30*(2), 356–370.

Allard, T., Dunn, L. H., & White, K. (2020). Negative reviews, positive impact: Consumer empathetic responding to unfair word of mouth. *Journal of Marketing, 84*(4). https://doi.org/10.1177/0022242920924389.

Arsenovic, J., Edvardsson, B., & Tronvoll, B. (2019). Moving toward collaborative service recovery: A multiactor orientation. *Service Science, 11*(3), 201–212.

Athwal, N., Istanbulluoglu, D., & McCormack, S. (2018). The allure of luxury brands' social media activities: A uses and gratifications perspective. *Information Technology and People, 33*(3), 603–625.

Azemi, Y., Ozuem, W., Howell, K. E., & Lancaster, G. (2019). An exploration into the practice of online service failure and recovery strategies in the Balkans. *Journal of Business Research, 94*, 420–431.

Babić Rosario, A., Sotgiu, F., de Valck, K., & Bijmolt, T. H. (2016). The effect of electronic word of mouth on sales: A meta-analytic review of platform, product, and metric factors. *Journal of Marketing Research, 53*(3), 297–318.

Babić-Rosario, A., Sotgiu, F., & de Valck, K. (2020). Conceptualizing the electronic word-of-mouth process: What we know and need to know about eWOM creation, exposure, and evaluation. *Journal of the Academy of Marketing Science, 48*(3), 422–448.

Balaji, M. S., Jha, S., Sengupta, A. S., & Krishnan, B. C. (2018). Are cynical customers satisfied differently? Role of negative inferred motive and customer participation in service recovery. *Journal of Business Research, 86,* 109–118.

Bambauer-Sachse, S., & Mangold, S. (2011). Brand equity dilution through negative online word-of-mouth communication. *Journal of Retailing and Consumer Services, 18*(1), 38–45.

Barakat, L. L., Ramsey, J. R., Lorenz, M. P., & Gosling, M. (2015). Severe service failure recovery revisited: Evidence of its determinants in an emerging market context. *International Journal of Research in Marketing, 32*(1), 113–116.

Barrett, L. F., & Russell, J. A. (1999). The structure of current affect: Controversies and emerging consensus. *Current Directions in Psychological Science, 8*(1), 10–14.

Bearden, W. O., Netemeyer, R. G., & Teel, J. E. (1989). Measurement of consumer susceptibility to interpersonal influence. *Journal of Consumer Research, 15*(4), 473–481.

Bell, C. R., & Zemke, R. E. (1987). Service breakdown: The road to recovery. *Management Review, 76*(10), 32.

Beneke, J., Mill, J., Naidoo, K., & Wickham, B. (2015). The impact of willingness to engage in negative electronic word-of-mouth on brand attitude: A study of airline passengers in South Africa. *Journal of Business and Retail Management Research, 9*(2), 68–84.

Berger, J. (2014). Word of mouth and interpersonal communication: A review and directions for future research. *Journal of Consumer Psychology, 24*(4), 586–607.

Berger, J., & Milkman, K. L. (2012). What makes online content viral? *Journal of Marketing Research, 49*(2), 192–205.

Berthon, P., Pitt, L., & Campbell, C. (2008). When customers create the ad. *California Management Review, 50*(4), 6–30.

Bhandari, M., & Rodgers, S. (2018). What does the brand say? Effects of brand feedback to negative eWOM on brand trust and purchase intentions. *International Journal of Advertising, 37*(1), 125–141.

Bickart, B., & Schindler, R. M. (2001). Internet forums as influential sources of consumer information. *Journal of Interactive Marketing, 15*(3), 31–40.

Blodgett, J. G., Wakefield, K. L., & Barnes, J. H. (1995). The effects of customer service on consumer complaining behavior. *Journal of Services Marketing, 9*(4), 31–42.

Boshoff, C. (1997). An experimental study of service recovery options. *International Journal of Service Industry Management, 8*(2), 110–130.

Bougoure, U. S., Russell-Bennett, R., Fazal-E-Hasan, S., & Mortimer, G. (2016). The impact of service failure on brand credibility. *Journal of Retailing and Consumer Services, 31,* 62–71.

Brady, M. K., Cronin, J. J., Jr., Fox, G. L., & Roehm, M. L. (2008). Strategies to offset performance failures: The role of brand equity. *Journal of Retailing, 84*(2), 151–164.

Brakus, J. J., Schmitt, B. H., & Zarantonello, L. (2009). Brand experience: What is it? How is it measured? Does it affect loyalty? *Journal of Marketing, 73*(3), 52–68.

Buda, R., & Zhang, Y. (2000). Consumer product evaluation: The interactive effect of message framing, presentation order, and source credibility. *Journal of Product & Brand Management, 9*(4), 229–242.

Burt, R. S. (1987). Social contagion and innovation: Cohesion versus structural equivalence. *American Journal of Sociology, 92*(6), 1287–1335.

Buttle, F. (2001). The CRM value chain. *Marketing Business, 96*(2), 52–5.

Campbell, C. (2014). *The negativity effect of consumer reviews and how to minimize its impact, review trackers.* Available at: http://www.reviewtrackers.com/negativity-effect-consumer-reviews-minimize-impact/.

Cantallops, A. S., & Salvi, F. (2014). New consumer behavior: A review of research on eWOM and hotels. *International Journal of Hospitality Management, 36,* 41–51.

Chatterjee, P. (2001). Online reviews: Do consumers use them? In M. C. Gilly, & J. Myers-Levy (Eds.), *ACR 2001 proceedings* (pp. 129–134). Association for Consumer Research. Available at SSRN: https://ssrn.com/abstract=900158.

Cheung, C. M., Lee, M. K., & Rabjohn, N. (2008). The impact of electronic word-of-mouth: The adoption of online opinions in online customer communities. *Internet Research: Electronic Networking Applications and Policy, 18*(3), 229–247.

Cheung, C. M., Lee, M. K., & Thadani, D. R. (2009, September). The impact of positive electronic word-of-mouth on consumer online purchasing decision. In *Proceedings of the Second World Summit on Knowledge Society, WSKS 2009, Vol. 5736 LNAI* (pp. 501–510). Springer.

Cheung, M. Y., Luo, C., Sia, C. L., & Chen, H. (2009b). Credibility of electronic word-of-mouth: Informational and normative determinants of on-line consumer recommendations. *International Journal of Electronic Commerce, 13*(4), 9–38.

Chevalier, J. A., & Mayzlin, D. (2006). The effect of word of mouth on sales: Online book reviews. *Journal of Marketing Research, 43*(3), 345–354.

Choi, B., & Choi, B. J. (2014). The effects of perceived service recovery justice on customer affection, loyalty, and word-of-mouth. *European Journal of Marketing, 46*(1/2), 108–131.

Christodoulides, G., Michaelidou, N., & Argyriou, E. (2012). Cross-national differences in e-WOM influence. *European Journal of Marketing, 46*(11/12), 1689–1709.

Corrigan, J. (2013, July 19). The benefits of user-generated content [Web log post]. http://raventools.com/blog/benefits-user-generated-content/.

Davidson, D. K. (2003). *Selling sin: The marketing of socially unacceptable products* (2nd ed.). Praeger.

de Kerviler, G., & Rodriguez, C. M. (2019). Luxury brand experiences and relationship quality for millennials: The role of self-expansion. *Journal of Business Research, 102*, 250–262.

De Wulf, K., Odekerken-Schröder, G., & Iacobucci, D. (2001). Investments in consumer relationships: A cross-country and cross-industry exploration. *Journal of Marketing, 65*(4), 33–50.

Deighton, J., Romer, D., & McQueen, J. (1989). Using drama to persuade. *Journal of Consumer Research, 16*(3), 335–343.

Dellarocas, C. (2006). Strategic manipulation of internet opinion forums: Implications for consumers and firms. *Management Science, 52*(10), 1577–1593.

Doh, S. J., & Hwang, J. S. (2009). How consumers evaluate eWOM (electronic word-of-mouth) messages. *CyberPsychology & Behavior, 12*(2), 193–197.

Dong, B., Evans, K. R., & Zou, S. (2008). The effects of customer participation in co-created service recovery. *Journal of the Academy of Marketing Science, 36*(1), 123–137.

Erdem, T., & Swait, J. (2004). Brand credibility, brand consideration, and choice. *Journal of Consumer Research, 31*(1), 191–198.

Filieri, R., & McLeay, F. (2014). E-WOM and accommodation: An analysis of the factors that influence travelers' adoption of information from online reviews. *Journal of Travel Research, 53*(1), 44–57.

Folkes, V. S. (1984). Consumer reactions to product failure: An attributional approach. *Journal of Consumer Research, 10*(4), 398–409.

Forman, C., Ghose, A., & Wiesenfeld, B. (2008). Examining the relationship between reviews and sales: The role of reviewer identity disclosure in electronic markets. *Information Systems Research, 19*(3), 291–313.

Freedman, J. L., Sears, D. O., & Carlsmith, J. M. (1981). *Social psychology*. Prentice-Hall, Inc.

Georgiou, S. N., & Stavrinides, P. (2008). Bullies, victims and bully-victims: Psychosocial profiles and attribution styles. *School Psychology International, 29*(5), 574–589.

Godes, D., & Mayzlin, D. (2004). Using online conversations to study word-of-mouth communication. *Marketing Science, 23*(4), 545–560.

Grégoire, Y., & Fisher, R. J. (2006). The effects of relationship quality on customer retaliation. *Marketing Letters, 17*(1), 31–46.

Grégoire, Y., & Fisher, R. J. (2008). Customer betrayal and retaliation: When your best customers become your worst enemies. *Journal of the Academy of Marketing Science, 36*(2), 247–261.

Gronroos, C. (1990). Relationship approach to marketing in service contexts: The marketing and organizational behavior interface. *Journal of Business Research, 20*(1), 3–11.

Gummesson, E. (1995). Relationship marketing: Its role in the service economy. *Understanding Services Management, 244,* 68.

Gupta, P., & Harris, J. (2010). How e-WOM recommendations influence product consideration and quality of choice: A motivation to process information perspective. *Journal of Business Research, 63*(9–10), 1041–1049.

Hajli, N. (2019). The impact of positive and negative valence on social commerce purchase intention. *Information Technology and People, 33*(2), 774–791.

Hansen, N., Kupfer, A. K., & Hennig-Thurau, T. (2018). Brand crises in the digital age: The short-and long-term effects of social media firestorms on consumers and brands. *International Journal of Research in Marketing, 35*(4), 557–574.

Harrigan, P., Evers, U., Miles, M. P., & Daly, T. (2018). Customer engagement and the relationship between involvement, engagement, self-brand connection and brand usage intent. *Journal of Business Research, 88,* 388–396.

Harris, K. E., Grewal, D., Mohr, L. A., & Bernhardt, K. L. (2006). Consumer responses to service recovery strategies: The moderating role of online versus offline environment. *Journal of Business Research, 59*(4), 425–431.

Hazée, S., Van Vaerenbergh, Y., & Armirotto, V. (2017). Co-creating service recovery after service failure: The role of brand equity. *Journal of Business Research, 74,* 101–109.

Heath, C., Bell, C., & Sternberg, E. (2001). Emotional selection in memes: The case of urban legends. *Journal of Personality and Social Psychology, 81*(6), 1028.

Herhausen, D., Ludwig, S., Grewal, D., Wulf, J., & Schoegel, M. (2019). Detecting, preventing, and mitigating online firestorms in brand communities. *Journal of Marketing, 83*(3), 1–21.

Ho-Dac, N. N., Carson, S. J., & Moore, W. L. (2013). The effects of positive and negative online customer reviews: Do brand strength and category maturity matter? *Journal of Marketing, 77*(6), 37–53.

Hoffman, L. W. (1977). Changes in family roles, socialization, and sex differences. *American Psychologist, 32*(8), 644.

Homburg, C., & Fürst, A. (2005). How organizational complaint handling drives customer loyalty: An analysis of the mechanistic and the organic approach. *Journal of Marketing, 69*(3), 95–114.

Hsu, C. L., Yu, L. C., & Chang, K. C. (2017). Exploring the effects of online customer reviews, regulatory focus, and product type on purchase intention: Perceived justice as a moderator. *Computers in Human Behavior, 69,* 335–346.

Johnson, J. W., & Rapp, A. (2010). A more comprehensive understanding and measure of customer helping behavior. *Journal of Business Research, 63*(8), 787–792.

Keller, K. L. (1993). Conceptualizing, measuring, and managing customer-based brand equity. *Journal of Marketing, 57*(1), 1–22.

Kelley, S. W., Hoffman, K. D., & Davis, M. A. (1993). A typology of retail failures and recoveries. *Journal of Retailing, 69*(4), 429.

Kim, S., Kandampully, J., & Bilgihan, A. (2018). The influence of eWOM communications: An application of online social network framework. *Computers in Human Behavior, 80,* 243–254.

Kordrostami, E., Liu-Thompkins, Y., & Rahmani, V. (2020). Investigating the influence of regulatory focus on the efficacy of online review volume versus valence. *European Journal of Marketing, 55*(1), 297–314.

Kotler, P. (1991). *Marketing management: Analysis, planning, implementation and control* (9th ed). Prentice-Hall International.

Kudeshia, C., & Kumar, A. (2017). Social eWOM: Does it affect the brand attitude and purchase intention of brands? *Management Research Review, 43*(6), 310–330.

Lazarus, R. S., & Folkman, S. (1987). Transactional theory and research on emotions and coping. *European Journal of Personality, 1*(3), 141–169.

Lee, M., Rodgers, S., & Kim, M. (2009). Effects of valence and extremity of eWOM on attitude toward the brand and website. *Journal of Current Issues & Research in Advertising, 31*(2), 1–11.

Levin, I. P. (1987). Associative effects of information framing. *Bulletin of the Psychonomics Society, 25,* 85–86.

Li, Y., Yang, K., Chen, J., Gupta, S., & Ning, F. (2019). Can an apology change after-crisis user attitude? The role of social media in online crisis management. *Information Technology & People, 32*(4), 802–827.

Liao, H. (2007). Do it right this time: The role of employee service recovery performance in customer-perceived justice and customer loyalty after service failures. *Journal of Applied Psychology, 92*(2), 475.

Litvin, S. W., Goldsmith, R. E., & Pan, B. (2008). Electronic word-of-mouth in hospitality and tourism management. *Tourism Management, 29*(3), 458–468.

Liu, B. (2006). A survey of credibility theory. *Fuzzy Optimization and Decision Making, 5*(4), 387–408.

Loken, B., & Roedder John, D. (1993). Diluting brand beliefs: When do brand extensions have a negative impact? *Journal of Marketing, 57*(3), 71–84.

Lord, C. G., Ross, L., & Lepper, M. R. (1979). Biased assimilation and attitude polarization: The effects of prior theories on subsequently considered evidence. *Journal of Personality and Social Psychology, 37*(11), 2098.

Low, G. S., & Lamb, C. W. (2000). The measurement and dimensionality of brand associations. *Journal of Product & Brand Management, 9*(6), 350–368.

Luo, X., Raithel, S., & Wiles, M. A. (2013). The impact of brand rating dispersion on firm value. *Journal of Marketing Research, 50*(3), 399–415.

MacInnis, D. J., & Folkes, V. S. (2017). Humanizing brands: When brands seem to be like me, part of me, and in a relationship with me. *Journal of Consumer Psychology, 27*(3), 355–374.

Mafael, A., Gottschalk, S. A., & Kreis, H. (2016). Examining biased assimilation of brand-related online reviews. *Journal of Interactive Marketing, 36*, 91–106.

Mattila, A. S. (2004). The impact of service failures on customer loyalty. *International Journal of Service Industry Management, 15*(2), 134–149.

Mattila, A. S., & Patterson, P. G. (2004). Service recovery and fairness perceptions in collectivist and individualist contexts. *Journal of Service Research, 6*(4), 336–346.

McFarland, R. G., Bloodgood, J. M., & Payan, J. M. (2008). Supply chain contagion. *Journal of Marketing, 72*(2), 63–79.

McGraw, A. P., Warren, C., & Kan, C. (2015). Humorous complaining. *Journal of Consumer Research, 41*(5), 1153–1171.

Mittal, V., Huppertz, J. W., & Khare, A. (2008). Customer complaining: The role of tie strength and information control. *Journal of Retailing, 84*(2), 195–204.

Nabi, R. L. (2003). Exploring the framing effects of emotion: Do discrete emotions differentially influence information accessibility, information seeking, and policy preference? *Communication Research, 30*(2), 224–247.

Nyer, P. U. (1997). A study of the relationships between cognitive appraisals and consumption emotions. *Journal of the Academy of Marketing Science, 25*(4), 296–304.

Oliver, R. L. (1980). A cognitive model of the antecedents and consequences of satisfaction decisions. *Journal of Marketing Research, 17*(4), 460–469.

Ozuem, W., & Azemi, Y. (2018). Online service failure and recovery strategies in luxury brands: A view from justice theory. In *Digital marketing strategies for fashion and luxury brands* (pp. 108–125). IGI Global.

Ozuem, W., Howell, K. E., & Lancaster, G. (2008). Communicating in the new interactive marketspace. *European Journal of Marketing, 42*(9–10), 1059–1083.

Ozuem, W., Patel, A., Howell, K. E., & Lancaster, G. (2017). An exploration of customers' response to online service recovery initiatives. *International Journal of Market Research, 59*(1), 97–116.

Ozuem, W., Thomas, T., & Lancaster, G. (2016). The influence of customer loyalty on small island economies: An empirical and exploratory study. *Journal of Strategic Marketing, 24*(6), 447–469.

Park, C. W., MacInnis, D. J., Priester, J., Eisingerich, A. B., & Iacobucci, D. (2010). Brand attachment and brand attitude strength: Conceptual and empirical differentiation of two critical brand equity drivers. *Journal of Marketing, 74*(6), 1–17.

Park, M., Im, H., & Kim, H. Y. (2018). "You are too friendly!" The negative effects of social media marketing on value perceptions of luxury fashion brands. *Journal of Business Research, 117,* 529–542.

Park, D. H., Lee, J., & Han, I. (2007). The effect of on-line consumer reviews on consumer purchasing intention: The moderating role of involvement. *International Journal of Electronic Commerce, 11*(4), 125–148.

Pennington, D. C. (2000). *Social cognition.* Routledge.

Pfeffer, J., Zorbach, T., & Carley, K. M. (2014). Understanding online firestorms: Negative word-of-mouth dynamics in social media networks. *Journal of Marketing Communications, 20*(1–2), 117–128.

Presi, C., Saridakis, C., & Hartmans, S. (2014). User-generated content behaviour of the dissatisfied service customer. *European Journal of Marketing, 28*(9–10), 1600–1625.

Purnawirawan, N., De Pelsmacker, P., & Dens, N. (2012). Balance and sequence in online reviews: How perceived usefulness affects attitudes and intentions. *Journal of Interactive Marketing, 26*(4), 244–255.

Rapp, A., Beitelspacher, L. S., Grewal, D., & Hughes, D. E. (2013). Understanding social media effects across seller, retailer, and consumer interactions. *Journal of the Academy of Marketing Science, 41*(5), 547–566.

Roggeveen, A. L., Tsiros, M., & Grewal, D. (2012). Understanding the co-creation effect: When does collaborating with customers provide a lift to service recovery? *Journal of the Academy of Marketing Science, 40*(6), 771–790.

Sabermajidi, N., Valaei, N., Balaji, M. S., & Goh, S. K. (2019). Measuring brand-related content in social media: A socialization theory perspective. *Information Technology & People, 33*(4), 1281–1302.

Sen, S., & Lerman, D. (2007). Why are you telling me this? An examination into negative consumer reviews on the web. *Journal of Interactive Marketing, 21*(4), 76–94.

Sheppes, G., Scheibe, S., Suri, G., & Gross, J. J. (2011). Emotion-regulation choice. *Psychological Science, 22*(11), 1391–1396.

Shin, D., Song, J. H., & Biswas, A. (2014). Electronic word-of-mouth (eWOM) generation in new media platforms: The role of regulatory focus and collective dissonance. *Marketing Letters, 25*(2), 153–165.

Smith, A. N., Fischer, E., & Yongjian, C. (2012). How does brand-related user-generated content differ across YouTube, Facebook, and Twitter? *Journal of Interactive Marketing, 26*(2), 102–113.

Smith, C. A., & Ellsworth, P. C. (1985). Patterns of cognitive appraisal in emotion. *Journal of Personality and Social Psychology, 48*(4), 813.

Sparks, B. A., & Browning, V. (2011). The impact of online reviews on hotel booking intentions and perception of trust. *Tourism Management, 32*(6), 1310–1323.

Spreng, R. A., Harrell, G. D., & Mackoy, R. D. (1995). Service recovery: Impact on satisfaction and intentions. *Journal of Services Marketing, 9*(1), 15–23.

Strizhakova, Y., Coulter, R. A., & Price, L. L. (2012). The young adult cohort in emerging markets: Assessing their glocal cultural identity in a global marketplace. *International Journal of Research in Marketing, 29*(1), 43–54.

Swaminathan, V., Sorescu, A., Steenkamp, J. B. E., O'Guinn, T. C. G., & Schmitt, B. (2020). Branding in a hyperconnected world: Refocusing theories and rethinking boundaries. *Journal of Marketing, 84*(2), 24–46. https://doi.org/10.1177/0022242919899905.

Tellis, G. J., MacInnis, D. J., & Tirunillai, S. (2020). What drives virality (sharing, spread) of YouTube video ads: Emotion vs brand prominence and information. *Marketing Science Working Paper Series, 83*(4) 1–20.

Thøgersen, J., Juhl, H. J., & Poulsen, C. S. (2009). Complaining: A function of attitude, personality, and situation. *Psychology & Marketing, 26*(8), 760–777.

Torres, J. L. S., Rawal, M., & Bagherzadeh, R. (2020). Role of brand attachment in customers' evaluation of service failure. *Journal of Product & Brand Management.* Available at: https://doi.org/10.1108/JPBM-03-2019-2293.

Tsao, W. C., Hsieh, M. T., Shih, L. W., & Lin, T. M. (2015). Compliance with eWOM: The influence of hotel reviews on booking intention from the perspective of consumer conformity. *International Journal of Hospitality Management, 46,* 99–111.

Van Schaik, P., & Ling, J. (2009). The role of context in perceptions of the aesthetics of web pages over time. *International Journal of Human Computer Studies, 67,* 79–89.

Verhagen, T., Nauta, A., & Feldberg, F. (2013). Negative online word-of-mouth: Behavioral indicator or emotional release? *Computers in Human Behavior, 29*(4), 1430–1440.

Wakefield, L. T., & Wakefield, R. L. (2018). Anxiety and ephemeral social media use in negative eWOM creation. *Journal of Interactive Marketing, 41,* 44–59.

Wang, Y., & Chaudhry, A. (2018). When and how managers' responses to online reviews affect subsequent reviews. *Journal of Marketing Research, 55*(2), 163–177.

Ward, J. C., & Ostrom, A. L. (2006). Complaining to the masses: The role of protest framing in customer-created complaint web sites. *Journal of Consumer Research, 33*(2), 220–230.

Wei, S., Ang, T., & Anaza, N. A. (2019). The power of information on customers' social withdrawal and citizenship behavior in a crowded service environment. *Journal of Service Management, 30*(1), 23–47.

Weitzl, W. J., & Hutzinger, C. (2019). Rise and fall of complainants' desires: The role of pre-failure brand commitment and online service recovery satisfaction. *Computers in Human Behavior, 97,* 116–129.

Weun, S., Beatty, S. E., & Jones, M. A. (2004). The impact of service failure severity on service recovery evaluations and post-recovery relationships. *Journal of Services Marketing, 18*(2), 133–146.

Yi, S., & Baumgartner, H. (2004). Coping with negative emotions in purchase-related situations. *Journal of Consumer Psychology, 14*(3), 303–317.

Yusuf, A. S., Che Hussin, A. R., & Busalim, A. H. (2018). Influence of e-WOM engagement on consumer purchase intention in social commerce. *Journal of Services Marketing, 32*(4), 493–504.

Zeelenberg, M., & Pieters, R. (2004). Beyond valence in customer dissatisfaction: A review and new findings on behavioral responses to regret and disappointment in failed services. *Journal of Business Research, 57*(4), 445–455.

Zeithaml, V. A., Berry, L. L., & Parasuraman, A. (1996). The behavioral consequences of service quality. *Journal of Marketing, 60*(2), 31–46.

Zheng, T., Youn, H., & Kincaid, C. S. (2009). An analysis of customers' e-complaints for luxury resort properties. *Journal of Hospitality Marketing & Management, 18*(7), 718–729.

CHAPTER 17

Opera as Luxury in Culture: The Marketing Impact of Digitalization

Nicola Bellini

INTRODUCTION

This paper deals with the marketing impact of digitalization in a cultural industry, namely in (Western) opera. We intend to provide a preliminary conceptual framework to analyze the process of digitalization in opera consumption, by exploring the analogies with digitalization in luxury markets. The analysis is based on a critical review of the relevant literature and on a very preliminary investigation including a limited number of informal interviews with opera managers and experts.

Two main issues are discussed. First, we consider digitalization as a tool for market expansion and possibly "democratization" through increased accessibility. Second, we look at the adoption of digital marketing approaches and at the development of opera-related content and communities in social networks.

N. Bellini (✉)
Scuola Superiore Sant'Anna, Pisa, Italy

© The Author(s), under exclusive license to Springer Nature   423
Switzerland AG 2021
W. Ozuem and S. Ranfagni (eds.), *The Art of Digital Marketing for
Fashion and Luxury Brands*,
https://doi.org/10.1007/978-3-030-70324-0_17

THE ASSUMPTION: OPERA AS A LUXURY PRODUCT

Our discussion, as well as its inclusion in this book, requires an introductory explanation of the main (and, to our knowledge, innovative) assumption behind our work, i.e. the analogy between opera attendance and luxury consumption.

Since the beginning of this century there has been a growing amount of published work (both research articles and handbooks) on the marketing of cultural institutions and, within this wider category, on the marketing of performing arts, including opera (Bernstein, 2014; Fraser & Fraser, 2014; Kolb, 2013). This growth has reflected the push towards greater "market orientation" in the management of opera houses (Jones, 2000), which is a consequence of the decreased ability of traditional sources of income (public subsidies, especially in Europe, and corporate sponsorships, especially in the US) to compensate for the structural inability of box office sales to pay for the costs of opera production.

The debate about opera marketing has been dominated by one issue: the renewal of audiences to offset the decline of attendance by traditional opera consumers and therefore the urgency to reach the large numbers of non-customers that feel rejected by the "strong cultural legitimacy" of this kind of performing art (Bourgeon-Renault, 2009; Di Fiore, 2010). Opera marketing (possibly within the theoretical framework of social marketing) was thus induced to focus on facilitating the access to opera, interpreting consumers' motivations and their (in)ability to translate them into action (Park & Yoon, 2017). As a matter of fact, however, the opera market is mature and declining, but far from disappearing. The quantity of operatic performances has not decreased during the last decades and, even more significantly, new opera houses are being built and older ones have been renovated (Fraser & Fraser, 2014).

There has been no easy extension of standard marketing concepts and toolboxes to the world of opera. This is due to some very problematic features of the opera business and in particular: the serious limitations to product development (in fact nowadays opera houses are working almost exclusively on a relatively small repertoire of works from the past, although more or less thoroughly reinterpreted); and the tensions between the cultural mission of the institutions and more "customer-driven" approaches in the planning of productions (Fraser & Fraser, 2014; Jones 2000; Sgourev 2012).

Suggesting the analogy between opera and luxury consumption is not totally new. The obvious link between high prices and the high social status of opera consumers leads in that direction. However, one can find only occasional and scattered reference to this connection in works concerning either luxury marketing (e.g. by Kapferer & Bastien, 2009) and opera (e.g. Fraser & Fraser, 2014). Opera is alternatively depicted either as a pricey pastime for wealthy and increasingly globalized audiences (Snowman, 2009) or as a "spirit feeding" luxury experience (Cristini et al., 2017).

To our knowledge, however, research has missed the opportunity to reframe opera in the new concept of "experiential luxury" and its emphasis on the symbolic, emotional, cultural and relational aspects of luxury consumption (Batat, 2019). Within this revised framework, new perspectives challenge the established knowhow about luxury, such as the "democratization" of luxury or the role of co-creation (Choi et al., 2016; Cristini et al., 2017). This paper suggests that new marketing insights may come from the interpretation of opera as a luxury experience, when these updated perspectives are considered.

Following the typology proposed by Seo and Buchanan-Oliver (2019), opera can fit in the two broad perspectives on how luxury can be conceptualized. Firstly, in a product-centric perspective, opera performances are the most complex and undoubtedly also the most expensive product of the performing arts sector. It often involves large numbers of people (orchestra, chorus, singers, stage directors and crew, props staff, venue crew, managers, administrative officers etc.). A new production would also imply costs related to the creative work and to the manufacturing of stage and costumes (Agid & Tarondeau, 2010; Trevisan, 2017).

Adding to this, in order to build or renovate opera houses huge investments are required, that are normally much higher than for other large ventures. This is due to the expected quality (of architectural design and of the interiors) and to increasing technical requirements, which are needed in order to increase the number of shows and therefore impact on the economic viability of the opera house.

The high cost of productions justifies the high prices of tickets. Attending an ordinary performance in one of the top opera houses may cost no less than 200 euros and up to 500: the excluding impact of prices is therefore unquestionable.

Secondly, in a consumer-centric perspective, opera attendance is a complex and highly immersive hedonic experience. The cultural value of the artwork combines with two dimensions of the luxury experience: the "luxury for yourself" (the excitement of participating to a memorable event in a special experiential setting) and the "luxury for others (to be seen at the opera, and to see famous personalities there)" (Kapferer & Bastien, 2009, p. 161). This relational dimension is the result of a centuries-long coexistence within opera houses of different social classes, physically distributed in the different areas of the hall. Historically, opera played a role in Western cultures and societies in representing and legitimating elites and power structures within the framework of a direct dialogue with popular masses: "opera's social performance has been never meaningless. On the contrary, its institutions, venues and promenades had been turned into a place for seeing and being seen, a place of taste and emotion, but, above all, the place of great signification, creation and enactment of imagined communities" (Kotnik, 2013).

Opera consumption fits quite well in several key streams of luxury marketing literature. E.g. motivations of opera attendance are consistent with self-congruency theory, i.e. as expression of the consumers' search for products (experiences) that they believe matching their self-image. This may be strengthened by the multicultural, international and transnational character of opera both as a product and as a production system, by the association of opera with luxury industry sponsors (Dalakas, 2009) and by the contextual link with other luxury consumptions (like the dress or the after-show dinner). Opera and opera house brands have been also integrated in luxury marketing strategies. Building on a long tradition of reciprocal influence between theatrical costumes and fashion, many illustrious designers have participated to opera productions by designing costumes, which in turn reflect some distinctive features of their style. Opera heritage may also be seen as emotional source of inspiration (like in the 2017 opera-inspired collection by Dolce and Gabbana, presented at La Scala theatre in Milan).

Furthermore, some specific segments of the luxury market may present more specific similarities, that can be useful for market analysis and segmentation. E.g. there are important analogies with luxury wine consumption (Bellini & Resnick, 2018), as for both opera and wine big spending must be combined with requirements of taste and knowledge.

The Impact of Digitalization: 1) Widening the Market for (and Democratizing?) Opera

Democratization is a major issue in contemporary luxury research. In a normative perspective, luxury scholars are investigating ways to balance the creation of "a sense of desirability" through widely distributed digital means and the exclusiveness "in terms of the selective distribution of the actual product" (Hennigs, Wiedmann, & Klarmann, 2012).

A reflection on opera democratization may contribute to this more general debate, also because—as already mentioned—opera history has been marked not by absolute exclusivity, but by the coexistence and co-consumption of different social groups. In modern times, opera houses were built as large venues with clearly separated spaces that allowed both co-attendance of performances and mutual visibility and recognition between elites and lower classes (Kotnik, 2013). Co-attendance was not only compatible with but strengthening the effect of social legitimization of the dominant social groups.

Although resilient in some countries (like in Italy or Austria with the tradition of "*loggione*" and "*Stehplätze*"), the loss of the popular, lower-income component had been progressive and apparently unstoppable in recent decades, contributing to the overall trend towards shrinking attendances. This combines with the aging of opera audiences, therefore introducing a generational issue: how to attract younger generations, seemingly hostile to (or simply scared by) the rituals of opera attendance and perceiving a growing distance between pop and classical music.

The democratization issue in opera emerged especially since the end of the 1960s, also in the wake of the changing socio-political climate. In order to counter the negative association of opera with dominant social classes exhibiting their power and wealth, opera managers and artists felt the need to "open" theatres and experiment socially inclusive (low cost or free) performances, usually addressed to "students and workers", but also to other potential market segments like tourists (Guachalla, 2017).

The aim of recovering the popular audience has been pursued also through some product innovation. E.g., rather than attending a whole opera, the least demanding and most popular features have been packaged in concerts including a selection of famous arias. "Classical crossover" have also emerged with spectacular events and iconic artists as bridges to pop music (the "Three Tenors" and "Pavarotti and Friends" events, Andrea Bocelli, Sarah Brightman, Rebecca Newman etc.).

Regarding the accessibility to the product, technology has played a major role already since the 1930s thanks to radio broadcasts of classical music, like in the hugely successful case of the NBC Symphony Orchestra (1937–1954) under the baton of Arturo Toscanini. From 1936 to 1964, more than 350 concerts were aired live on Monday in Italy under the label of a famous wine and vermouth company (Martini & Rossi), involving practically all the most relevant opera artists of the time.

A decisive contribution came from the recording industry, notwithstanding the lack of the visual dimension. With the improvement of sound fidelity, recordings were able to spread much more rapidly than in the past also some major artistic innovations, as witnessed by the Maria Callas phenomenon. Her 1953 EMI recording of Giacomo Puccini's "Tosca" was a huge commercial success and still today is one of the best-selling opera recordings.

A significant step forward took place with the emergence of visual media and of the TV (Pérez, 2012; Senici, 2009, 2010). Besides some earlier occasional filming of opera (or concert) performances, the implementation of video magnetic recording allowed to produce operas in studios and, increasingly, for recording live events in opera houses. The latter made possible to "participate" also to some unique, memorable events (Puccini's "Turandot" being performed within the Beijing Forbidden City in 1998, the 1976 boos to Carlos Kleiber conducting "Otello" in Milan etc.). TV broadcasts have been produced and realized mostly by public rather than commercial broadcasters, like PBS in the USA, and more recently by specialized satellite and pay-tv channels, like Arte, Classica, Medici TV, Mezzo etc. (Morris, 2010).

Parallel to this, opera films realized the convergence with the aesthetics and technical potentials of the movie industry. While early operatic adaptations were realized already in the 1930s, opera films reached high points especially in the 1980s and 1990s with directors such as Ingmar Bergman or Franco Zeffirelli. Furthermore, the interest of visual media in opera and the contamination between the two led also to some interesting, although isolated experiments, e.g. the short series of operas produced by Andrea Andermann and broadcasted live "in the original settings and times" (starting with the 1992 "Tosca") and the unique "Traviata" at the Zurich Central Station in 2008 (Morris, 2010).

Visual recordings have been "stored" and diffused on videocassettes, later through DVDs and BluRay discs and now by on-demand streaming services. Digital supports have not only improved the video and sound quality, but they have allowed for additional features: multi-language subtitles, supporting documentation, behind-the-scene footage, additional videos, interviews to artists etc. As a result, DVDs realized an opportunity rarely experimented in earlier times (with the pioneering exception of the educational features added to the 1958 Solti's recording of Wagner's "Ring"), i.e. to use technology in order to provide "enhanced" opera experiences.

Yet, notwithstanding all of this, the gap between the "real" opera experience and all these surrogates remained unfilled, because of the unresolvable opposition of "the theatricality of the stage to the realism of cinema and television", the loss of "spontaneity and uniqueness" and the physical absence of the "community of spectators" (Morris, 2010). In recent years, however, different forms of opera digitalization may have opened a radically new scenario (Radigales, 2013).

Because of the digitalization of movie theatres, an opportunity has emerged for the digital delivery also of "non-traditional content" such as sports and arts. Opera could profit from unprecedented quality of HD video and special surround audio (at levels unattainable in private settings) and from the "sense of the now" (Morris, 2010) due to simultaneity with the real performance. Rather than a mere packaged surrogate, operas live in cinemas "are like an alternative opera experience", that is especially effective for some productions (also due to the interaction with digital technologies increasingly used on stage). Adding to this, there is the feeling of being nonetheless part of a collective experience shared with the other viewers convened to the movie theatre (Tommasini, 2013).

Thus, digitalization marks a clear discontinuity and opens to new challenges. According to one author, "in the early twenty-first century, [its] spatial and conceptual mobility allows opera to transgress, break down, or creatively adapt the seeming divide between the live and the digital" (Kreuzer, 2019). This new kind of mediatization "does not, a priori, free opera from aura. It represents, however, a formidable chance to challenge the entanglement of opera and tradition" (Cachopo, 2018).

The most important experience in this field has been realized by the Metropolitan Opera in New York (Elberse & Perez, 2009; Heyer, 2008). The first broadcast took place in December 2006. In the 2019–2020 season, the live broadcast of MET operas was announced to reach 2200 screens in over 70 countries around the globe. This means hundreds of thousands additional viewers per production. In 2013 the MET leadership estimated that their audience had quadrupled thanks to these broadcasts (Tommasini, 2013). The other opera house that has most consistently committed to this approach is the Royal Opera House (Covent Garden) in London. Here again figures are impressive: in the 2019–2020 season, ROH operas were being watched in 1600 movie theatres in 53 countries.

The impact of these experiences is only partially known. Early surveys (that are mostly focused on the New York Met case) highlighted the significant, but overall limited impact in terms of generating new and younger opera audiences. Most attendees are "moderate and frequent opera goers", resulting in an extension of "operagoing life of older customers". This will concern "second and third tier" customers that may not access live performances on a more regular basis, because of their limited income and/or because they live in places that are distant form the opera house (Goodman, Lenihan, & Rathore, 2011; Opera America, 2008; Tommasini, 2013; Van Eeden, 2011; Van Riet, 2011). More recent surveys are however not available, and evidence is missing about the possible evolution (and consolidation?) of opera live broadcasts in cinema as a truly alternative experience.

The evolution of this "new" opera market is therefore left open to further investigation. Considering the high barriers to entry (due to the exceptional organizational and technological requirements), this new market is likely to be dominated by a handful of opera houses and/or networks of them. Notwithstanding the superiority of the real experience, we are heading to a point where "real live" performances of so many minor opera houses (e.g. in peripheral or small cities) are directly and locally competing with the cinema across the street, where one can watch world-class artists play "HD live". The choice in favor of the "real live" performance may be not so obvious (cf. Vladica & Davis, 2013).

Strengthening the ability of a greater number of opera producers to meet these challenges is thus a potential matter for policy consideration. So far, public support has limited itself to internet (live and on demand) streaming and educational activities. This is the case of the OperaVision project (2017–2021, www.operavision.eu) offering a platform with free-view, online performances of 29 participating opera houses from 19 countries, as well as free resources for young audiences and for artistic career development. The EU supports this project with a 2 million euros grant by through the "Creative Europe" program. At a different scale, the Regional government of Emilia Romagna (Italy) is financing the three-year "OperaStreaming" program (2019–2021, https://operastreaming.

com), offering live streaming of productions by the eight opera houses active in the region. The rationale of the project combines the objective of providing "a service aimed at disadvantaged sections of the public in the fruition of the theatres' activities" and the cultural promotion of the region in the field of opera productions. The program is a follow-up of a previous 2012 experience ("TeatroNet"), supporting also the setting up of the technological infrastructure.

Lastly, a number of experimentations are exploring the creative potential linked to "hypermediacy" (Morris, 2010) and enhanced experiences (Reichl et al., 2016), as well as to the reorganization of the production process to improve the geographical accessibility of the opera experience (e.g. the substitution of traditional touring with remote orchestra performances supporting live signing).

In conclusion, these preliminary findings suggest a prudent approach to the hypothesis of a technology-driven democratization. Digitalization may certainly be instrumental to grater inclusivity, also through more updated ways to create "curiosity" about opera (like the virtual reality experience of the "magic Butterfly" project at Welsh National opera in 2017–2018). However, an alternative hypothesis emerges (and is proposed for further testing), i.e. that digitalization may originate alternative ways of consumption *integrating* traditional attendance, especially of those market segments of operagoers that are unable to be in opera houses more than a few times a year (because of physical distance or limited purchasing power).

The Impact of Digitalization: 2) the Role of Social Networks

Like in the luxury industry, digital marketing approaches have been increasingly implemented in the world of opera, raising similar questions about the tensions between exclusivity and the level of inclusion that is made possible by web accessibility. In luxury online brand communities have emerged as a web-based evolution of traditional brand communities in all cases where consumption has a positive and strong impact on the social identity of individual members (Brogi et al., 2013; Helal & Ozuem, 2018; Kim & Lee, 2017). In the case of opera, online communities are also emerging around the main brands of the world of opera and they may be interpreted as the contemporary surrogate of more traditional and deeply rooted forms of social sharing of operatic experiences, that were diffused especially in the popular section of the audiences ("the fans") (Benzecry 2011; Fraser & Fraser 2014).

The borders of these communities are quite blurred. The hard core of these communities is normally centered around the local theatre and the geographical spread of members is likely to correspond to its physical market. Nonetheless, a few "benchmark" opera houses will refer to wider communities (either nationally or internationally). At the same time, significant crossover may be expected between opera lovers' communities and those related to other performing arts, such as drama or classical music

Opera houses are now present in several social networks like Facebook, YouTube, Twitter and Instagram. The commitment to social networks is far from homogeneous with some opera houses emerging as more active and with different emphasis on the options provided by individual platforms. Table 17.1 compares the number of followers for selected opera houses. Data are not strictly comparable as some houses produce also non opera performances (concerts, ballets etc.) or, like in the case of Sidney, they work as a more general cultural hub. Still differences are significant, especially when these data are analyzed in relation to the ranking and reputation (most prestigious opera houses are not necessarily the most digitally active) and when data are compared with benchmarks provided by major performing art institutions. E.g. we notice that in New York the digital activity of the opera house is greater than that of the most important orchestra, while the opposite occurs in Berlin between the Philharmoniker and the three local opera houses.

Institutional actors use social networks systematically as alternative channels to communicate "one-way" information about events, plans, contingent information (like the cancellation of events, changes in the artists' cast) etc. However, opera houses have increasingly understood that effective social media marketing requires facilitating interaction, collaboration and content sharing (Kim & Ko, 2012). While somehow puzzled by the "democratizing" nature of social media, luxury marketers have experienced the positive effects in strengthening customer engagement through quality interactions (Hennigs et al., 2012; Pentina, Guilloux, & Micu, 2018).

A preliminary look at the presence of opera houses in social medias apparently confirms the emergence of similar approaches. Out of the five dimensions of social media marketing identified by Kim and Ko (2012) in luxury fashion, two seem to prevail: entertainment and trendiness.

Table 17.1 Social networks' communities of selected opera houses (official accounts, thousands of followers, August 2020)

Opera House	Facebook	Twitter	YouTube	Instagram
Royal Opera House, London	1415	205	851	736
Welsh National Opera, Cardiff	14	34	3	5
Opéra national de Paris	349	254	84	342
Opéra national de Lyon	48	4	3	12
Gran Teatre del Liceu, Barcelona	63	25	21	44
Teatro alla Scala, Milan	383	311	26	263
Teatro del Maggio Musicale Fiorentino, Florence	58	11	1	17
Teatro La Fenice, Venice	301	67	71	55
Arena di Verona	417	27	10	37
Théatre Royal de la Monnaie, Brussels	31	9	3	10
De Nationale Opera, Amsterdam	34	16	62	54
Deutsche Oper Berlin	42	23	2	14
Staatsoper Unter den Linden, Berlin	34	24	6	64
Komische Oper Berlin	33	14	5	13
Bayerische Staatsoper, Munich	63	27	35	52
Wiener Staatsoper, Vienna	126	13	10	90
Salzburger Festspiele, Salzburg	113	29	3	30
Opernhaus Zurich	47	24	5	28
Metropolitan Opera House, New York	611	239	156	403
Lyric Opera of Chicago	66	35	5	40
San Francisco Opera	49	92	5	42
Los Angeles Opera	60	39	5	48
Teatro Colòn, Buenos Aires	419	110	46	310
Sydney Opera House	2122	143	98	148
Benchmarks				
Berliner Philharmoniker	1504	150	356	311
New York Philharmonic	471	439	40	97
Royal Shakespeare Company	471	177	68	184

Source Author's elaboration on data from social network platforms

The former is the result of the wide use (especially on Facebook, Instagram and YouTube) of images and videos. These may be trailers of incoming productions, commentaries and explanations by musicians, interviews with artists or memories of related past events (including the complete recording of past performances). Materials may go beyond the strict relationship with performances, in order to involve communities in the life of music production, e.g. through additional features (e.g.

Masterclasses) or creative storytelling (e.g., the "3e scène" short movies produced by the Paris Opéra). In some cases, the opera house brand is consistently associated with a popular artist. A good example is provided by the Royal Opera House systematic use of its Music Director, Antonio Pappano, as a communicative, friendly and inspiring guide to opera fans.

Regarding trendiness, social media are instrumental to keep "globalized" opera fans up to date on new productions, emerging artists etc. and to provide meanings and appropriate emphasis to outstanding events compared to more routine repertoire (as shown by the year-long promotion of the debut by star tenor Jonas Kaufmann in the title role of Verdi's "Otello" at Covent Garden in June 2017).

The interactivity dimension is probably not (yet?) developed to the extent that is otherwise detectable for luxury brands. It is, of course, not absent. Opera houses encourage the sharing of opera attendance experiences and conversations between operagoers, by reposting comments to performances or by incentives, as mentioned by Jones (2016) in the case of Arizona Opera. According to some exploratory studies, this is linked to the relevance of eWOM also in this field (Hausmann & Poelmann, 2016).

This phenomenon is complemented by the role played by a number of specialized external media (opera magazines and blogs), fully or partially operating on the web, that are also important sources of information and shape the fans' opinion with their reviews. However, it is also likely that, like in luxury, *passive* social media practices ("lurking": Leban et al., 2020) are relevant: opera fans may in fact be happy to merely follow, rather than contribute, and to realize a kind of virtual consumption, as exemplified by the practice of YouTube "playlists".

Social media have made possible to manage difficulties and controversies that could affect the brand reputation of involved opera houses, like those concerning inappropriate behavior by world-famous artists in the wake of the "MeToo" movement (e.g. in the 2019 charges of sexual harassment against Placido Domingo). Later, social networks have given support to the gradual "rehabilitation" of the artist, by discussing the imbalance between the allegations about his misconduct and his unparalleled contribution to the arts.

Social networks accounts are also held by individual artists. Although the size of their communities is definitely incomparable to that of pop singers and even of the most popular "crossover" artists, their figures can

Table 17.2 Facebook followers of the official accounts of selected opera singers (August 2020)

Artist	Followers ('000)
Placido Domingo	1334
Anna Netrebko	363
Cecilia Bartoli	218
Thomas Hampson	197
Renée Fleming	159
Jonas Kaufmann	148
Elina Garanca	138
Joyce Di Donato	109
Benchmarks	
Andrea Bocelli	4317
Sarah Brightman	1168

Source Author's elaboration on data from social network platforms

be more relevant than the ones of several opera houses and they also appear to have a more global character (Table 17.2).

The engagement of opera artists reflects a consolidated belief that social network activities are a necessary promotional tool and an effective way to maintain a constant flow of information towards the communities of their fans (Jones, 2016; Meachem, 2018). Correspondingly singers' official accounts focus on self-promotion, by providing information about performances and recordings as well as images and video clips. Some accounts include elements of a more personal character: the artist shares backstage and personal stories, with related images and videos. In these cases, they create opportunities for a more personal and empathic interaction, that is not limited to professional achievements.

Finally, an apparently minor phenomenon concerns the many (but smaller) spontaneous communities activated by opera fans, that are especially active on Instagram or YouTube to share images and audio-video elements of the playlists.

In conclusion, a robust analysis of opera-related online communities is clearly missing. The comparison with luxury brand communities highlights significant similarities, but also some interesting differences. The first one is related to the territorial dimension that seems still quite relevant for opera houses (but less so for opera artists). Secondly, at this stage there is not enough evidence of the transformational impact of "digital prosumption" that has been identified in the case of luxury. This leads to an essential research question, that is clearly unanswered so far, i.e.

to what extent we are just witnessing a technological update of communication channels between providers and consumers or a more complex evolution, where the dynamics of online communities impact on opera brands in terms of loyalty, awareness and associations.

Within this framework, we will also need to understand the impact of the COVID-19 pandemics. Like with other businesses, online communities have helped to keep the relationship with customers alive at a time of lockdown and closed theatres. This has been undoubtedly a time for experimentations, ranging from the attempt to establish more empathic relations between the artists and their audience to unprecedented online events (e.g. the "At-Home Gala" of the Metropolitan Opera in April 2020). It is of course too early to identify possible implications for the future of online communities, although the statements by operas managers convey a new and diffused awareness of the importance of online communities as a strategic asset. To what extent this will be an integral part of future marketing strategies, in a way similar to what happened for luxury, is yet to be seen.

Conclusions and Managerial Implications

In this paper we looked at two dimensions of digitalization in opera. Both discussions have significant management implications that derive from the analogy between opera and luxury.

Digitalization has been and will be instrumental to market penetration. Opera managers should probably escape the trap of the traditional and somewhat ideological "obsession" on market expansion and consider digitalization as a way to complement the traditional opera experience for specific market segments that, for a variety of reasons, cannot afford more than limited attendance to live shows, but are still eager to "consume" the luxury of opera. In other words, digital opera may be effective in increasing consumption levels and brand loyalty for consumers that belong to middle-class, average-income social groups and/or are physically peripheral, i.e. live in "second-tier" cities with respect to major opera houses.

Digital marketing has the potential to renew on a wider scale "opera fans" communities around opera houses and singers. With possible exceptions (that would deserve further specific investigation), one-way promotion seems to prevail, and more complex, interactive and "dialogic" exchanges (Mahoney & Tang, 2017) are definitely less frequent.

Although we may expect that membership impacts on social identities (as it used to do in the past: Benzecry, 2011), participation is still mostly passive. Managerial challenges are therefore especially high, especially in an effort—that is visible in a few cases—to integrate the digitalization of communications with the digitalization of products.

REFERENCES

Agid, P., & Tarondeau, J. (2010). *The management of opera: An international comparative study*. London: Plagrave Macmillan.

Batat, W. (2019). *The new luxury experience*. Springer.

Bellini, N., & Resnick, E. (2018). 12 The luxury turn in wine tourism. In N. Bellini, C. Clergeau, & O. Etcheverria (Eds.), *Gastronomy and local development: The quality of products, places and experiences*. London: Routledge.

Benzecry, C. E. (2011). *The opera fanatic: Ethnography of an obsession*. University of Chicago Press.

Bernstein, J. (2014). *Standing room only: Marketing insights for engaging performing arts audiences*. Springer.

Bourgeon-Renault, D. (2009). Le marketing des arts du spectacle vivant. In D. Bourgeon-Renault (Ed.), *Marketing de l'Art et de la Culture. Spectacle vivant, patrimoine et industries culturelles* (pp. 139–174). Paris: Dunod.

Brogi, S., Calabrese, A., Campisi, D., Capece, G., Costa, R., & Di Pillo, F. (2013). The effects of online brand communities on brand equity in the luxury fashion industry. *International Journal of Engineering Business Management, 5,* 5–32.

Cachopo, J. P. (2018). The aura of opera reproduced: Fantasies and traps in the age of the cinecast. *The Opera Quarterly, 34*(4), 266–283.

Choi, E., Ko, E., & Kim, A. J. (2016). Explaining and predicting purchase intentions following luxury-fashion brand value co-creation encounters. *Journal of Business Research, 69*(12), 5827–5832.

Cristini, H., Kauppinen-Räisänen, H., Barthod-Prothade, M., & Woodside, A. (2017). Toward a general theory of luxury: Advancing from workbench definitions and theoretical transformations. *Journal of Business Research, 70,* 101–107.

Dalakas, V. (2009). Consumer response to sponsorships of the performing arts. *Journal of Promotion Management, 15*(1–2), 204–211.

Di Fiore, A. (2010). Slaying the phantoms of Italy's opera. *Harvard Business Review*, Reprint H00S0X.

Elberse, A., & Perez, C. (2009). *Case study: The metropolitan opera*. Harvard Business School.

Fraser, P., & Fraser, I. (2014). Creating the opera habit: Marketing and the experience of opera. In D. O'Reilly, R. Rentschler, & T. A. Kirchner (Eds.). (2014). *The Routledge companion to arts marketing*. Routledge.

Goodman, L., Lenihan, J., & Rathore, O. (2011). *Met: Live in HD analysis and marketing plan*. Retrieved from https://www.slideshare.net/lorraineg oodman2/live-in-hd-analysis-amp-marketing-plan.

Guachalla, A. (2017). Social inclusion and audience development at the Royal Opera House: A tourist perspective. *International Journal of Culture, Tourism and Hospitality Research, 11*(3), 436–449.

Hausmann, A., & Poellmann, L. (2016). eWOM in the performing arts: exploratory insights for the marketing of theaters. *Arts and the Market, 6*(1), 11–123.

Helal, G., & Ozuem, W. (2018). Social identity matters: Social media and brand perceptions in the fashion apparel and accessories industries. In Ozuem, W., & Azemi, Y. (Eds.), *Digital marketing strategies for fashion and luxury brands*. IGI Global.

Hennigs, N., Wiedmann, K. P., & Klarmann, C. (2012). Luxury brands in the digital age—Exclusivity versus ubiquity. *Marketing Review St. Gallen, 29*(1), 30–35.

Heyer, P. (2008). Live from the met: Digital broadcast cinema, medium theory, and opera for the masses. *Canadian Journal of Communication, 33*(4), 591–604.

Jones, J. (2016). *Social media, marketing, and the opera singer*. Arizona State University.

Jones, L. (2000). Market orientation—A case study of three UK opera companies. *International Journal of Nonprofit and Voluntary Sector Marketing, 5*(4), 348–364.

Kapferer, J. N., & Bastien, V. (2009). *The luxury strategy*. London: Kogan Page.

Kim, A. J., & Ko, E. (2012). Do social media marketing activities enhance customer equity? An empirical study of luxury fashion brand. *Journal of Business Research, 65*(10), 1480–1486.

Kim, J., & Lee, K. H. (2017). Influence of integration on interactivity in social media luxury brand communities. *Journal of Business Research, 99*, 422–429.

Kolb, B. M. (2013). *Marketing for cultural organizations: New strategies for attracting audiences*. Routledge.

Kotnik, V. (2013). The adaptability of opera: when different social agents come to common ground. *International Review of the Aesthetics and Sociology of Music*, 303–342.

Kreuzer, G. (2019). Operatic Configurations in the Digital Age. *The Opera Quarterly, 35*(1–2), 130–134.

Leban, M., Seo, Y., & Voyer, B. G. (2020). Transformational effects of social media lurking practices on luxury consumption. *Journal of Business Research, 116*, 514–521.

Mahoney, L. M., & Tang, T. (2017). *Strategic social media: From marketing to social change*. John Wiley & Sons.

Meachem, L. (2018). *Social media strategy for musicians.* Retrieved from https://thebaritoneblog.com/2018/08/01/social-media-strategy-for-musicians/.

Morris, C. (2010). Digital diva: Opera on video. *The Opera Quarterly, 26*(1), 96–119.

Opera America. (2008). *The metropolitan Opera Live in HD: Who attends, and why?.* Download from https://web.archive.org/web/20120502032044/http://www.operaamerica.org/content/research/Met%20HD%20Article.pdf.

Park, H. S., & Yoon, H. (2017). Facilitating public access to the arts: Applying the motivation, opportunity, and ability framework to the case of the UK Royal Opera House. *Journal of Arts & Humanities, 6*(7), 1–12.

Pentina, I., Guilloux, V., & Micu, A. C. (2018). Exploring social media engagement behaviors in the context of luxury brands. *Journal of Advertising, 47*(1), 55–69.

Pérez, H. (Ed.). (2012). *Opera and video: Technology and spectatorship.* Bern: Peter Lang.

Radigales, J. (2013). Media literacy and new entertainment venues: The case of opera in movie theatres. *Communication & Society/Comunicación y Sociedad, 26*(3), 160–170.

Reichl, P. et al. (2016). *The salome experience: Opera live streaming and beyond.* In Proceedings of the 2016 CHI Conference Extended Abstracts on Human Factors in Computing Systems (pp. 728–737).

Senici, E. (2009). *Il video d'opera "dal vivo": testualizzazione e 'liveness' nell'era digitale* (pp. 273–312). XVI: Il Saggiatore musicale.

Senici, E. (2010). Porn style?: Space and time in live opera videos. *The Opera Quarterly, 26*(1), 63–80.

Seo, Y., & Buchanan-Oliver, M. (2019). Constructing a typology of luxury brand consumption practices. *Journal of Business Research, 99*, 414–421.

Sgourev, S. V. (2012). The dynamics of risk in innovation: A premiere or an encore? *Industrial and Corporate Change, 22*(2), 549–575.

Snowman, D. (2009). *The gilded stage: A social history of opera.* Atlantic Books Ltd.

Tommasini, A. (2013, March). A success in HD, but at what cost? In *New York Times.* Download from www.nytimes.com/2013/03/15/arts/music/mets-hd-broadcasts-success-but-at-what-cost.html.

Trevisan, P. (2017). *Reshaping Opera: A critical reflection on arts management.* Cambridge: Cambridge Scholars Publishing.

van Eeden, S. (2011). *The impact of The Met: Live in HD on local opera attendance*. University of British Columbia.

Van Riet, K. (2011). Opera at the cinema. Ghent: Kinepolis Group. Retrieved from https://www.slideshare.net/ETMGhent/opera-at-the-cinema.

Vladica, F., & Davis, C. H. (2013). Value propositions of opera and theater live in cinema. In *World Media and Economics Conference*. Download from http://www.learningsynergy.com/documents/LSCinema.pdf.

Index

A

Accessibility, 223–225, 232, 234–236
Active participation, 107, 108, 113, 119
Active users, 117, 154, 166
Adidas, 380
Advertising, 137, 139, 143
Anonymity, 94
Appropriateness, 137, 138, 143
Assortment strategy, 7, 20
Asymmetrical assortment, 7
Attitudinal loyalty, 159, 160, 162, 168, 169, 180, 184–186, 190, 191
Augmented reality (AR), 377, 380, 386
Authenticity, 87, 96, 97, 248

B

Back office operations, 13
Balenciaga, 381
Beacon technologies, 377
Behavioural competences, 307, 316

Behavioural loyalty, 159, 161, 165, 166, 168, 184, 186, 190, 191
Big data, 299, 301, 302, 311, 312
Brand awareness, 347, 349, 351, 355, 357
Brand commitment, 115, 185
Brand communication, 275, 280, 290
Brand community, 156, 157, 431, 435
Brand credibility, 410, 413
Brand equity, 33, 39, 40, 42, 44
Brand identity, 275, 281, 282, 284, 285, 287, 288, 290
Brand image, 37, 39, 42, 43, 273–277, 281, 282, 284, 286, 289
Brand influence, 154
Brand knowledge, 39–42, 44
Brand loyalty, 180, 182–186, 188
Brand mentions, 117, 122, 123
Brand positioning, 133, 146
Brand preference, 154, 162, 168
Brand-related eWOM, 405–407, 409
Brand-related participation, 117

Brand relationship, 163
Brand resonance model, 33, 40
Brand switching, 180, 181, 186–189
Brand value, 350
Brand websites, 156
Burberry, 378, 382, 386

C
Chaffey and Chadwick, 206
Chaffey and Smith, 206
Chanel, 385, 386
Change reluctance, 185
Channel choice, 7
Channel integration, 34, 37, 38, 374, 376
Channel-specific pricing, 7
Channel switching, 11
Chevalier and Mayzlin (2006), 254
China, 346, 348, 351, 352, 354, 356, 357
Chinese market, 65
Chinese marketplace, 346–348, 357
Cloud computing technology, 301, 302
Co-created service recovery, 411
Co-creation, 86
Co-creation recovery strategy, 258
Collaboration, 86, 87, 97
Community members, 55
Community touchpoints, 373
Competences, 300, 307–309, 312–314, 316, 324, 325, 328–330, 334
Competences in fashion sector, 307, 312
Competitive environment, 135
Conformity, 400
Conspicuous perspective, 354
Consumer behaviour, 180, 201, 203, 209
Consumer-centric perspective, 425

Consumer image, 275, 290
Consumer perspective, 277
Consumer segment, 347
Consumers evaluation, 400, 406
Consumer-to-brand engagement, 158
Consumer-to-consumer communication, 54
Consumer-to-consumer engagement, 158
Content-oriented social media, 60
Corporate touchpoints, 373
Covid-19, 199, 201, 209, 212, 214, 215
Creative brand image, 133, 135, 136, 145, 146
Creative control, 146
Creative leaders, 139, 141
Creative marketing, 132, 134, 138, 144
Creativity inspiration, 135, 141
Creativity theory, 139, 140, 145
Credibility, 398–400, 407, 410
Cross-channel retail, 4, 5
Cultural industry, 423, 432
Cultural value, 425
Culture, 346, 352, 354, 355
Customer–brand interaction, 120, 349
Customer-based brand equity (CBBE), 33, 34, 39, 40, 43, 44
Customer complaint, 244
Customer engagement, 432
Customer focused strategy, 202, 210, 211, 215
Customer goals, 110, 111, 119
Customer integration, 5
Customer interaction, 5, 6, 18
Customer journey, 365–367, 370, 371, 373, 374, 387–389
Customer loyalty, 108, 123, 154, 160
Customer loyalty conceptualisation, 160
Customer-owned touchpoints, 370

Customer participation, 107–112, 117, 123
Customer touchpoints, 34, 36
Customization, 67

D
Decision-making process, 223, 224, 233–235
De Keyser et al. (2020), 371
Democratisation, 350, 352
Democratizing, 427, 432
Differentiation, 86
Digital disruption, 181
Digital factory, 301, 304, 332
Digital fashion, 301, 304, 305, 307, 309, 310, 314, 316, 327, 329, 330, 332, 333
Digital fashion process, 305, 316
Digital integration, 201, 207, 208, 210, 215
Digitalisation, 3, 346, 348, 350–352, 356, 357, 429, 431, 436, 437
Digital manufacturing, 321
Digital marketing, 200–204, 206–208, 210, 211, 215, 216, 303, 304, 310, 316, 324, 325, 327
Digital media, 58
Digital opera, 423, 429, 431, 432, 436
Digital skills, 309, 321
Digital technology, 203, 208
Digital transformation, 306, 308
Dior, 381
Direct channels, 31
Disconfirmation paradigm, 12
Disruptive innovation, 182, 191
Dissonance theory, 12
Distribution channels, 32, 40–42
Distributive justice, 254, 404
Domain-related/specialist competences, 309

Drivers of online customer experience, 369

E
E-buyer, 320
E-commerce, 3, 20, 36, 37, 43
Effects of negative eWOM, 398, 402, 403, 407–409
Electronic word of mouth (eWOM), 221–227, 232–236, 247, 248, 254, 397–402, 405–409, 412
Emotions, 87, 91
Empathy, 84, 95
Ethics, 278
eWOM and service failure, 398, 401–403, 405, 407, 408, 412
Experiential luxury, 425, 426
Expertise-specific, 146
Extrinsic motivation, 142, 146

F
Failure severity, 404, 410
Farfetch, 380, 384
Fashion bloggers, 82–87, 91–93, 95–98
Fashion brands, 244, 248, 251, 259, 260
Fashion industry, 19, 234, 235, 302, 305, 306, 309, 311, 314, 316, 330, 375, 397, 398
Fashion supply chain, 302
Followers, 83, 85–87, 90, 95, 116, 121, 123
Functional utility, 187, 189, 190

G
Generation X, 202
Generation Y, 202
Generation Z, 280
Green conspicuousness, 279

Greenwashing, 278
Group identity, 94

H
Hashtags, 122
Holistic experience, 34, 35
Homophily social influence, 224, 225, 227, 232, 234
Human resource management (HRM), 300, 313, 329–331, 334

I
Identification, 56
Incremental creativity, 140, 142, 144
Industry 4.0, 300, 302, 306, 308, 309, 312–314, 316, 324, 330, 333–335
Influencer marketing, 52, 61
Informational justice, 254, 255, 404
Information quality, 400
Information seekers, 115, 116, 119
Informativeness, 225, 227, 232
Informative value, 223, 224, 234
Instagram, 83, 84, 86, 87, 432, 433, 435
In-store customer experience, 346, 357, 365, 367, 369, 378, 379, 381
Integrated marketing communication (IMC), 132, 133, 135, 136
Integration quality, 13–16, 18, 20, 21, 23, 24
Intended audience, 117, 120
Interactional justice, 254, 255, 404
Interactive channels, 31
Interactive experience, 156, 158
Interactive kiosks, 377
Interactive platforms, 345
Internet celebrities, 60, 66–69
Internet of things (IoT), 182, 301, 326

Internet technology, 53
Intrinsic motivation, 139, 145
Italy, 227

K
Kim and Ko (2012), 432

L
Leadership creativity, 139–141
Lifestyle product, 81, 82
L'Oreal, 386
Low-cost brands, 38, 39
Loyalty intentions, 155, 164, 168–170
Lurkers, 115, 166
Luxury brand, 38, 39, 132–136, 138, 144, 146, 179–181, 190, 375, 378, 383, 385–387, 389
Luxury characteristics, 274, 276, 374, 381, 382, 389
Luxury consumption, 424–426
Luxury demand, 355, 357
Luxury fashion, 108–110, 114, 116, 120–124, 131–134, 136–142, 144–147, 200–202, 204, 206, 207, 209, 210, 212, 213, 215, 216, 273, 275, 276, 291, 345–352, 357, 358
Luxury fashion retail, 32, 43
Luxury marketing, 425, 426
Luxury smartphones, 180, 182, 183, 190

M
Market disruptions, 181, 189, 190
Marketing communication, 31, 40, 41
Methodological competences, 309
Mid-priced brands, 39
Millennials, 109, 119–123, 155, 156, 159–167, 169, 170, 245, 247, 251, 258–260, 279, 350, 351
Mobile application, 36, 38, 39

Motivations for negative eWOM, 402, 403, 408
Multichannel environment, 37
Multichannel retail, 4, 5

N

Negative brand experiences, 398, 405, 407, 412
Negative electronic word-of-mouth, 398, 401, 402, 407–409, 412
Negative word-of-mouth, 246, 253, 368
Netnography, 282
Network marketing, 68
Network ties, 116, 117
Non-brand-related participation, 117
Nordstrom, 379, 380
Normative social influence, 187, 225–227, 232, 234, 249

O

Omnichannel brand management, 135, 146
Omnichannel customer experience, 366, 374
Omnichannel customers' service perception, 4, 19
Omnichannel customer typology, 21
Omnichannel distribution, 41
Online brand communities (OBCs), 107–120, 122–124, 153–170
Online consumer engagement, 158
Online Customer Experience (OCE), 365, 367–369, 384–387
Online promotions, 8
Online relationships, 154
Online service failure, 246, 257, 260
Online service fulfilment, 8, 9
Online touchpoints, 372–374, 384
Opera, 423–432, 434–436
Opera heritage, 426

Opera market, 424, 430
Opera-related online communities, 423, 435
Opinion-giving, 221, 222, 225, 226
Opinion leaders, 52–54, 58–61, 66, 69, 70, 84, 92, 93
Opinion-seeking, 221–227, 232–236
Opinion sharing, 357
Optimal level, 6
Original content, 85
Originality, 137, 138, 141, 143

P

Participation effort, 117, 120
Participation motives, 119
Participation willingness, 117, 118
Passive users, 117, 154, 161
Peer-to-peer communication, 223
Peer-to-peer influence, 234
Perceived critical mass, 117
Perceived ease of use, 225, 227, 232, 234
Perceived justice, 254, 255, 398, 399, 403, 404, 410, 413
Perceived level of risk, 188
Perceived service quality, 12, 13, 18
Personal communications, 32
Personal competences, 309
Persuasion, 188
Post-pandemic era, 210, 215
Pre-pandemic, 213
Pricing strategy, 7, 8
Procedural justice, 254, 404
Product-centric perspective, 425
Product channels, 156
Product characteristics, 188
Professionalism, 87, 93
Psychological attachment, 154, 157
Purchase intention, 185, 187, 223, 226, 227, 232–234, 400, 406, 407, 409, 410, 413
Purchasing decisions, 155, 156

Q
Quality, 425, 429, 432

R
Radical creativity, 140, 142, 144–146
Recovery strategy, 253, 255, 257, 258, 260, 398, 403, 404, 409, 410
Reference groups, 58
Risk taking, 136, 139–141, 145

S
Salvatore Ferragamo, 275, 280, 281, 289, 290
Self-branding, 86
Self-enhancement, 190
Self-matching pricing, 8
Sense of belonging, 154, 164
Sentiment analysis, 91
Service failure, 244–246, 249, 253–260, 398, 401–405, 407–413
Service quality attributes, 13
Service recovery strategies, 254, 255, 258
Shared values, 113
Shopping experience, 33–37, 41–43
Short videos, 52, 56, 57, 62–68, 70
Single-channel retail, 20
Skills, 299–301, 307–314, 316, 323, 325, 328–332, 334, 335
Smart factories, 299
SNs involvement, 223–225, 227, 232, 234, 235
SNs Type, 227, 235
Social capital, 84, 95, 96, 98
Social change, 189, 190
Social commerce, 51–53, 60, 61, 69
Social competences, 309
Social cues, 223–225, 232, 234, 235
Social distance, 110

Social eWOM, 223, 224, 226, 227, 232–235
Social/external touchpoints, 370, 371
Social identification, 113
Social identity, 155, 162
Social identity theory, 189, 190
Social influence, 187
Social influence theory (SIT), 58, 159, 161, 163, 164, 186, 246
Socialisation, 159, 170
Socialisers, 116
Social issues, 89
Social marketing, 325
Social media, 31, 34, 39, 107–110, 112–114, 116, 117, 119–123, 153–156, 158, 160–164, 166, 169, 170, 201–204, 206–216, 223, 225, 234, 235, 245, 247, 249, 251–253, 255, 257–260, 397, 399, 412
Social media influencers, 52, 60, 66–68
Social media marketing (SMM), 345, 348, 350, 356, 432
Social media platforms, 52, 54, 56–58, 60, 62, 64–70
Social mobility, 189
Social networks (SNs), 38, 43, 222–229, 232–235, 423, 432–434
Social relationship, 234
Social sharing, 431
Social web, 89–91
Society-centric stratergy, 210, 213
Sociocultural context, 354
SOSTAC©, 206
Spurious loyalty, 185
Stakeholders, 137, 140
Status, 85, 92
Status consumption, 155, 162
Stimulus-organism-response (S-O-R) model, 224–226, 234

Strategy, 202, 204–211
Strauss and Frost, 206
Subjective norm, 249
Susceptibility, 225, 227, 234
Sustainability, 273–281, 287, 289, 290
Sustainable brand identity, 275, 284, 287
Sustainable luxury, 274, 278, 279, 290
Sustainable strategy, 199, 276, 290
Sustainable thinking, 281, 289, 290
Switching behaviour, 180, 183, 187
Symbolic value, 187, 347

T
Tablet devices, 34, 36
Tagging, 84, 85
Target, 379, 380, 382, 383, 389
TCQ framework, 371
Team creativity, 141
Technical competences, 307, 309, 316, 325, 326
Technical service failure, 401
Text mining, 282, 289
T-LAB, 283
Tommy Hilfiger, 381
TOMS, 379
Total Cost Management (TCM), 373
Touchpoints, 365, 367, 370–375, 379, 383, 385, 388
Traditional/physical retail, 31, 32, 36
Traditional video, 63, 64
Trendsetters, 84, 89
Trust, 248–250
Twitter, 88, 90

U
United Kingdom (UK), 207, 244, 245, 249–252
USA, 82, 90
User-generated content (UGC), 245–249, 252, 255, 260, 281, 397

V
Valence, 248, 254
Valence in online reviews, 399, 401, 402, 406, 407, 412
Value, 200, 209–212, 214–216
Viral marketing, 89, 90
Virtual assistance, 377
Virtual community, 53, 55, 56, 58–60, 65, 67, 70
Visual media, 428

W
Web 1.0, 202, 204
Web 2.0, 202, 204
Web 3.0, 202
Web 4.0, 202
Web 5.0, 202, 204
Web of Thought, 204, 205
WeChat, 356
We-intentions, 111
Word of mouth (WOM), 221, 222

Y
YouTube, 432–435

Z
Zara, 381

CPSIA information can be obtained
at www.ICGtesting.com
Printed in the USA
LVHW081926080123
736723LV00008B/773